part 1

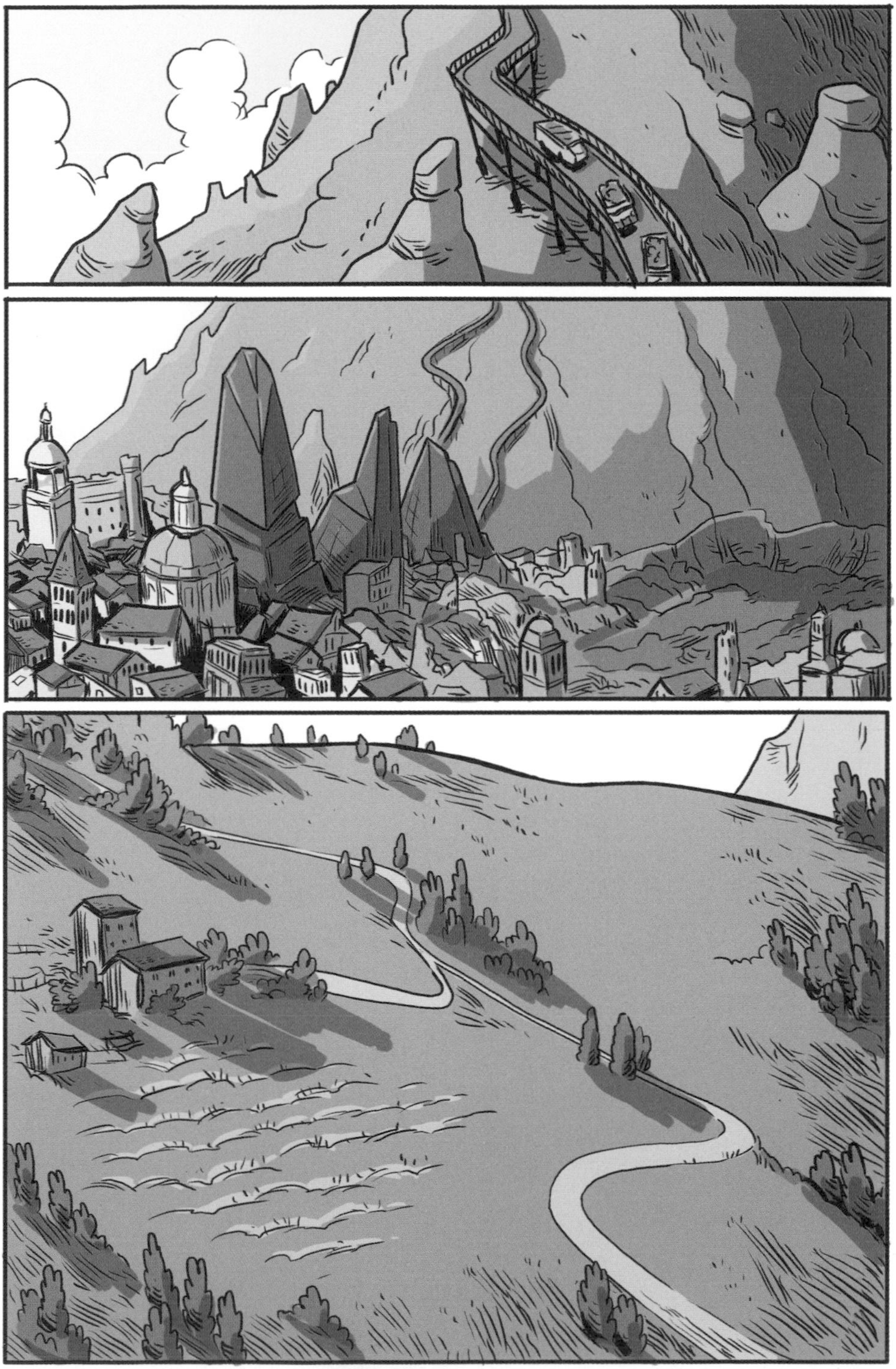

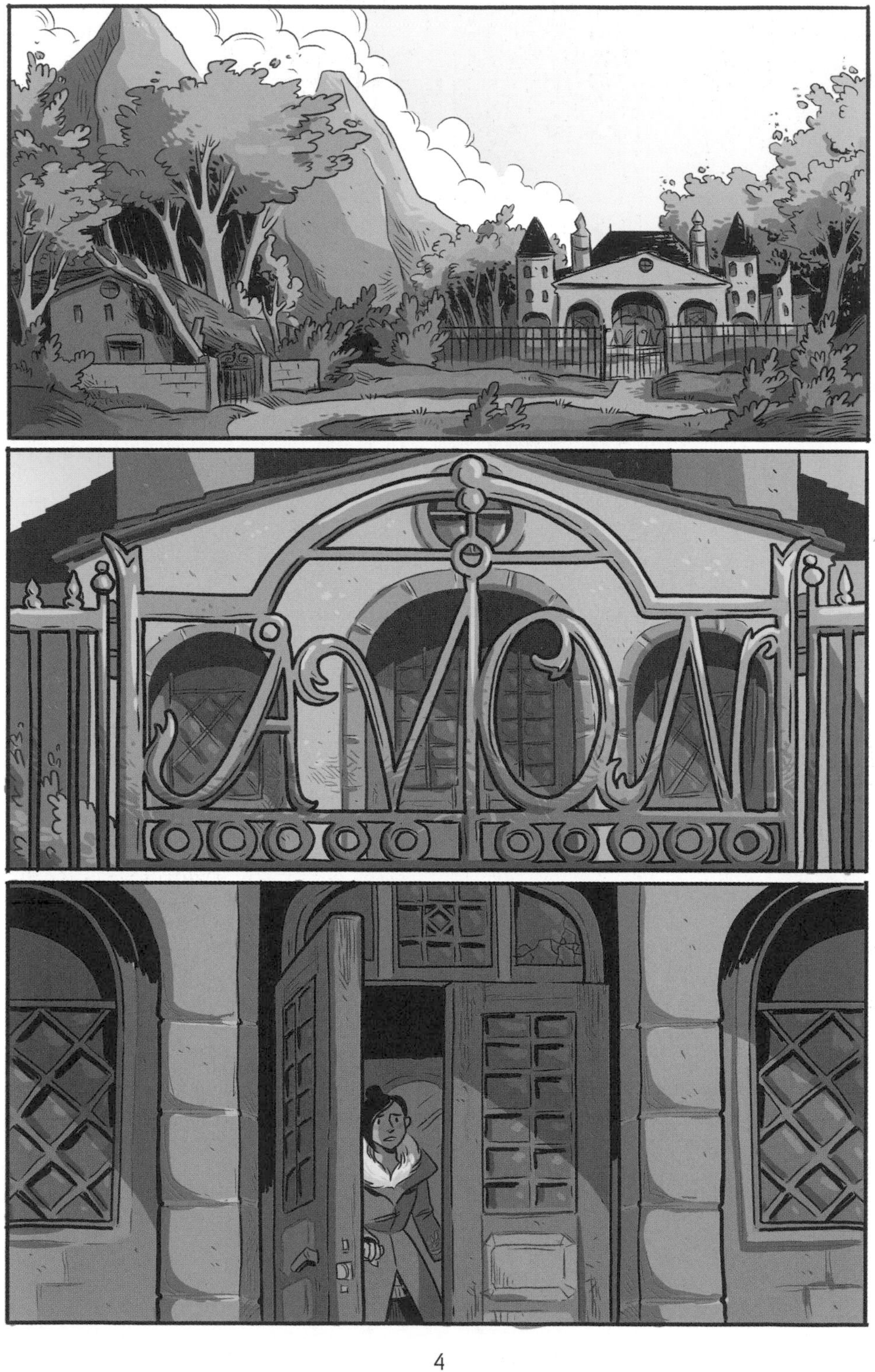

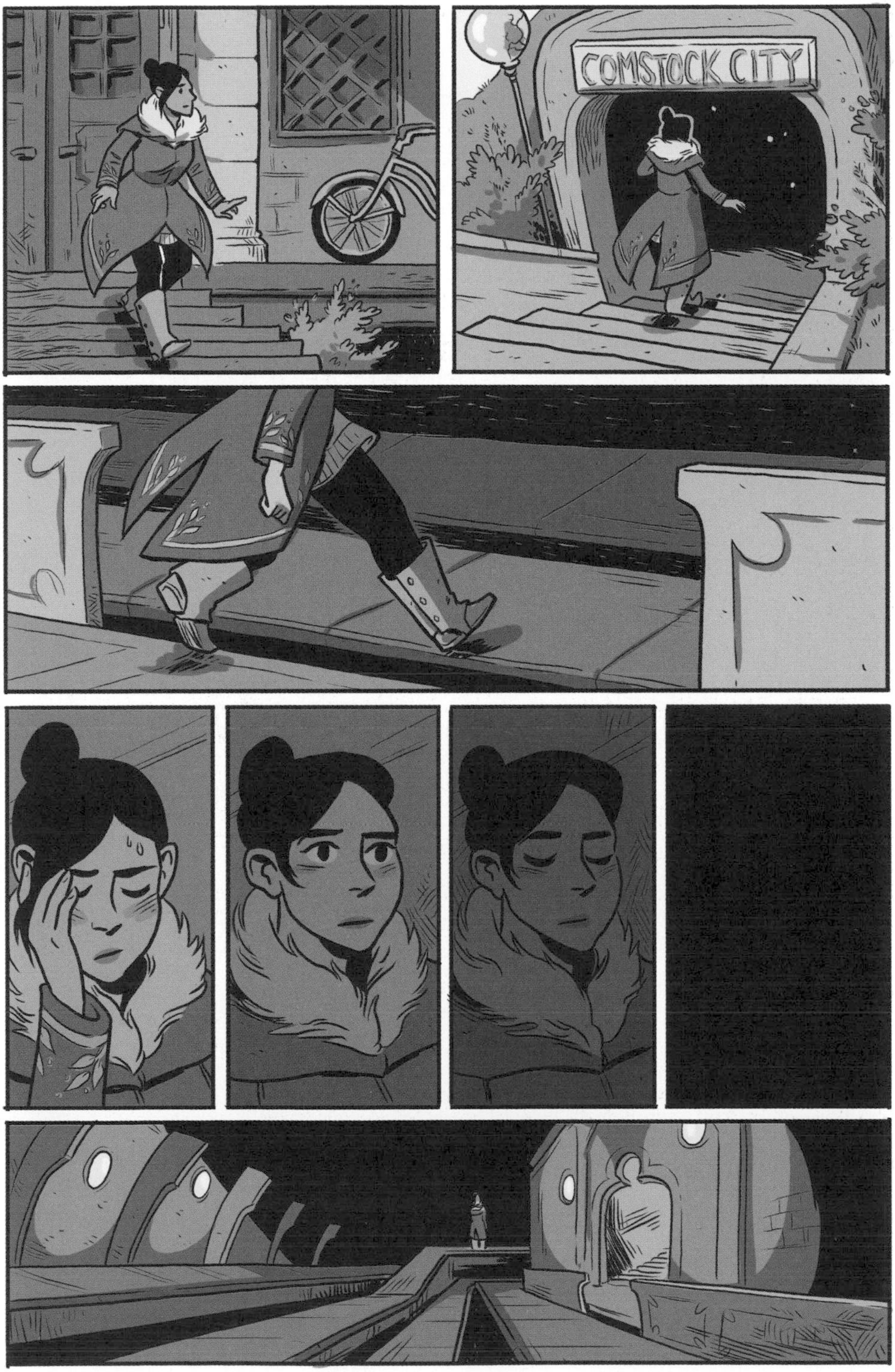
COMSTOCK CITY

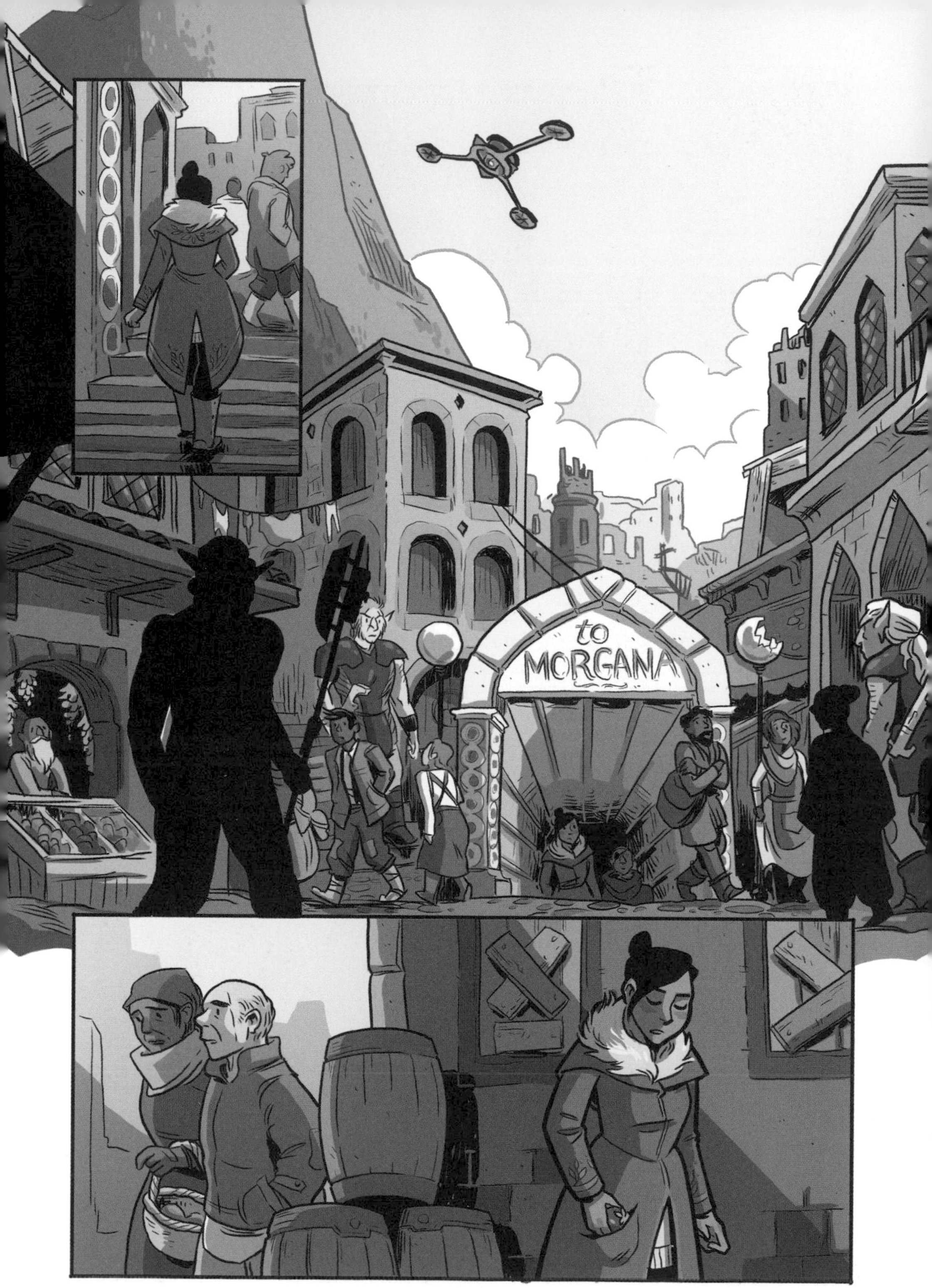
to
MORGANA

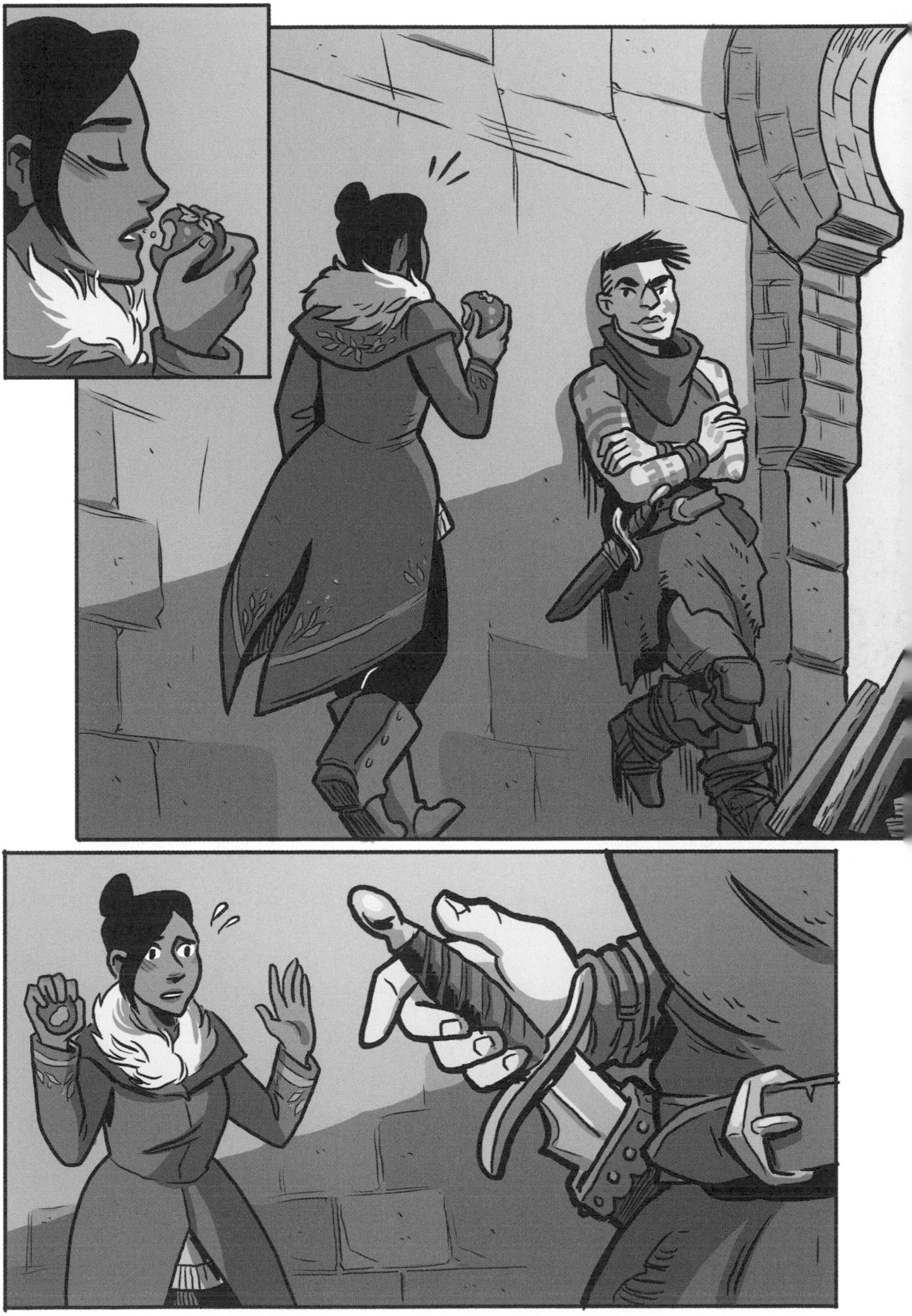

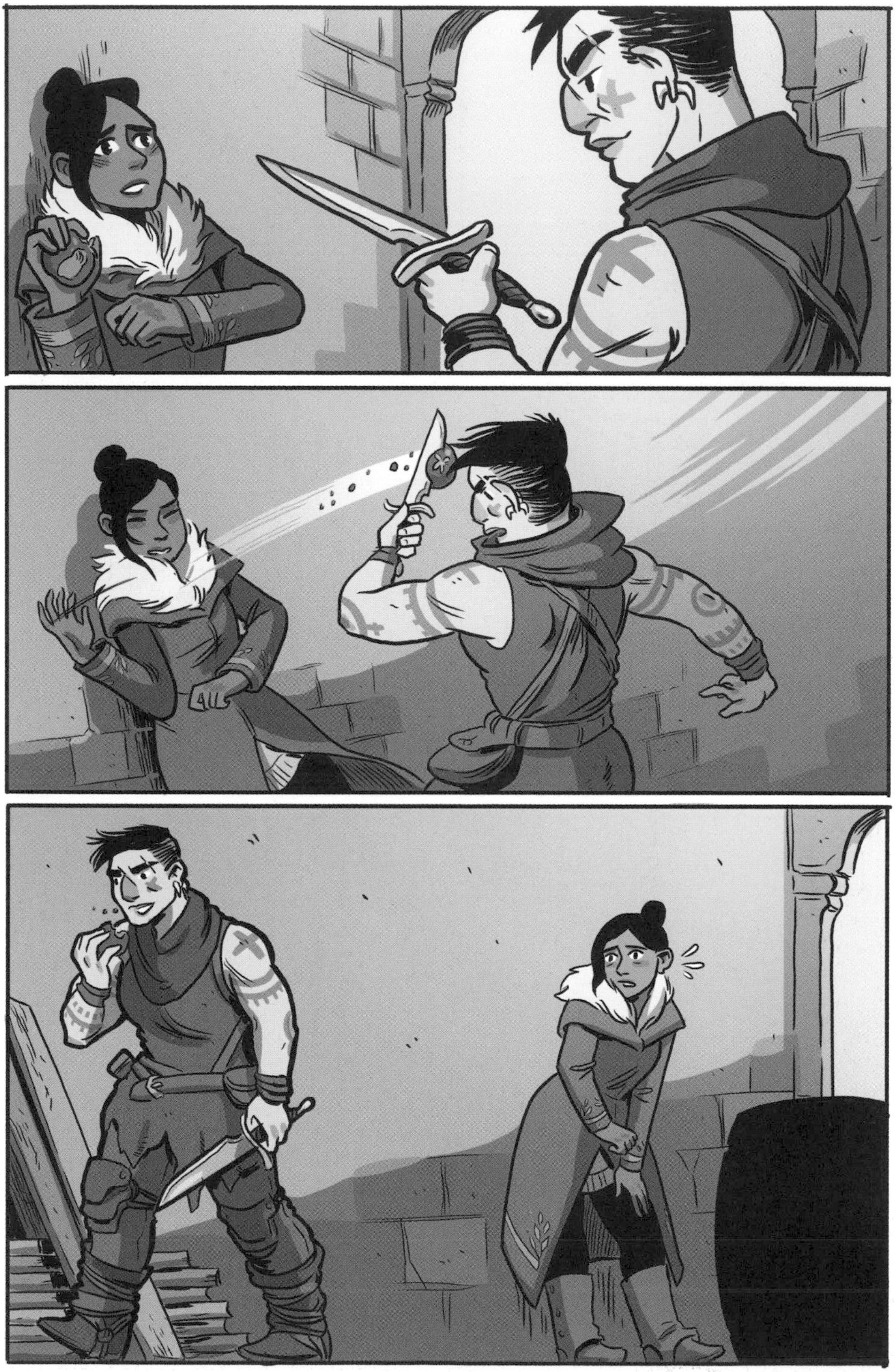

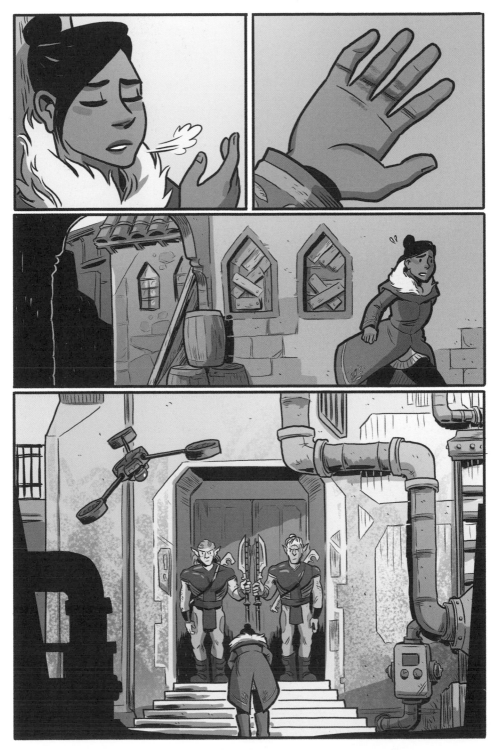

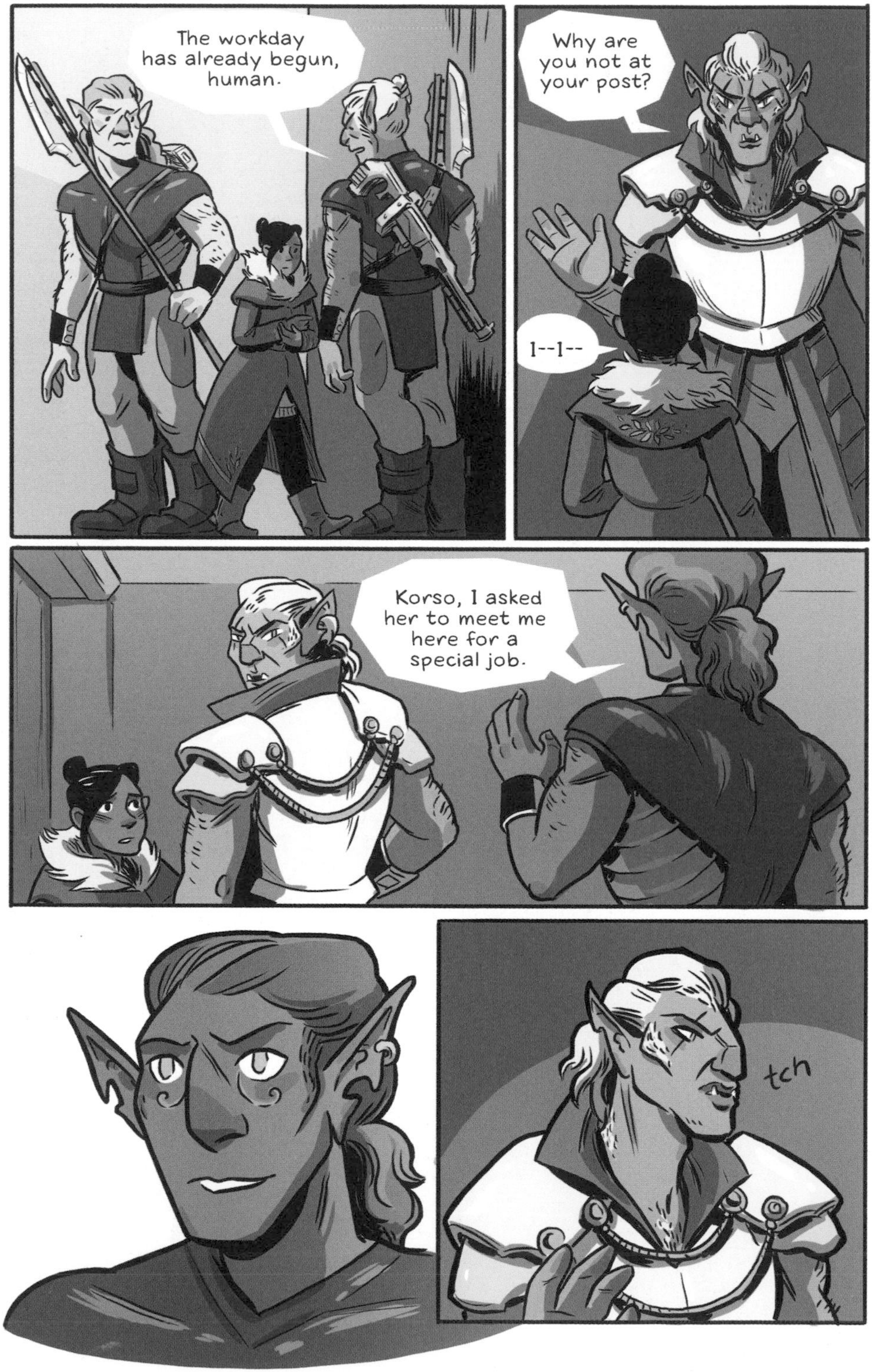

The workday has already begun, human.
Why are you not at your post?
I--I--
Korso, I asked her to meet me here for a special job.
tch

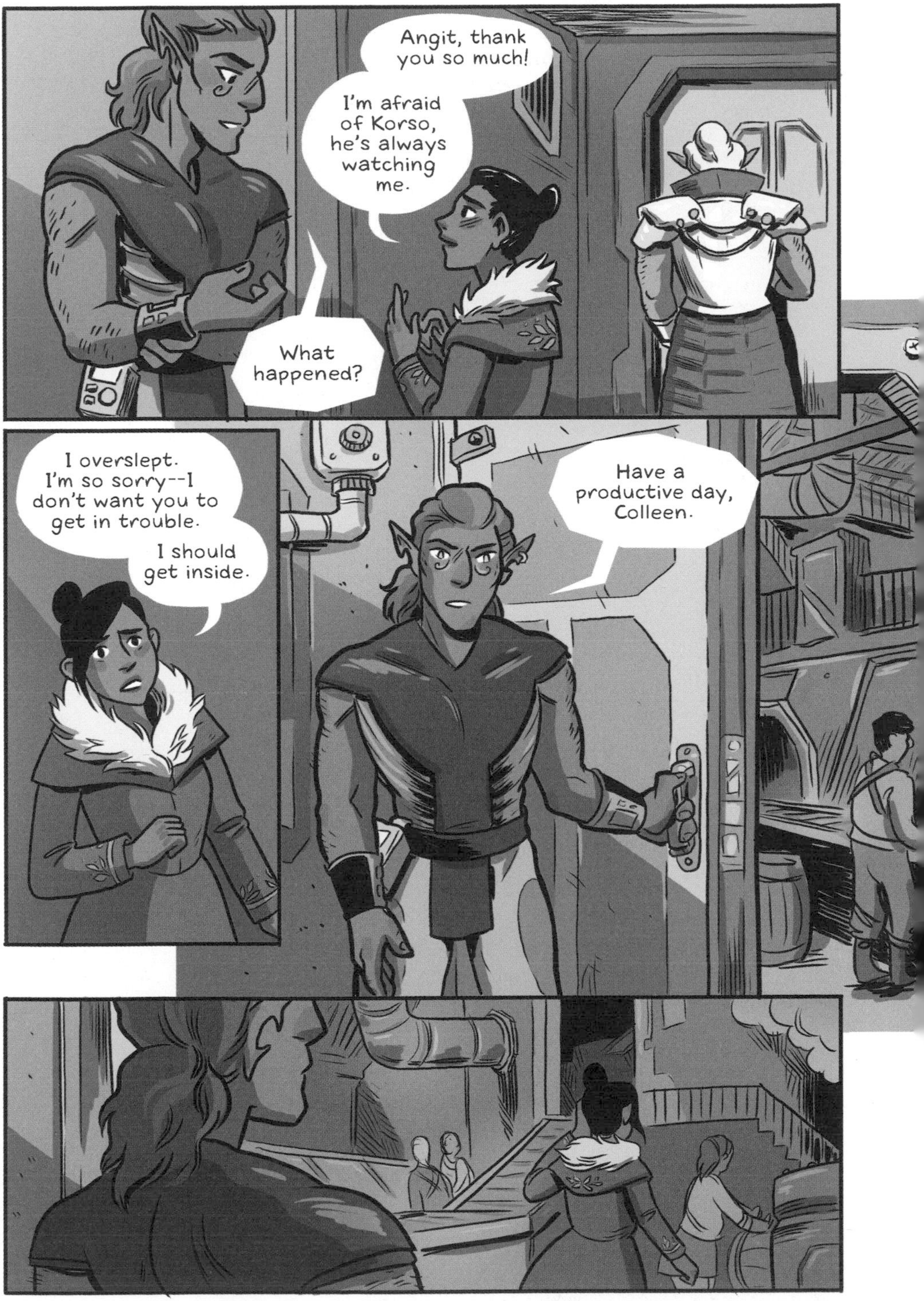
Angit, thank you so much!
I'm afraid of Korso, he's always watching me.
What happened?
I overslept. I'm so sorry--I don't want you to get in trouble.
I should get inside.
Have a productive day, Colleen.

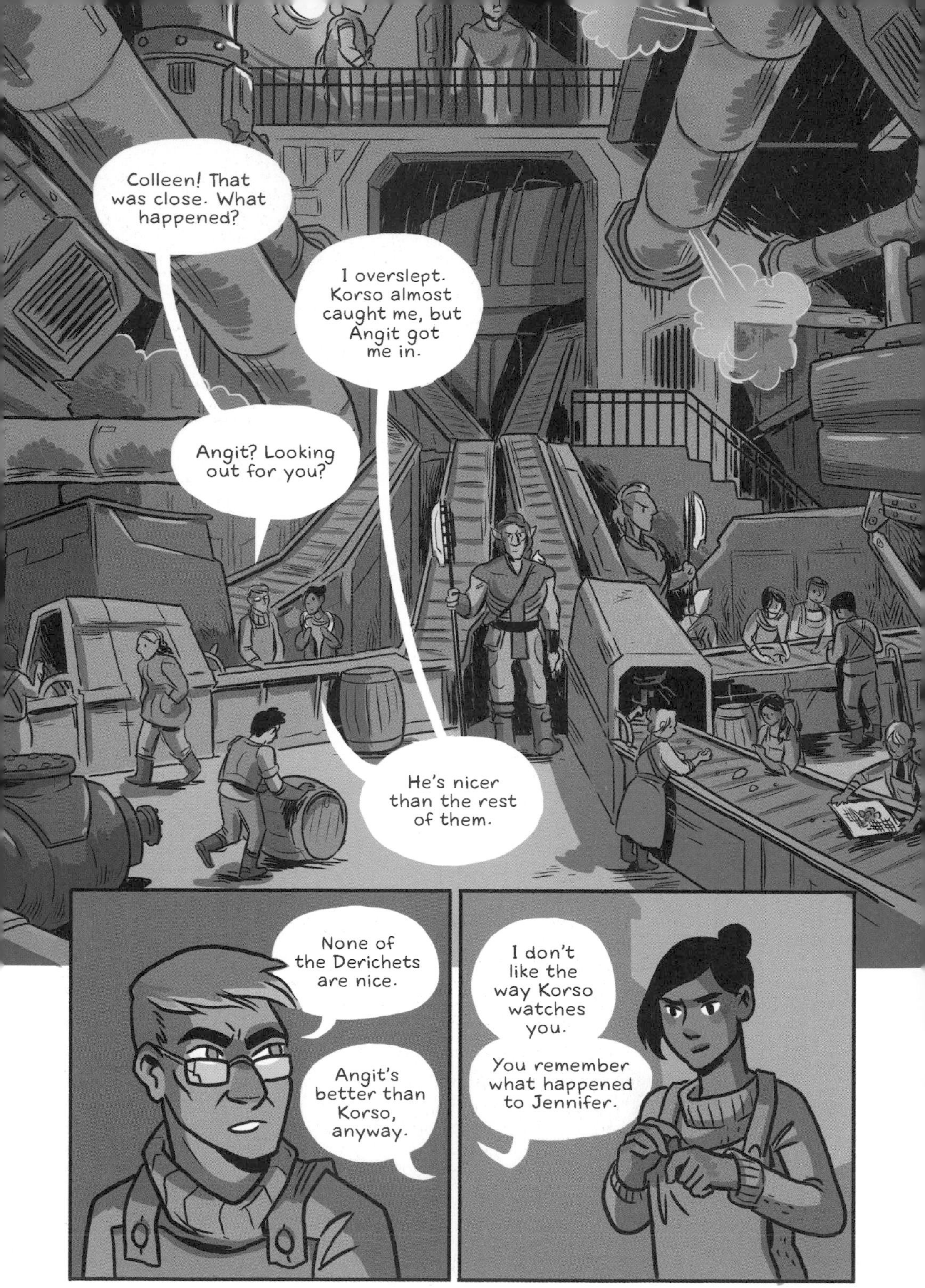
Colleen! That was close. What happened?
I overslept. Korso almost caught me, but Angit got me in.
Angit? Looking out for you?
He's nicer than the rest of them.
None of the Derichets are nice.
Angit's better than Korso, anyway.
I don't like the way Korso watches you.
You remember what happened to Jennifer.

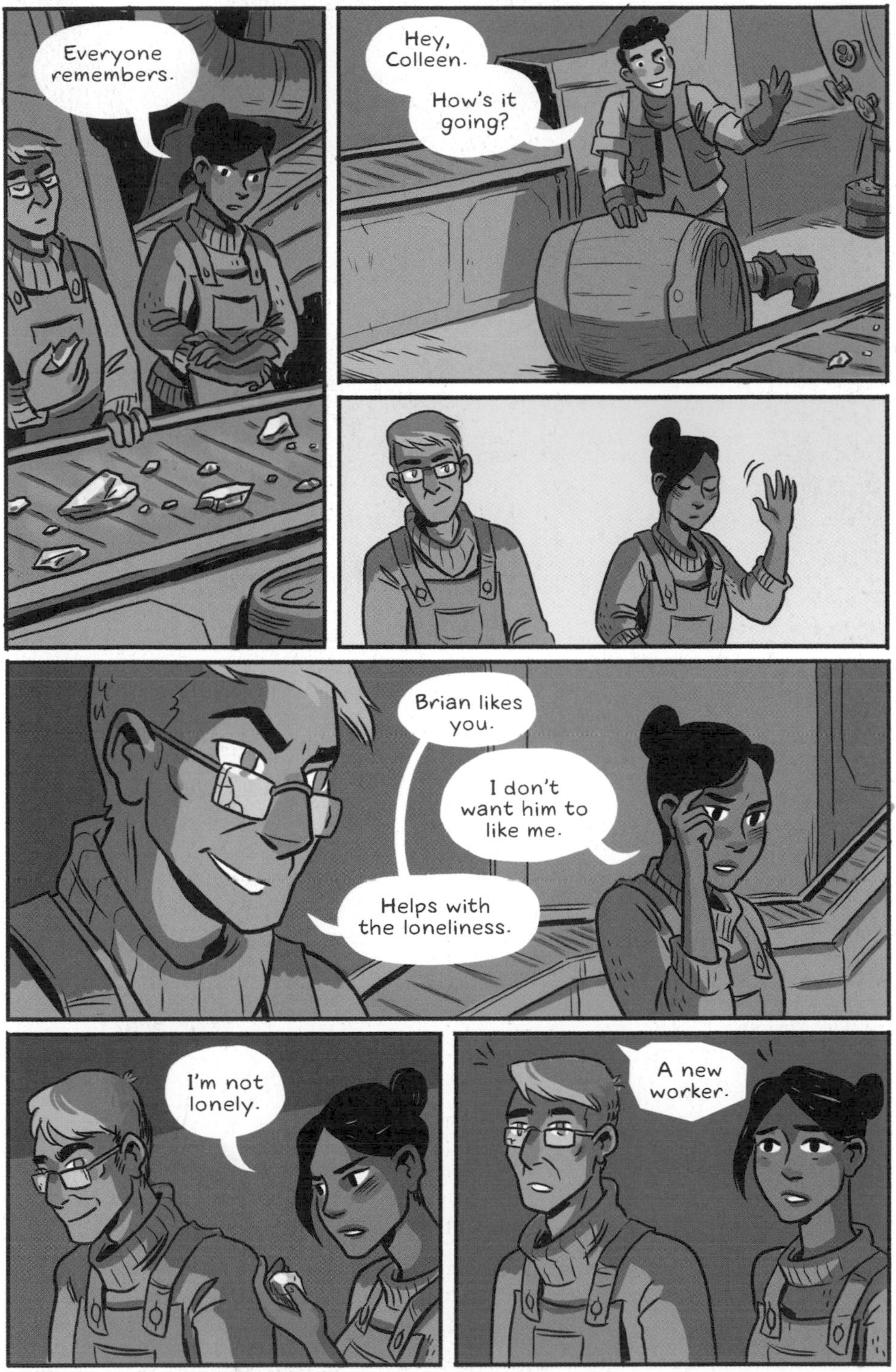
Everyone remembers.
Hey, Colleen.
How's it going?
Brian likes you.
I don't want him to like me.
Helps with the loneliness.
I'm not lonely.
A new worker.

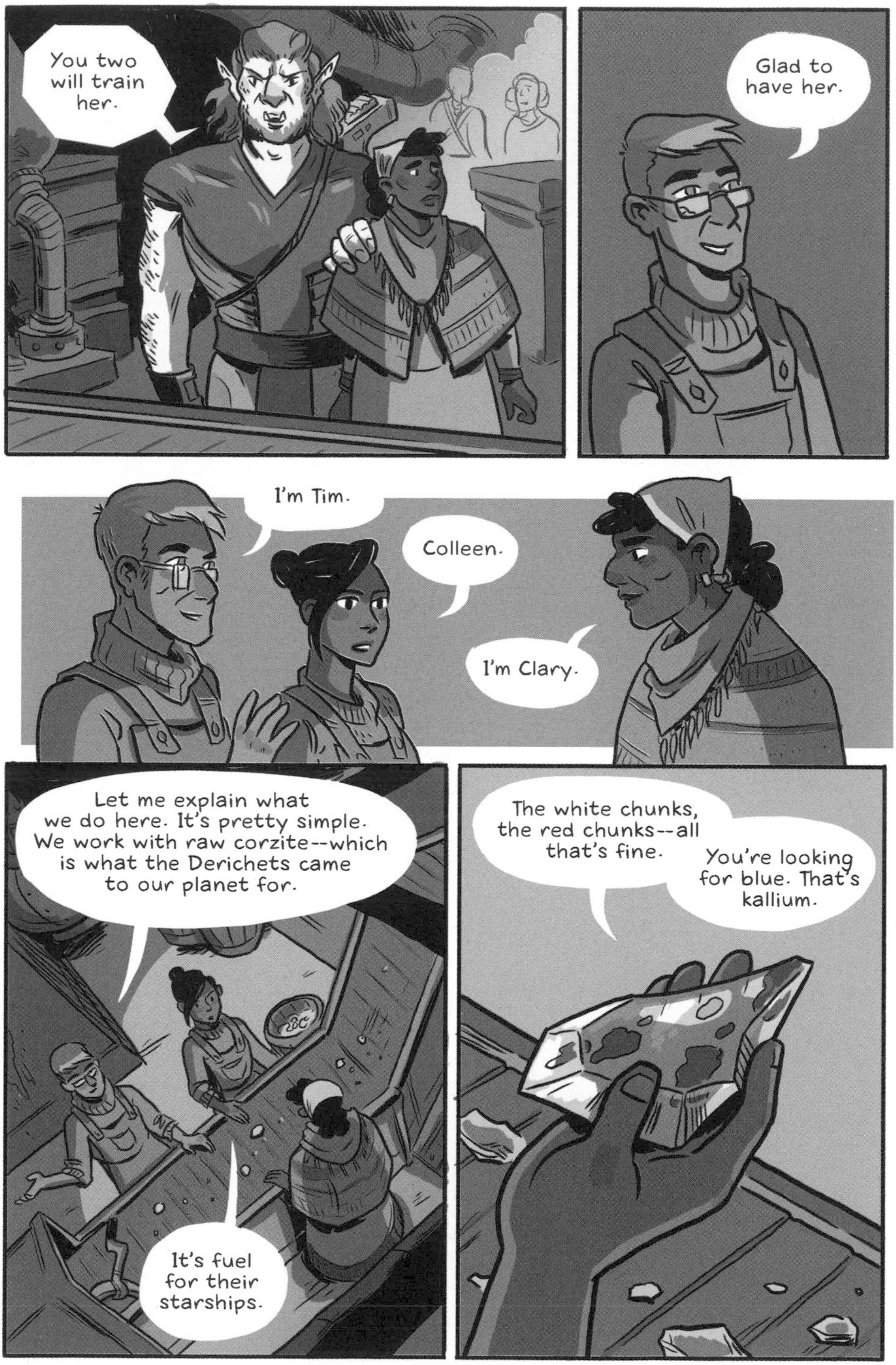
You two will train her.
Glad to have her.
I'm Tim.
Colleen.
I'm Clary.
Let me explain what we do here. It's pretty simple. We work with raw corzite--which is what the Derichets came to our planet for.
It's fuel for their starships.
The white chunks, the red chunks--all that's fine.
You're looking for blue. That's kallium.

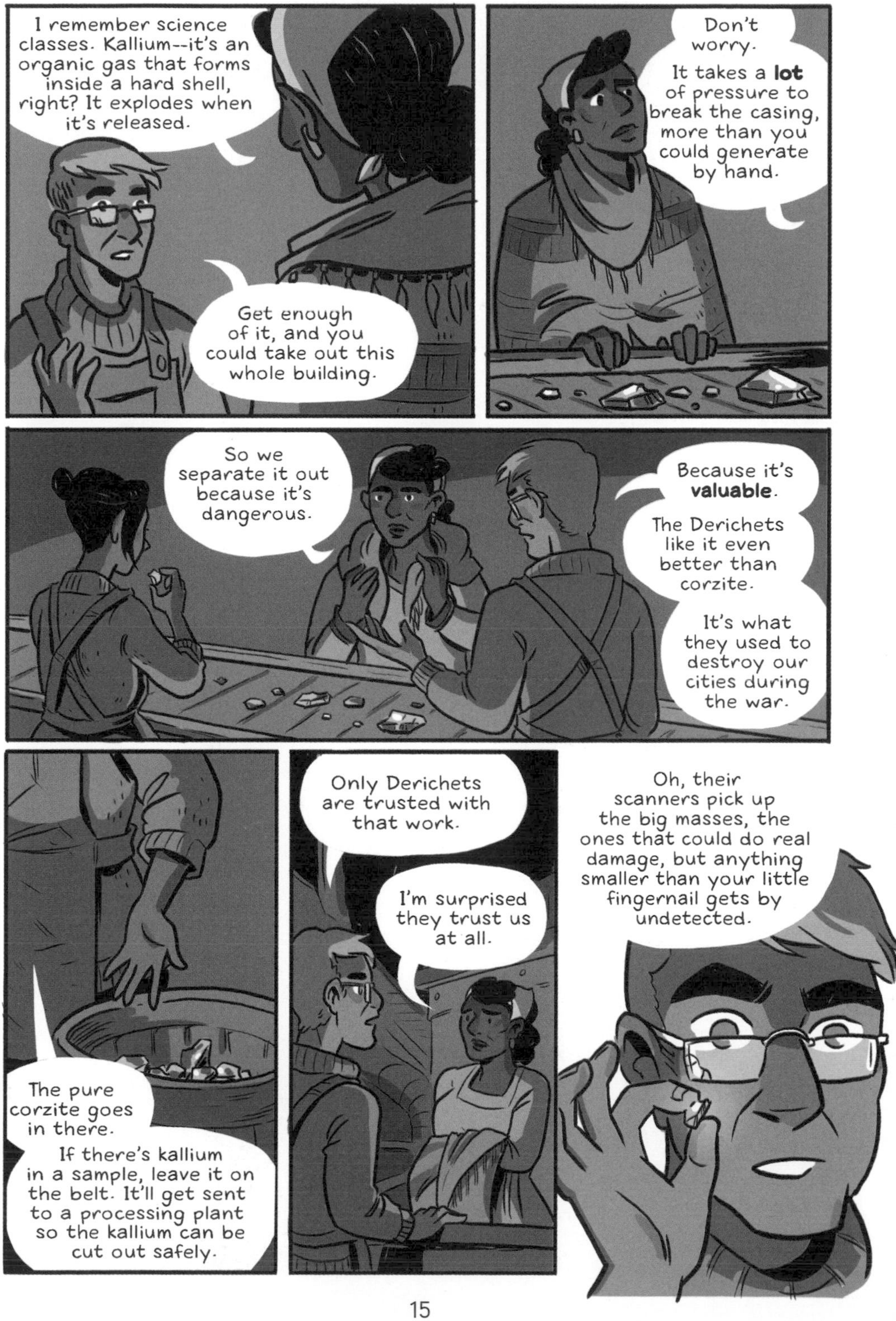
I remember science classes. Kallium--it's an organic gas that forms inside a hard shell, right? It explodes when it's released.
Get enough of it, and you could take out this whole building.
Don't worry.
It takes a **lot** of pressure to break the casing, more than you could generate by hand.
So we separate it out because it's dangerous.
Because it's **valuable**.
The Derichets like it even better than corzite.
It's what they used to destroy our cities during the war.
The pure corzite goes in there.
If there's kallium in a sample, leave it on the belt. It'll get sent to a processing plant so the kallium can be cut out safely.
Only Derichets are trusted with that work.
I'm surprised they trust us at all.
Oh, their scanners pick up the big masses, the ones that could do real damage, but anything smaller than your little fingernail gets by undetected.

All right. I think I've got it.

So, what brings you here?

Couldn't make a go of it on the farm anymore--the land's all poisoned. So my husband and our son and I came to the city last week to look for jobs.

You know it's dangerous, here in Comstock City.

I know. Chromatti everywhere--

Mostly they just fight with other Chromatti gangs, but if you get in their way, they'll kill you. The Derichets, on the other hand...

And sometimes not-so-young girls.

And young men disappear. They're conscripted for the mines.

I heard that young girls disappear sometimes.

I know it's dangerous. But we have to eat. I have to have a job.

16

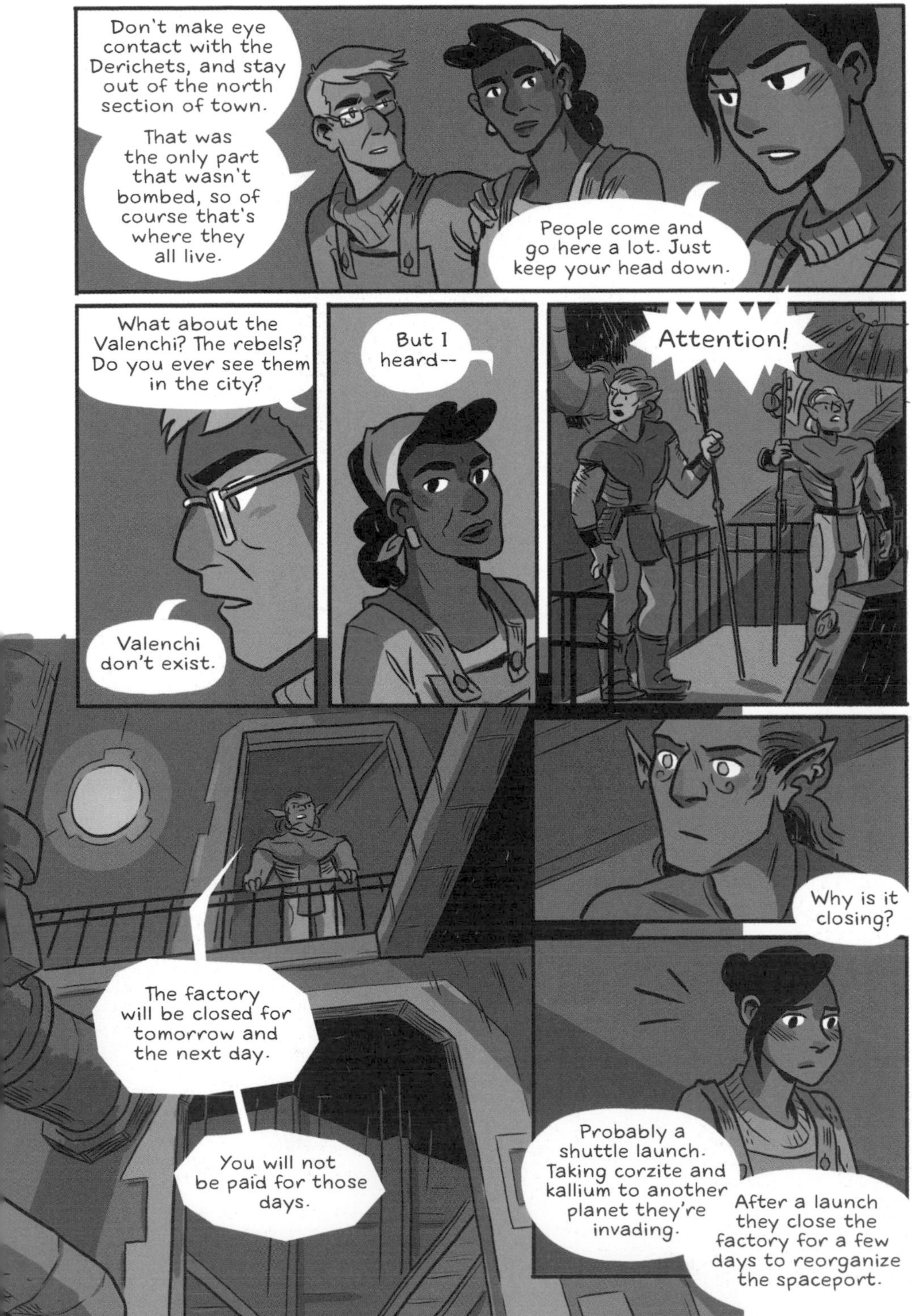
Don't make eye contact with the Derichets, and stay out of the north section of town.
That was the only part that wasn't bombed, so of course that's where they all live.
People come and go here a lot. Just keep your head down.
What about the Valenchi? The rebels? Do you ever see them in the city?
Valenchi don't exist.
But I heard--
Attention!
The factory will be closed for tomorrow and the next day.
You will not be paid for those days.
Why is it closing?
Probably a shuttle launch. Taking corzite and kallium to another planet they're invading.
After a launch they close the factory for a few days to reorganize the spaceport.

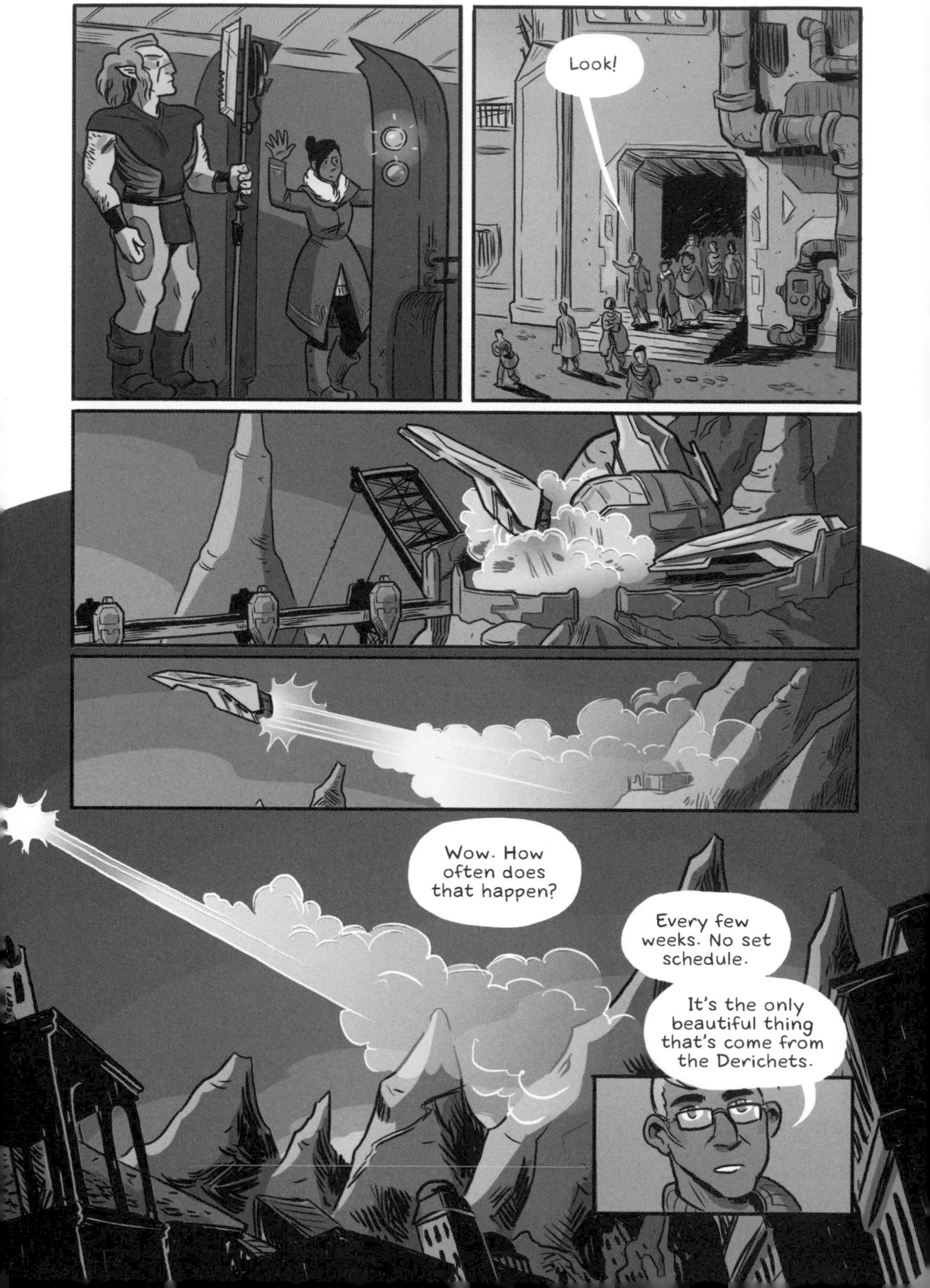
Look!
Wow. How often does that happen?
Every few weeks. No set schedule.
It's the only beautiful thing that's come from the Derichets.

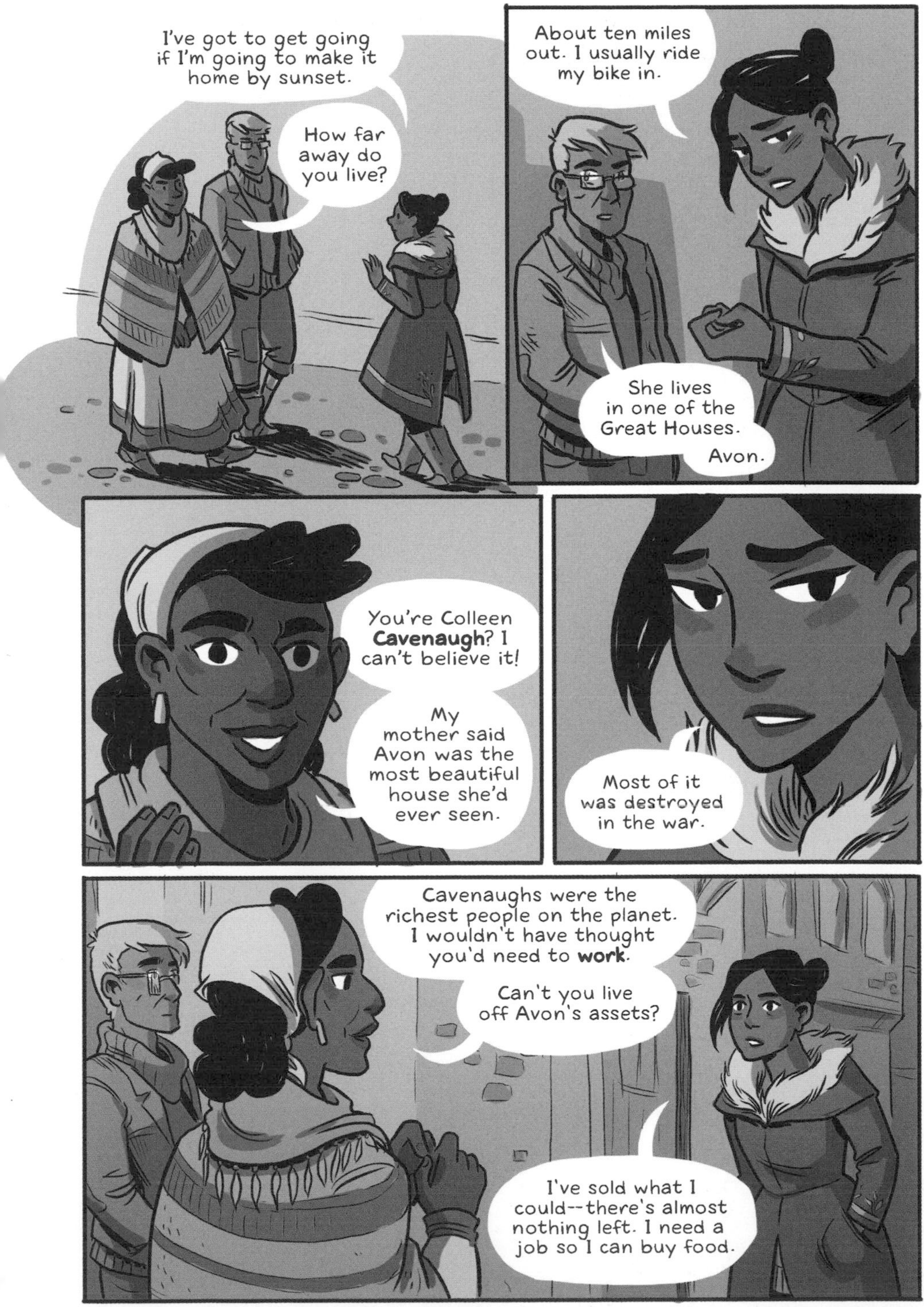
I've got to get going if I'm going to make it home by sunset.
How far away do you live?
About ten miles out. I usually ride my bike in.
She lives in one of the Great Houses.
Avon.
You're Colleen **Cavenaugh**? I can't believe it!
My mother said Avon was the most beautiful house she'd ever seen.
Most of it was destroyed in the war.
Cavenaughs were the richest people on the planet. I wouldn't have thought you'd need to **work**.
Can't you live off Avon's assets?
I've sold what I could--there's almost nothing left. I need a job so I can buy food.

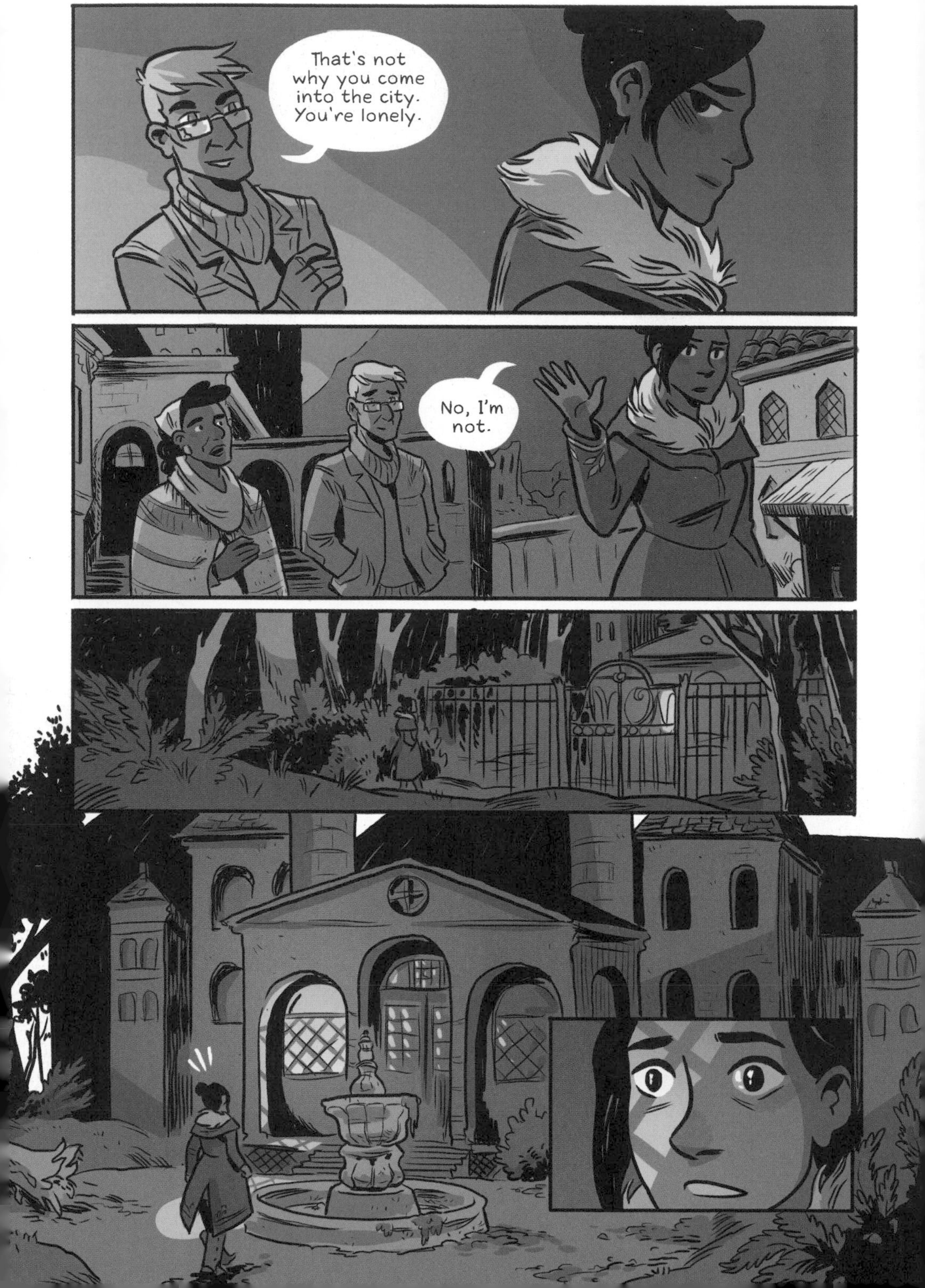
That's not why you come into the city. You're lonely.
No, I'm not.

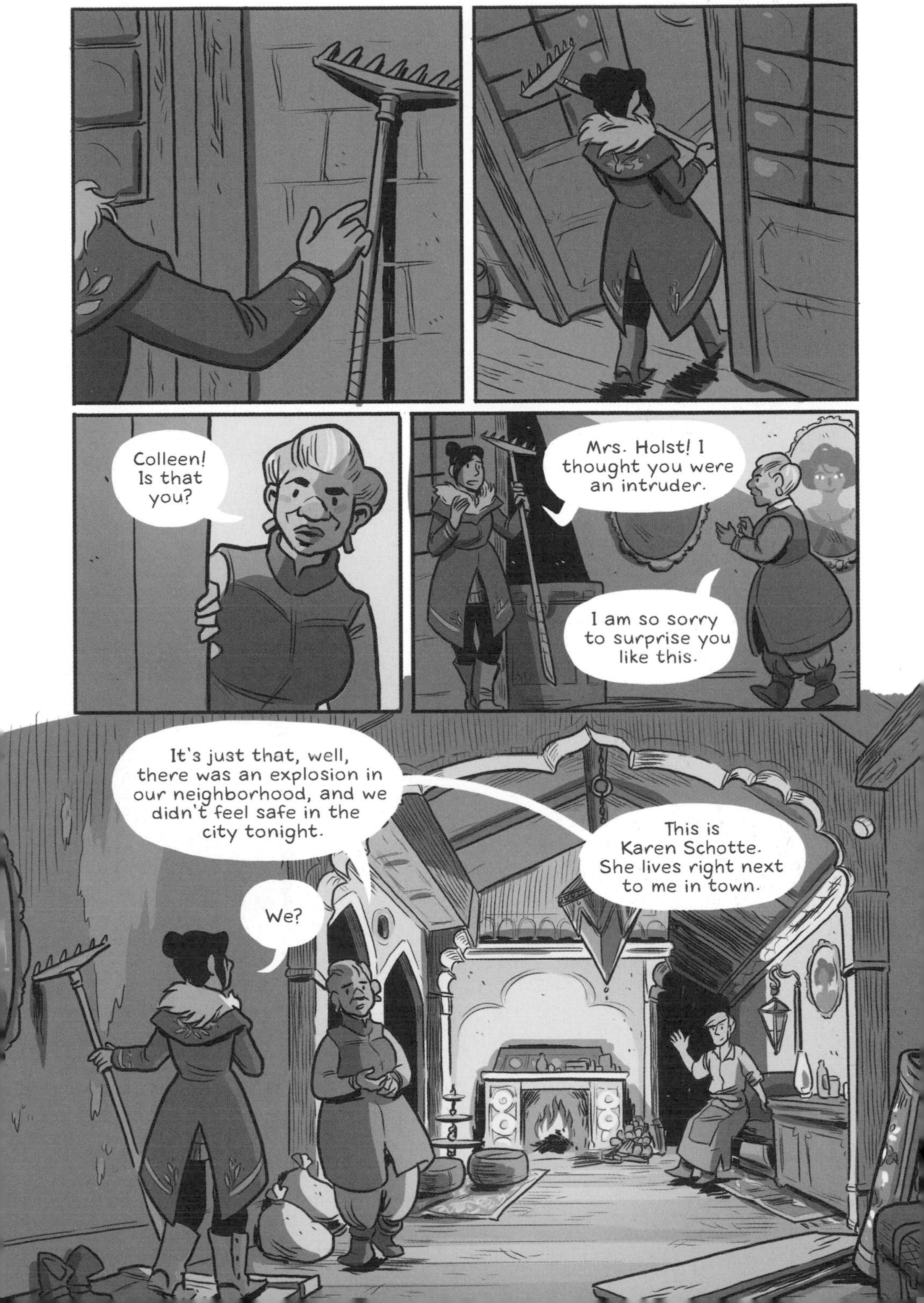

Colleen! Is that you?
Mrs. Holst! I thought you were an intruder.
I am so sorry to surprise you like this.
It's just that, well, there was an explosion in our neighborhood, and we didn't feel safe in the city tonight.
This is Karen Schotte. She lives right next to me in town.
We?

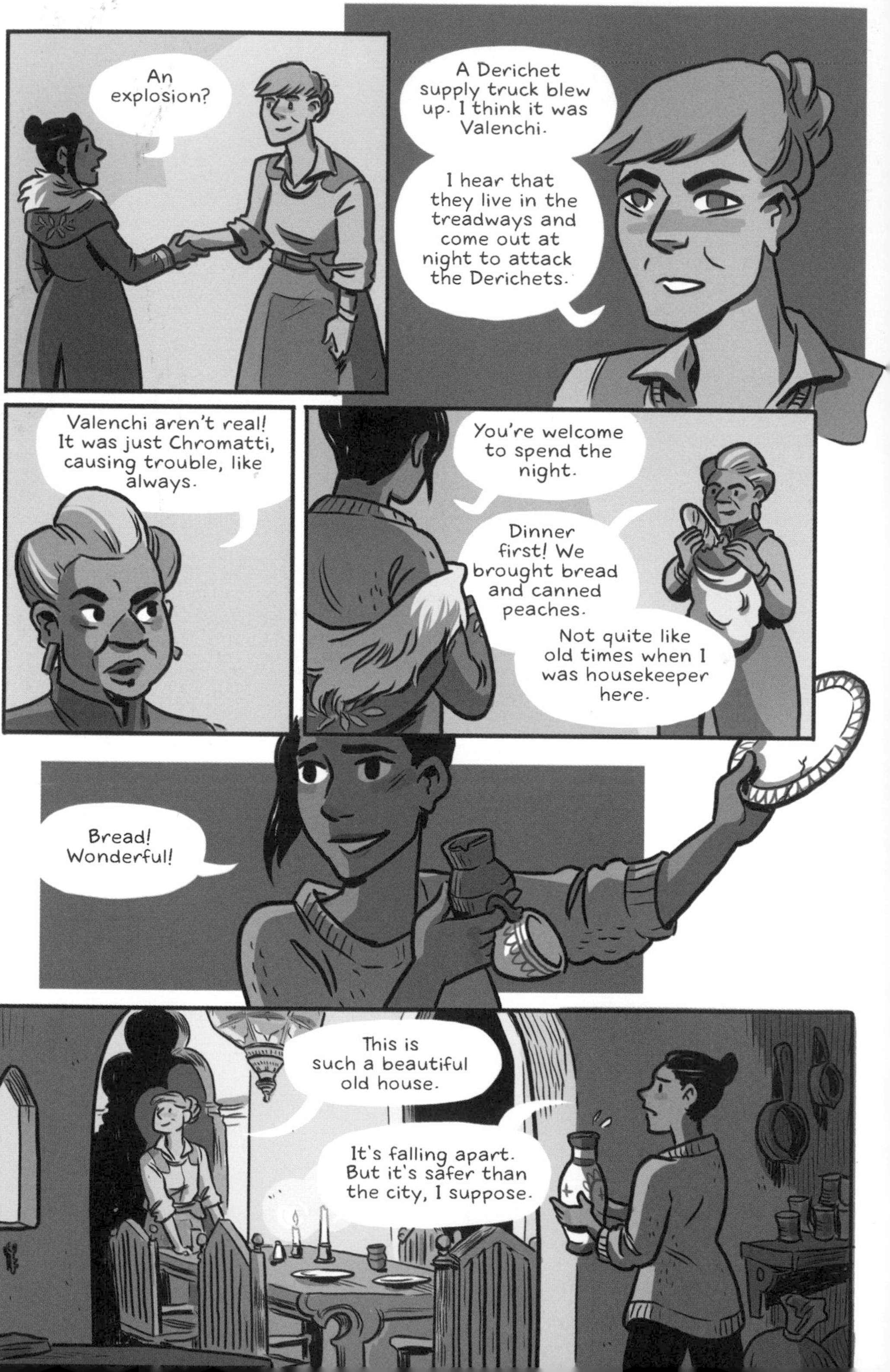
An explosion?
A Derichet supply truck blew up. I think it was Valenchi.
I hear that they live in the treadways and come out at night to attack the Derichets.
Valenchi aren't real! It was just Chromatti, causing trouble, like always.
You're welcome to spend the night.
Dinner first! We brought bread and canned peaches.
Not quite like old times when I was housekeeper here.
Bread! Wonderful!
This is such a beautiful old house.
It's falling apart. But it's safer than the city, I suppose.

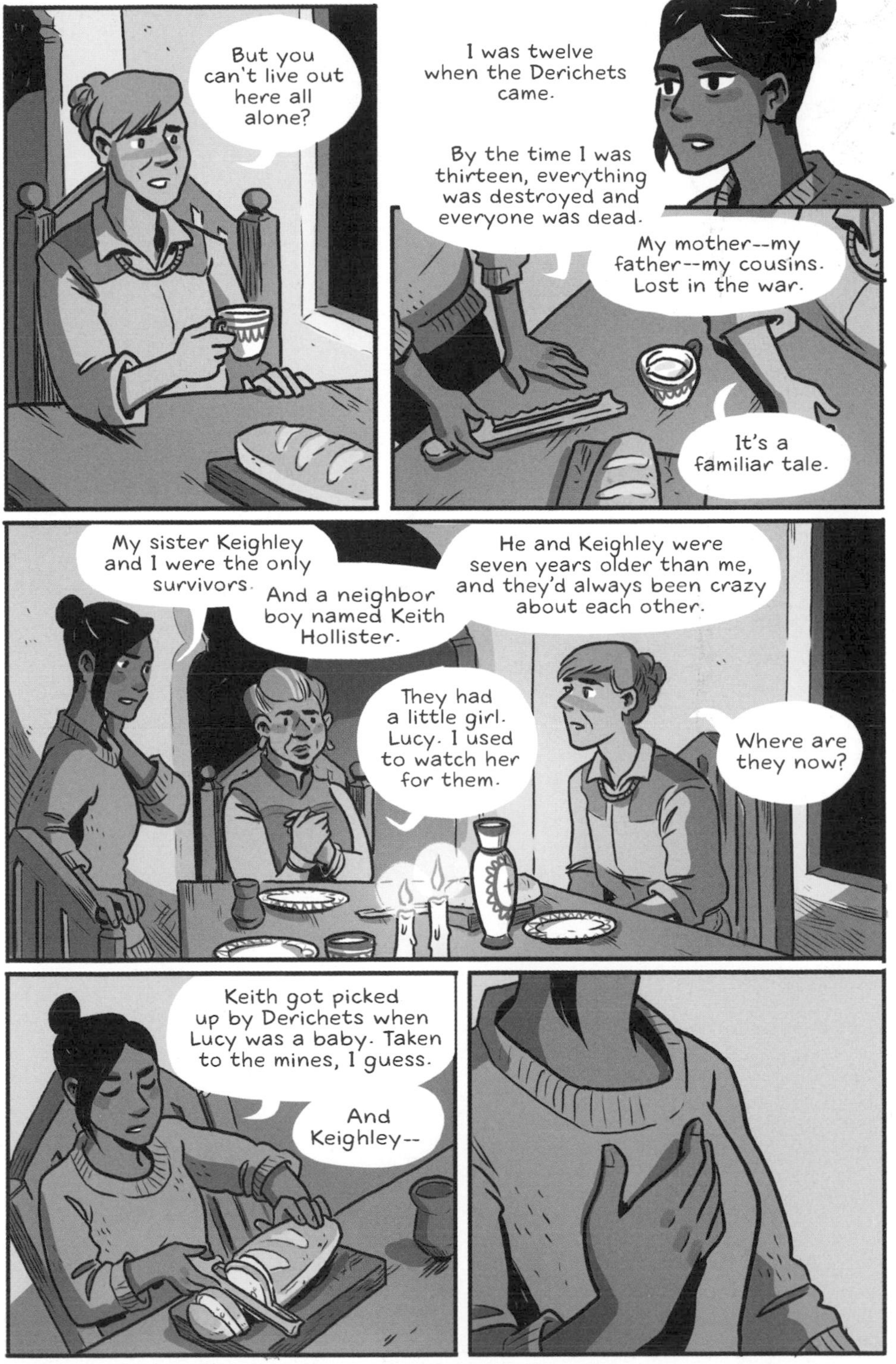
But you can't live out here all alone?
I was twelve when the Derichets came.
By the time I was thirteen, everything was destroyed and everyone was dead.
My mother--my father--my cousins. Lost in the war.
It's a familiar tale.
My sister Keighley and I were the only survivors.
And a neighbor boy named Keith Hollister.
He and Keighley were seven years older than me, and they'd always been crazy about each other.
They had a little girl. Lucy. I used to watch her for them.
Where are they now?
Keith got picked up by Derichets when Lucy was a baby. Taken to the mines, I guess.
And Keighley--

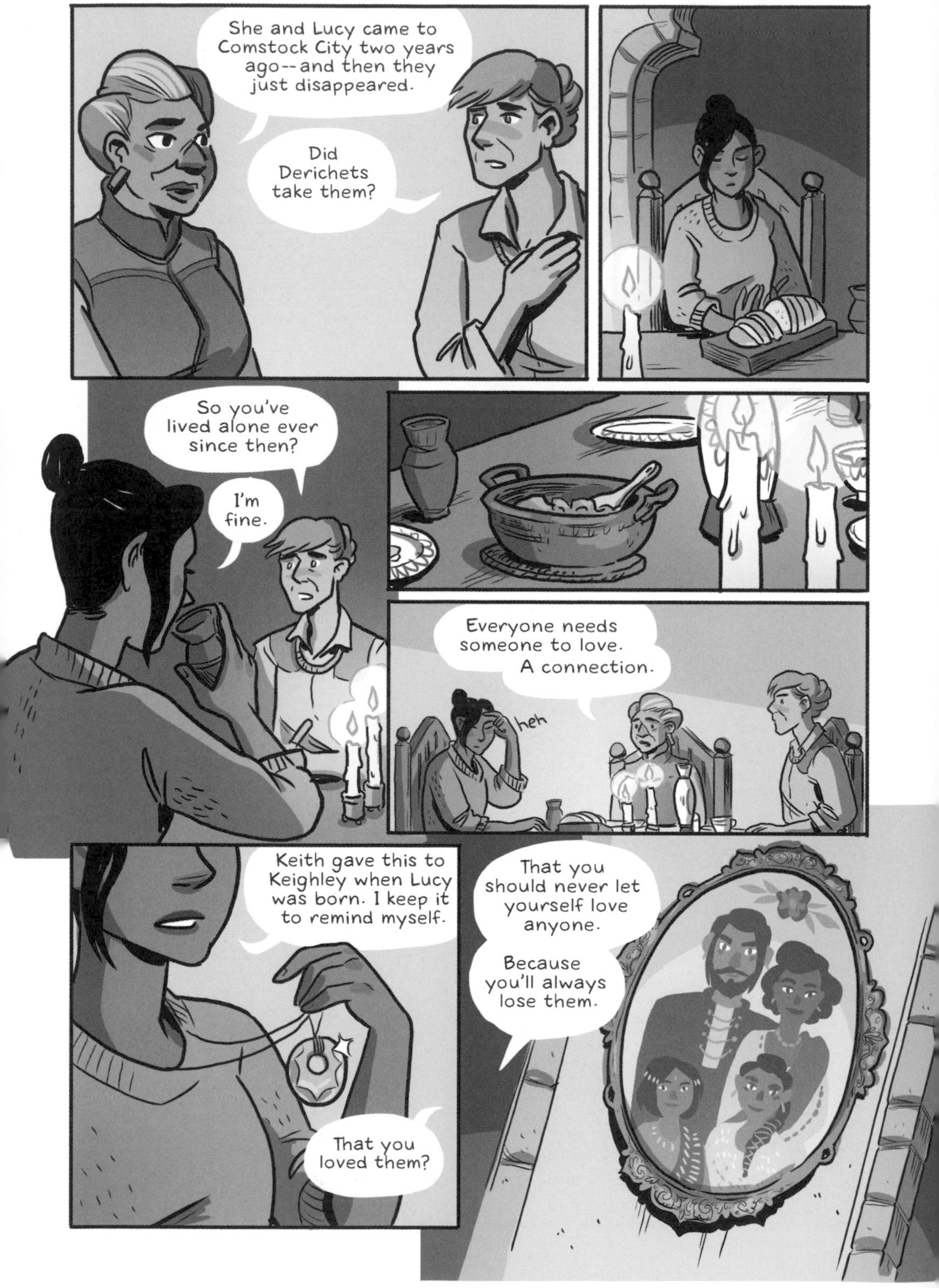

She and Lucy came to Comstock City two years ago--and then they just disappeared.
Did Derichets take them?
So you've lived alone ever since then?
I'm fine.
Everyone needs someone to love. A connection.
heh
Keith gave this to Keighley when Lucy was born. I keep it to remind myself.
That you loved them?
That you should never let yourself love anyone.
Because you'll always lose them.

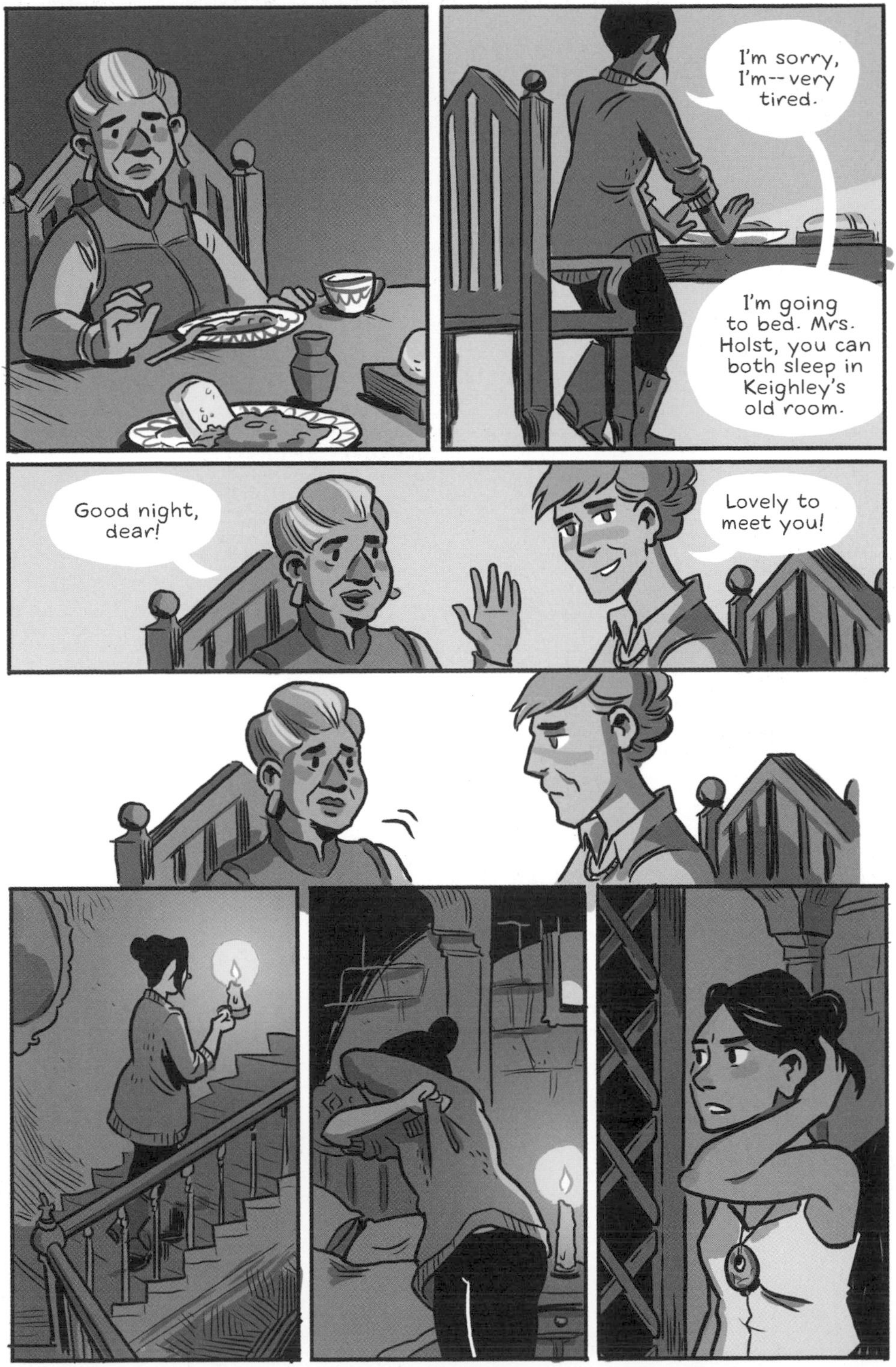
I'm sorry, I'm--very tired.
I'm going to bed. Mrs. Holst, you can both sleep in Keighley's old room.
Good night, dear!
Lovely to meet you!

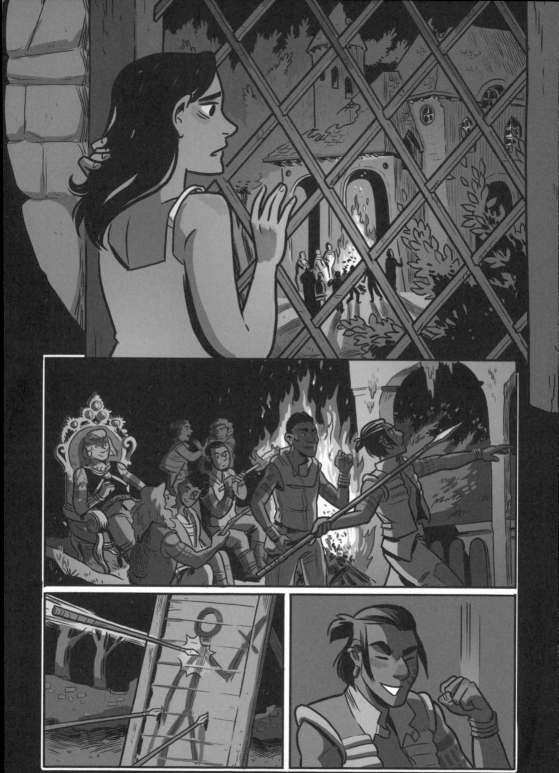

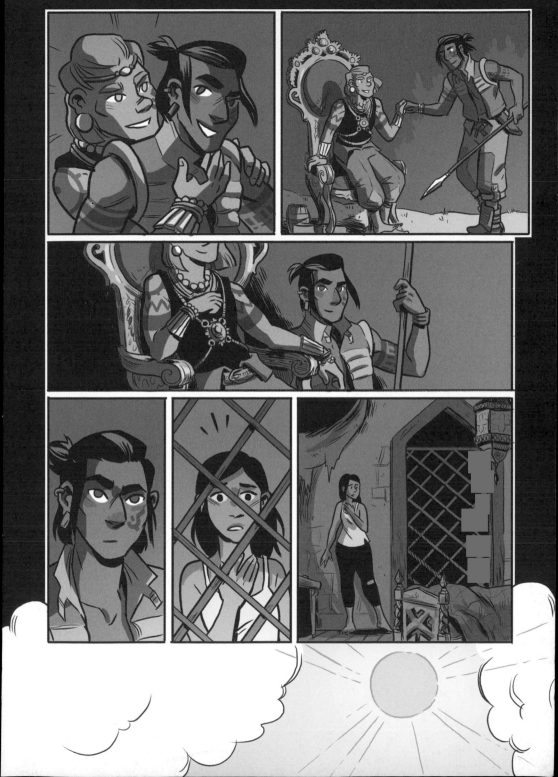

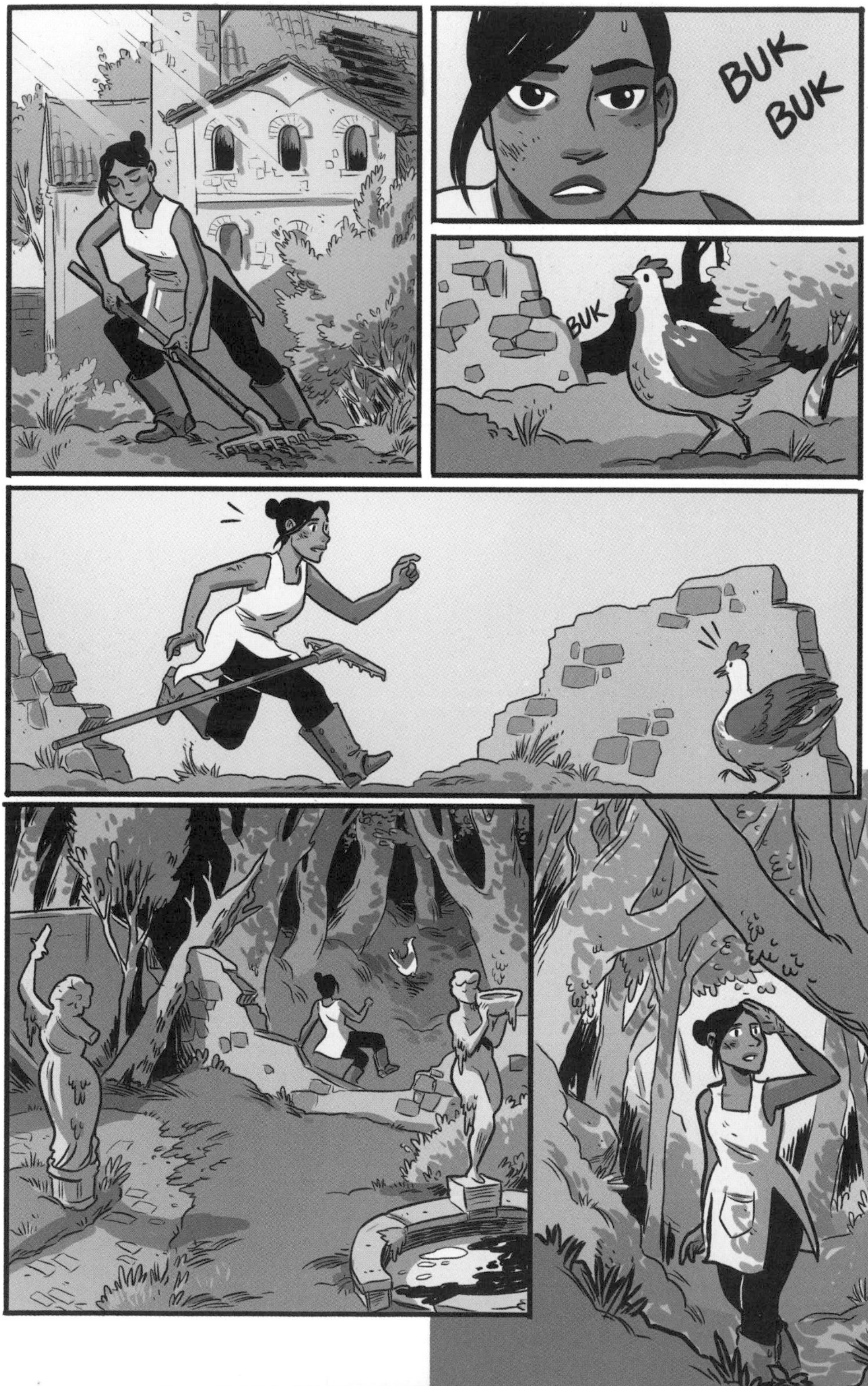
BUK
BUK
BUK

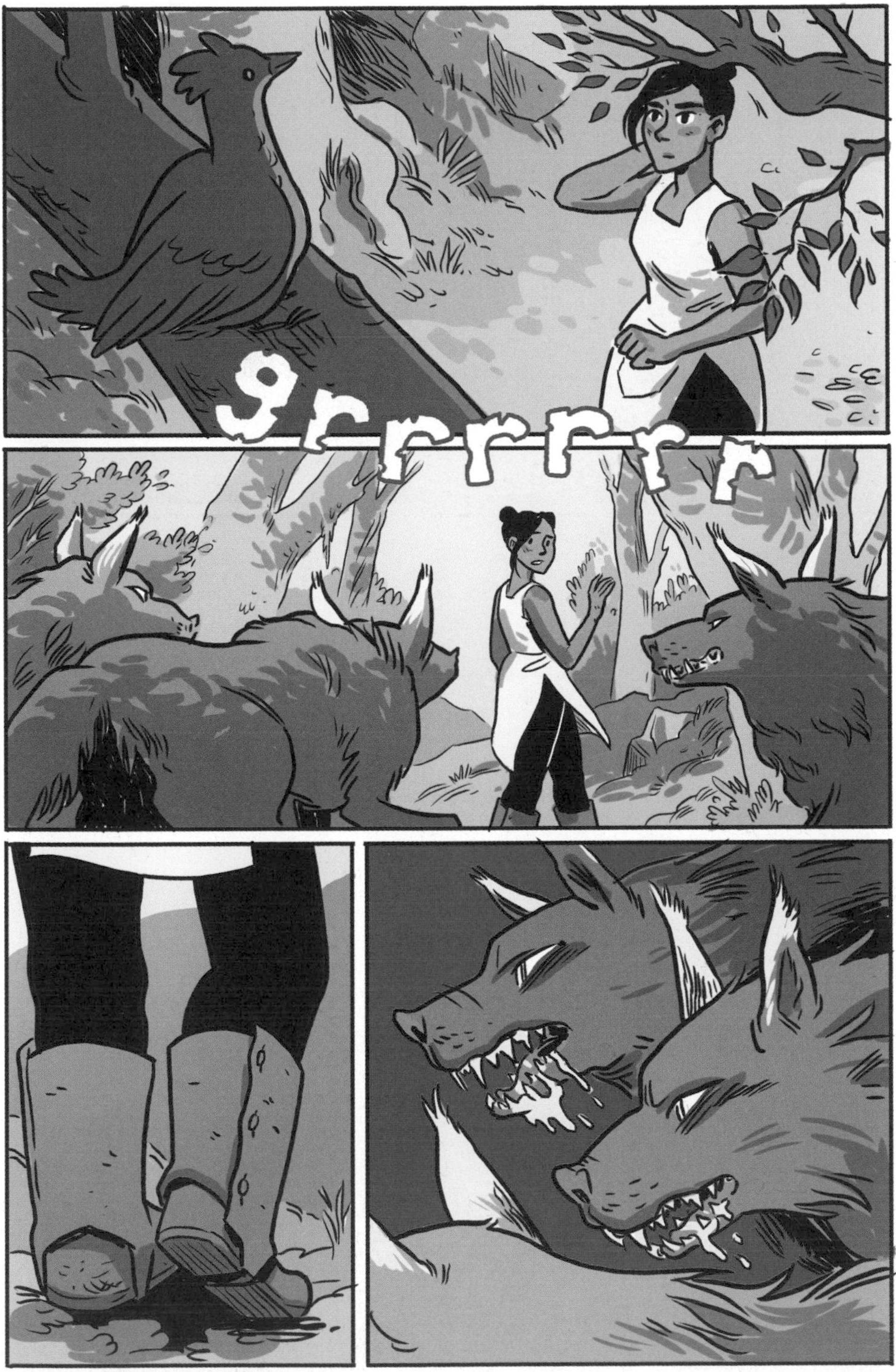
grrrrrr

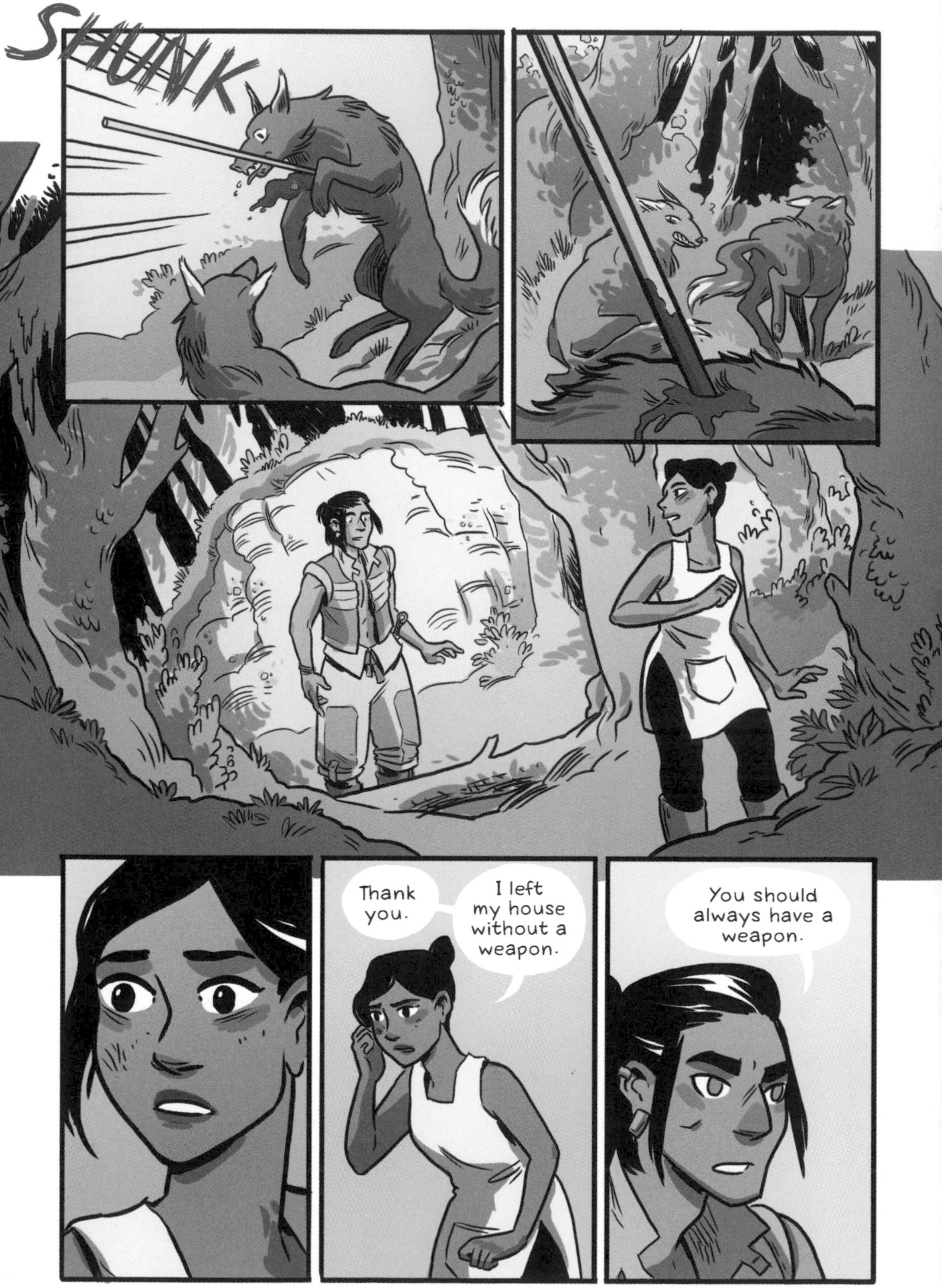
SHUNK
Thank you.
I left my house without a weapon.
You should always have a weapon.

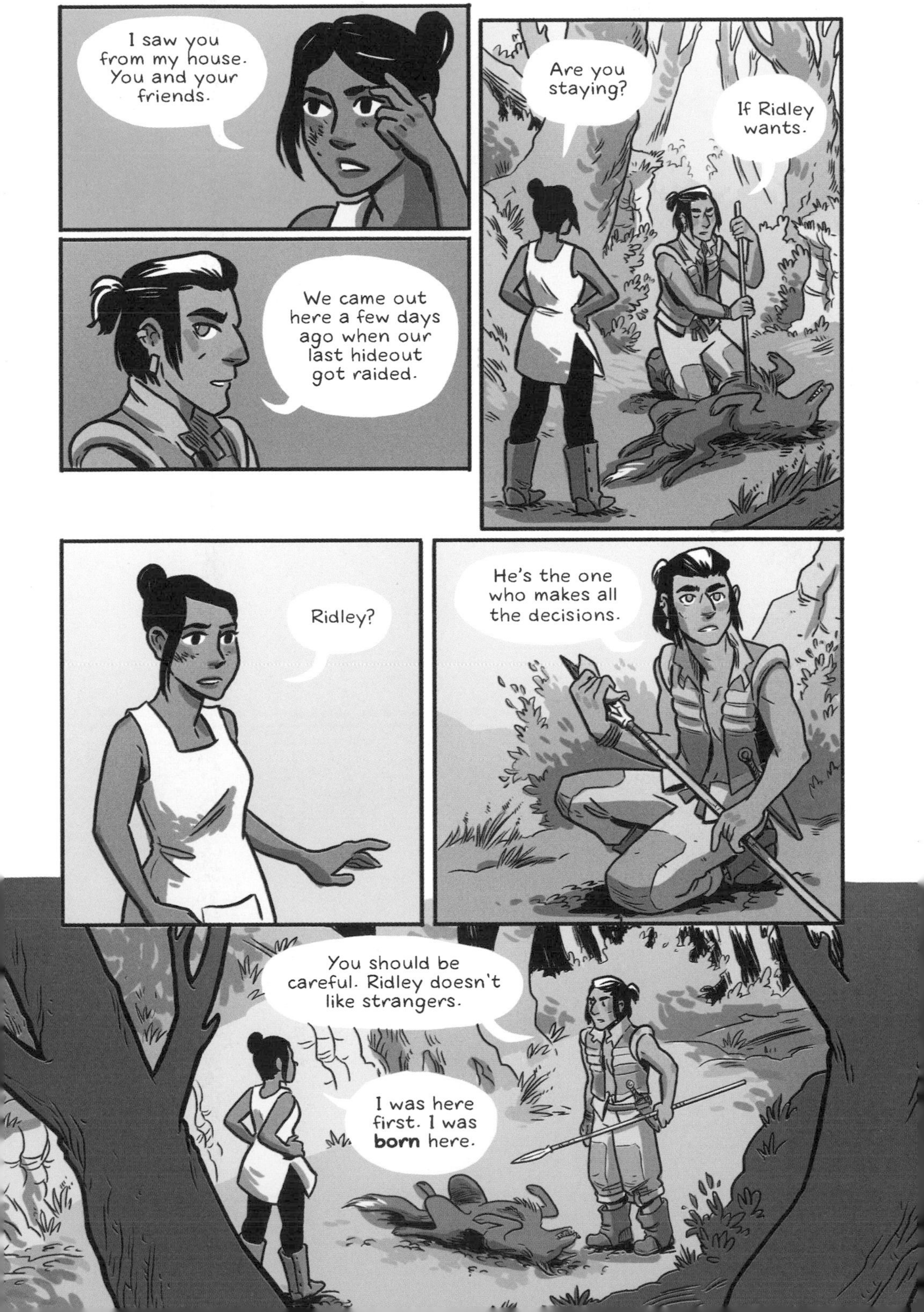
I saw you from my house. You and your friends.
We came out here a few days ago when our last hideout got raided.
Are you staying?
If Ridley wants.
Ridley?
He's the one who makes all the decisions.
You should be careful. Ridley doesn't like strangers.
I was here first. I was **born** here.

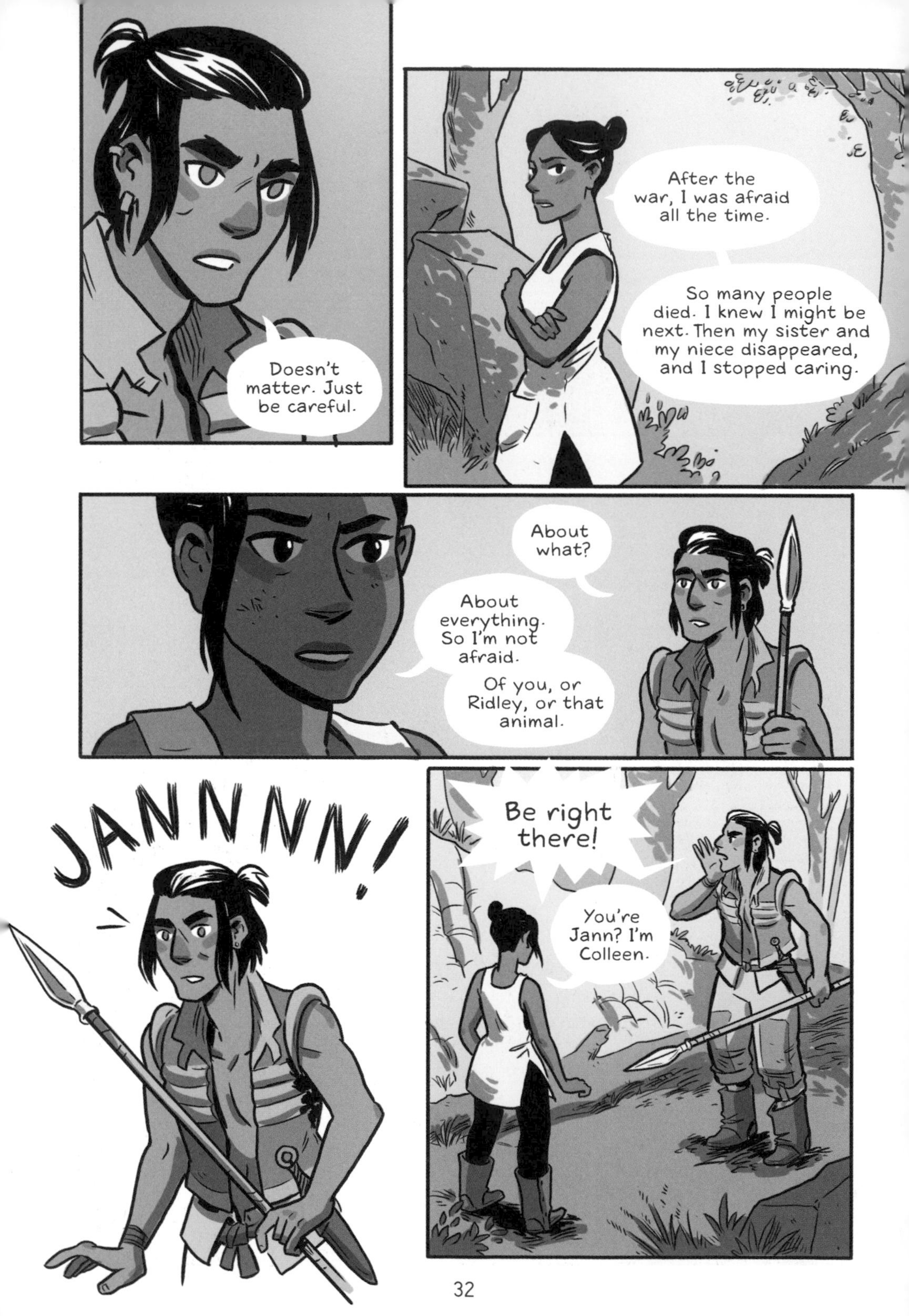
Doesn't matter. Just be careful.
After the war, I was afraid all the time.
So many people died. I knew I might be next. Then my sister and my niece disappeared, and I stopped caring.
About what?
About everything. So I'm not afraid.
Of you, or Ridley, or that animal.
JANNNN!
Be right there!
You're Jann? I'm Colleen.

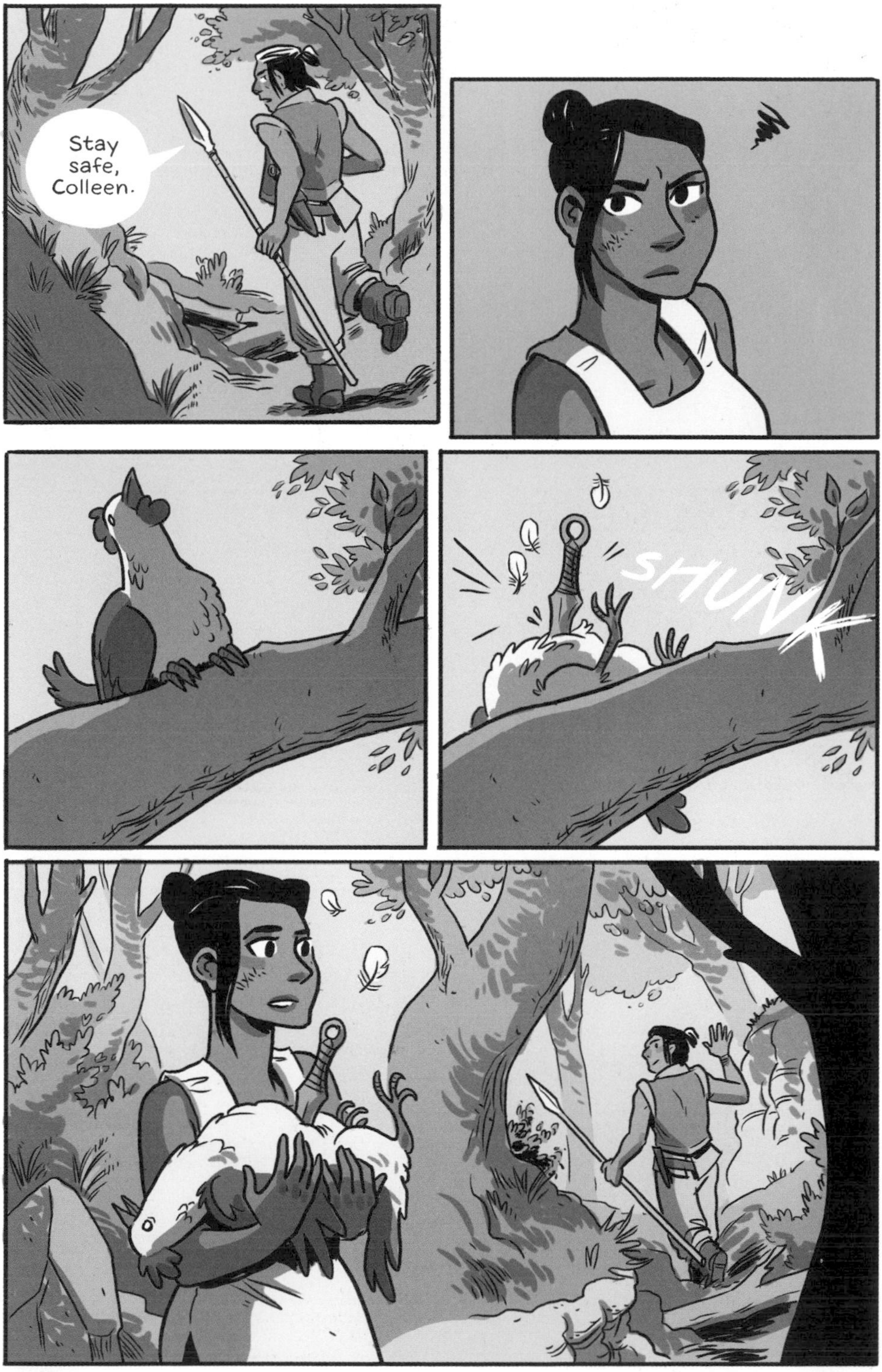
Stay safe, Colleen.
SHUNK

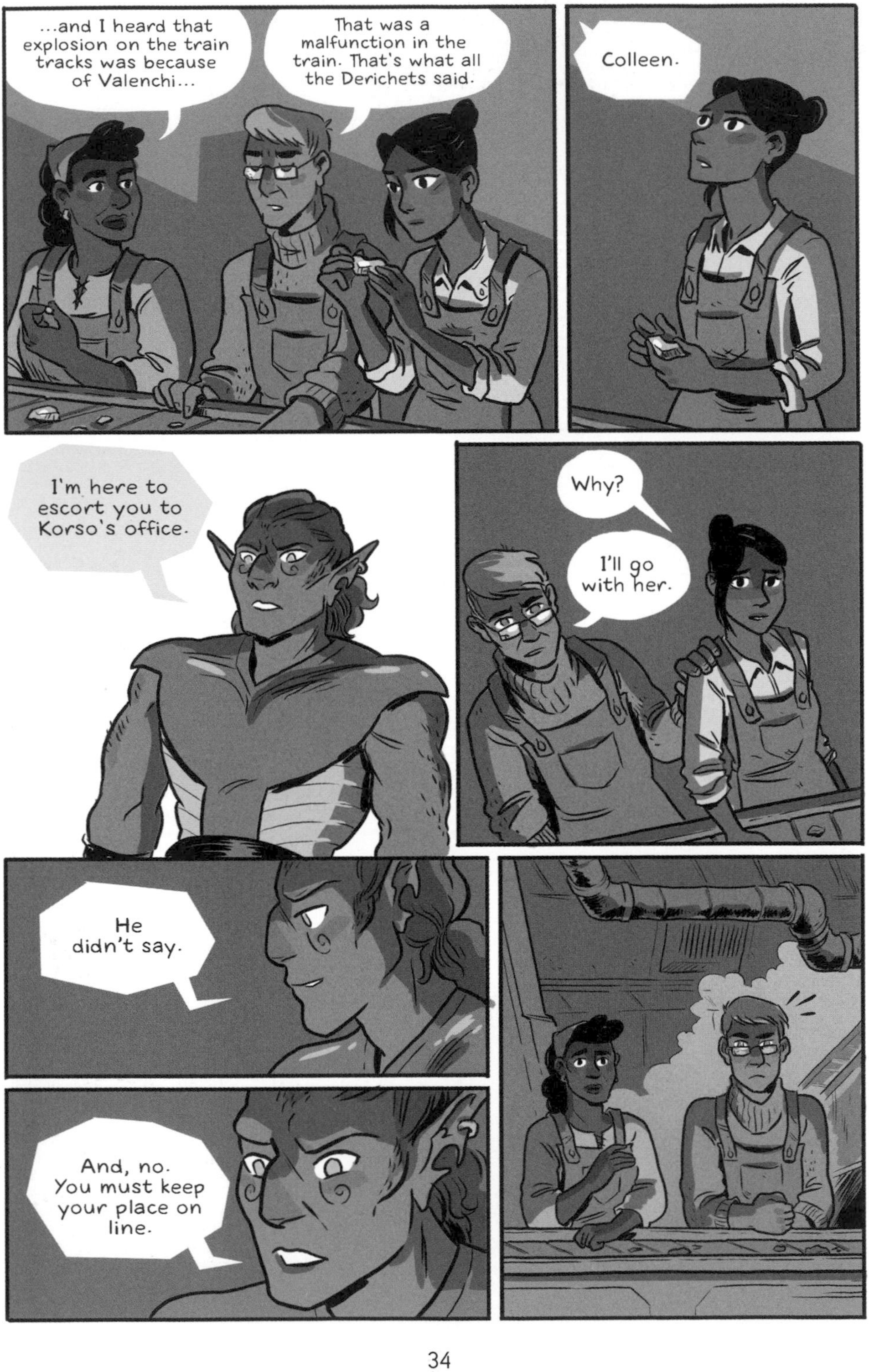
...and I heard that explosion on the train tracks was because of Valenchi...
That was a malfunction in the train. That's what all the Derichets said.
Colleen.
I'm here to escort you to Korso's office.
Why?
I'll go with her.
He didn't say.
And, no. You must keep your place on line.

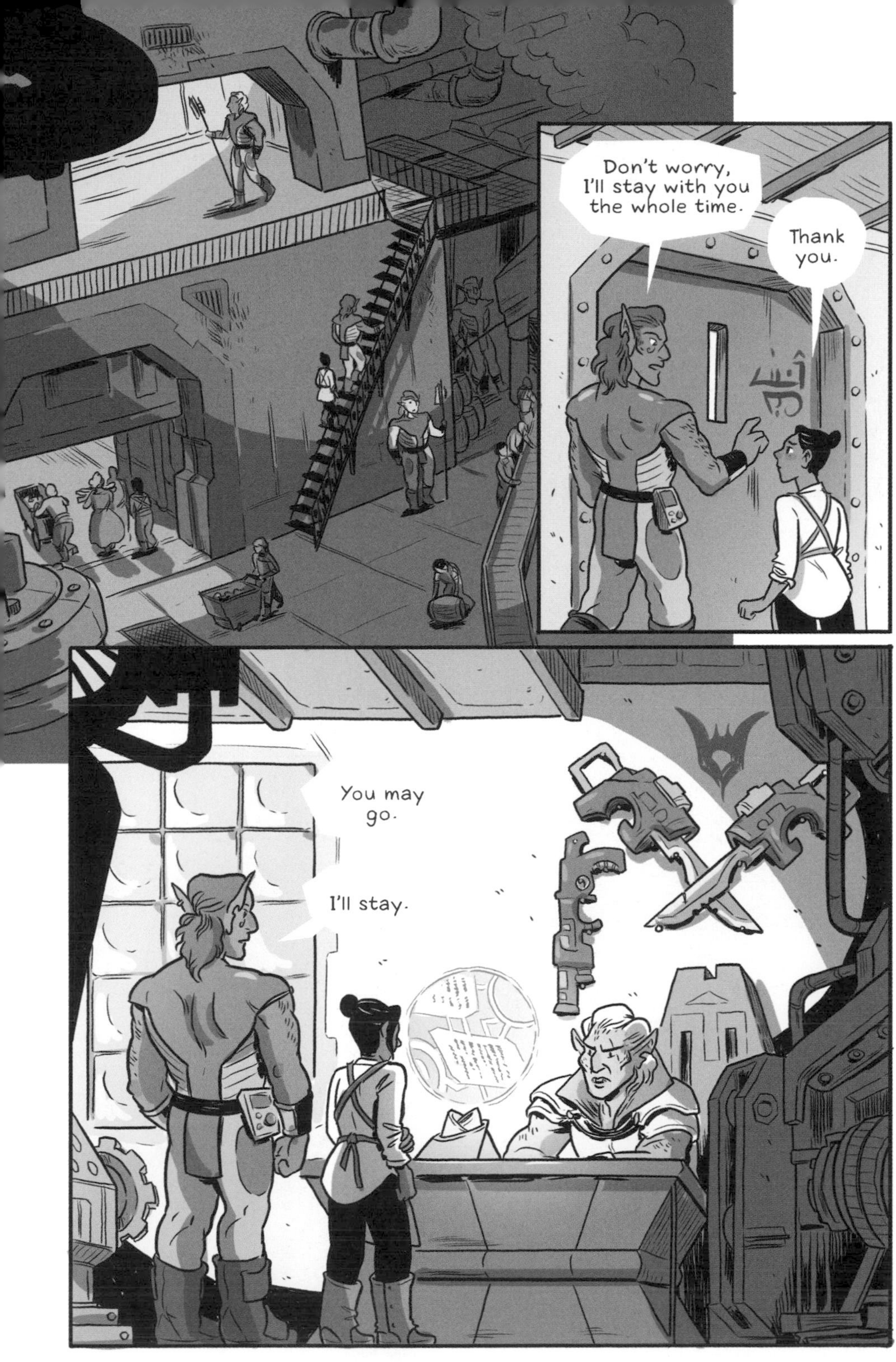
Don't worry, I'll stay with you the whole time.
Thank you.
You may go.
I'll stay.

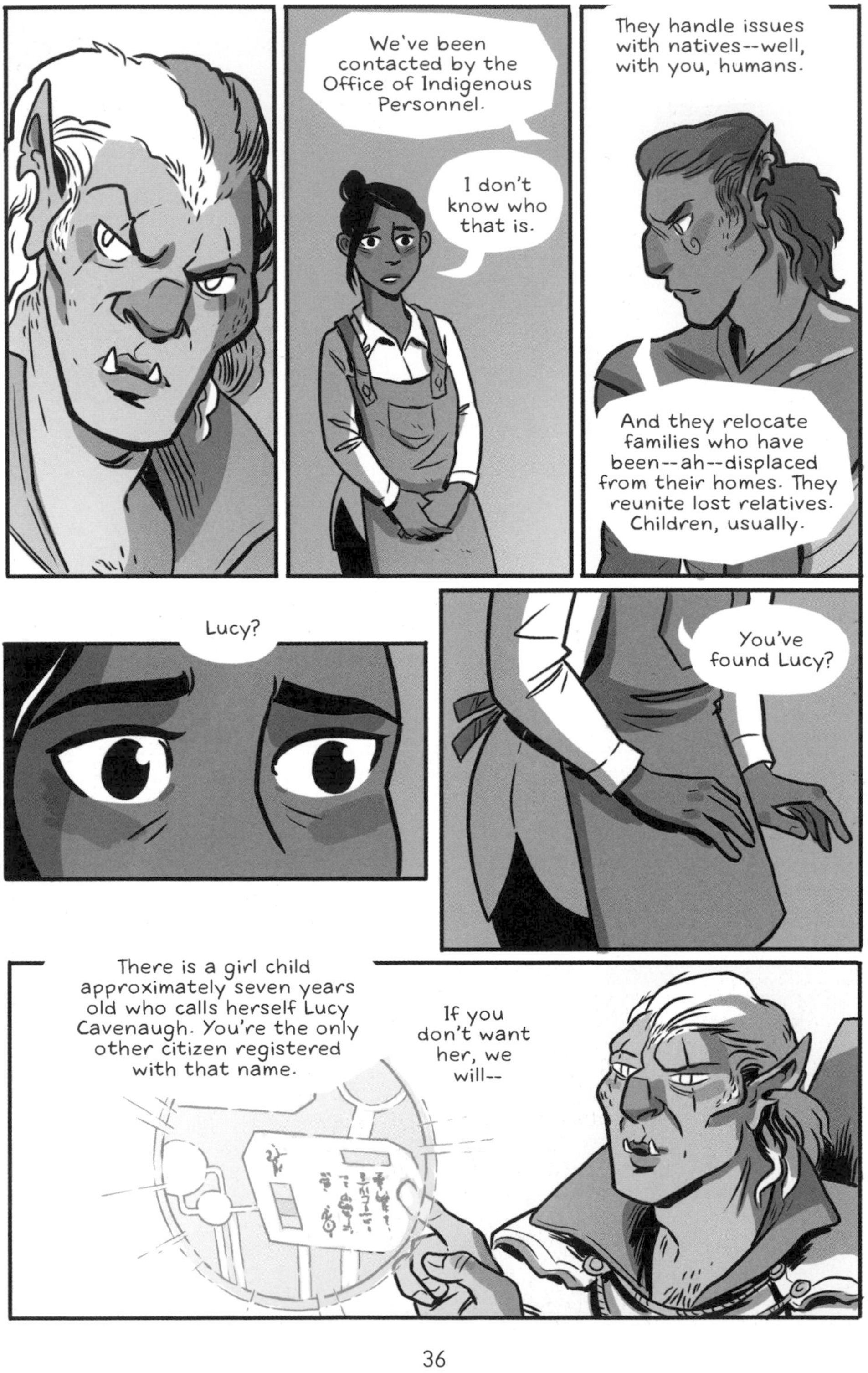
We've been contacted by the Office of Indigenous Personnel.
I don't know who that is.
They handle issues with natives--well, with you, humans.
And they relocate families who have been--ah--displaced from their homes. They reunite lost relatives. Children, usually.
Lucy?
You've found Lucy?
There is a girl child approximately seven years old who calls herself Lucy Cavenaugh. You're the only other citizen registered with that name.
If you don't want her, we will--

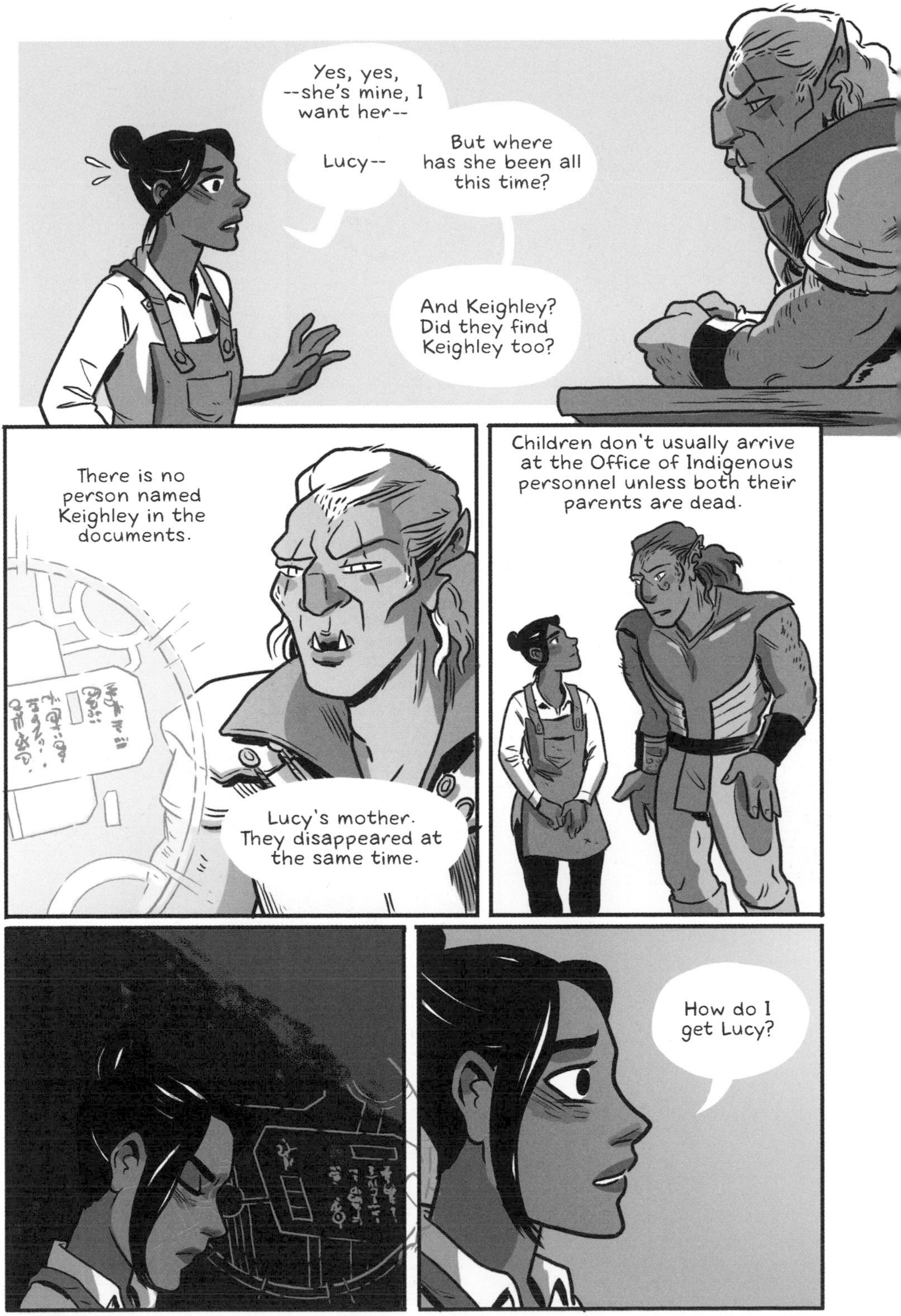
Yes, yes, --she's mine, I want her--
Lucy--
But where has she been all this time?
And Keighley? Did they find Keighley too?
There is no person named Keighley in the documents.
Lucy's mother. They disappeared at the same time.
Children don't usually arrive at the Office of Indigenous personnel unless both their parents are dead.
How do I get Lucy?

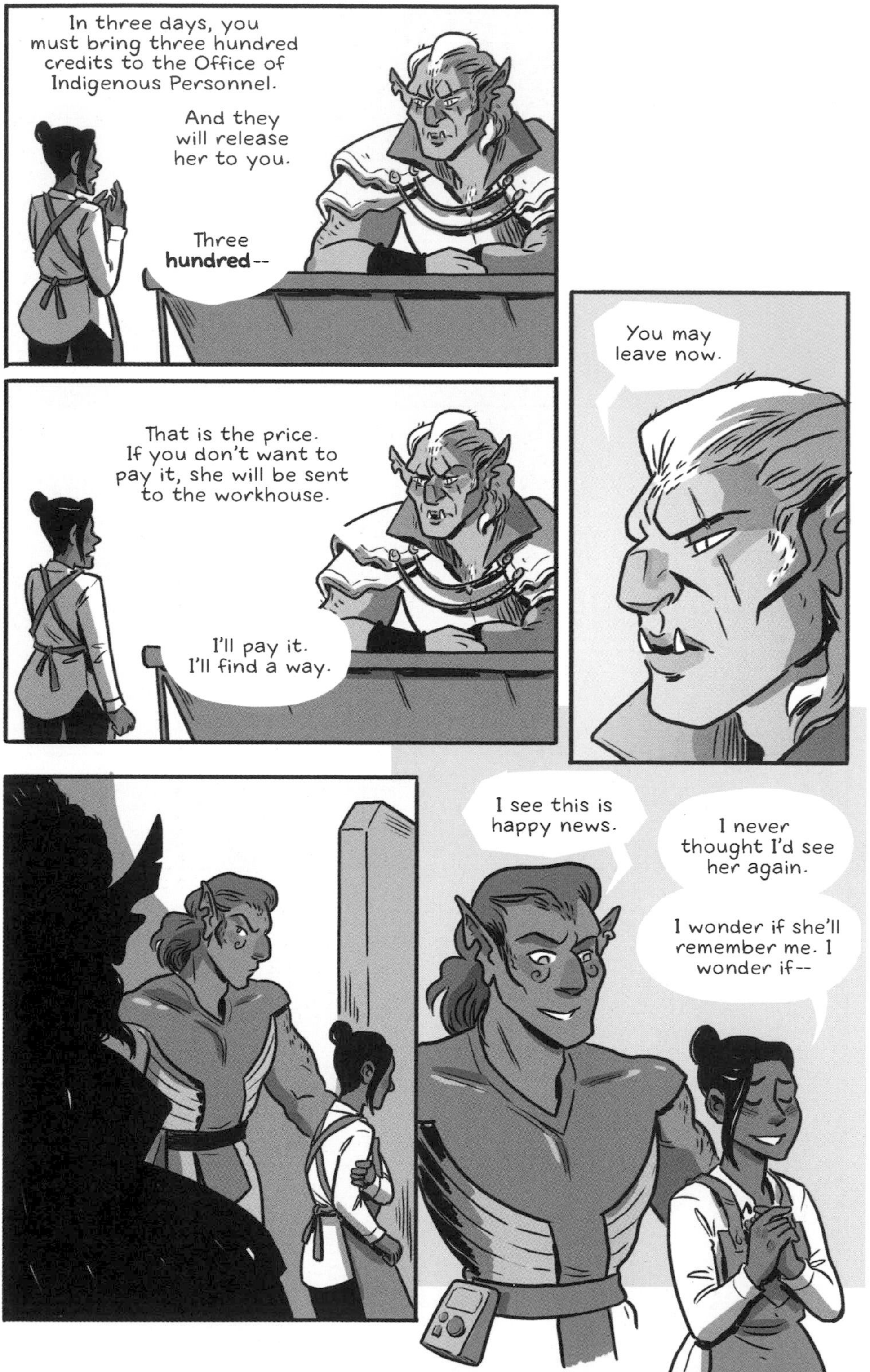
In three days, you must bring three hundred credits to the Office of Indigenous Personnel.
And they will release her to you.
Three **hundred**--
You may leave now.
That is the price. If you don't want to pay it, she will be sent to the workhouse.
I'll pay it. I'll find a way.
I see this is happy news.
I never thought I'd see her again.
I wonder if she'll remember me. I wonder if--

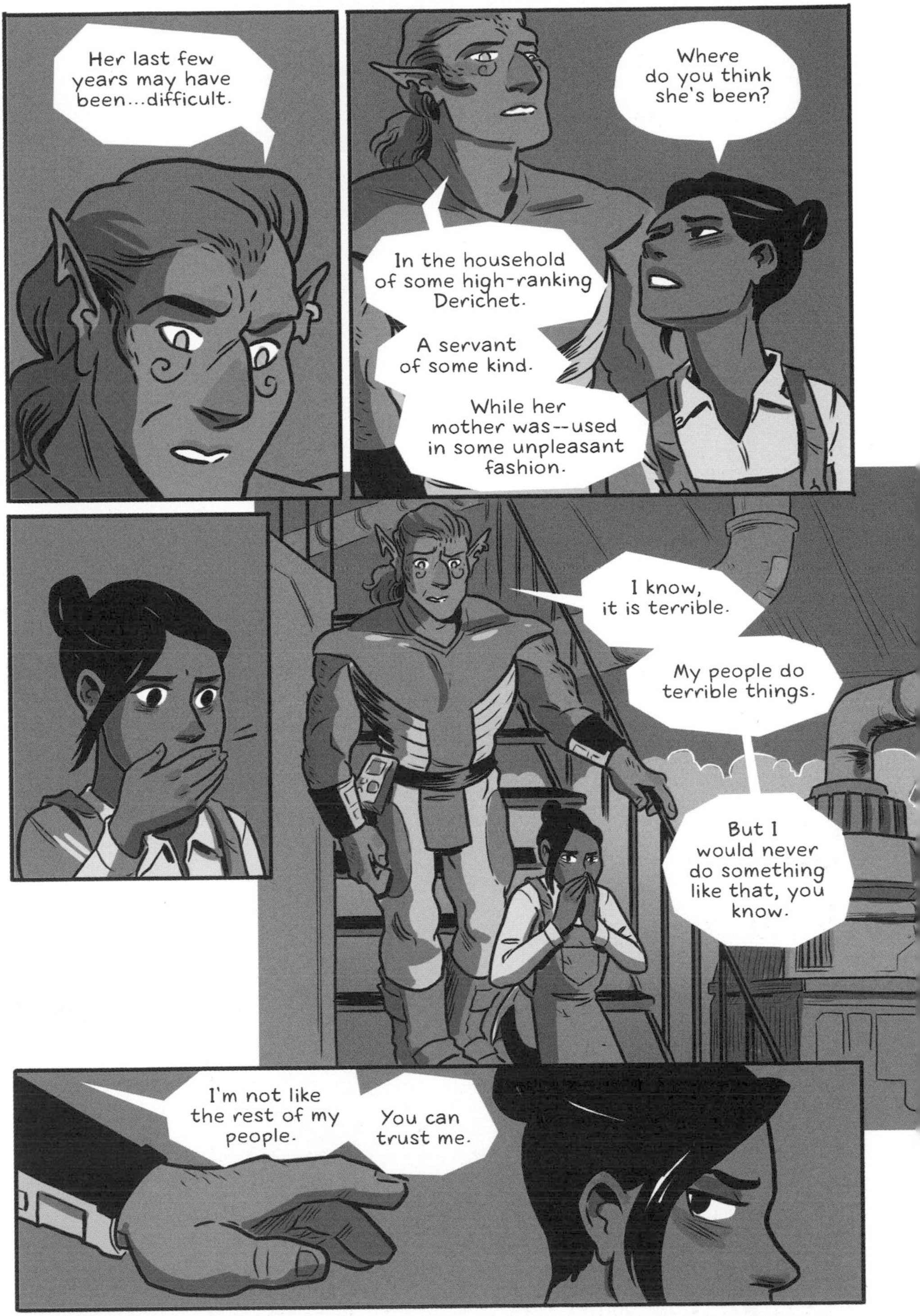
Her last few years may have been...difficult.
Where do you think she's been?
In the household of some high-ranking Derichet.
A servant of some kind.
While her mother was--used in some unpleasant fashion.
I know, it is terrible.
My people do terrible things.
But I would never do something like that, you know.
I'm not like the rest of my people.
You can trust me.

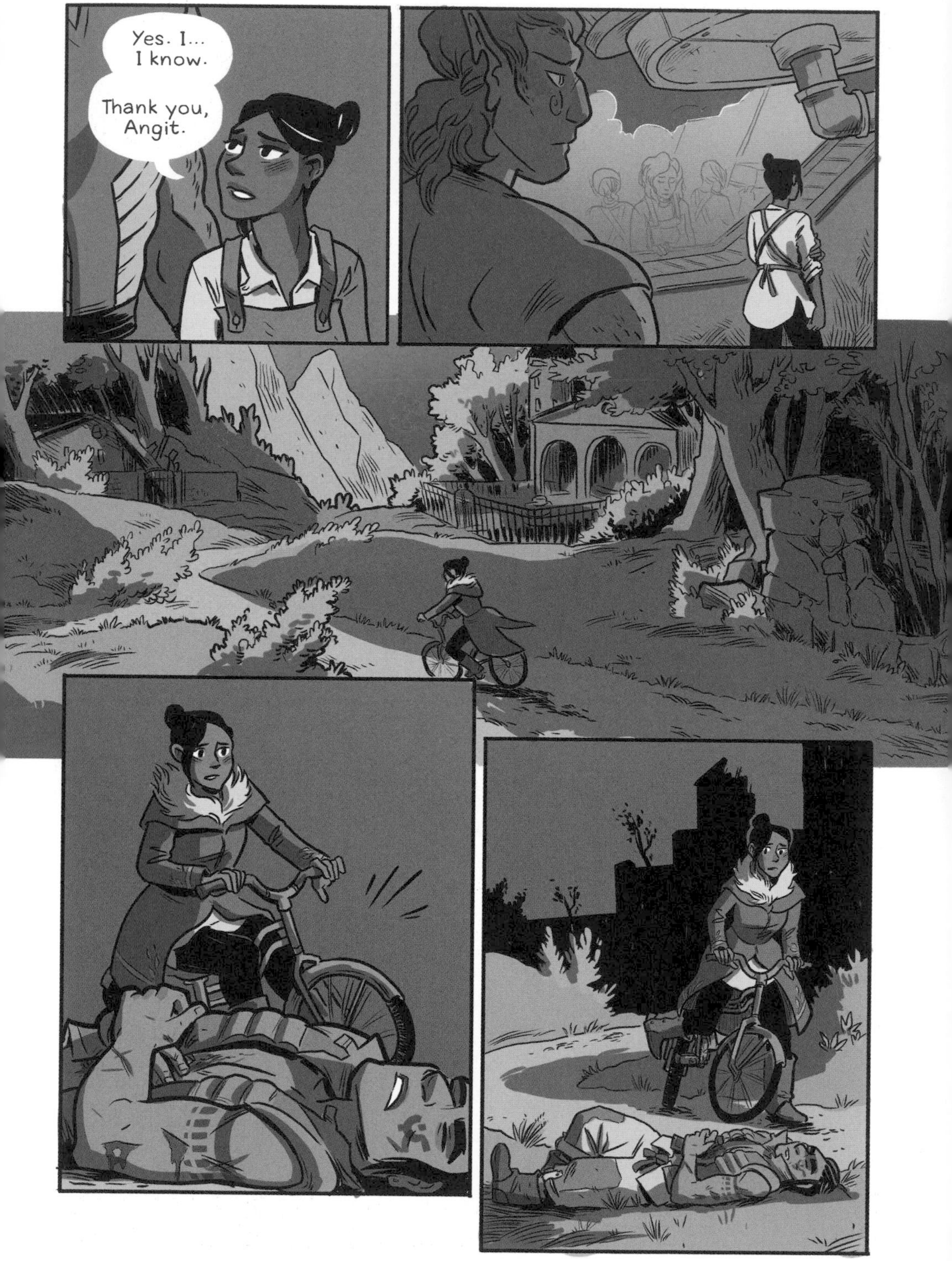
Yes. I... I know.
Thank you, Angit.

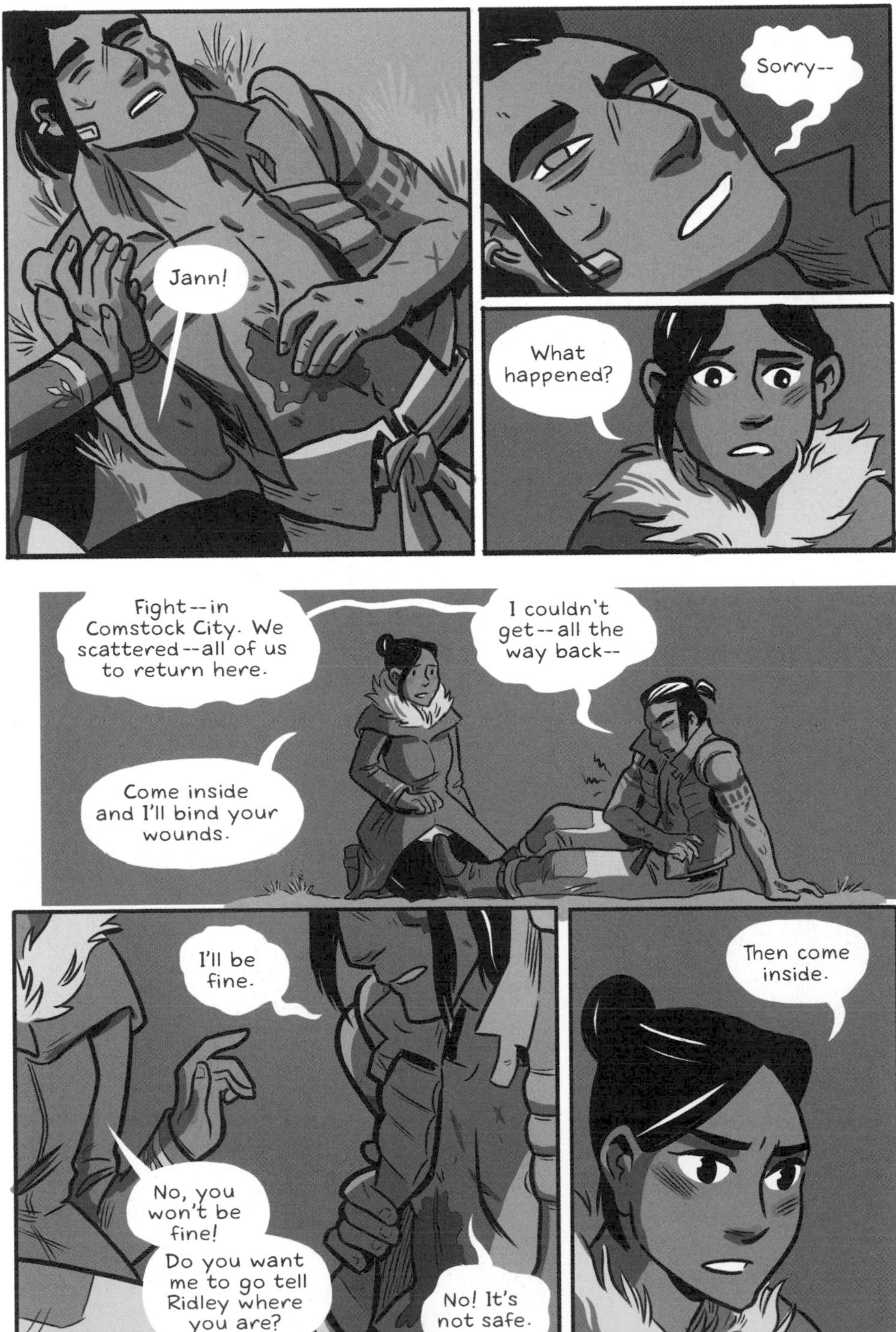
Jann!
Sorry--
What happened?
Fight--in Comstock City. We scattered--all of us to return here.
I couldn't get--all the way back--
Come inside and I'll bind your wounds.
I'll be fine.
No, you won't be fine!
Do you want me to go tell Ridley where you are?
No! It's not safe.
Then come inside.

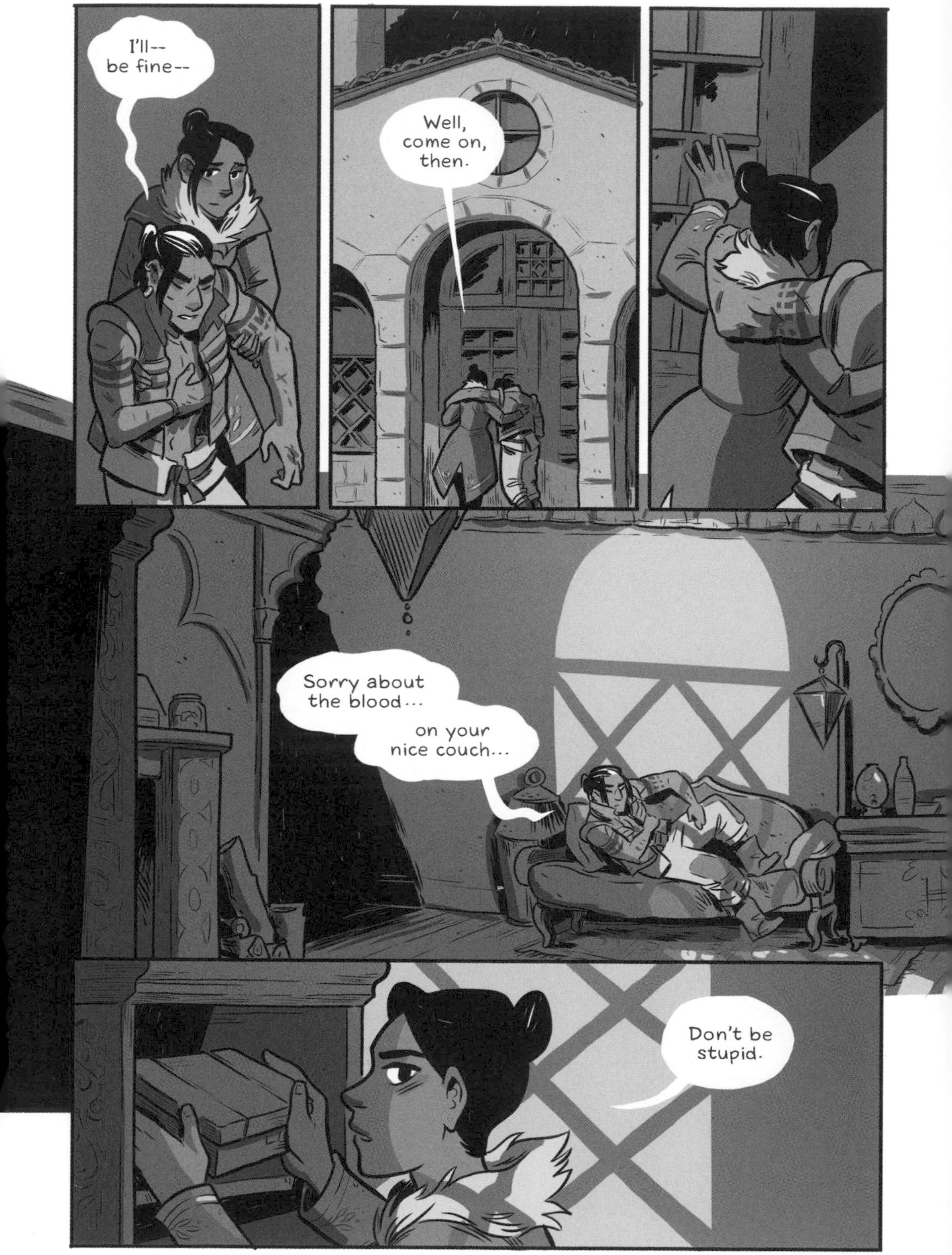
I'll--
be fine--
Well, come on, then.
Sorry about the blood...
on your nice couch...
Don't be stupid.

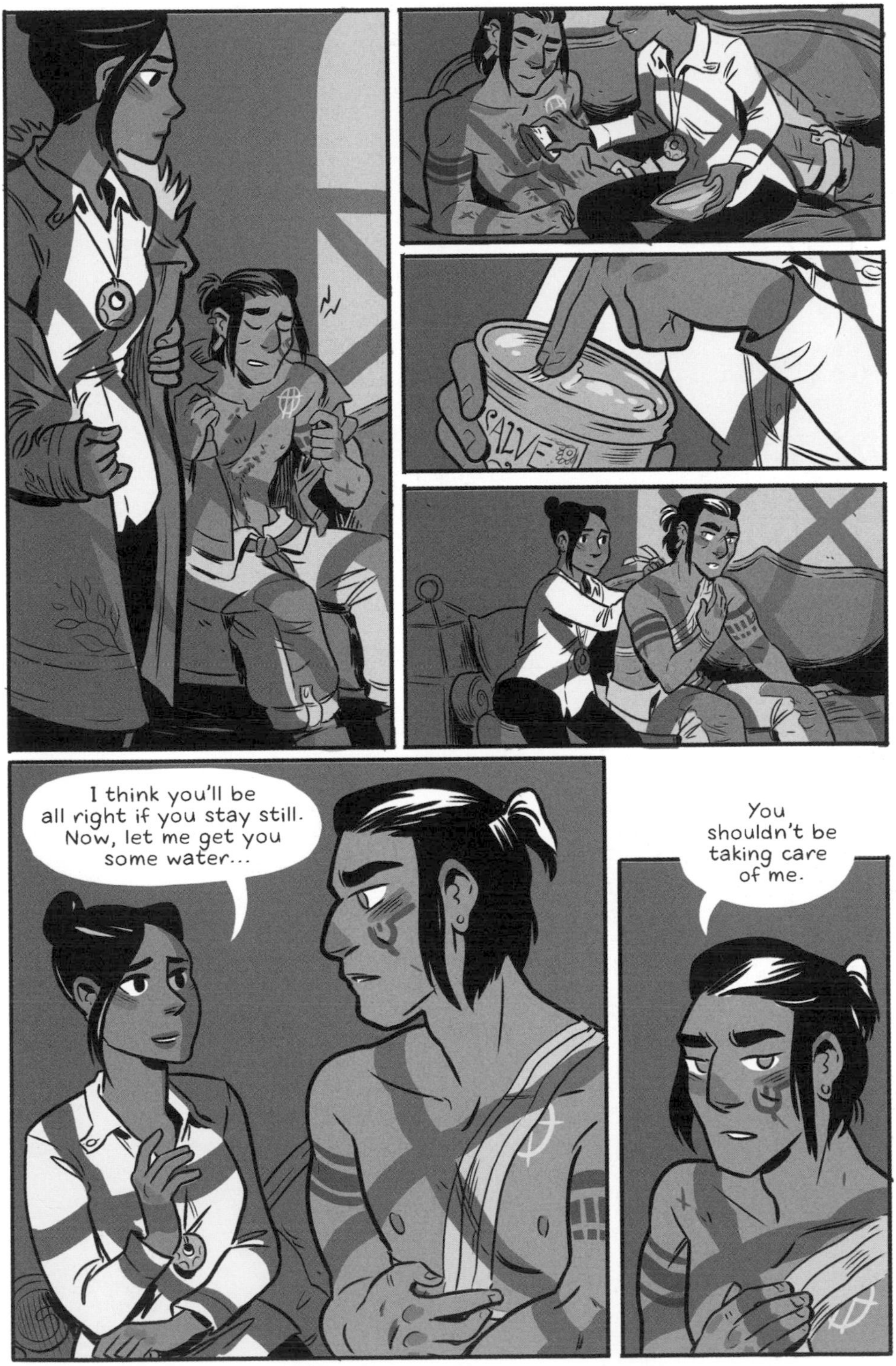
SALVE
I think you'll be all right if you stay still. Now, let me get you some water...
You shouldn't be taking care of me.

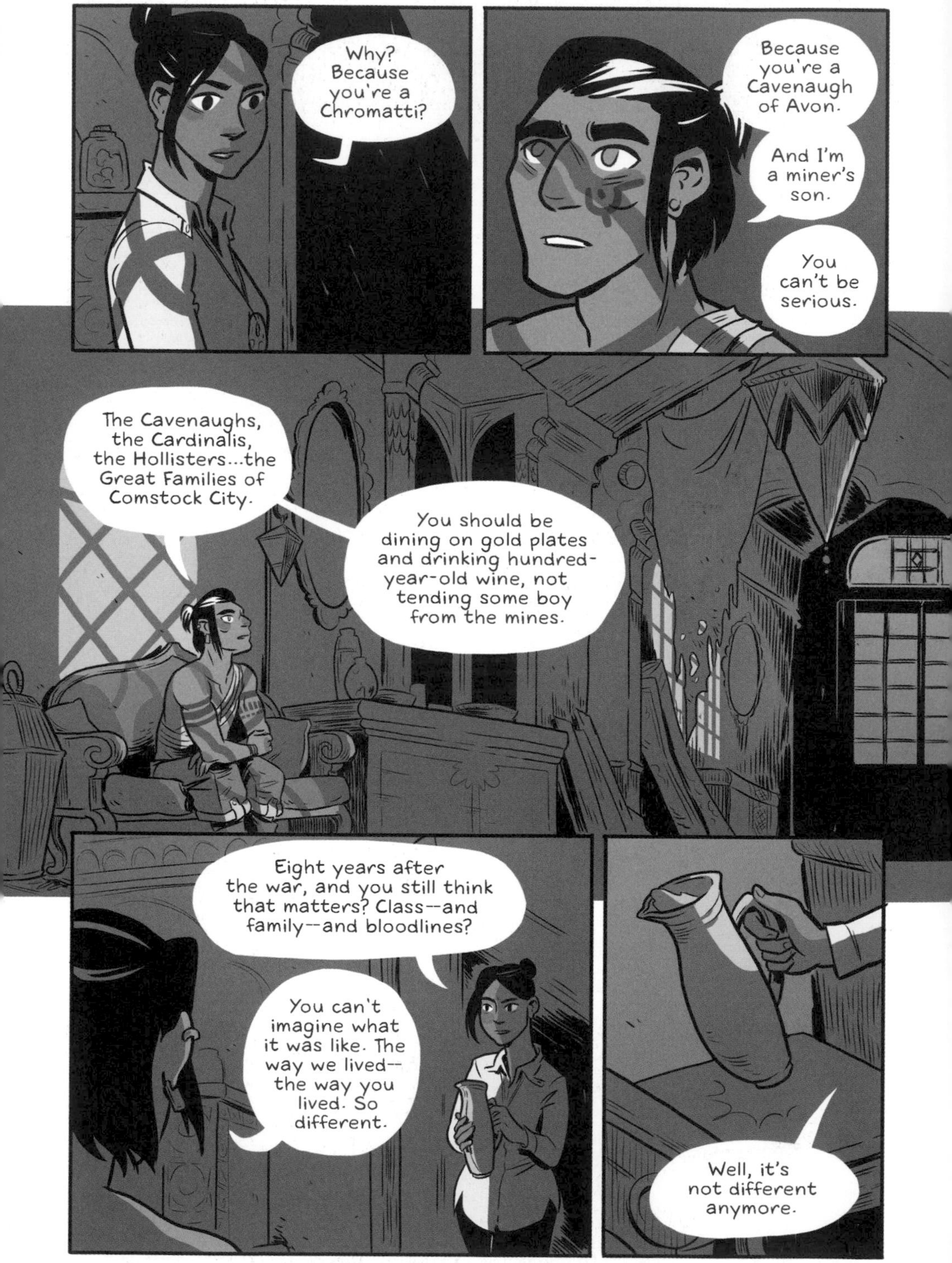
Why? Because you're a Chromatti?
Because you're a Cavenaugh of Avon.
And I'm a miner's son.
You can't be serious.
The Cavenaughs, the Cardinalis, the Hollisters...the Great Families of Comstock City.
You should be dining on gold plates and drinking hundred-year-old wine, not tending some boy from the mines.
Eight years after the war, and you still think that matters? Class--and family--and bloodlines?
You can't imagine what it was like. The way we lived--the way you lived. So different.
Well, it's not different anymore.

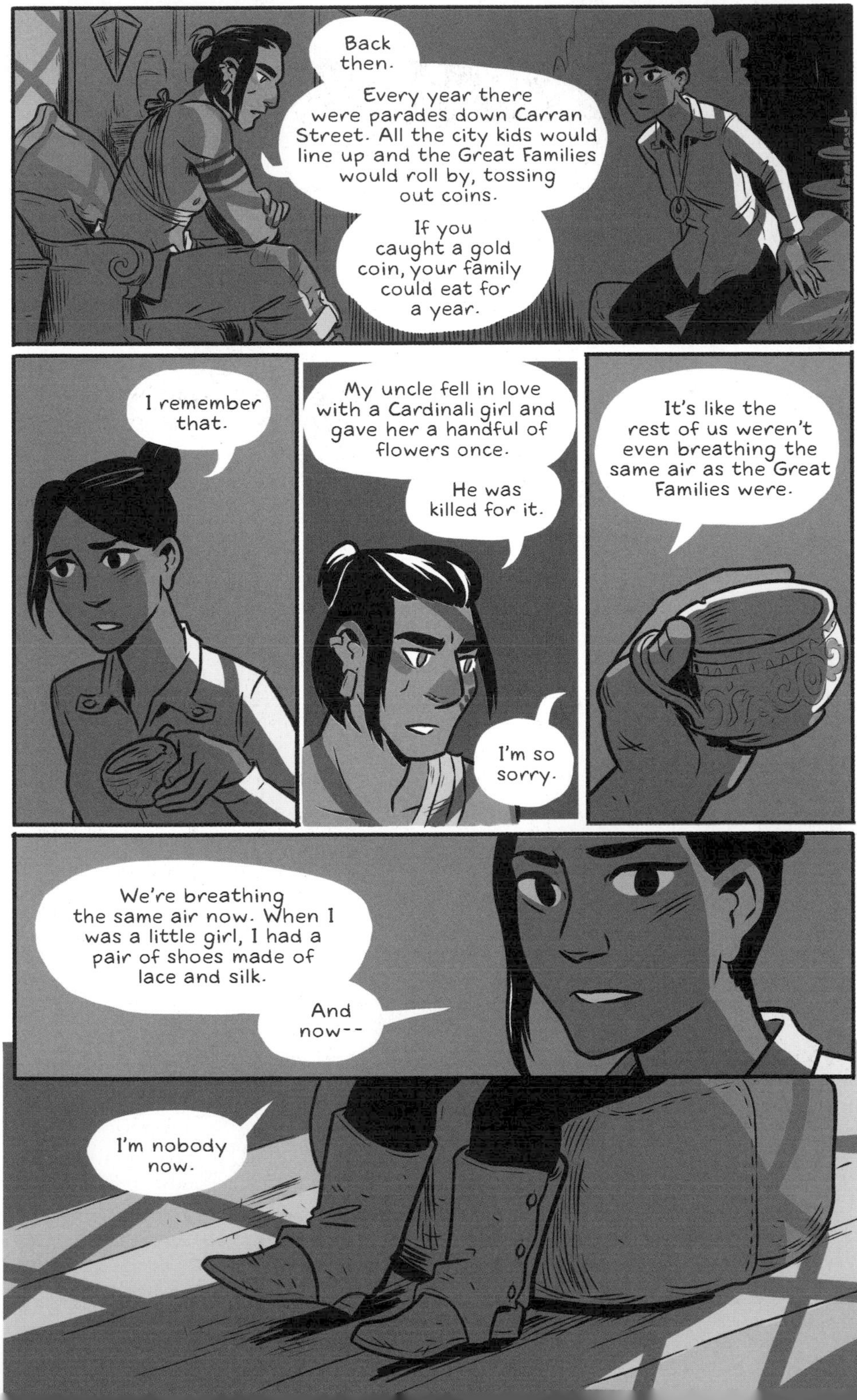
Back then.
Every year there were parades down Carran Street. All the city kids would line up and the Great Families would roll by, tossing out coins.
If you caught a gold coin, your family could eat for a year.
I remember that.
My uncle fell in love with a Cardinali girl and gave her a handful of flowers once.
He was killed for it.
I'm so sorry.
It's like the rest of us weren't even breathing the same air as the Great Families were.
We're breathing the same air now. When I was a little girl, I had a pair of shoes made of lace and silk.
And now--
I'm nobody now.

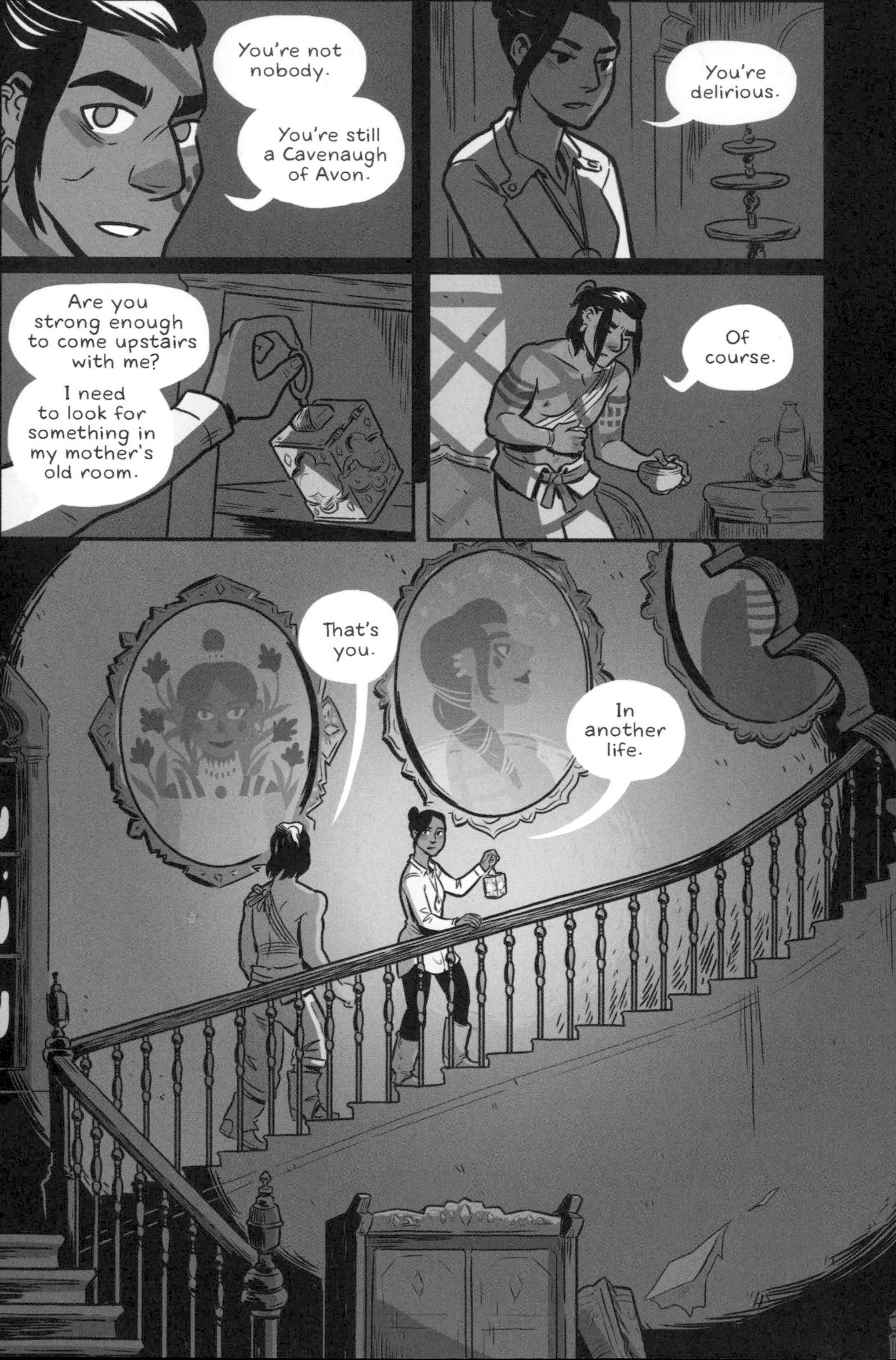
You're not nobody.
You're still a Cavenaugh of Avon.
You're delirious.
Are you strong enough to come upstairs with me?
I need to look for something in my mother's old room.
Of course.
That's you.
In another life.

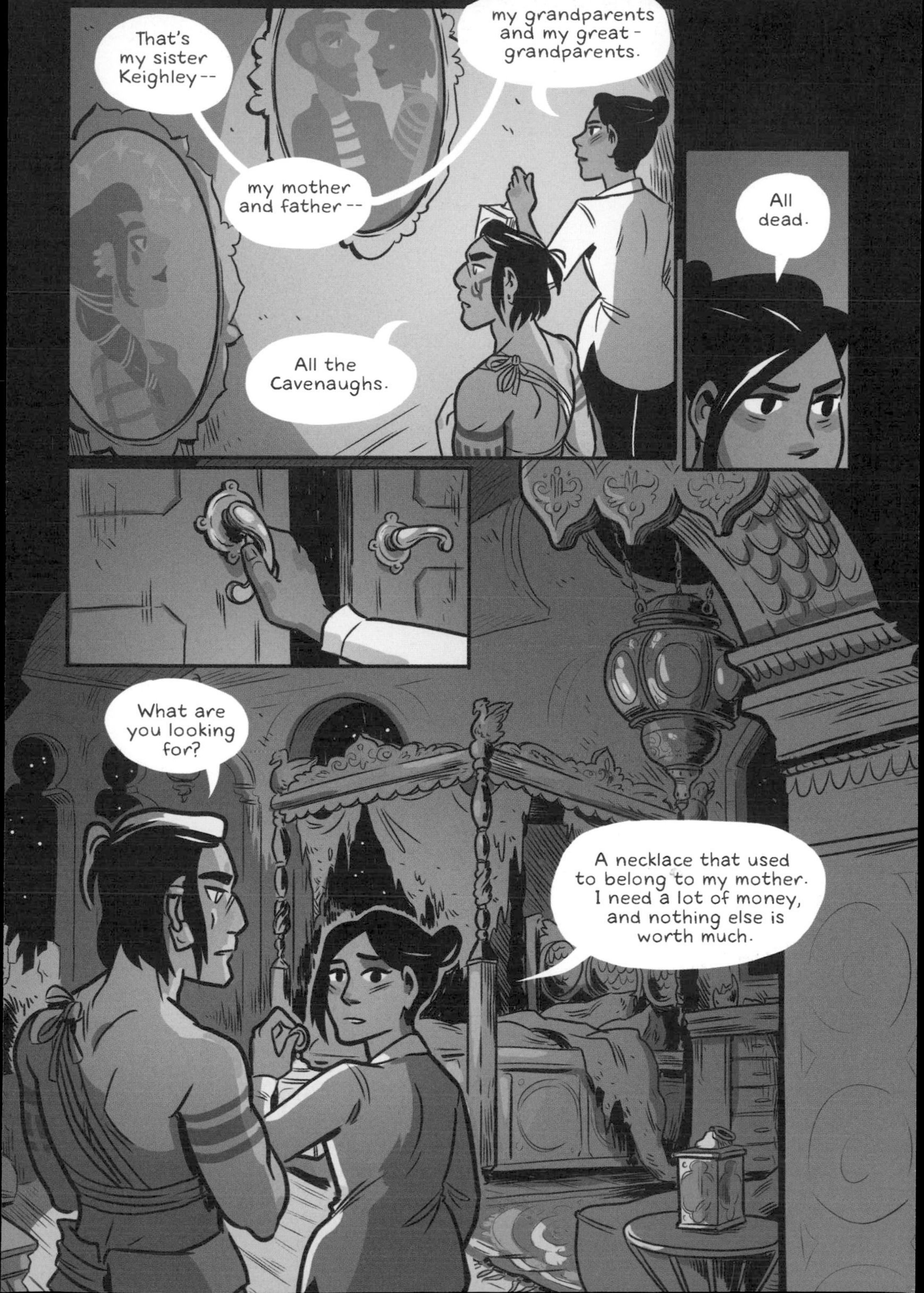
That's my sister Keighley--
my mother and father--
my grandparents and my great-grandparents.
All the Cavenaughs.
All dead.
What are you looking for?
A necklace that used to belong to my mother. I need a lot of money, and nothing else is worth much.

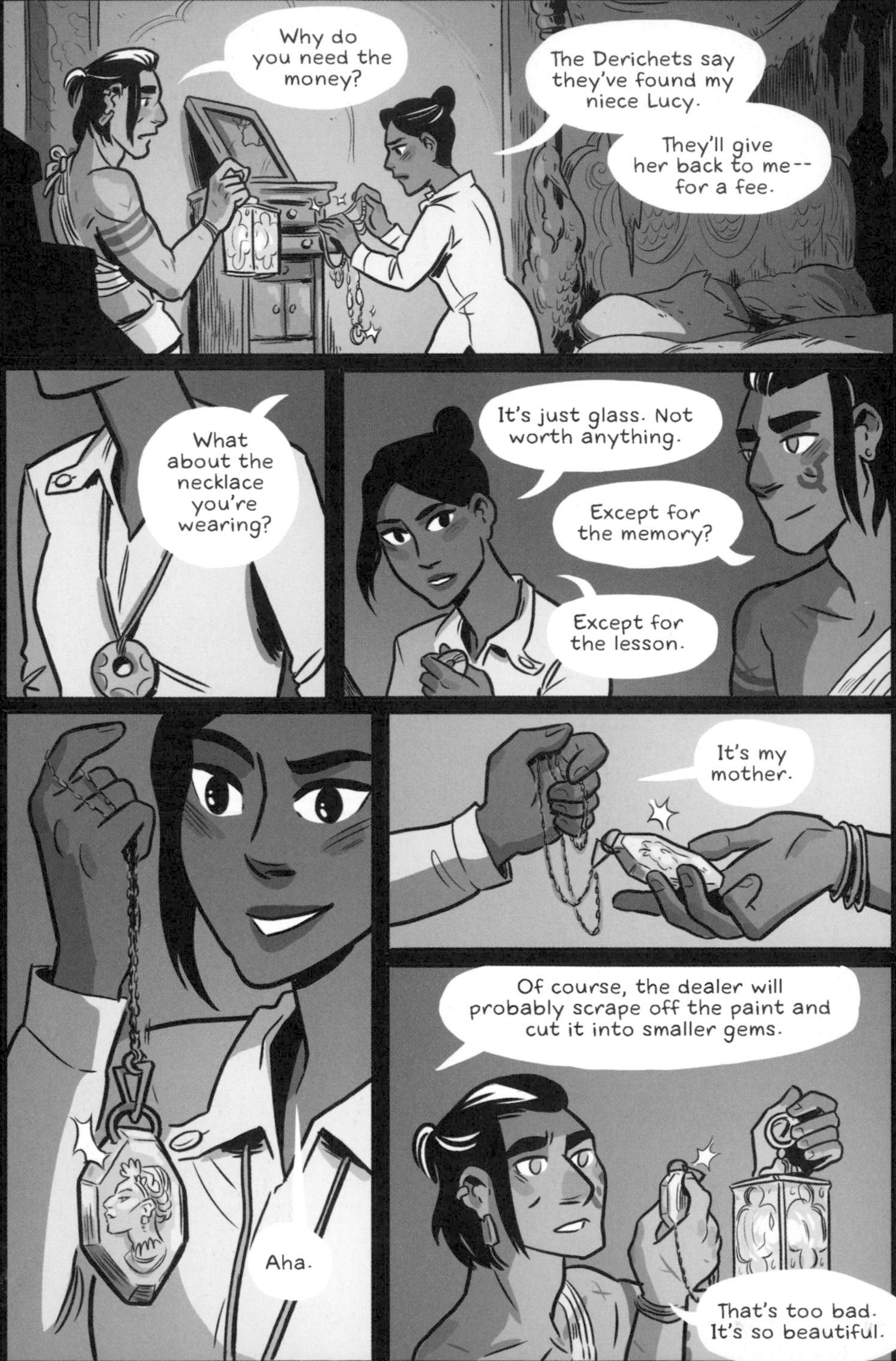
Why do you need the money?
The Derichets say they've found my niece Lucy.
They'll give her back to me-- for a fee.
What about the necklace you're wearing?
It's just glass. Not worth anything.
Except for the memory?
Except for the lesson.
Aha.
It's my mother.
Of course, the dealer will probably scrape off the paint and cut it into smaller gems.
That's too bad. It's so beautiful.

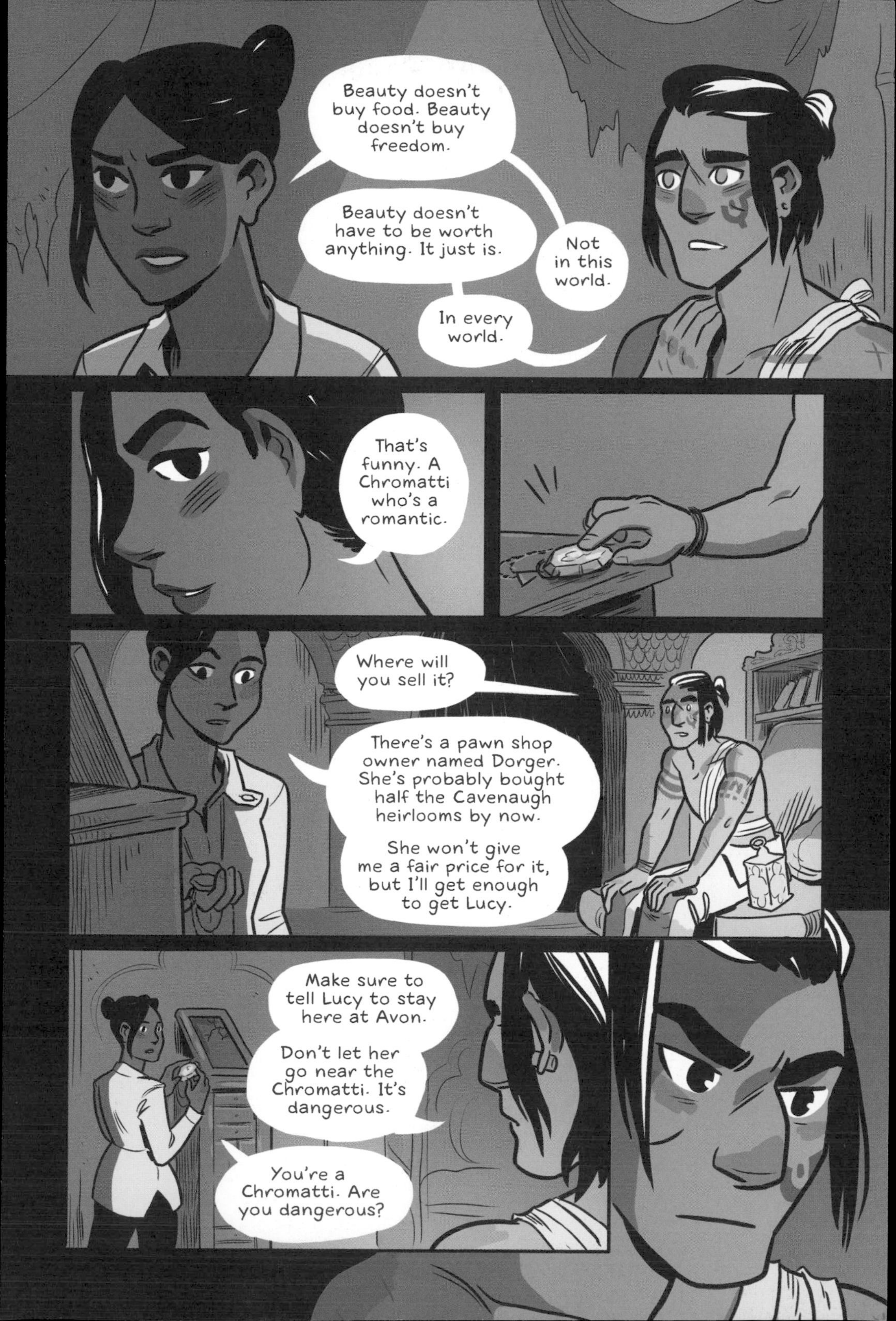
Beauty doesn't buy food. Beauty doesn't buy freedom.
Beauty doesn't have to be worth anything. It just is.
Not in this world.
In every world.
That's funny. A Chromatti who's a romantic.
Where will you sell it?
There's a pawn shop owner named Dorger. She's probably bought half the Cavenaugh heirlooms by now.
She won't give me a fair price for it, but I'll get enough to get Lucy.
Make sure to tell Lucy to stay here at Avon.
Don't let her go near the Chromatti. It's dangerous.
You're a Chromatti. Are you dangerous?

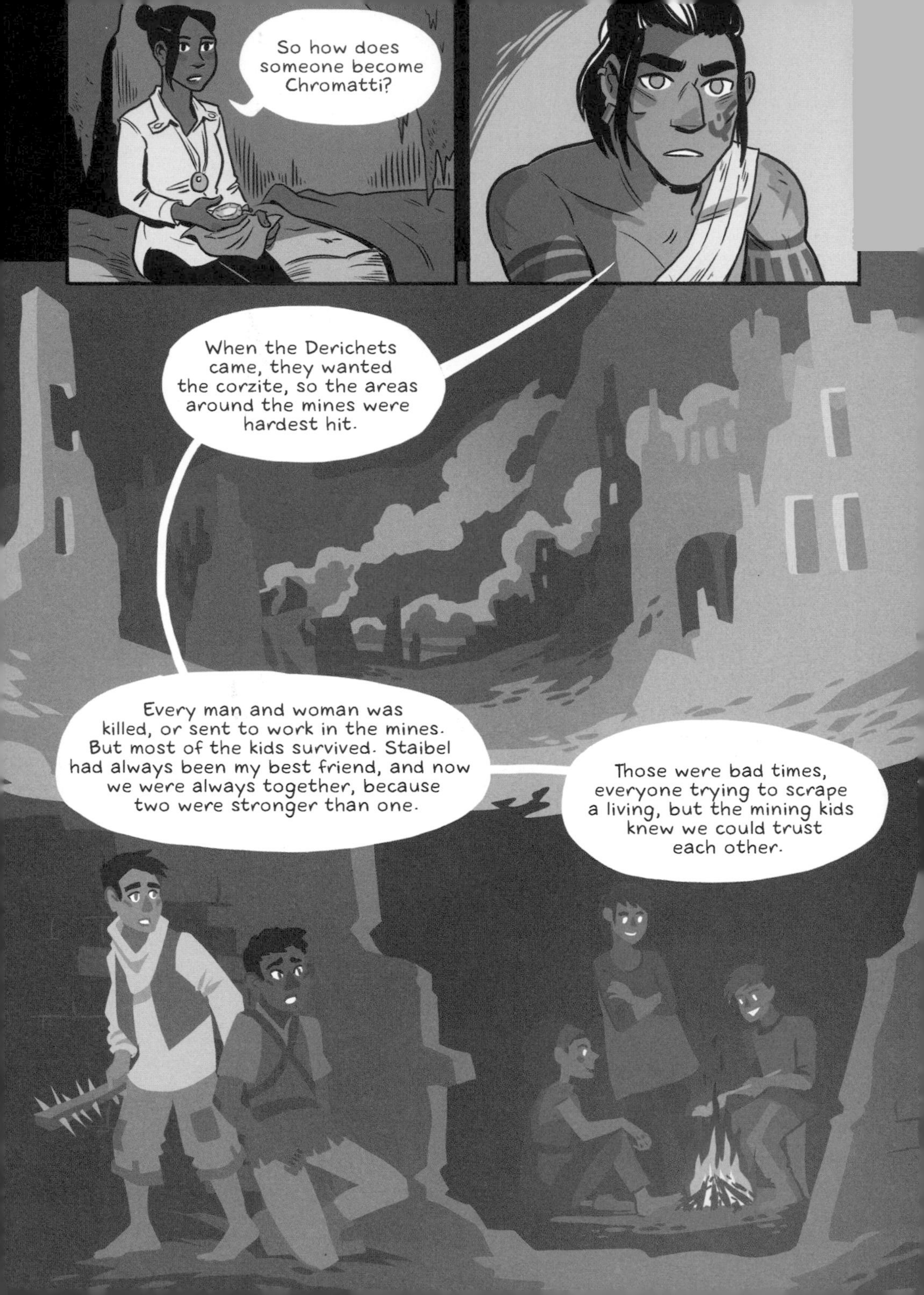
So how does someone become Chromatti?
When the Derichets came, they wanted the corzite, so the areas around the mines were hardest hit.
Every man and woman was killed, or sent to work in the mines. But most of the kids survived. Staibel had always been my best friend, and now we were always together, because two were stronger than one.
Those were bad times, everyone trying to scrape a living, but the mining kids knew we could trust each other.

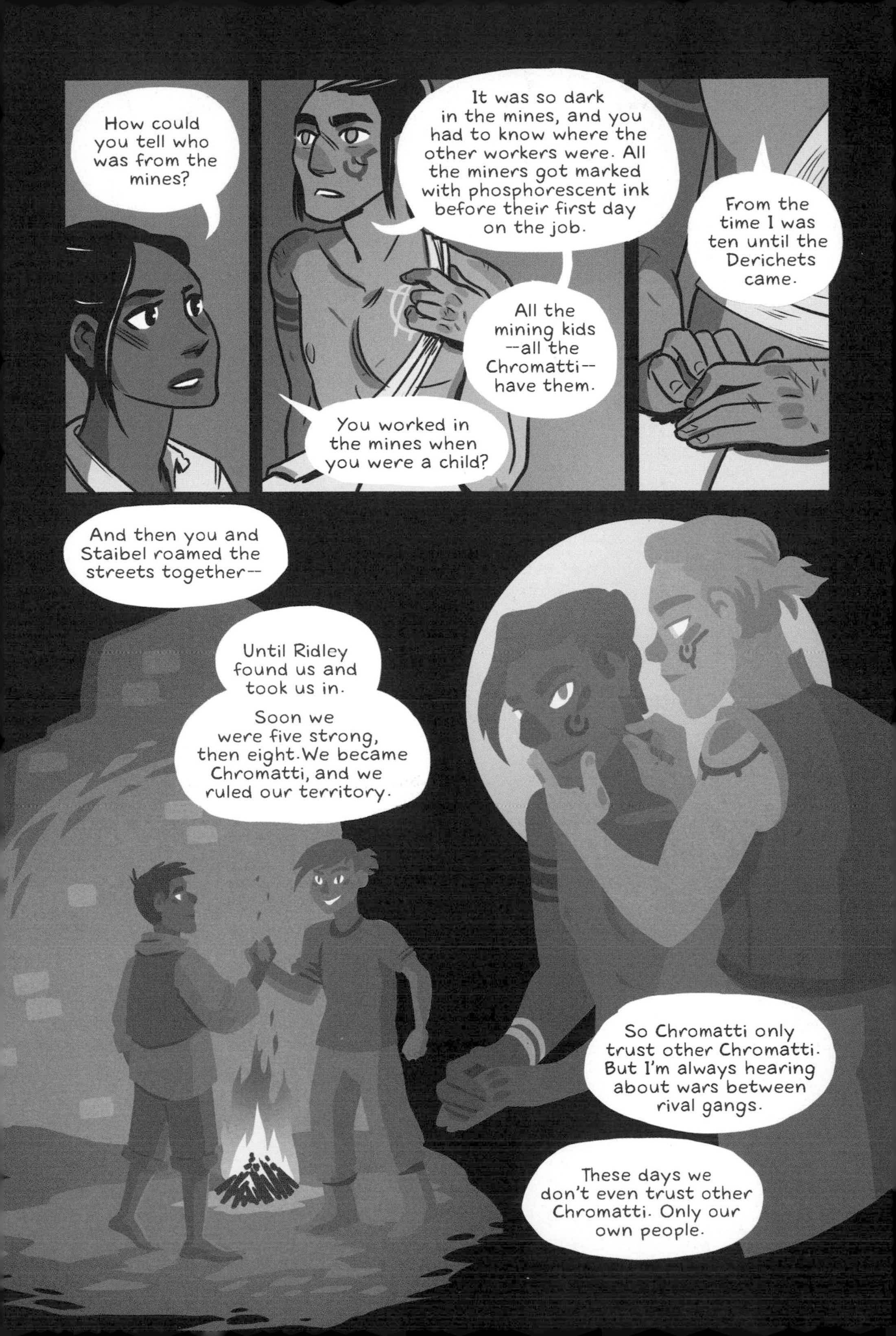

How could you tell who was from the mines?
It was so dark in the mines, and you had to know where the other workers were. All the miners got marked with phosphorescent ink before their first day on the job.
All the mining kids --all the Chromatti-- have them.
You worked in the mines when you were a child?
From the time I was ten until the Derichets came.
And then you and Staibel roamed the streets together--
Until Ridley found us and took us in.
Soon we were five strong, then eight. We became Chromatti, and we ruled our territory.
So Chromatti only trust other Chromatti. But I'm always hearing about wars between rival gangs.
These days we don't even trust other Chromatti. Only our own people.

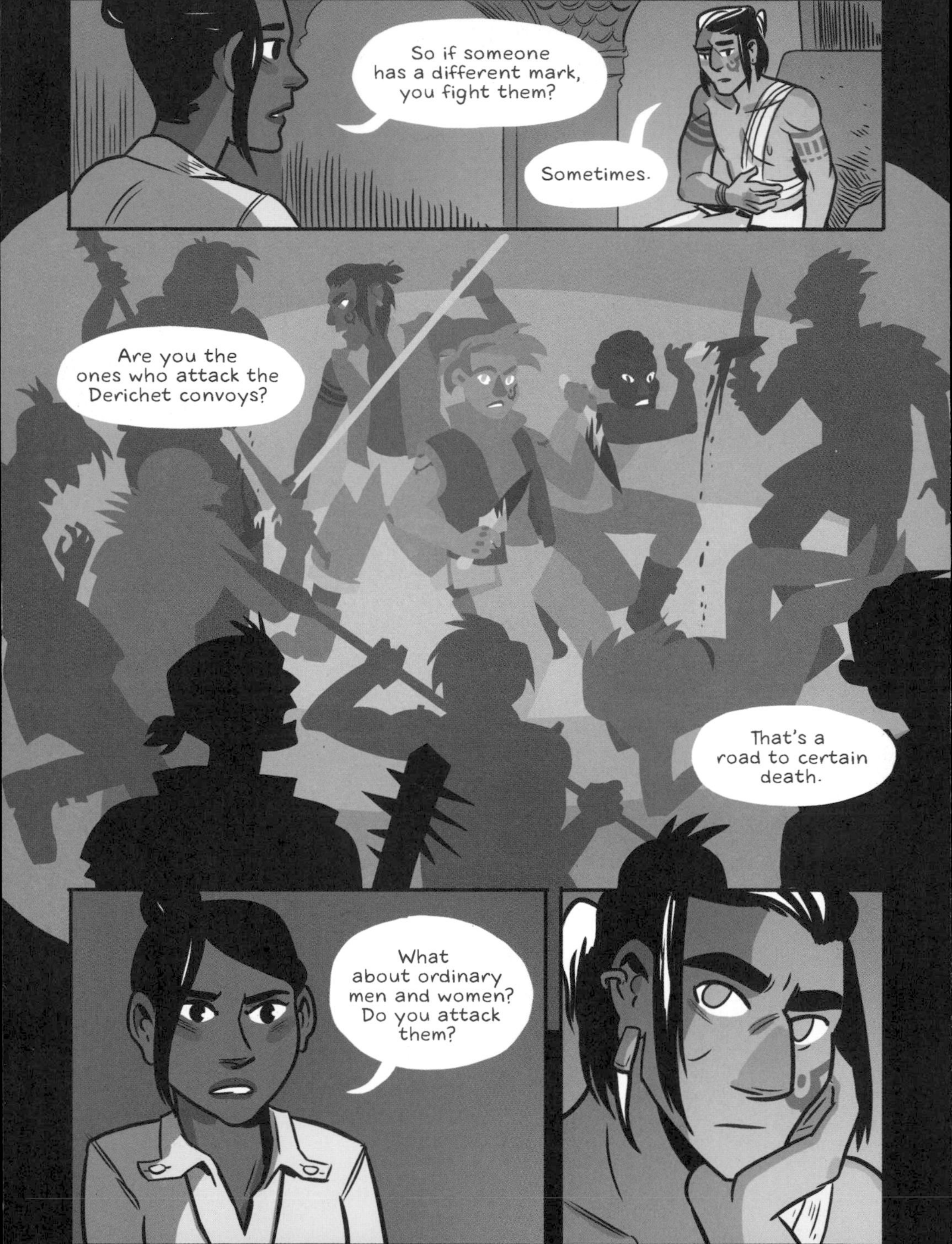
So if someone has a different mark, you fight them?
Sometimes.
Are you the ones who attack the Derichet convoys?
That's a road to certain death.
What about ordinary men and women? Do you attack them?

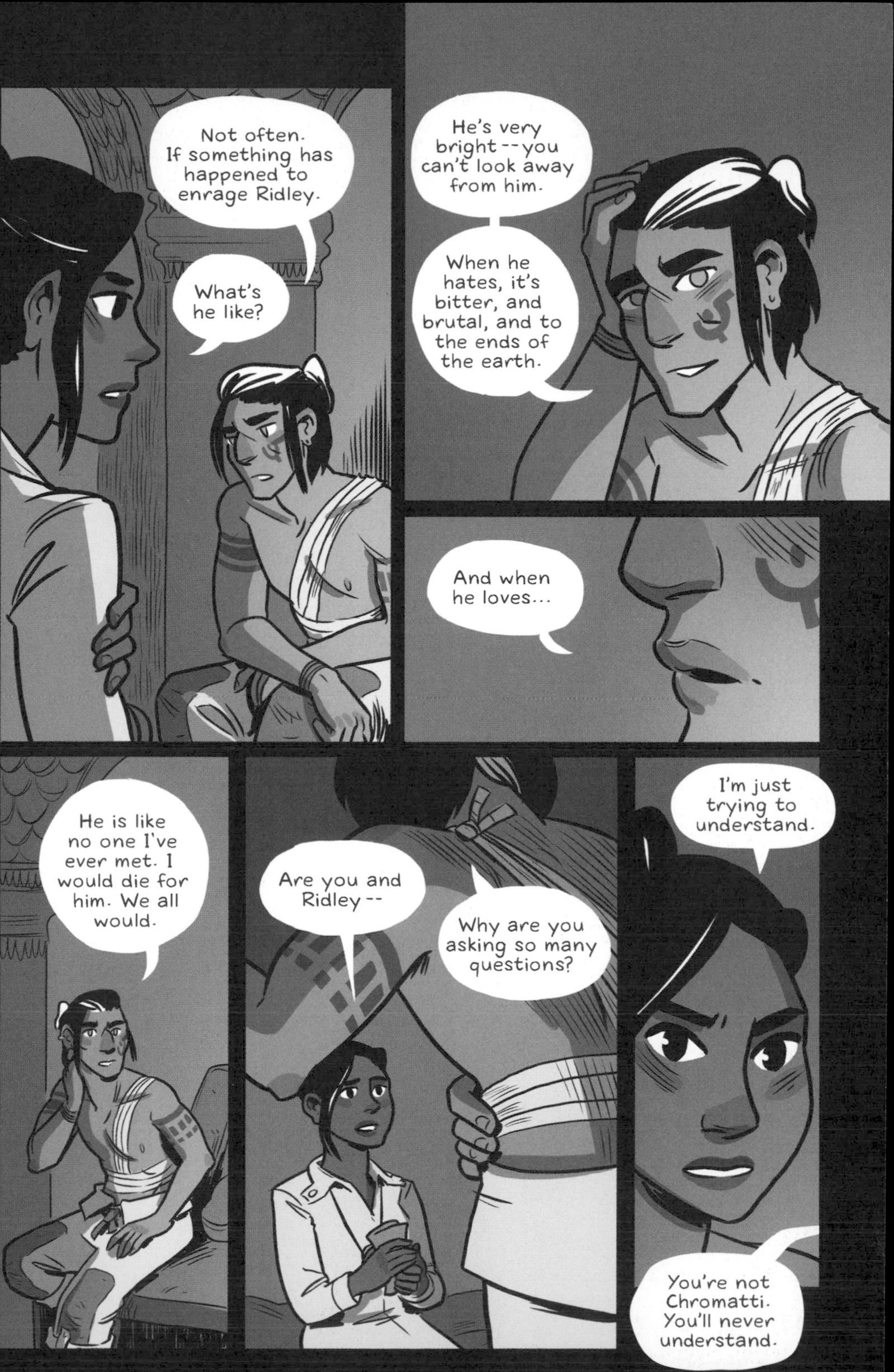

Not often. If something has happened to enrage Ridley.
What's he like?
He's very bright--you can't look away from him.
When he hates, it's bitter, and brutal, and to the ends of the earth.
And when he loves...
He is like no one I've ever met. I would die for him. We all would.
Are you and Ridley--
Why are you asking so many questions?
I'm just trying to understand.
You're not Chromatti. You'll never understand.

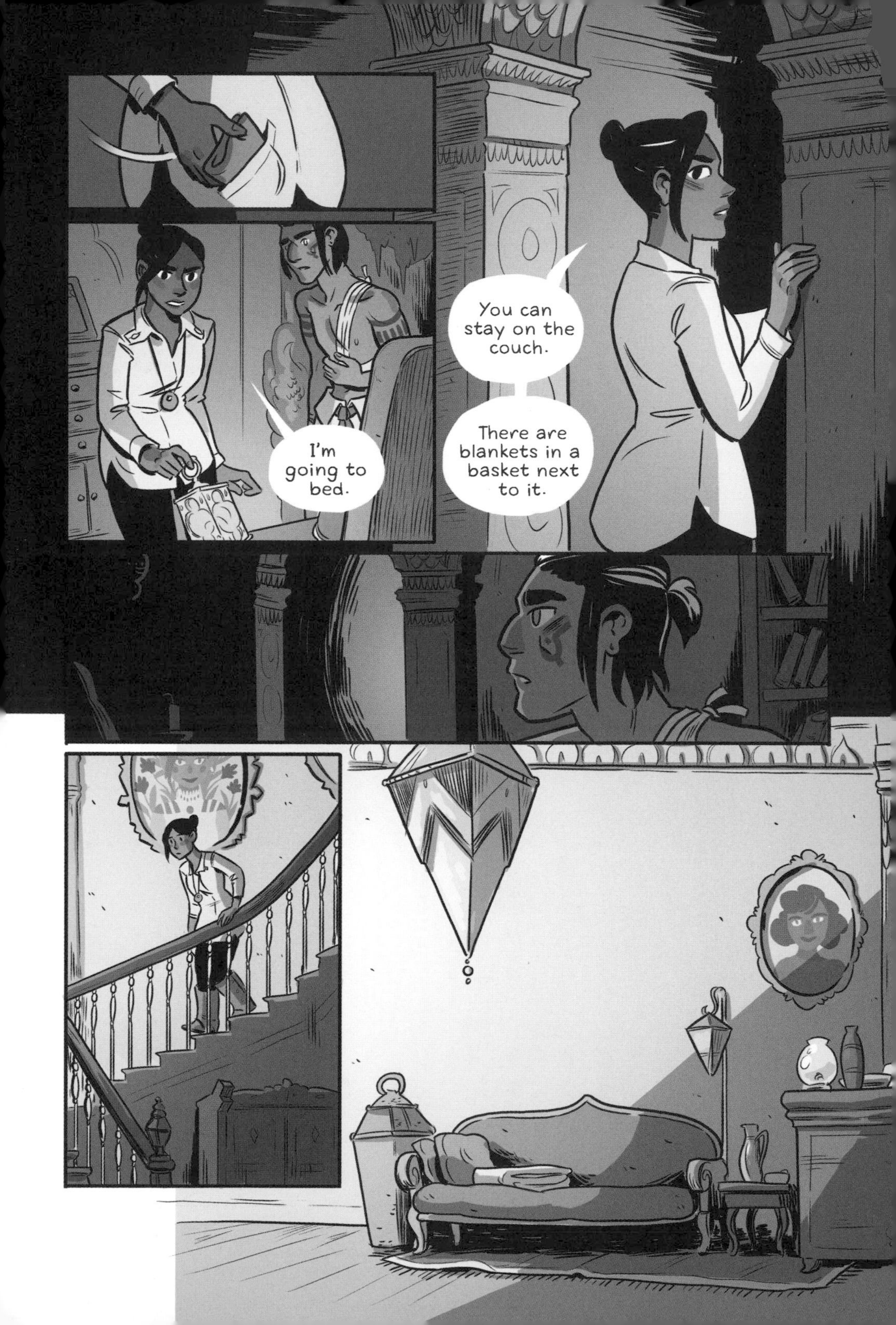
I'm going to bed.
You can stay on the couch.
There are blankets in a basket next to it.

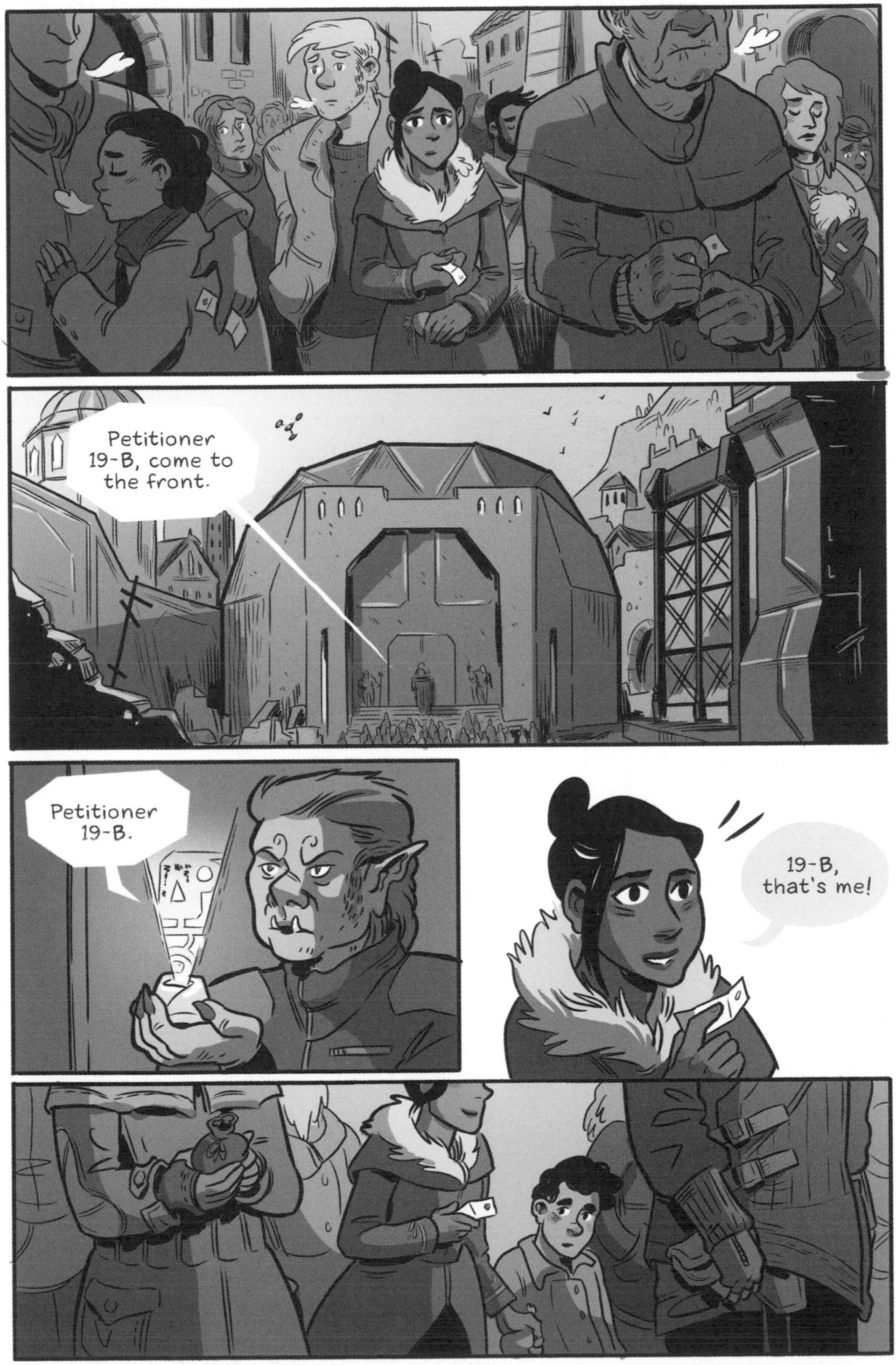
Petitioner 19-B, come to the front.
Petitioner 19-B.
19-B, that's me!

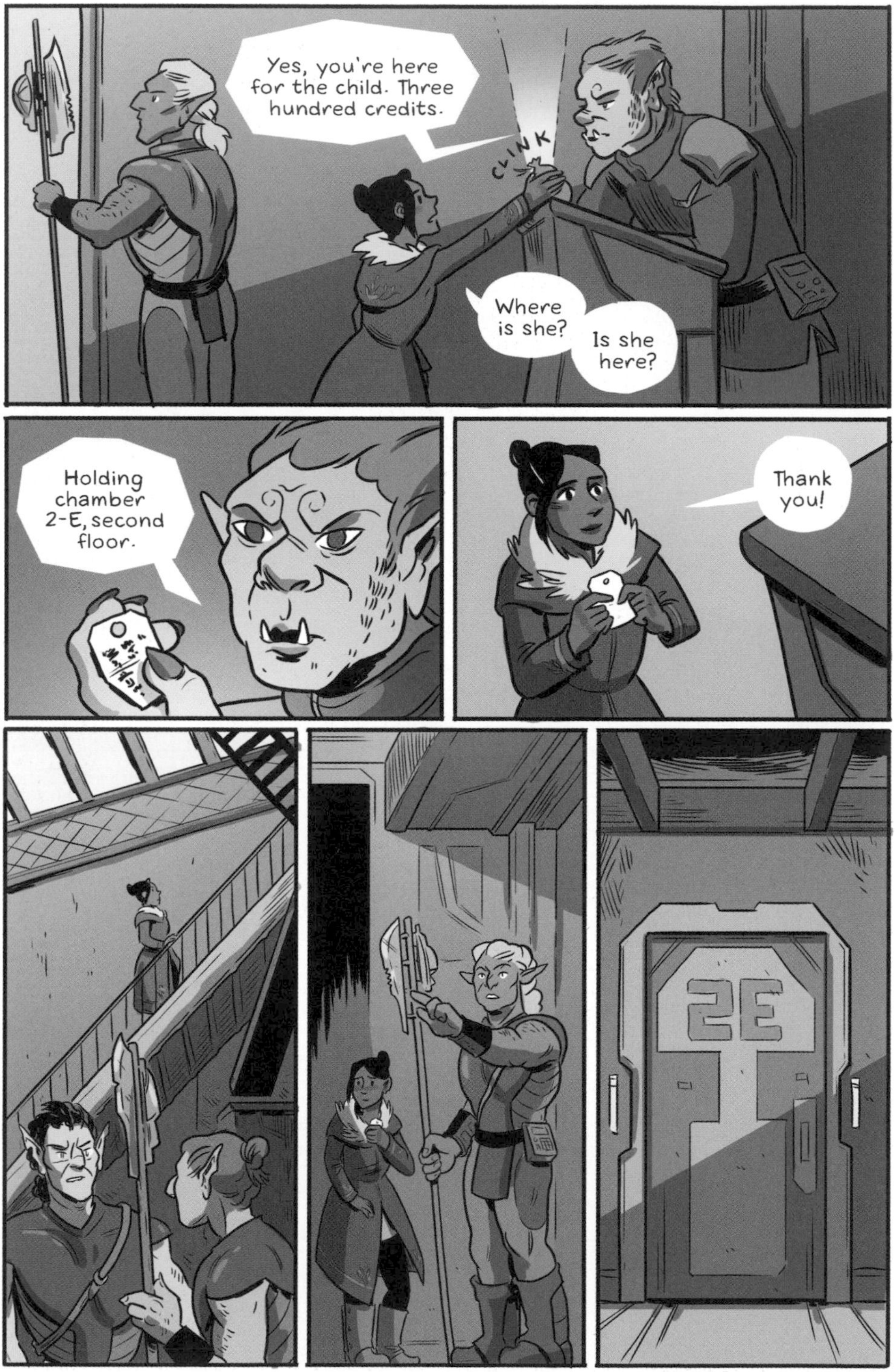
Yes, you're here for the child. Three hundred credits.
CLINK
Where is she?
Is she here?
Holding chamber 2-E, second floor.
Thank you!
2E

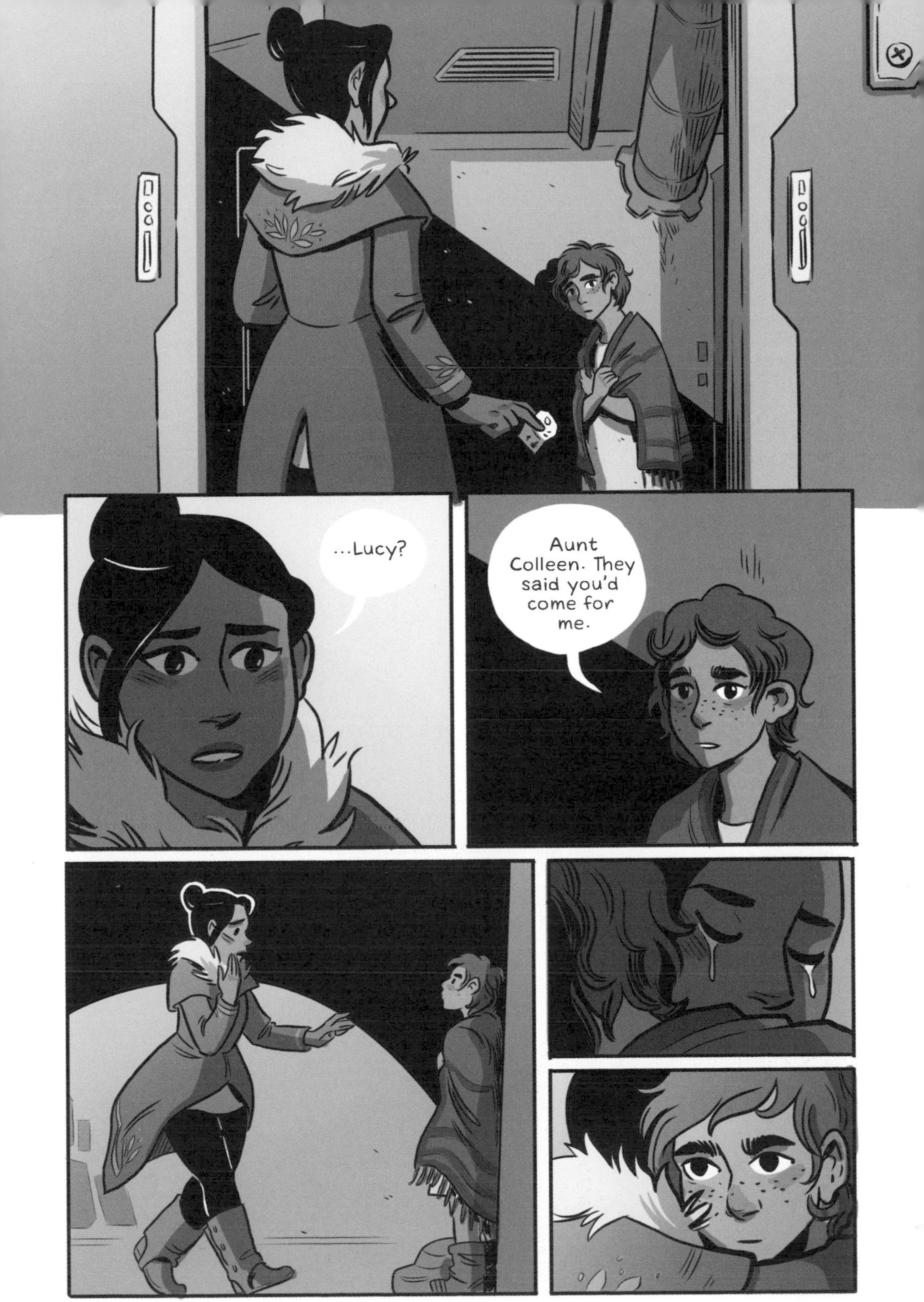
...Lucy?
Aunt Colleen. They said you'd come for me.

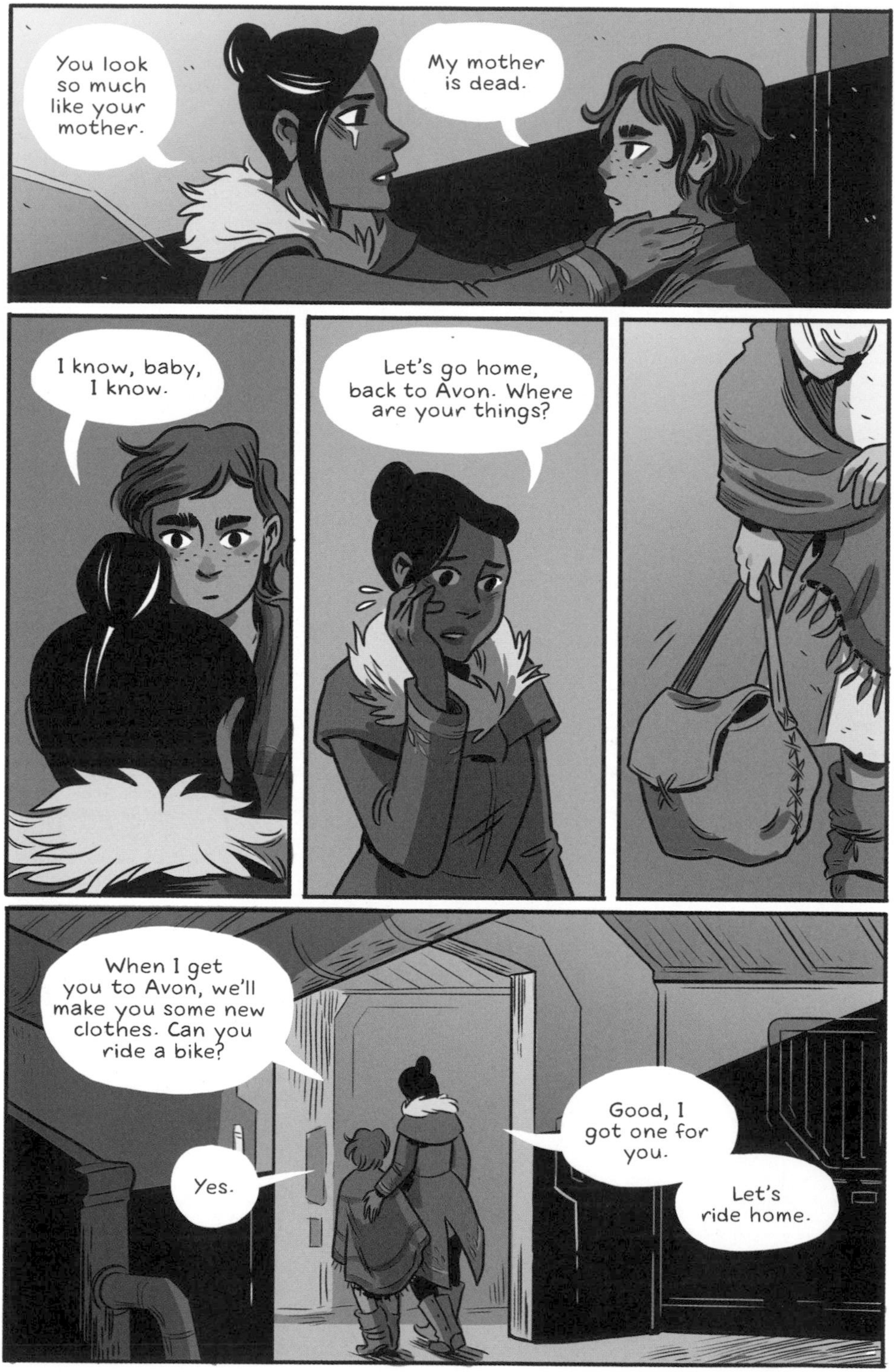
You look so much like your mother.
My mother is dead.
I know, baby, I know.
Let's go home, back to Avon. Where are your things?
When I get you to Avon, we'll make you some new clothes. Can you ride a bike?
Yes.
Good, I got one for you.
Let's ride home.

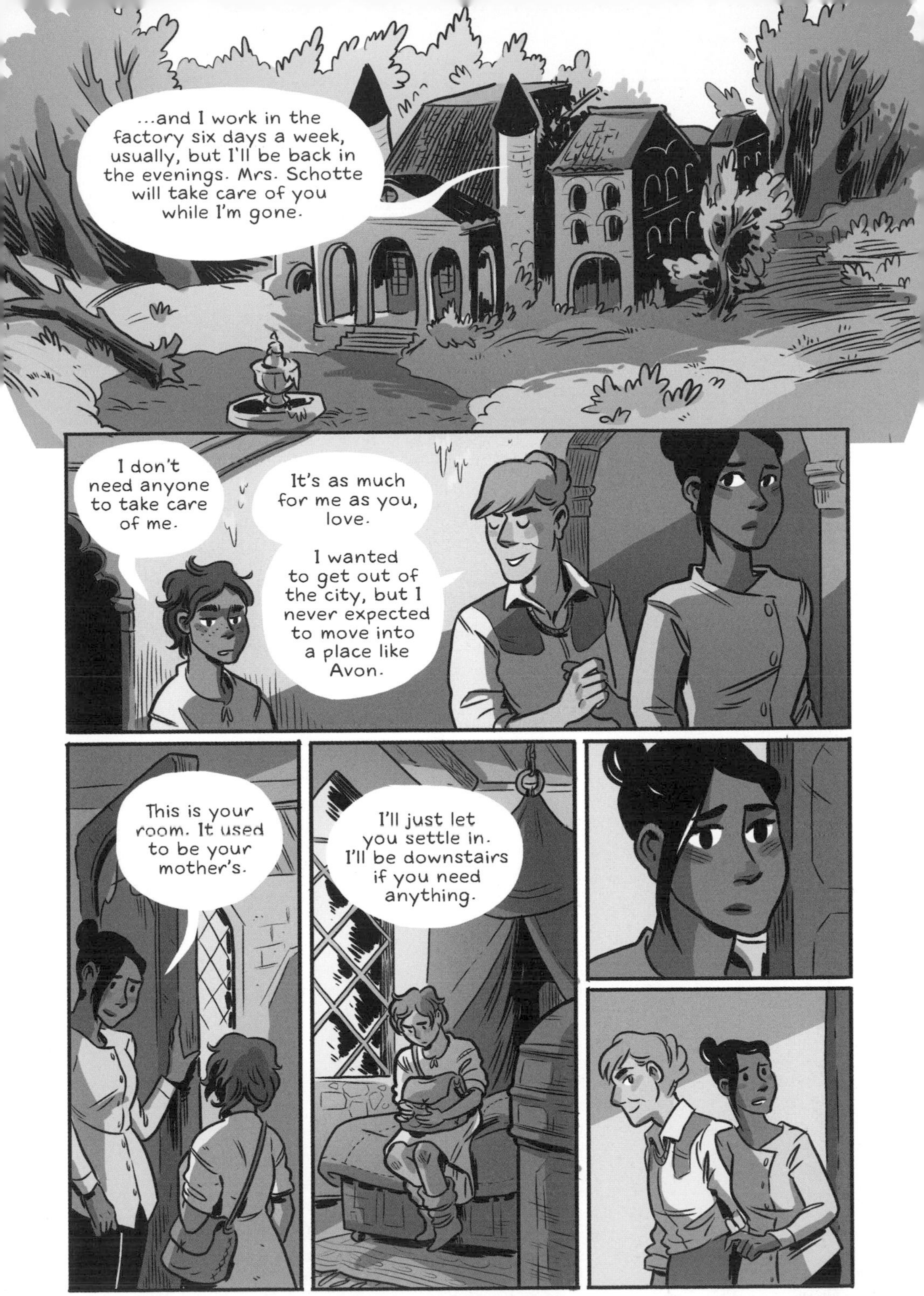
...and I work in the factory six days a week, usually, but I'll be back in the evenings. Mrs. Schotte will take care of you while I'm gone.
I don't need anyone to take care of me.
It's as much for me as you, love.
I wanted to get out of the city, but I never expected to move into a place like Avon.
This is your room. It used to be your mother's.
I'll just let you settle in. I'll be downstairs if you need anything.

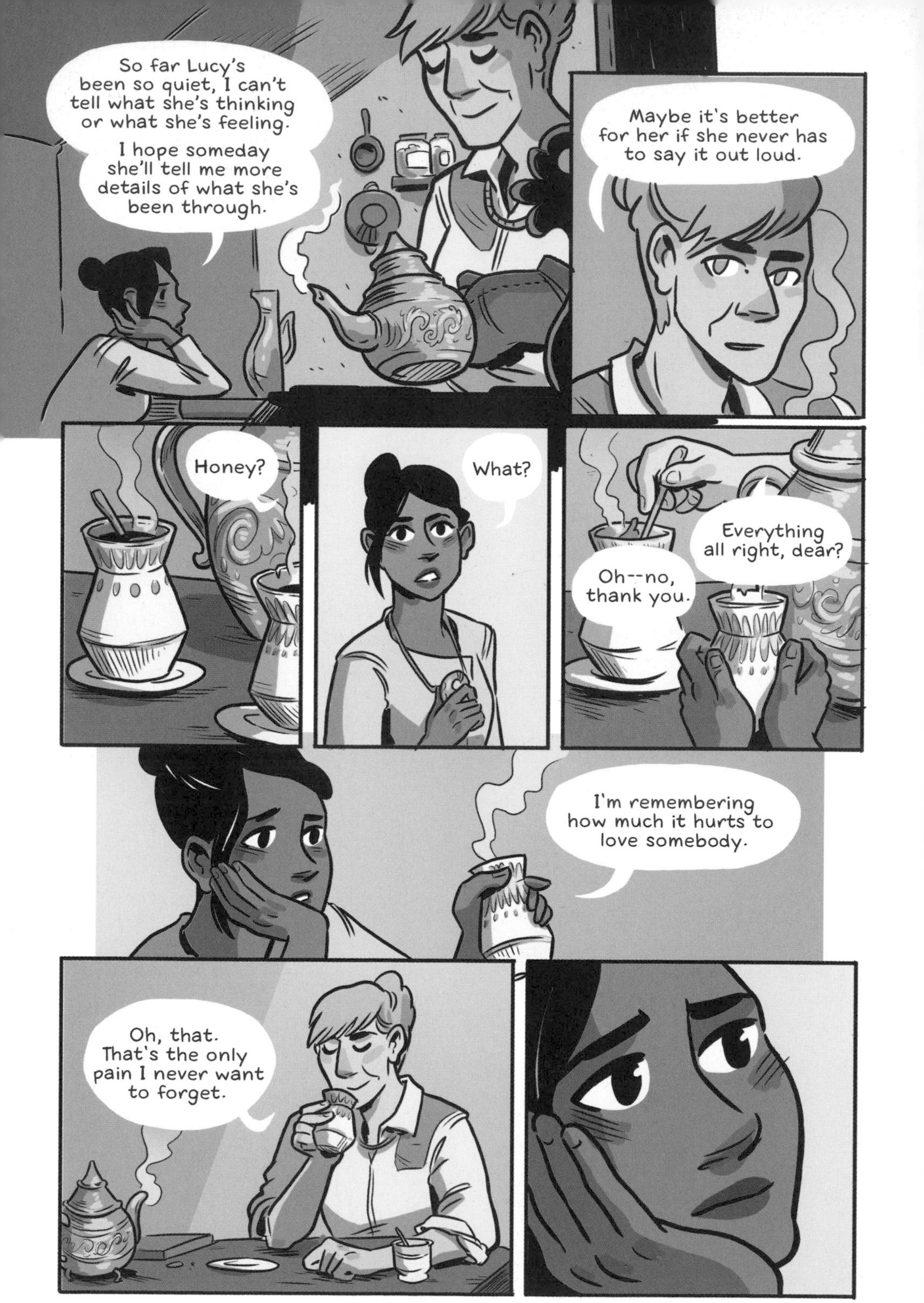
So far Lucy's been so quiet, I can't tell what she's thinking or what she's feeling.
I hope someday she'll tell me more details of what she's been through.
Maybe it's better for her if she never has to say it out loud.
Honey?
What?
Everything all right, dear?
Oh--no, thank you.
I'm remembering how much it hurts to love somebody.
Oh, that. That's the only pain I never want to forget.

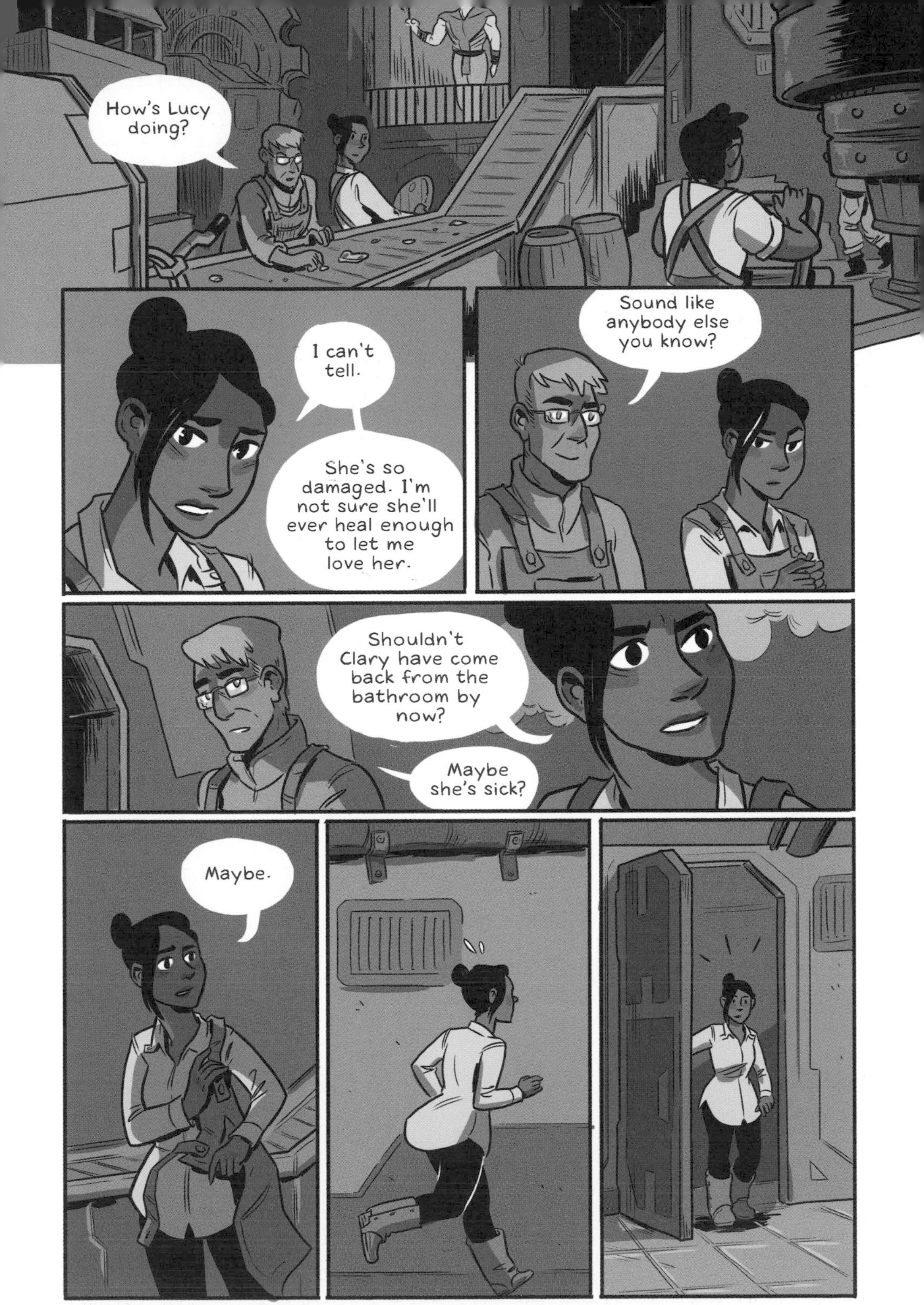
How's Lucy doing?
I can't tell.
She's so damaged. I'm not sure she'll ever heal enough to let me love her.
Sound like anybody else you know?
Shouldn't Clary have come back from the bathroom by now?
Maybe she's sick?
Maybe.

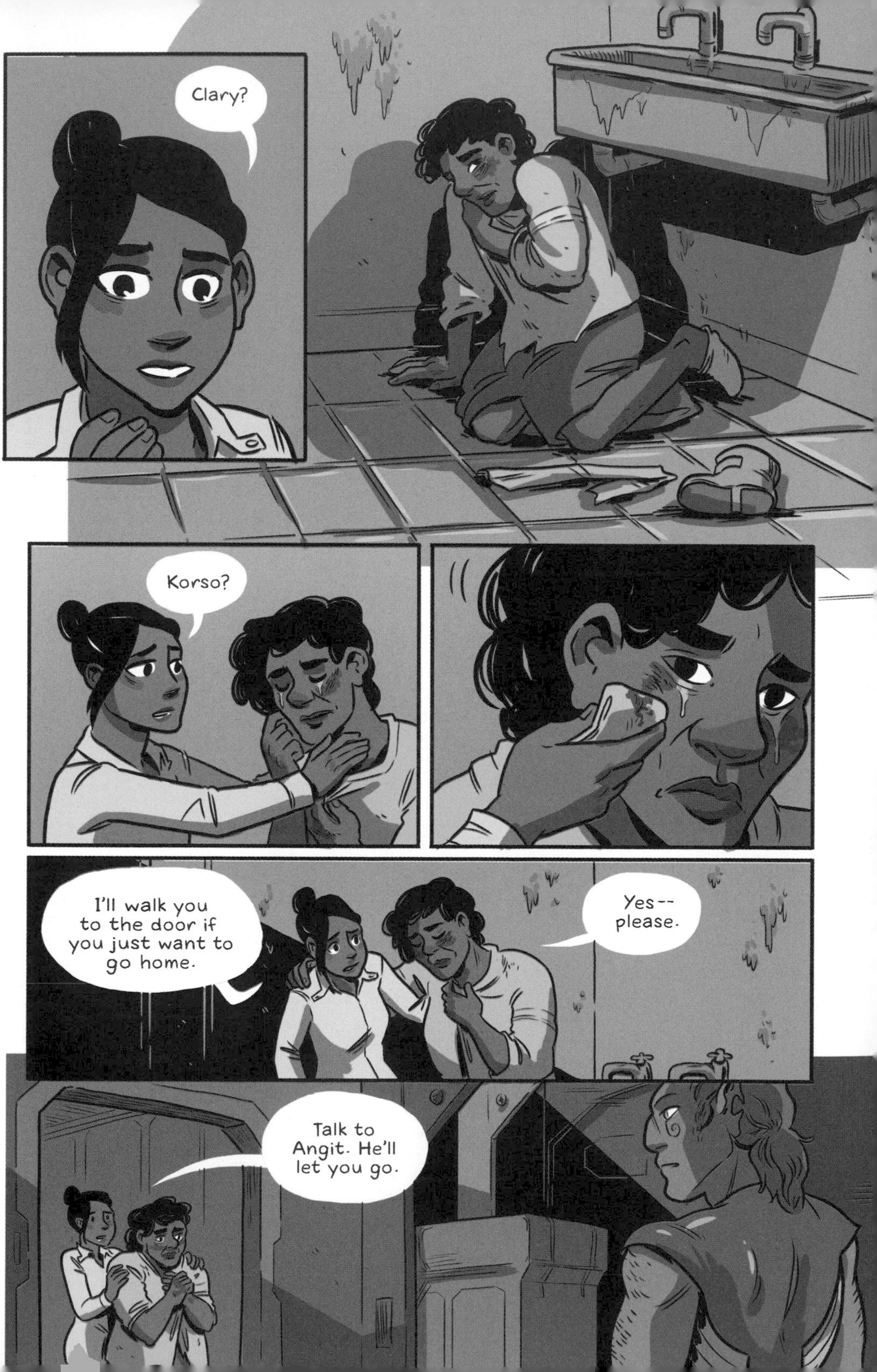
Clary?
Korso?
I'll walk you to the door if you just want to go home.
Yes--please.
Talk to Angit. He'll let you go.

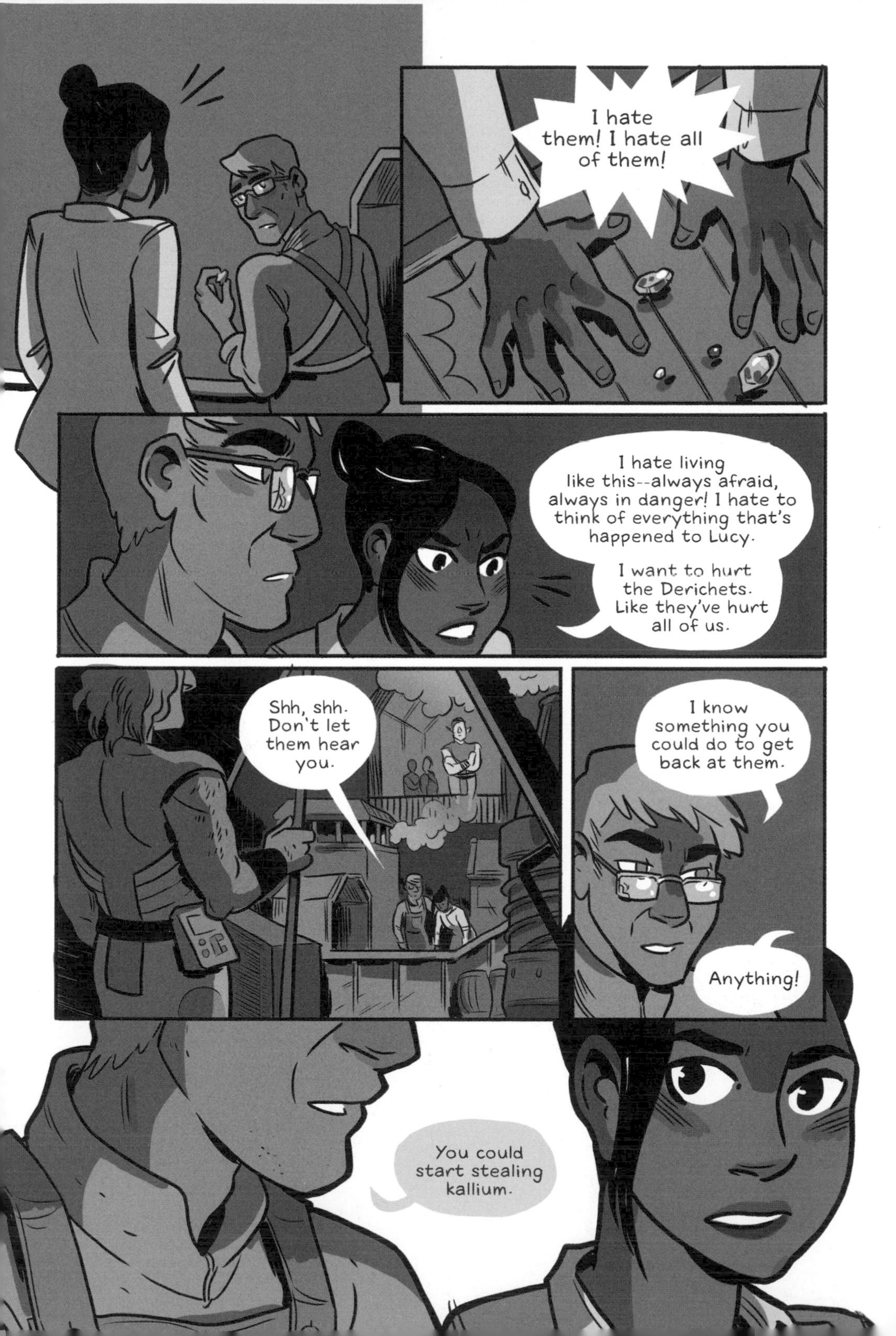
I hate them! I hate all of them!
I hate living like this--always afraid, always in danger! I hate to think of everything that's happened to Lucy.
I want to hurt the Derichets. Like they've hurt all of us.
Shh, shh. Don't let them hear you.
I know something you could do to get back at them.
Anything!
You could start stealing kallium.

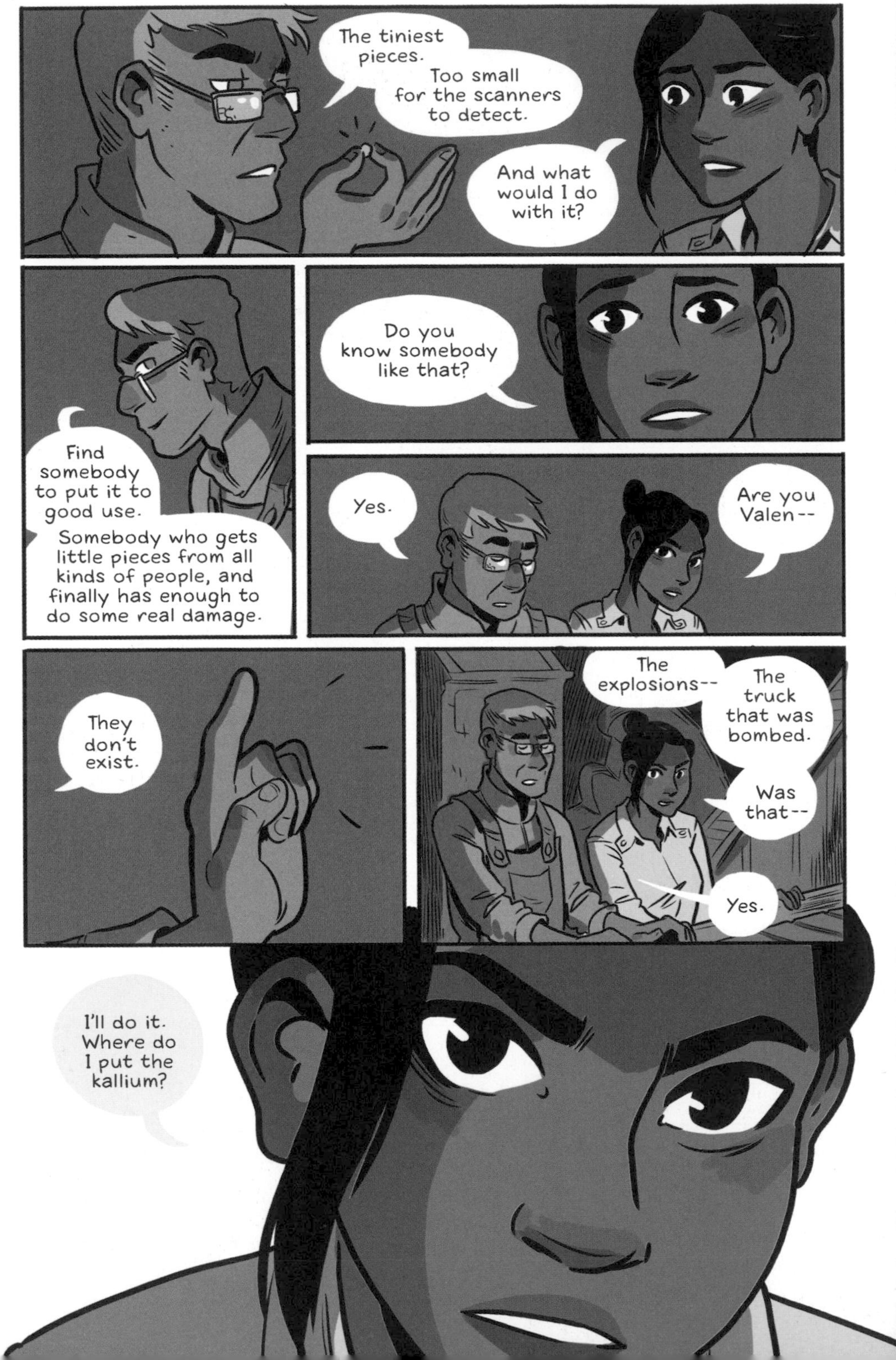
The tiniest pieces.
Too small for the scanners to detect.
And what would I do with it?
Find somebody to put it to good use.
Somebody who gets little pieces from all kinds of people, and finally has enough to do some real damage.
Do you know somebody like that?
Yes.
Are you Valen--
They don't exist.
The explosions--
The truck that was bombed.
Was that--
Yes.
I'll do it. Where do I put the kallium?

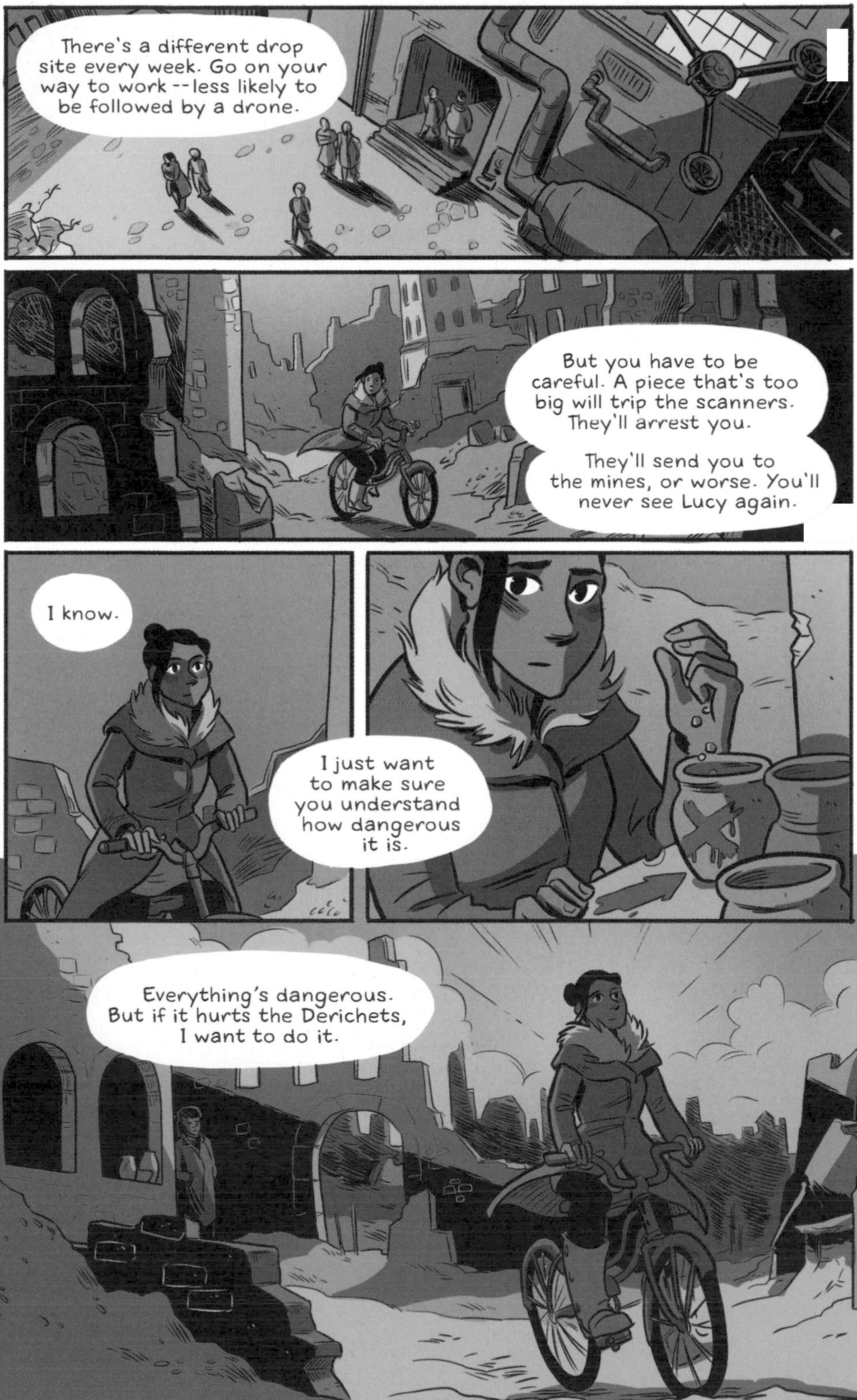
There's a different drop site every week. Go on your way to work --less likely to be followed by a drone.
But you have to be careful. A piece that's too big will trip the scanners. They'll arrest you.
They'll send you to the mines, or worse. You'll never see Lucy again.
I know.
I just want to make sure you understand how dangerous it is.
Everything's dangerous. But if it hurts the Derichets, I want to do it.

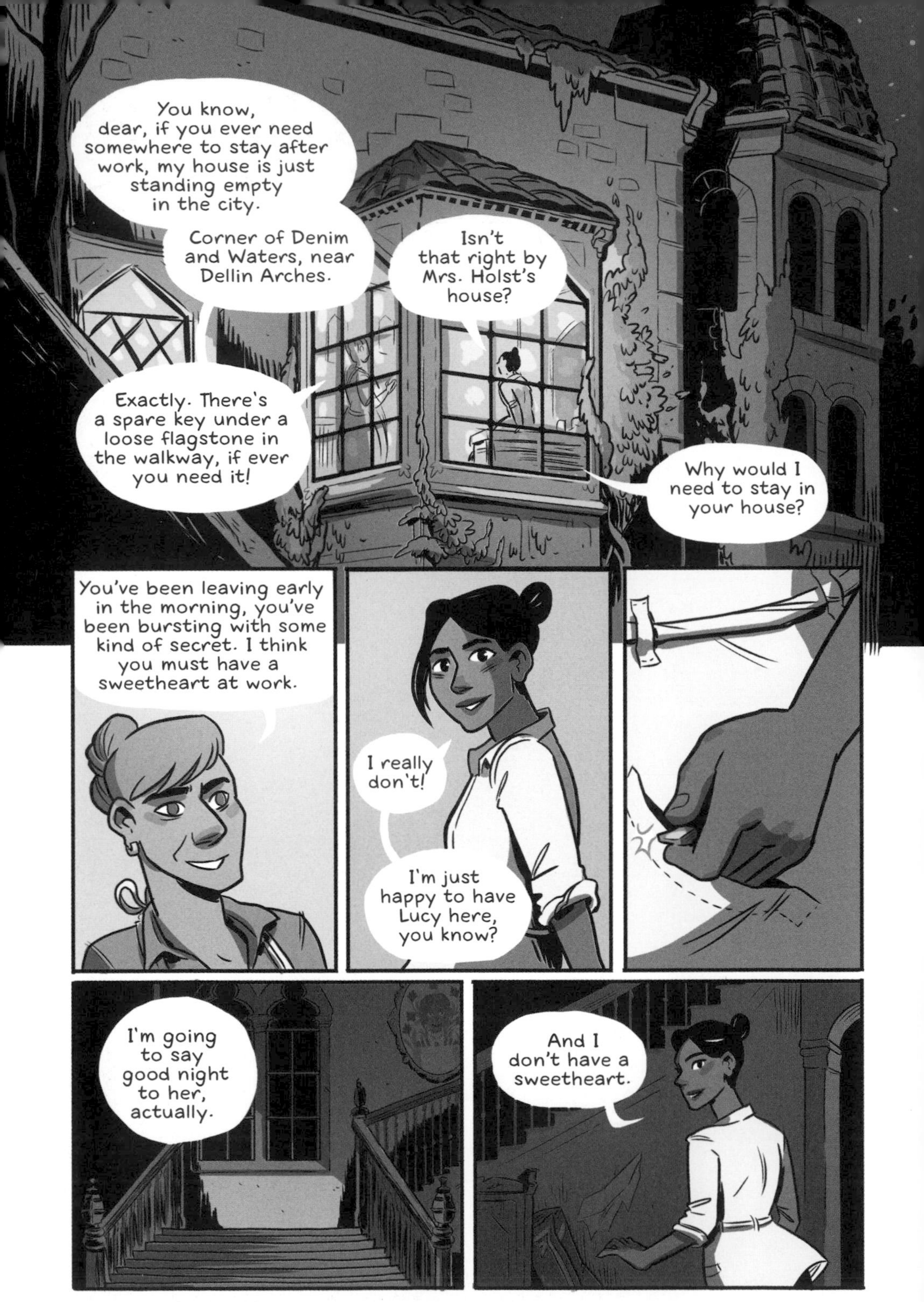
You know, dear, if you ever need somewhere to stay after work, my house is just standing empty in the city.
Corner of Denim and Waters, near Dellin Arches.
Isn't that right by Mrs. Holst's house?
Exactly. There's a spare key under a loose flagstone in the walkway, if ever you need it!
Why would I need to stay in your house?
You've been leaving early in the morning, you've been bursting with some kind of secret. I think you must have a sweetheart at work.
I really don't!
I'm just happy to have Lucy here, you know?
I'm going to say good night to her, actually.
And I don't have a sweetheart.

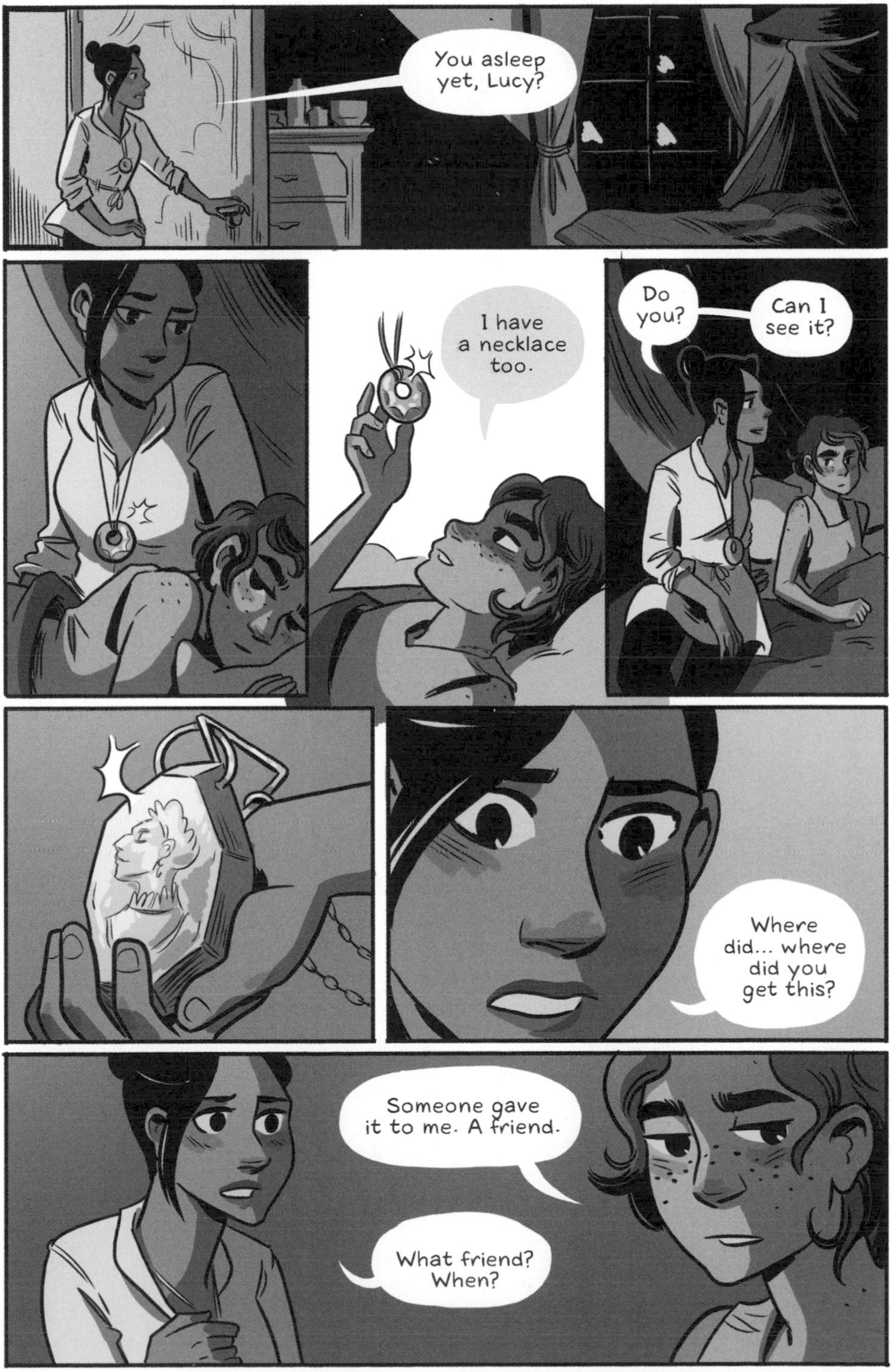
You asleep yet, Lucy?
I have a necklace too.
Do you?
Can I see it?
Where did... where did you get this?
Someone gave it to me. A friend.
What friend? When?

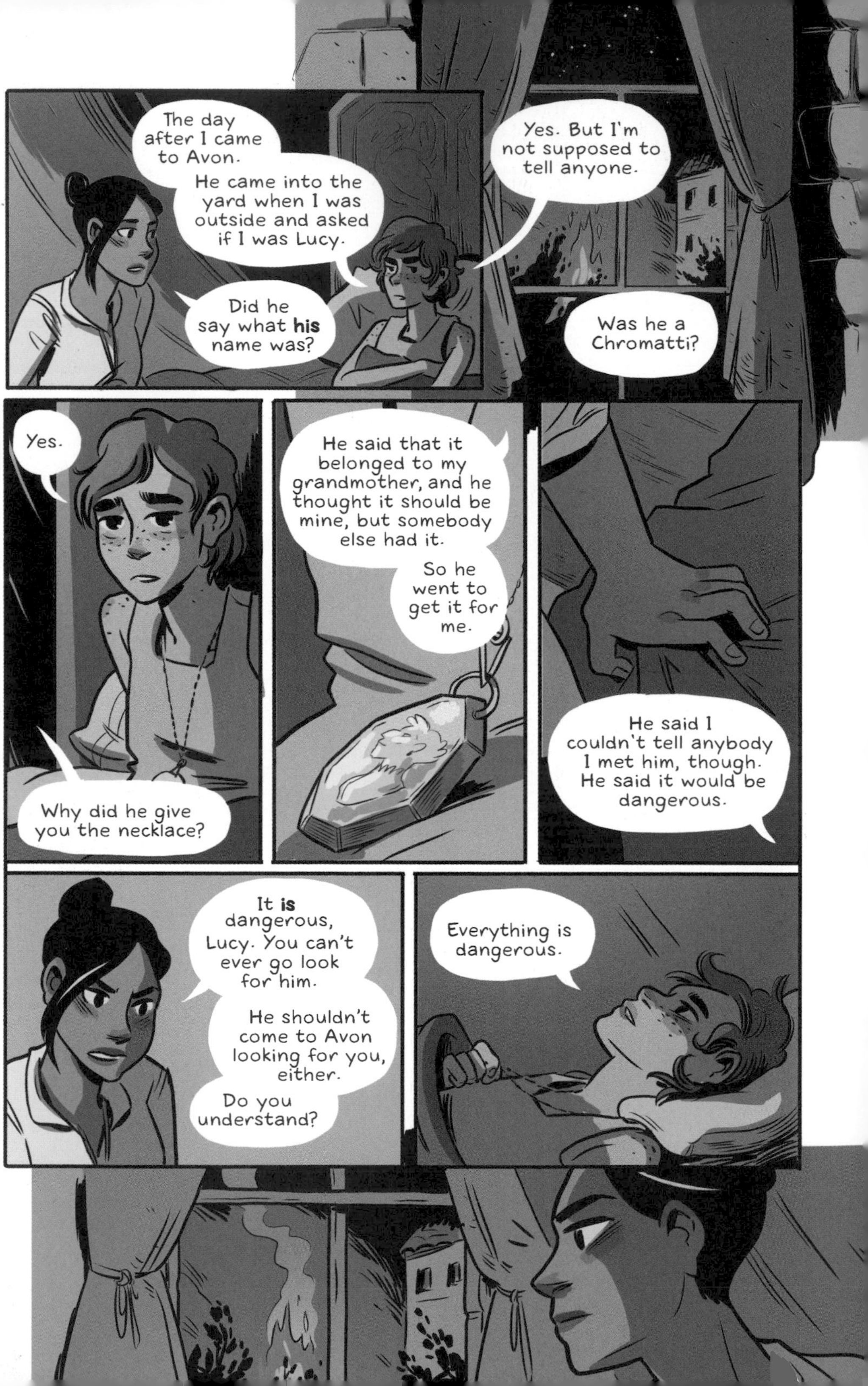
The day after I came to Avon.
He came into the yard when I was outside and asked if I was Lucy.
Did he say what **his** name was?
Yes. But I'm not supposed to tell anyone.
Was he a Chromatti?
Yes.
Why did he give you the necklace?
He said that it belonged to my grandmother, and he thought it should be mine, but somebody else had it.
So he went to get it for me.
He said I couldn't tell anybody I met him, though. He said it would be dangerous.
It **is** dangerous, Lucy. You can't ever go look for him.
He shouldn't come to Avon looking for you, either.
Do you understand?
Everything is dangerous.

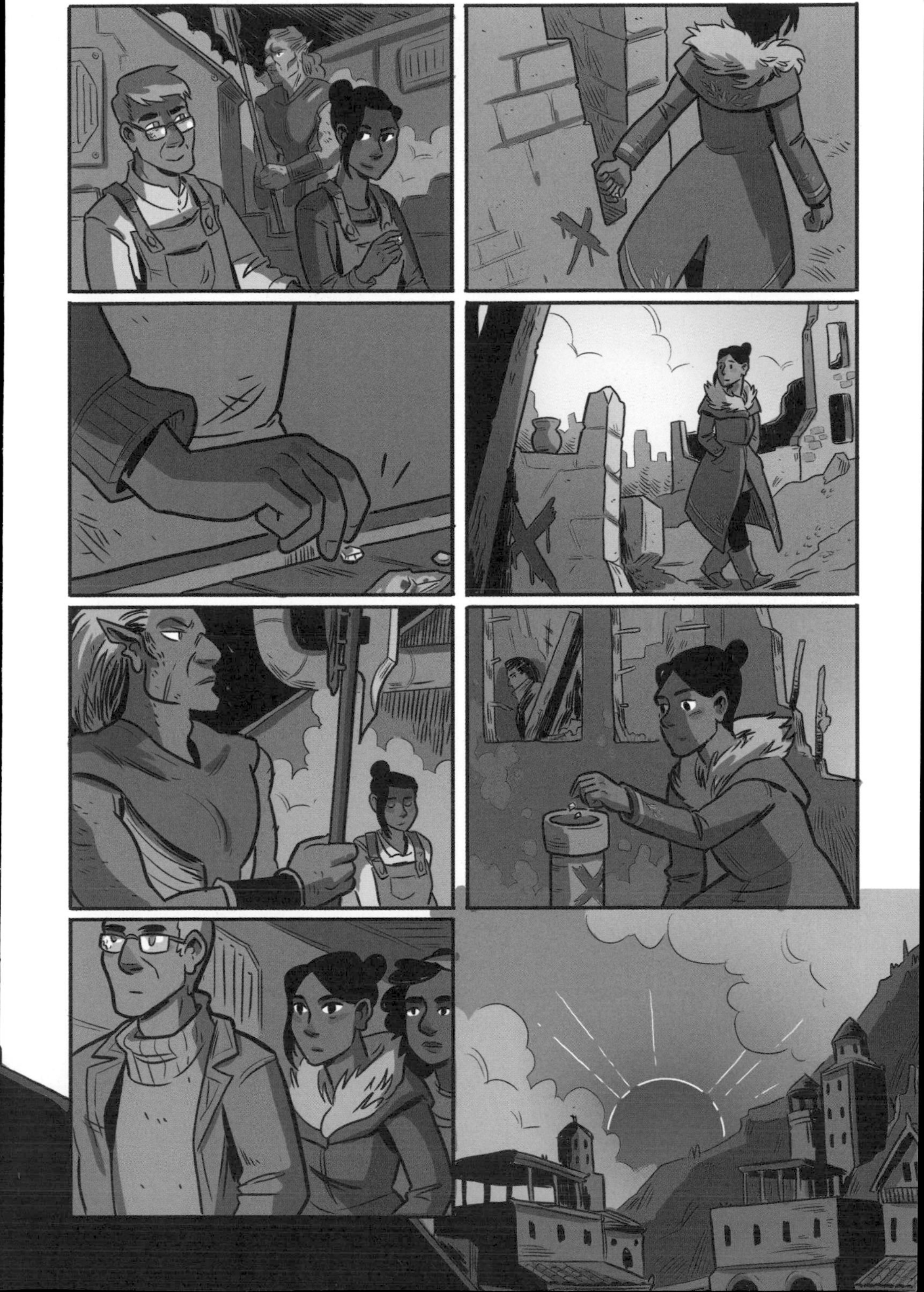

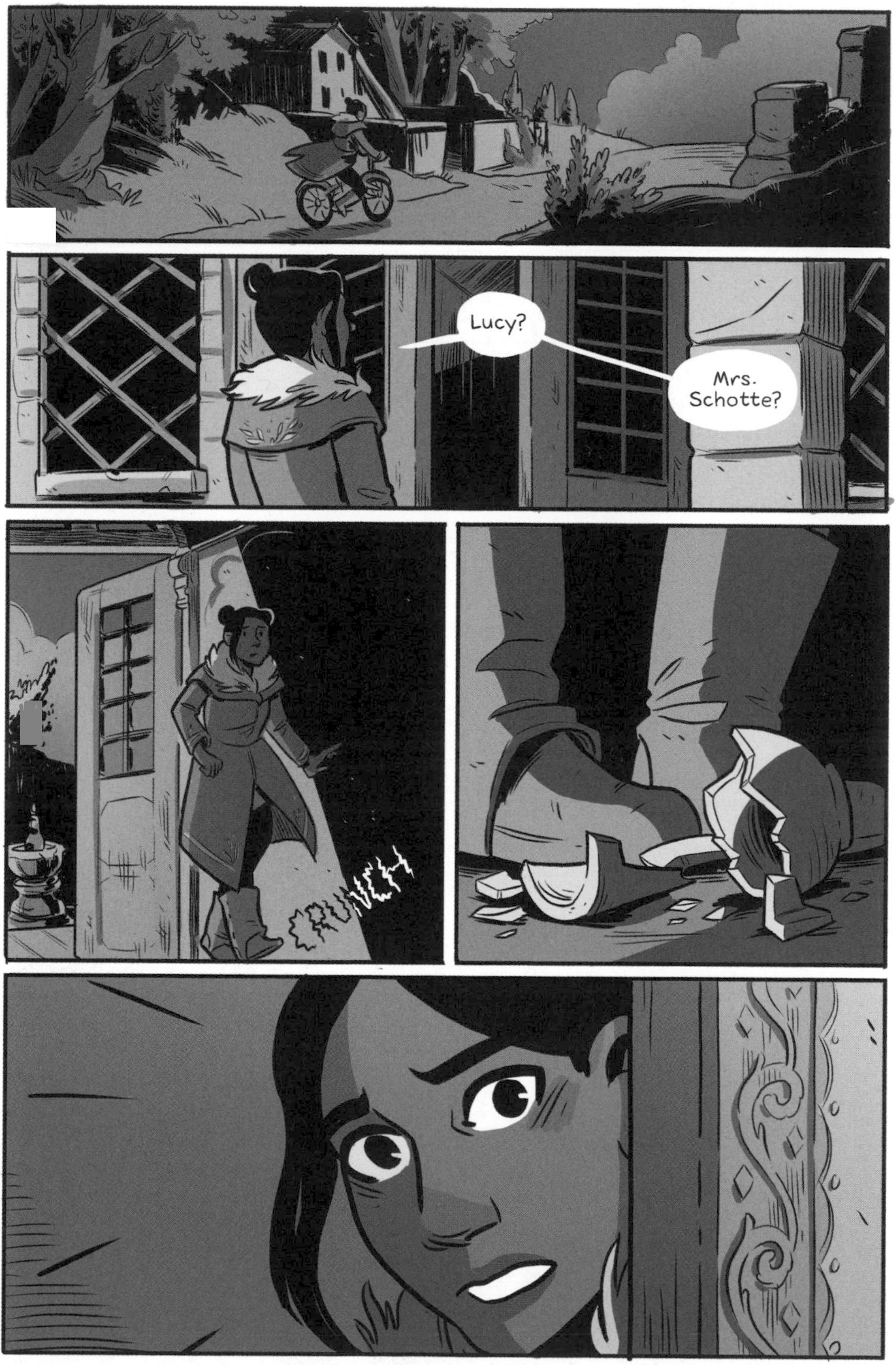
Lucy?
Mrs. Schotte?
CRUNCH

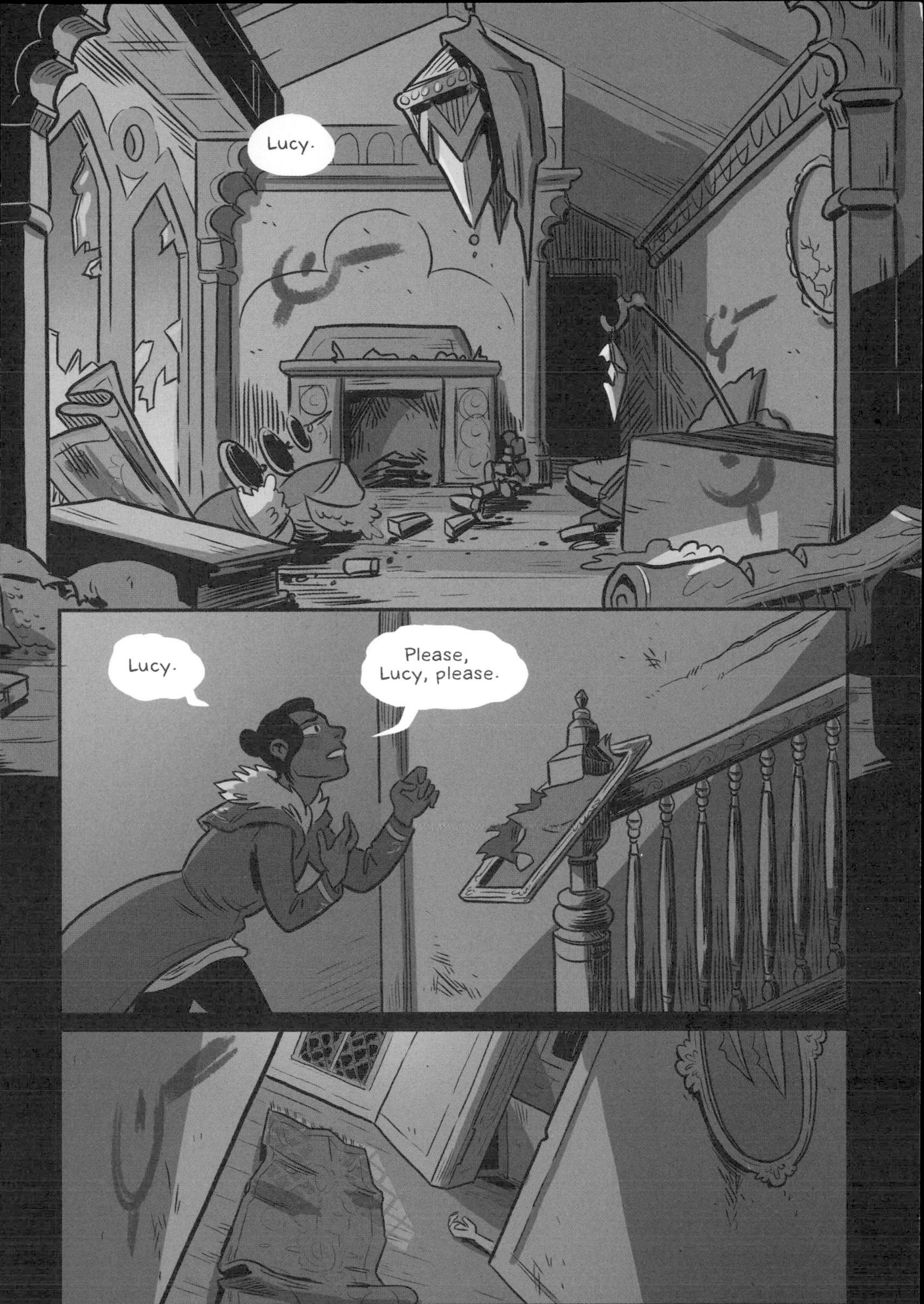
Lucy.
Lucy.
Please, Lucy, please.

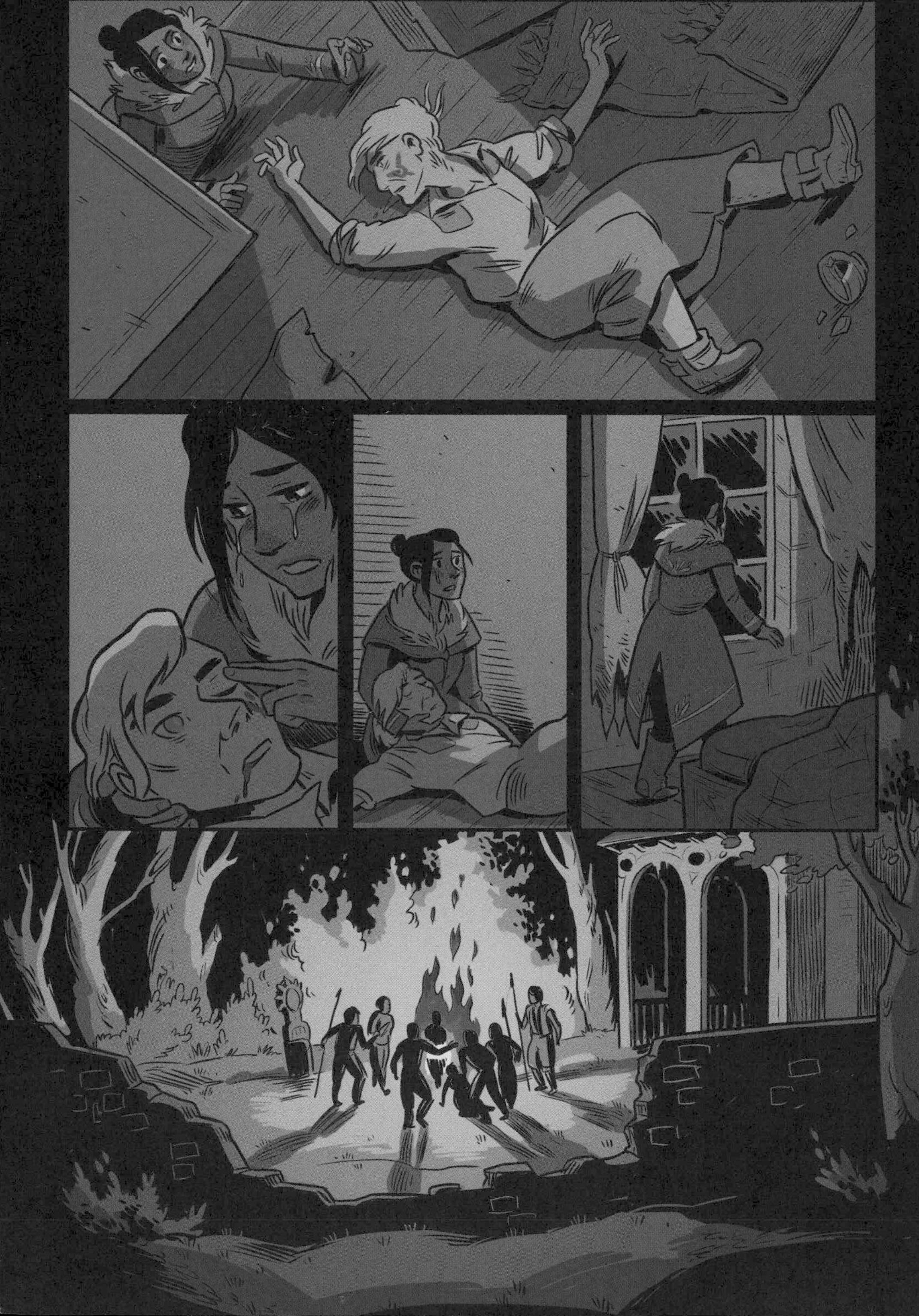

part 2

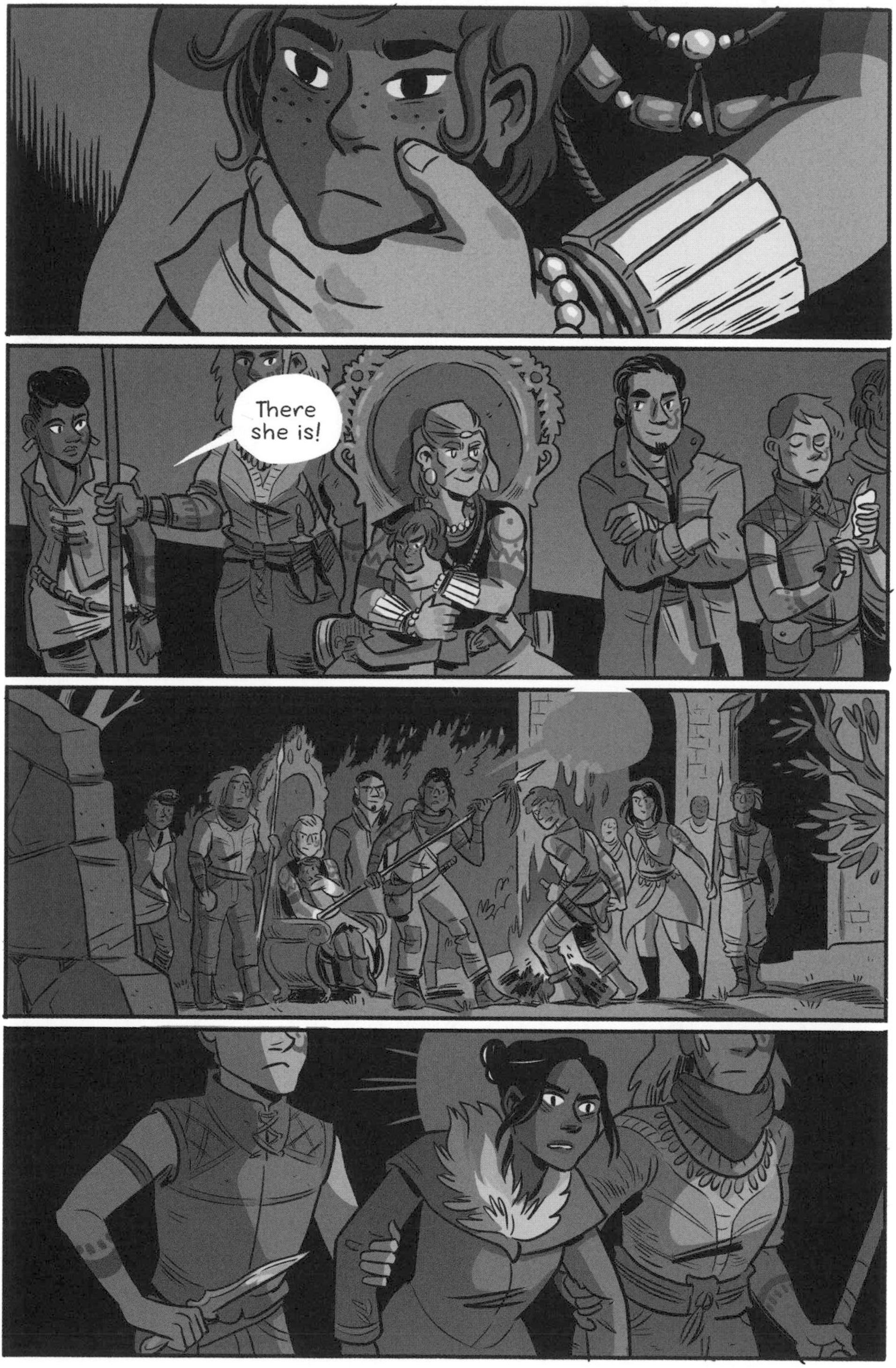
There she is!

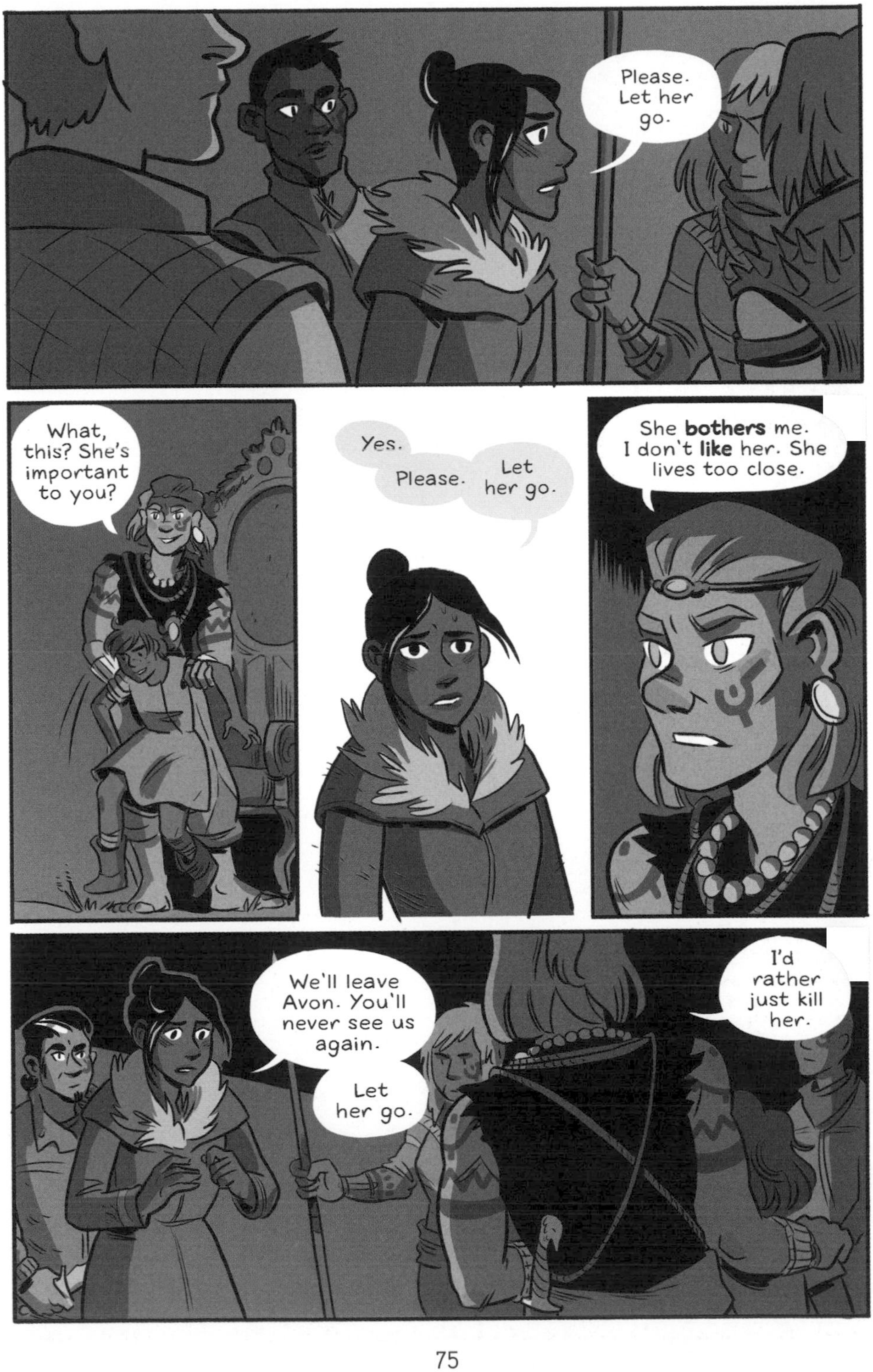
Please. Let her go.
What, this? She's important to you?
Yes.
Please.
Let her go.
She **bothers** me. I don't **like** her. She lives too close.
We'll leave Avon. You'll never see us again.
Let her go.
I'd rather just kill her.

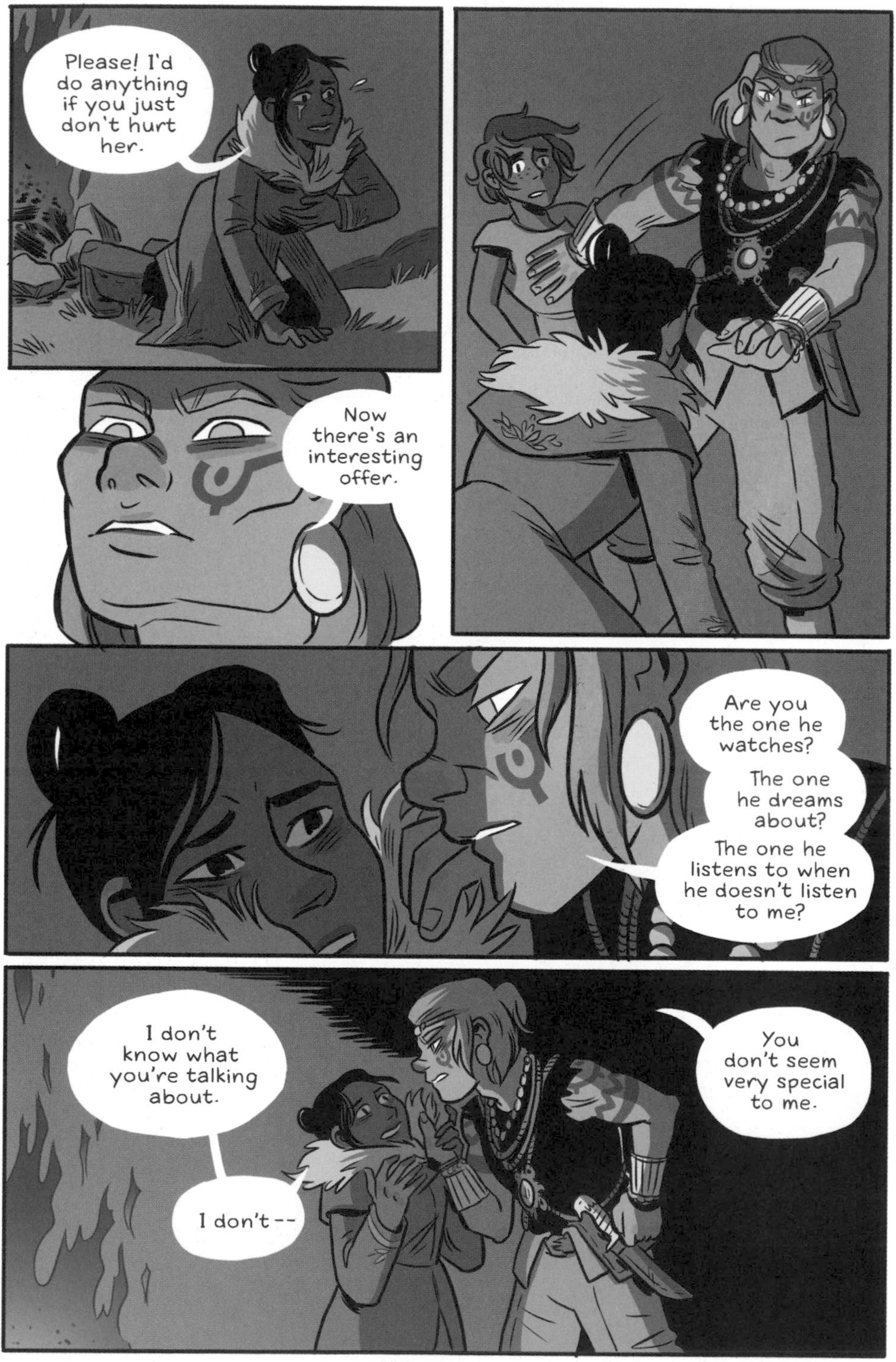
Please! I'd do anything if you just don't hurt her.
Now there's an interesting offer.
Are you the one he watches?
The one he dreams about?
The one he listens to when he doesn't listen to me?
I don't know what you're talking about.
I don't--
You don't seem very special to me.

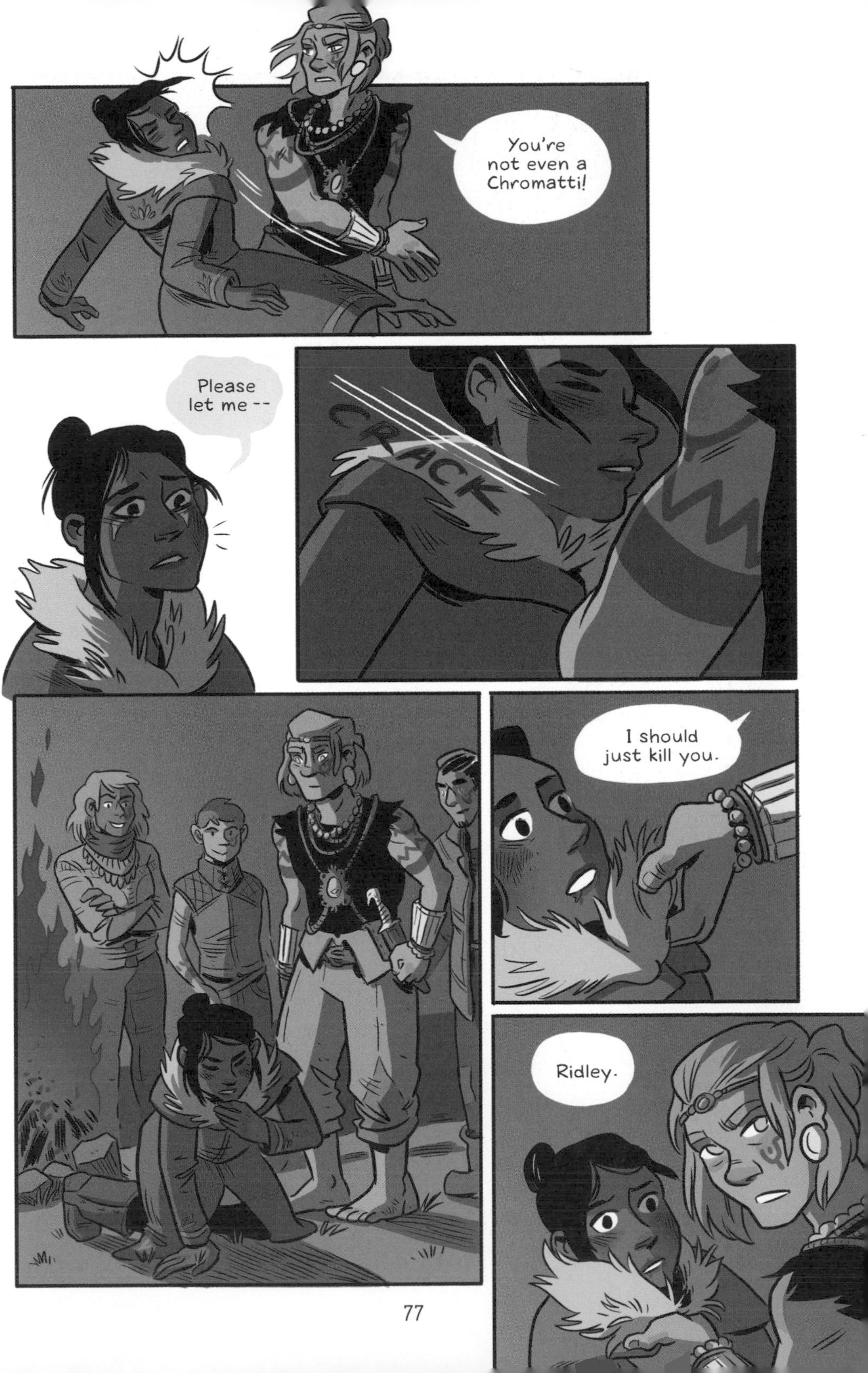
You're not even a Chromatti!
Please let me --
CRACK
I should just kill you.
Ridley.

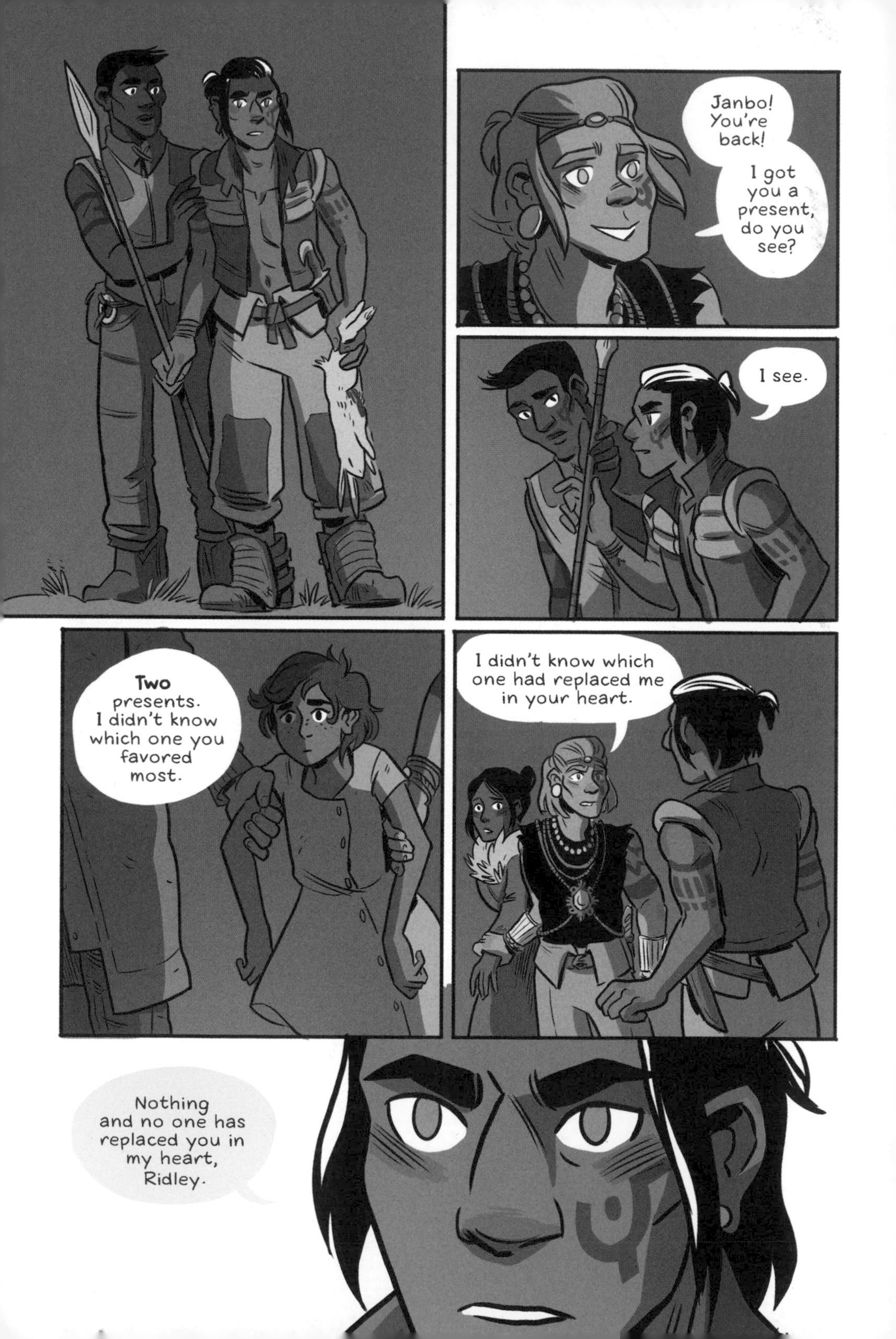
Janbo! You're back!
I got you a present, do you see?
I see.
Two presents. I didn't know which one you favored most.
I didn't know which one had replaced me in your heart.
Nothing and no one has replaced you in my heart, Ridley.

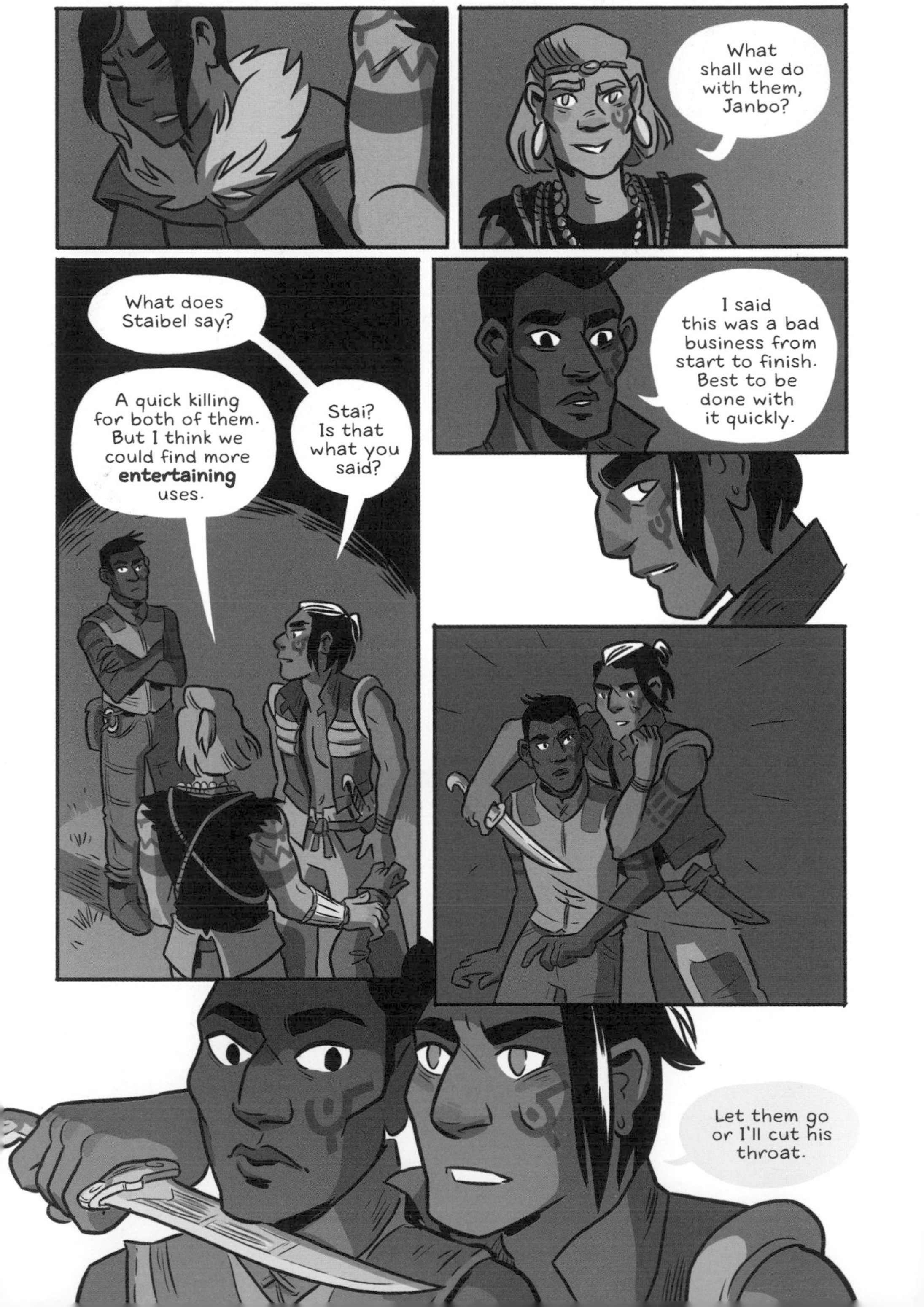
What shall we do with them, Janbo?
What does Staibel say?
A quick killing for both of them. But I think we could find more **entertaining** uses.
Stai? Is that what you said?
I said this was a bad business from start to finish. Best to be done with it quickly.
Let them go or I'll cut his throat.

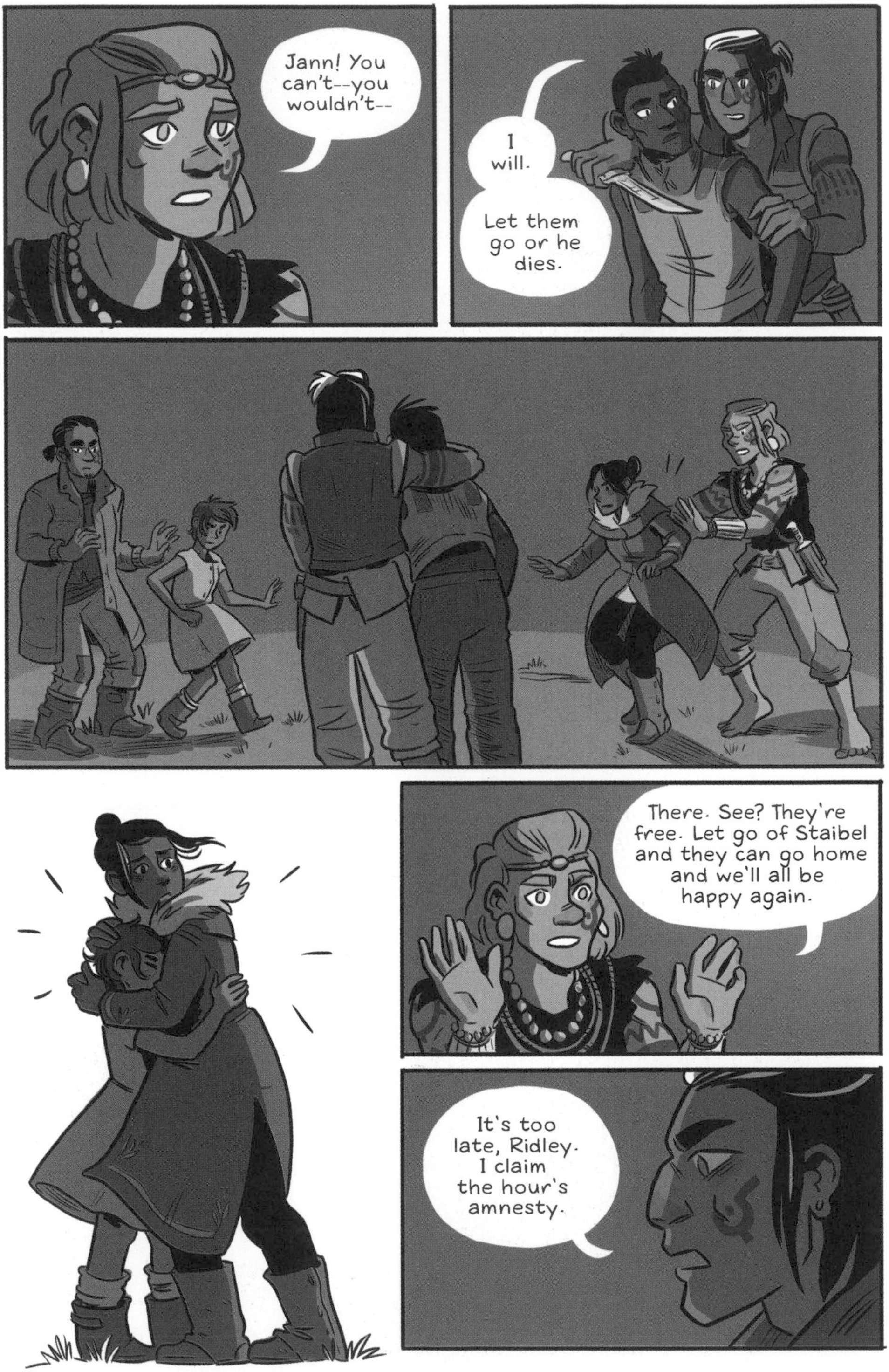

Jann! You can't--you wouldn't--
I will.
Let them go or he dies.
There. See? They're free. Let go of Staibel and they can go home and we'll all be happy again.
It's too late, Ridley. I claim the hour's amnesty.

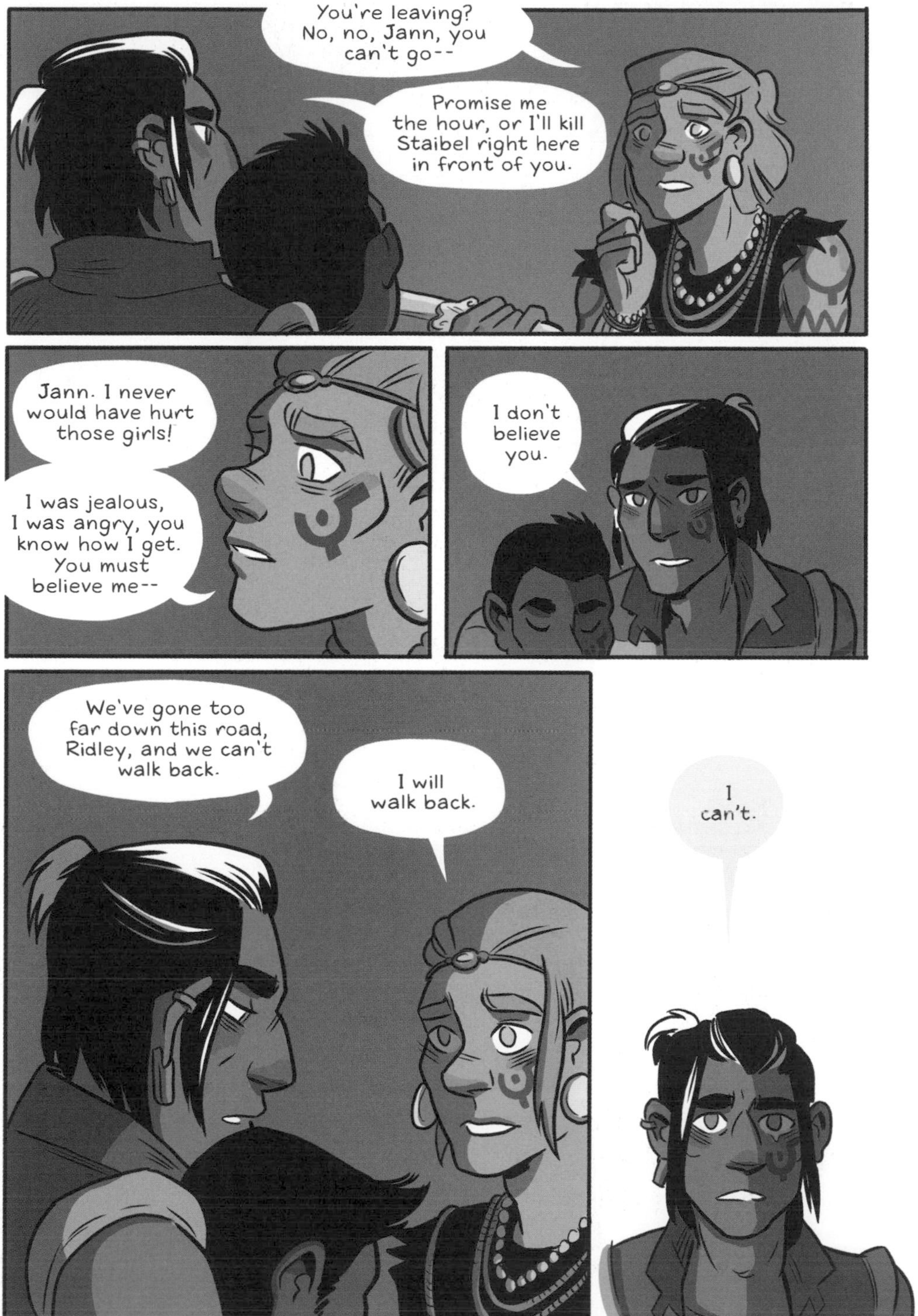

You're leaving? No, no, Jann, you can't go--
Promise me the hour, or I'll kill Staibel right here in front of you.
Jann. I never would have hurt those girls!
I was jealous, I was angry, you know how I get. You must believe me--
I don't believe you.
We've gone too far down this road, Ridley, and we can't walk back.
I will walk back.
I can't.

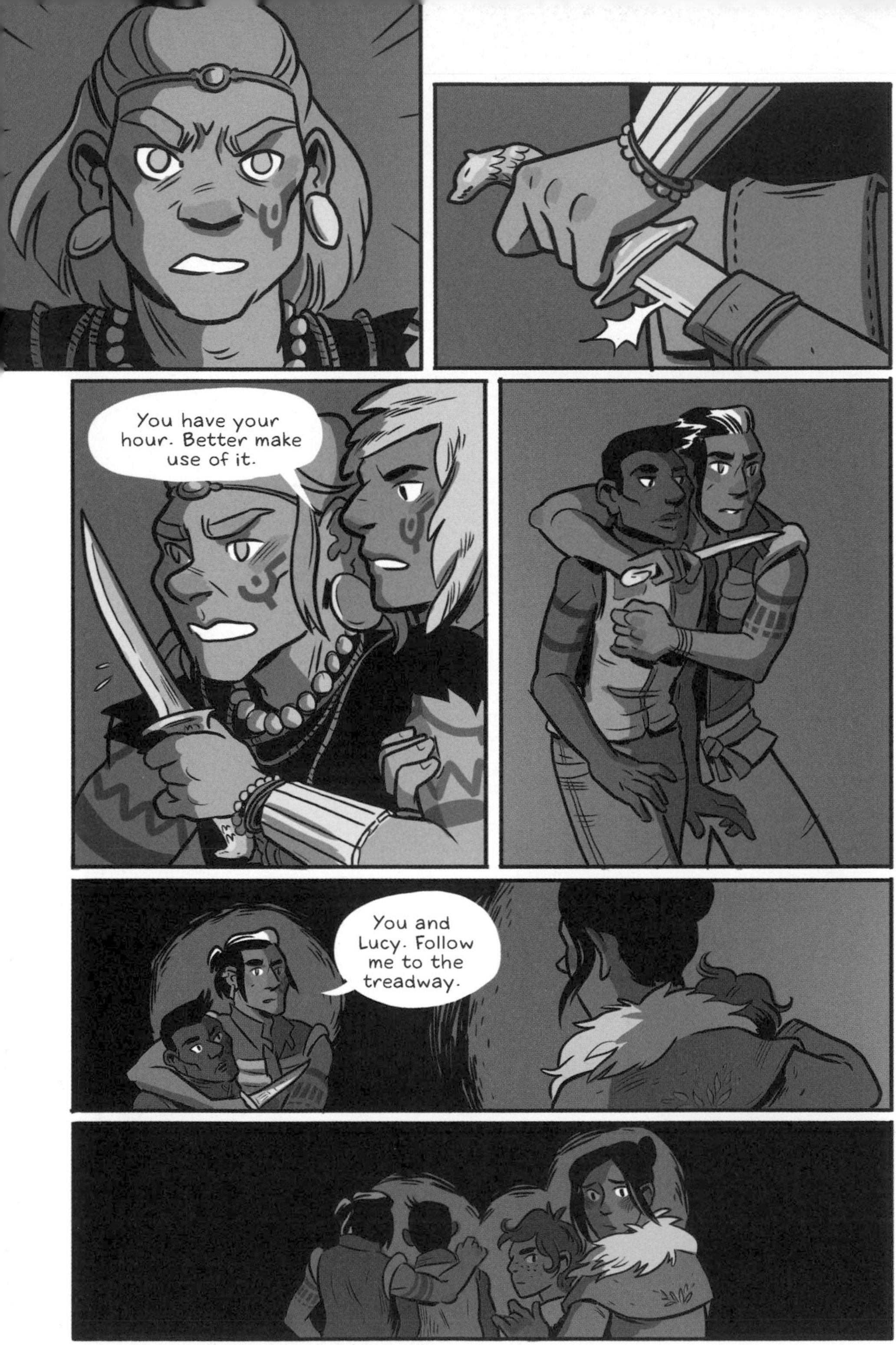
You have your hour. Better make use of it.
You and Lucy. Follow me to the treadway.

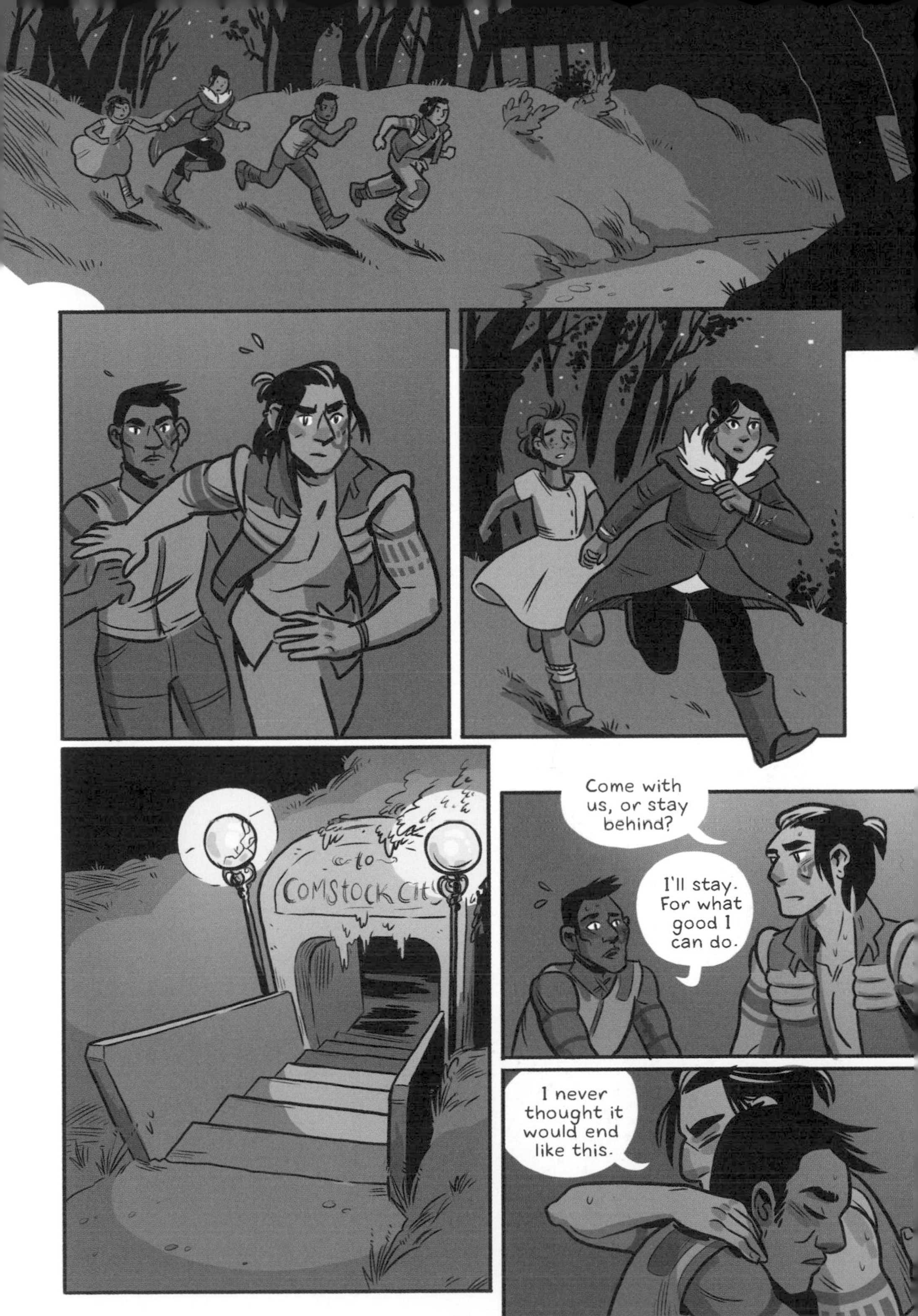
to
COMSTOCK CITY
Come with us, or stay behind?
I'll stay. For what good I can do.
I never thought it would end like this.

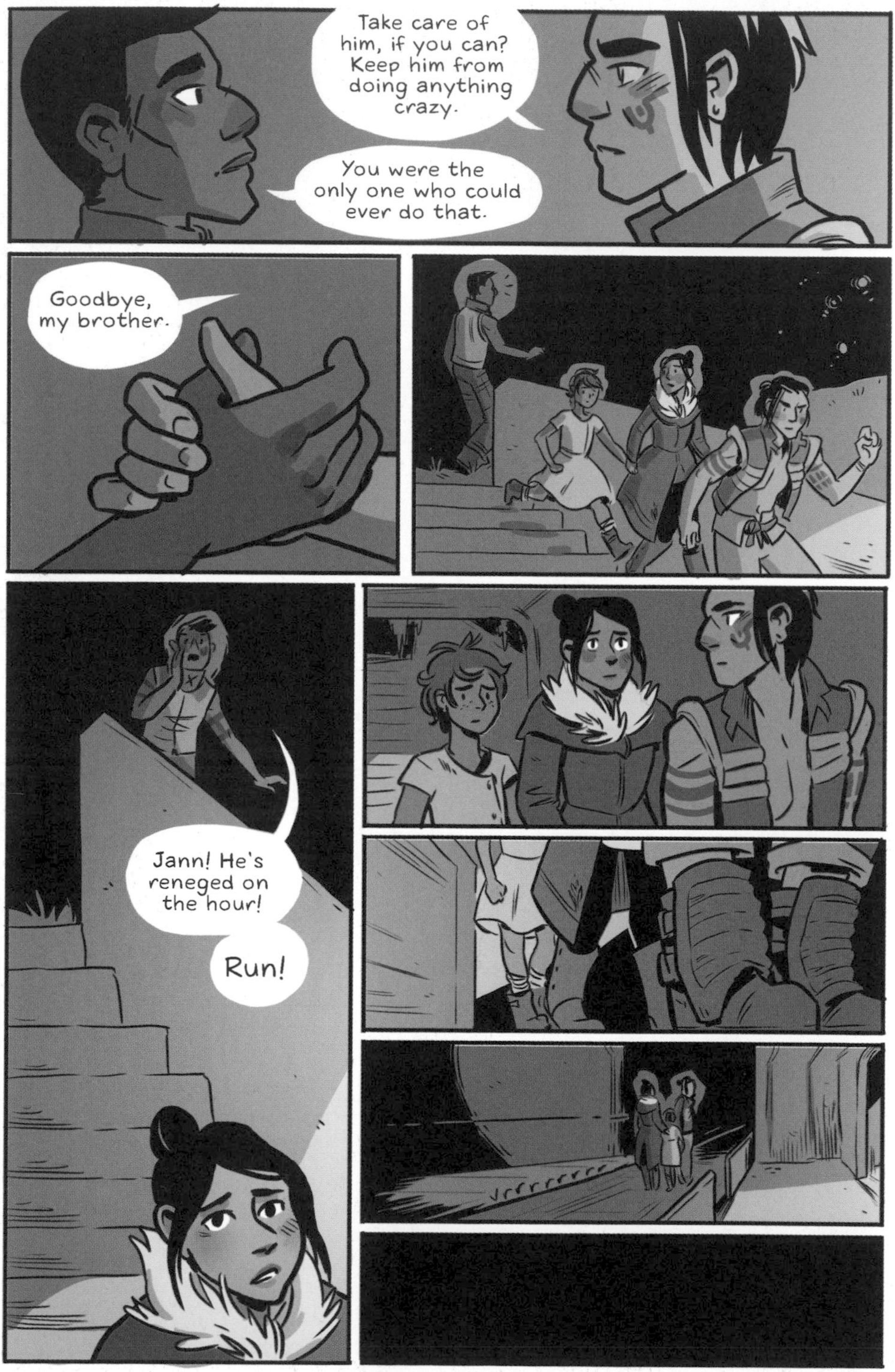
Take care of him, if you can? Keep him from doing anything crazy.
You were the only one who could ever do that.
Goodbye, my brother.
Jann! He's reneged on the hour!
Run!

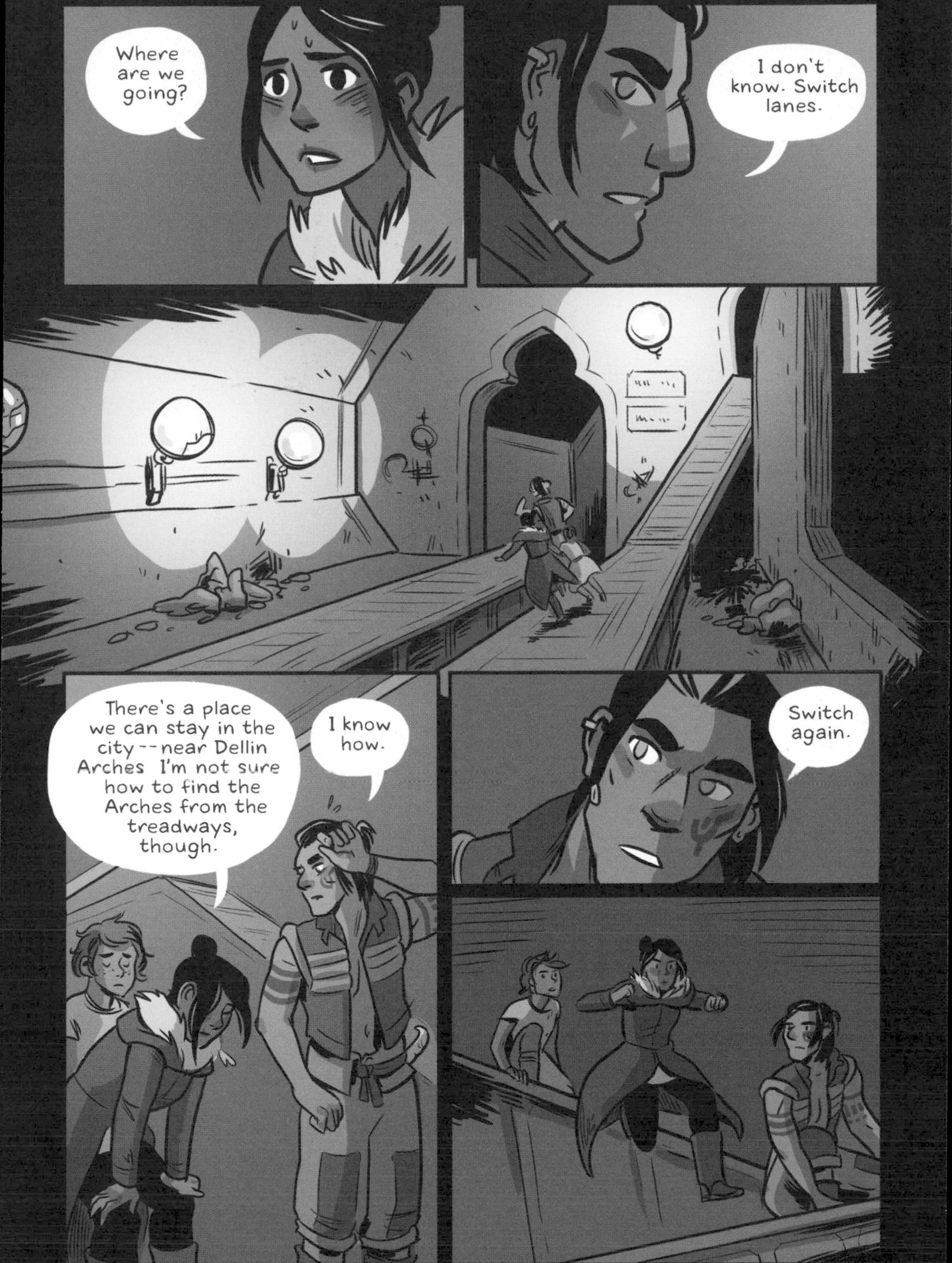

Where are we going?
I don't know. Switch lanes.
There's a place we can stay in the city--near Dellin Arches I'm not sure how to find the Arches from the treadways, though.
I know how.
Switch again.

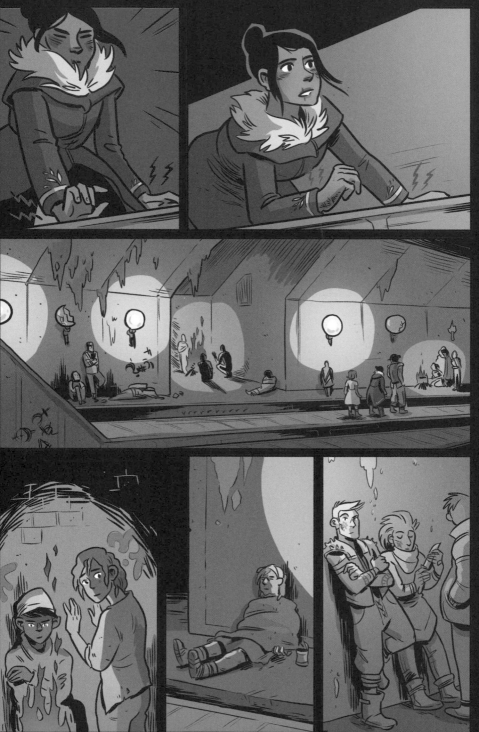

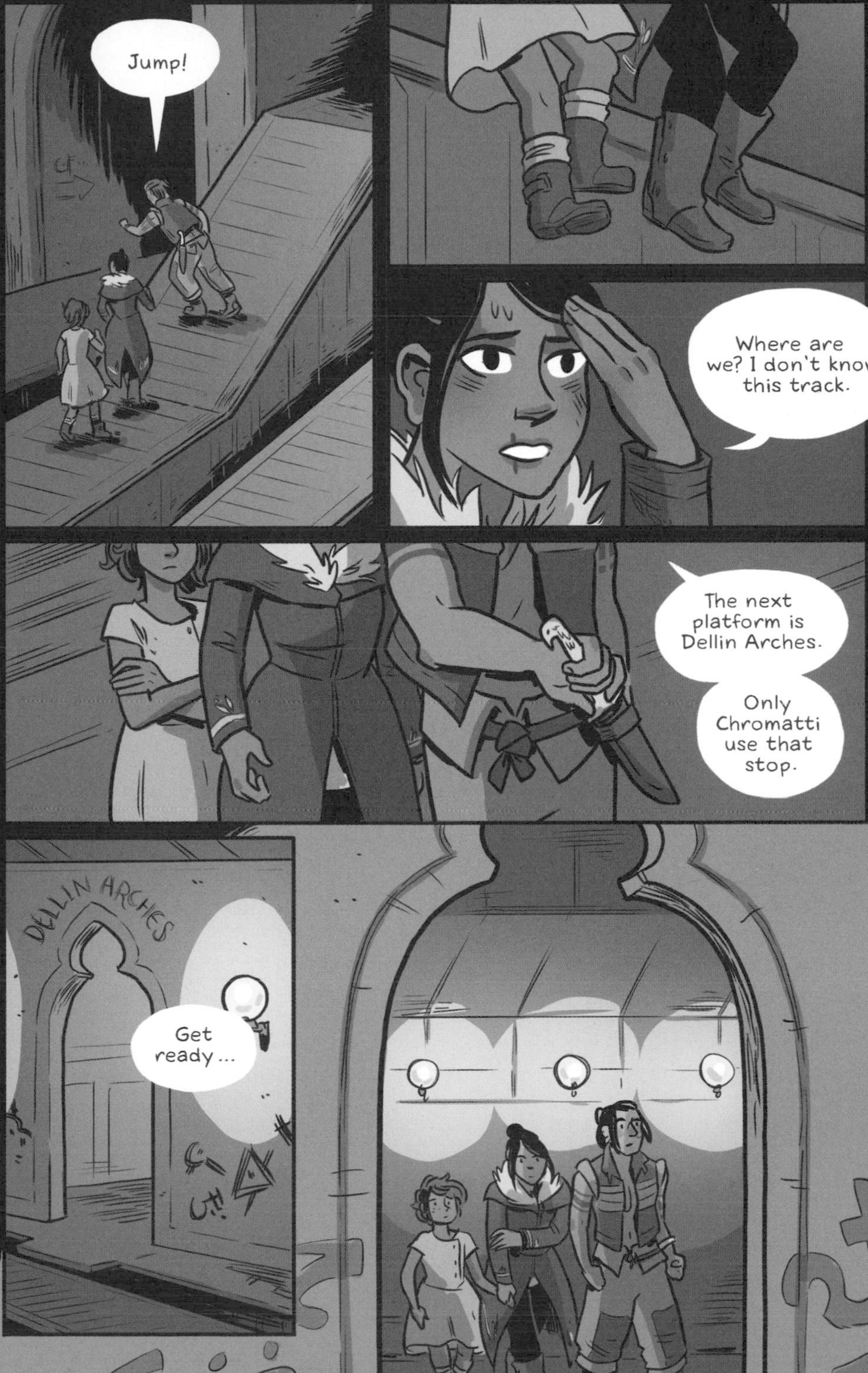
Jump!
Where are we? I don't know this track.
The next platform is Dellin Arches.
Only Chromatti use that stop.
DELLIN ARCHES
Get ready...

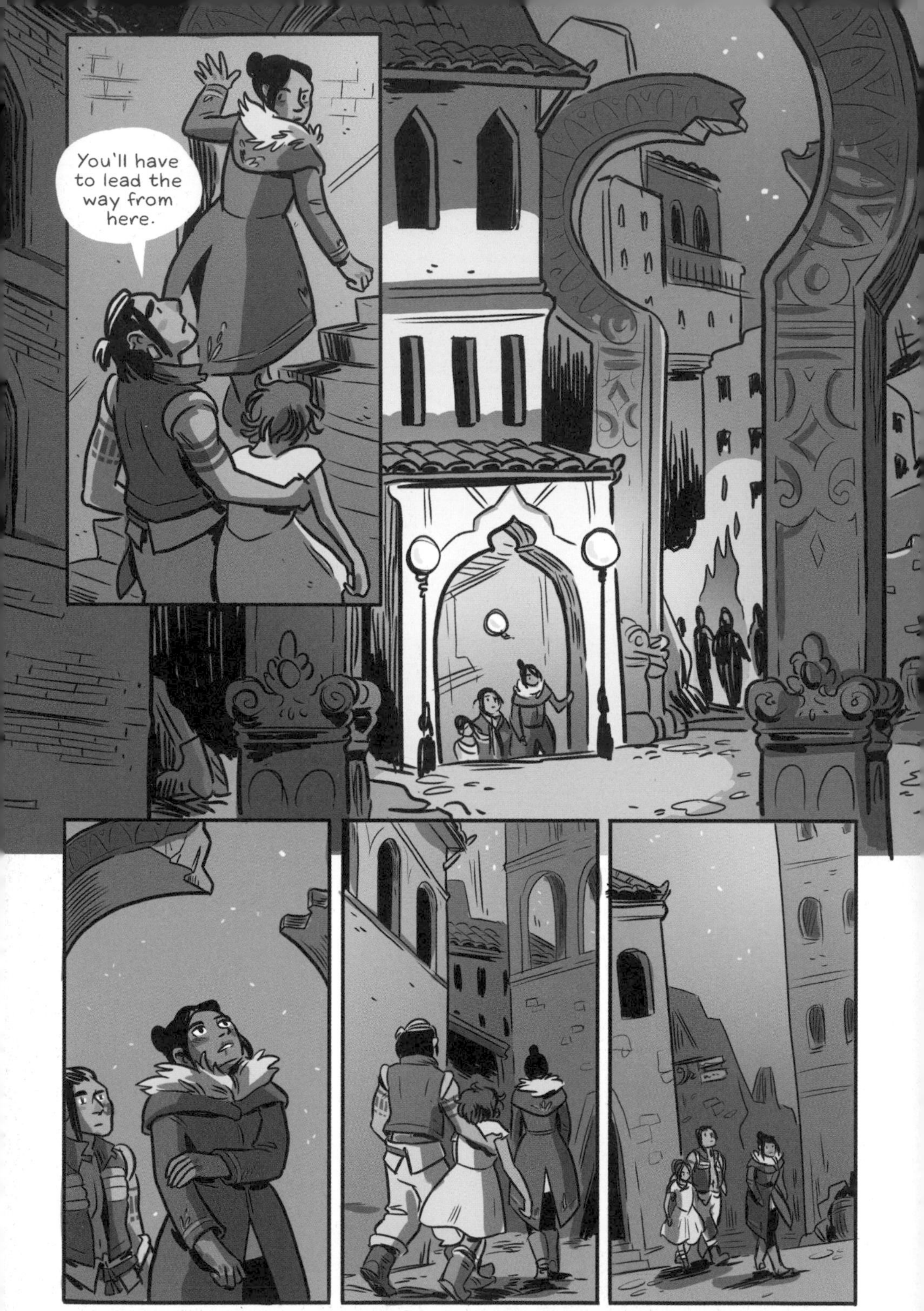
You'll have to lead the way from here.

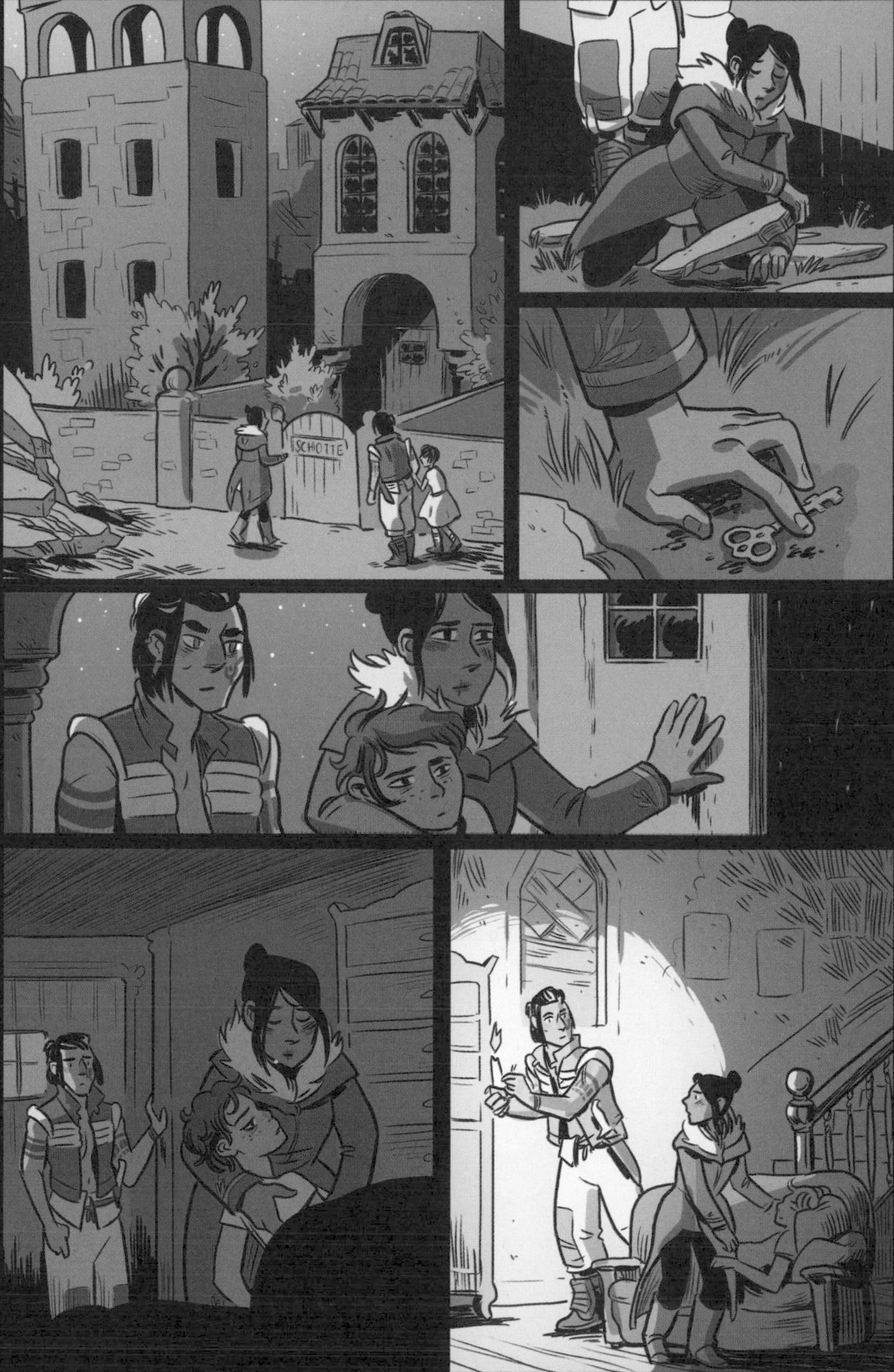
SCHIOTTE

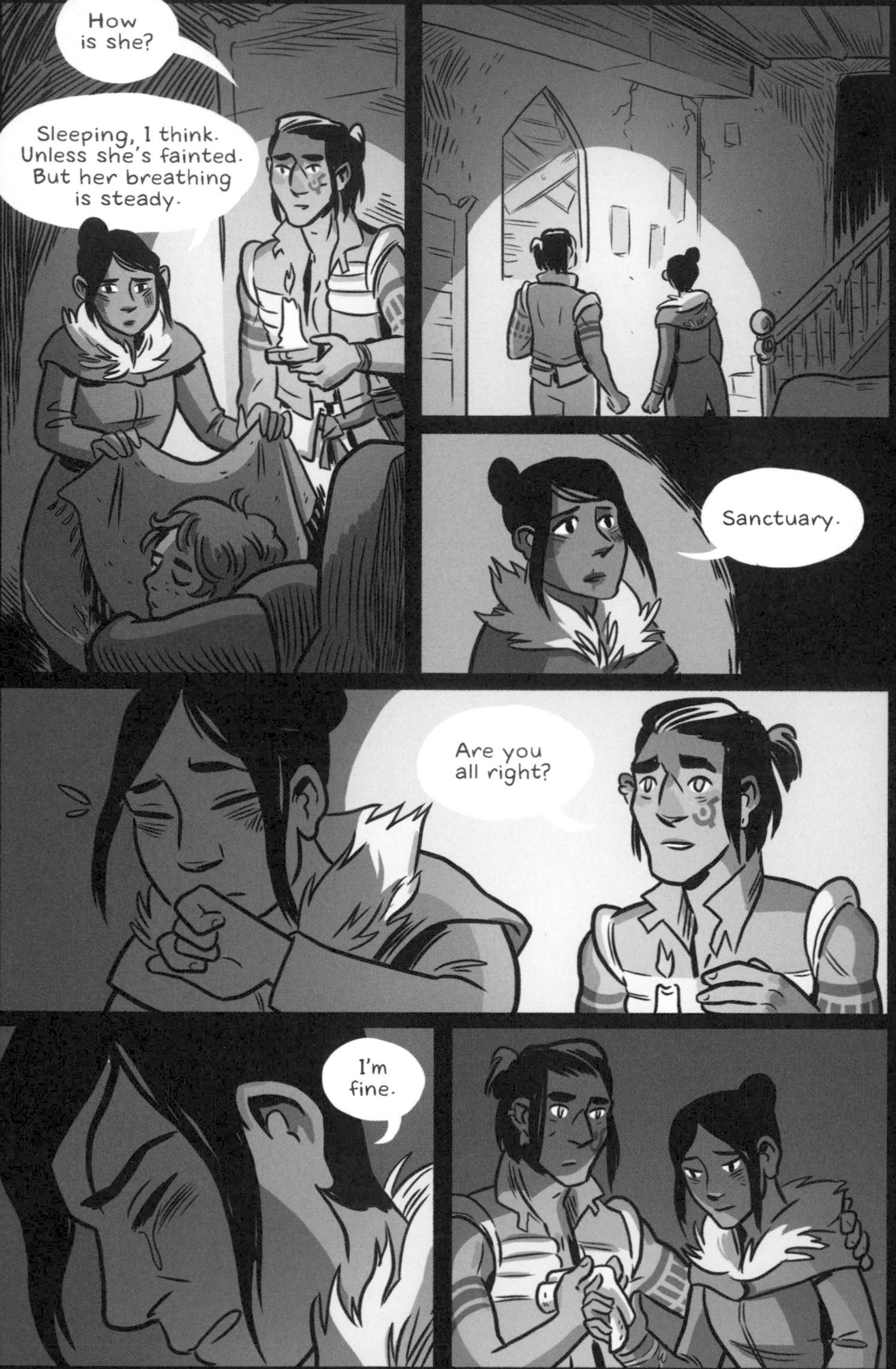
How is she?
Sleeping, I think. Unless she's fainted. But her breathing is steady.
Sanctuary.
Are you all right?
I'm fine.

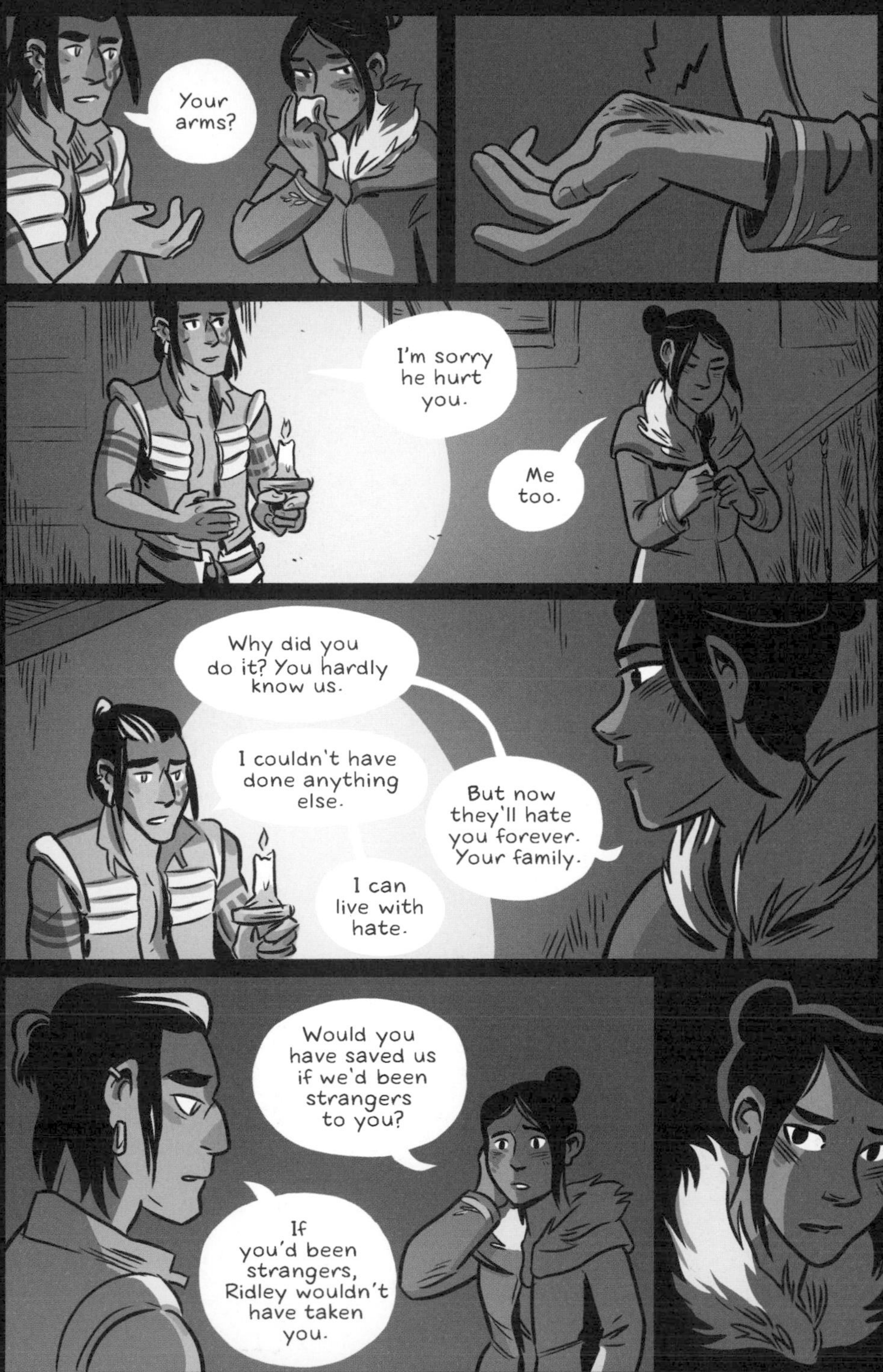
Your arms?
I'm sorry he hurt you.
Me too.
Why did you do it? You hardly know us.
I couldn't have done anything else.
But now they'll hate you forever. Your family.
I can live with hate.
Would you have saved us if we'd been strangers to you?
If you'd been strangers, Ridley wouldn't have taken you.

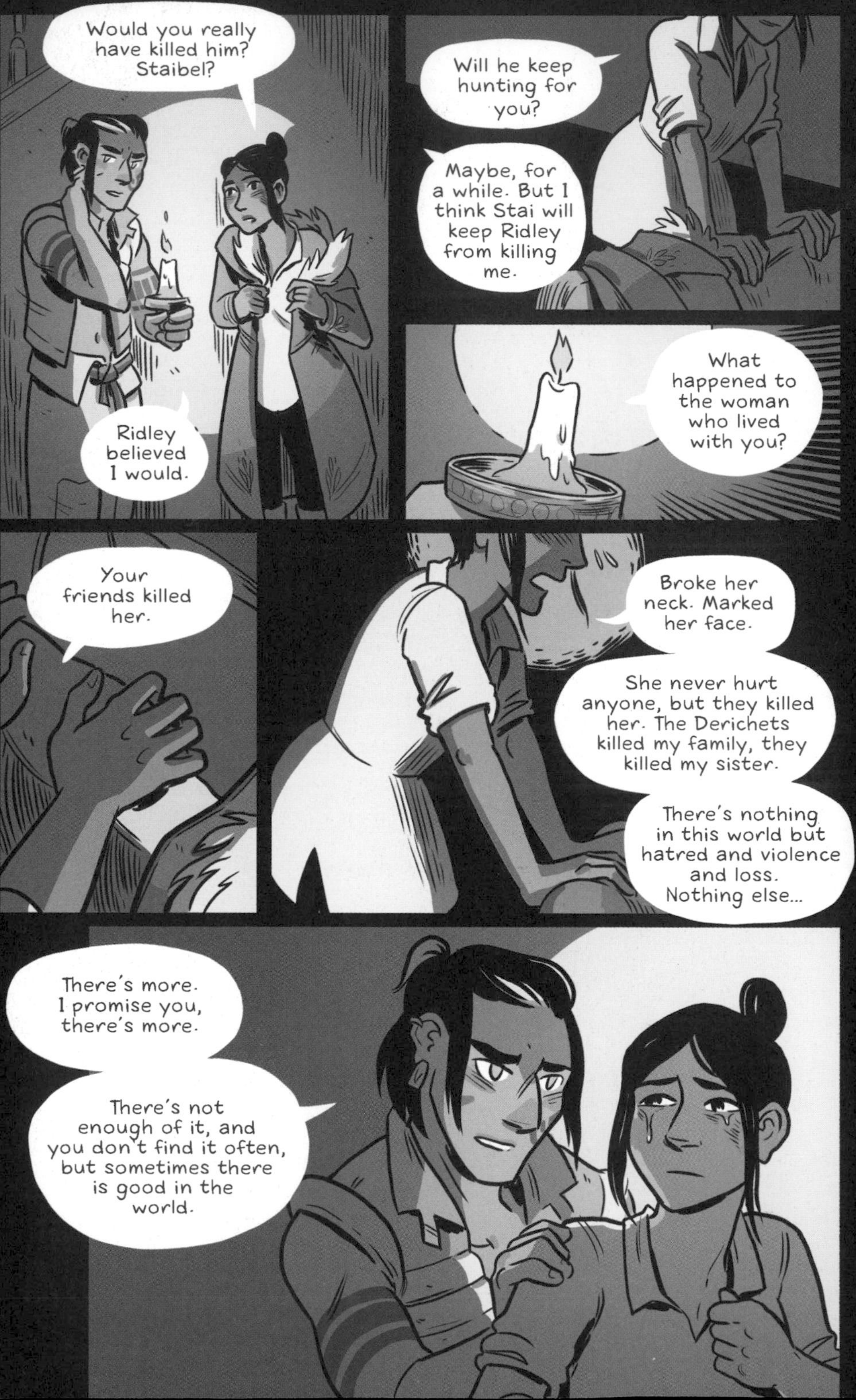
Would you really have killed him? Staibel?
Ridley believed I would.
Will he keep hunting for you?
Maybe, for a while. But I think Stai will keep Ridley from killing me.
What happened to the woman who lived with you?
Your friends killed her.
Broke her neck. Marked her face.
She never hurt anyone, but they killed her. The Derichets killed my family, they killed my sister.
There's nothing in this world but hatred and violence and loss. Nothing else...
There's more. I promise you, there's more.
There's not enough of it, and you don't find it often, but sometimes there is good in the world.

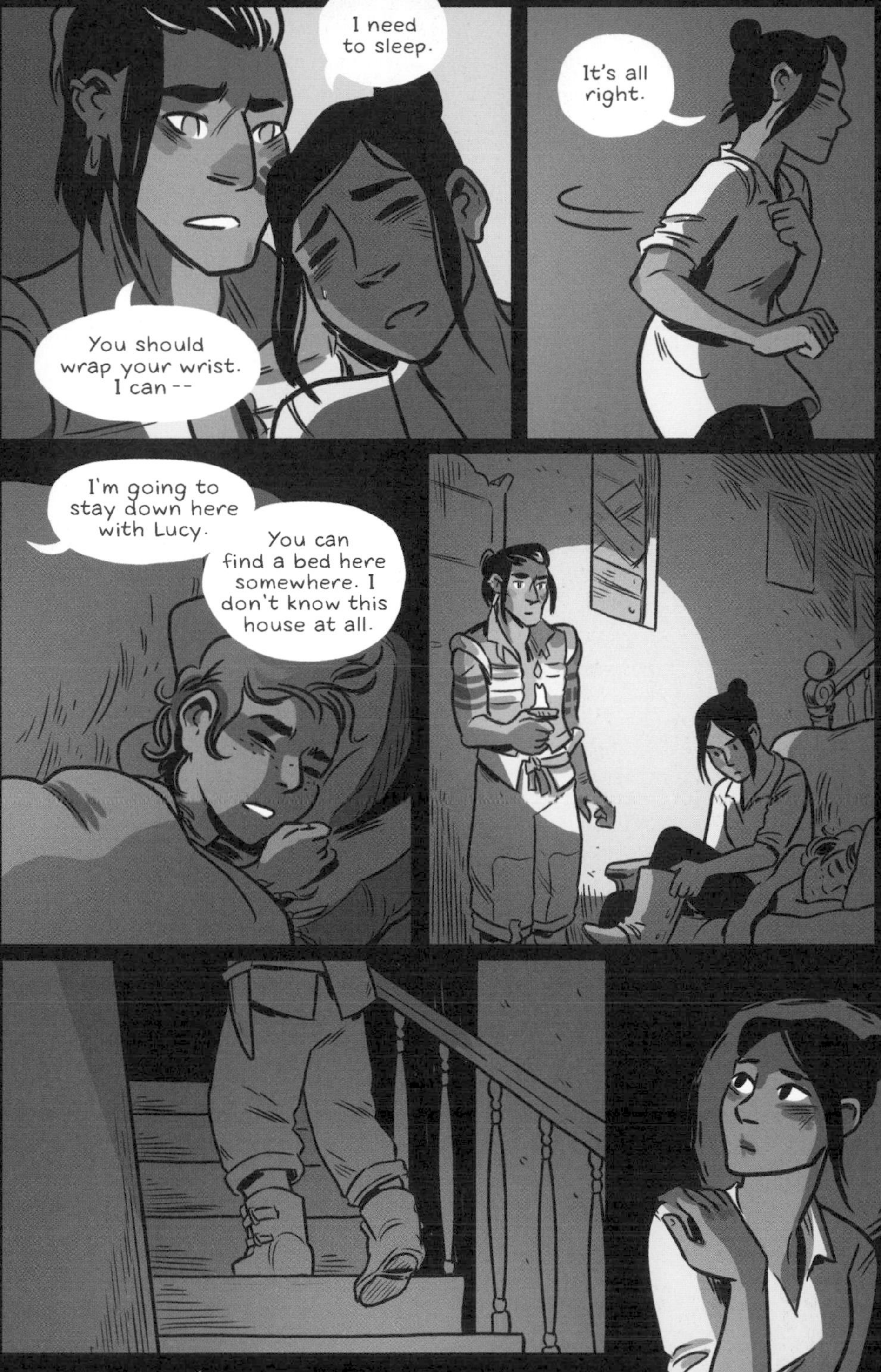
I need to sleep.
You should wrap your wrist. I can--
It's all right.
I'm going to stay down here with Lucy.
You can find a bed here somewhere. I don't know this house at all.

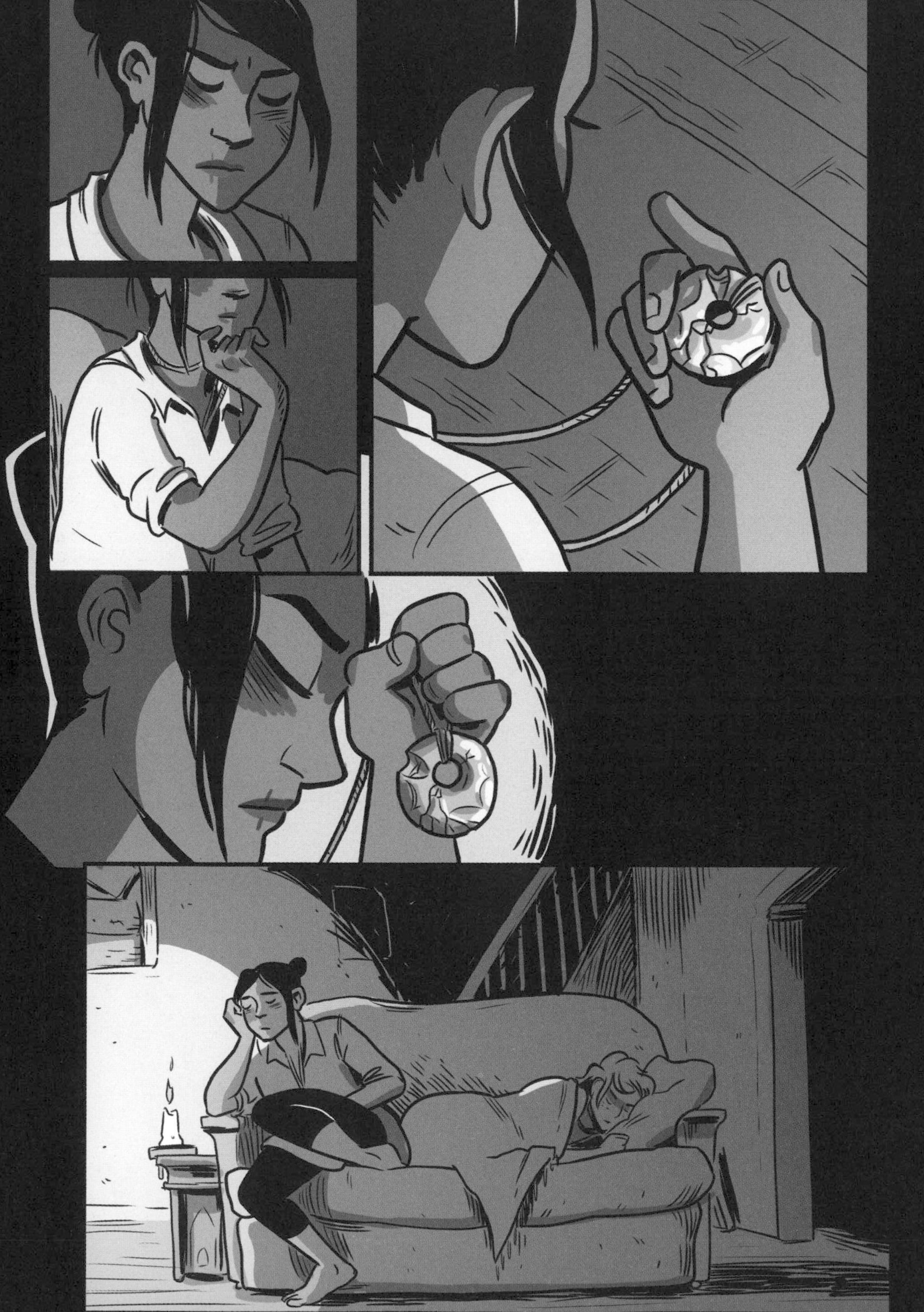

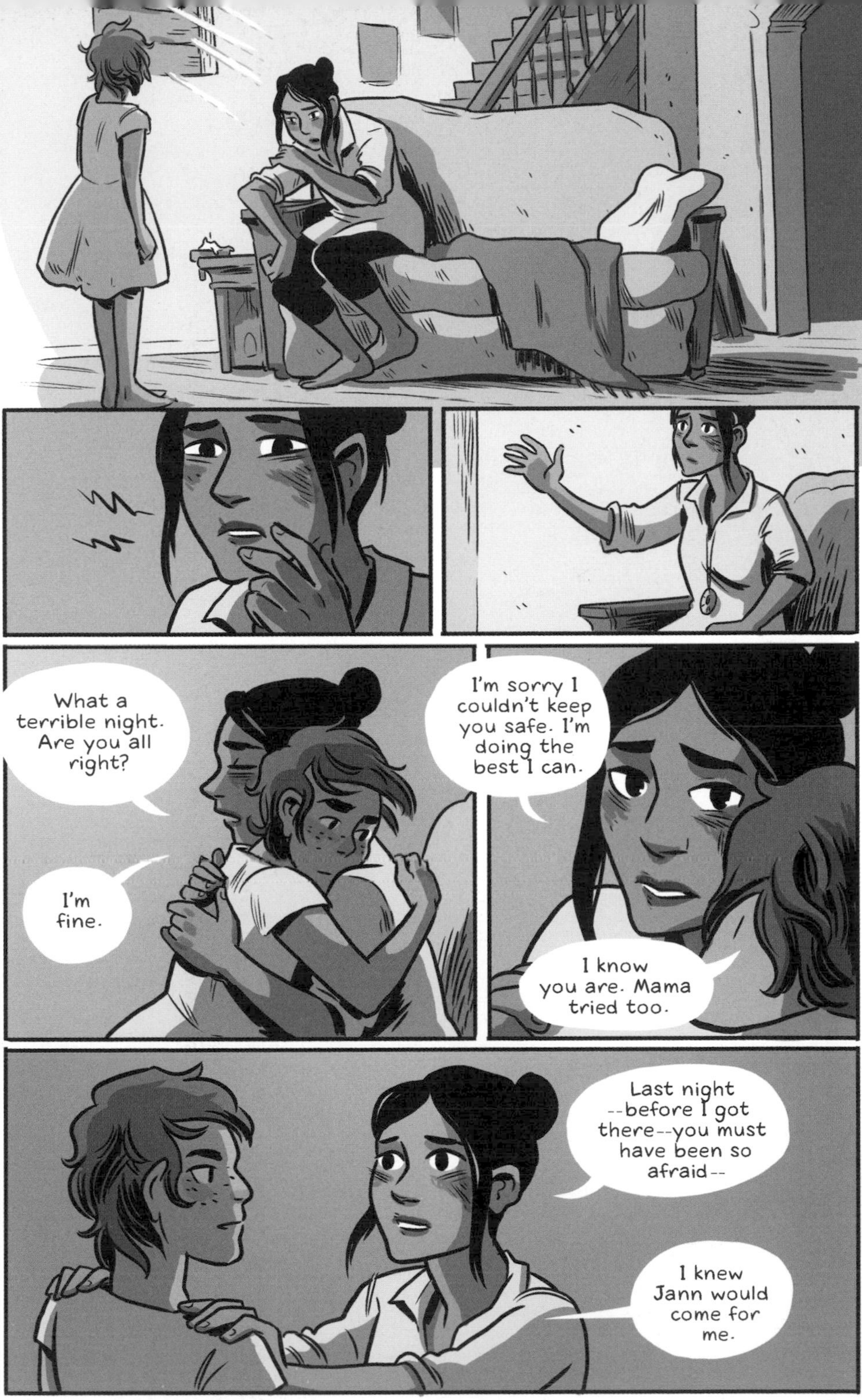
What a terrible night. Are you all right?
I'm fine.
I'm sorry I couldn't keep you safe. I'm doing the best I can.
I know you are. Mama tried too.
Last night --before I got there--you must have been so afraid--
I knew Jann would come for me.

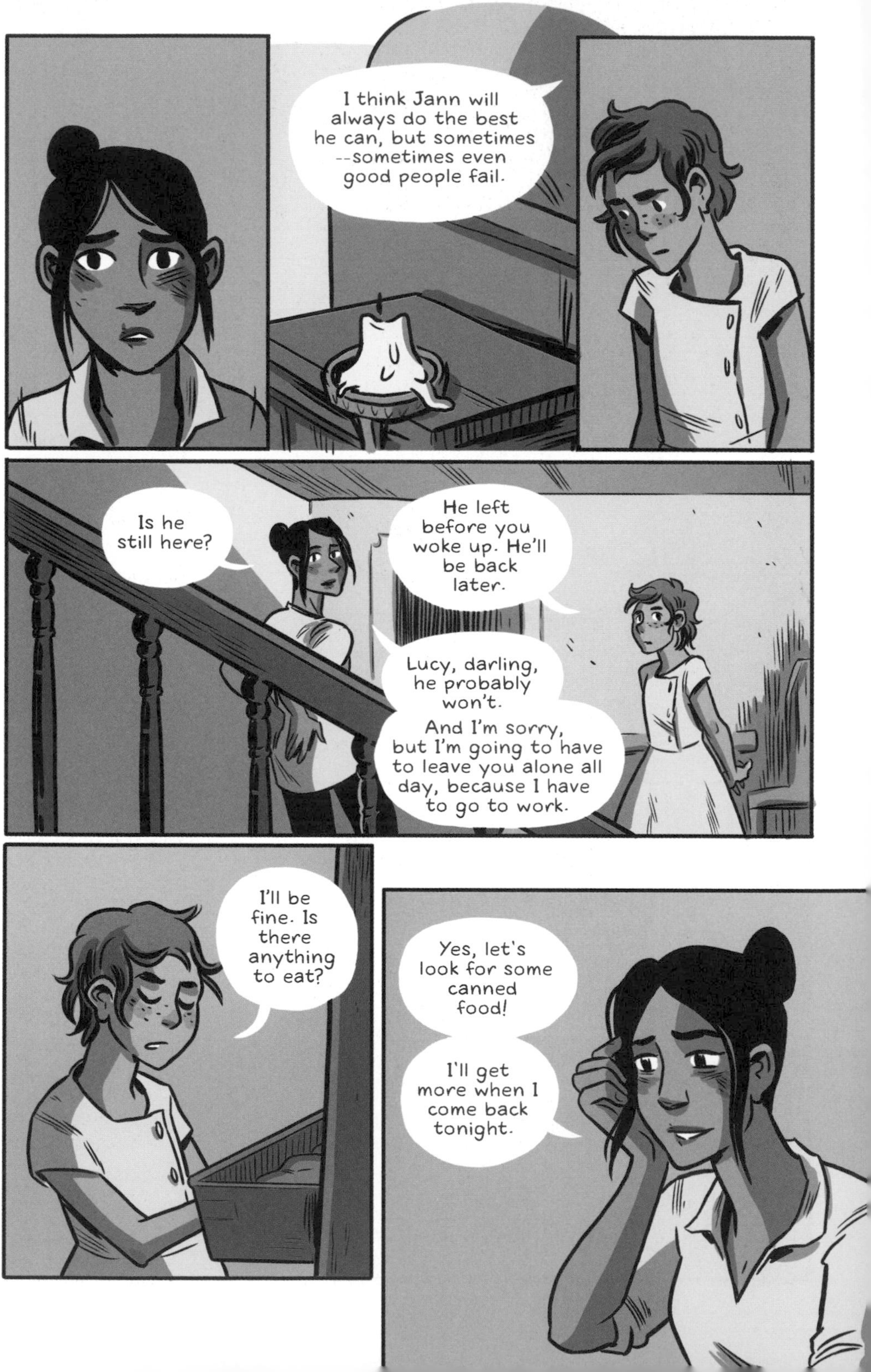
I think Jann will always do the best he can, but sometimes --sometimes even good people fail.
Is he still here?
He left before you woke up. He'll be back later.
Lucy, darling, he probably won't.
And I'm sorry, but I'm going to have to leave you alone all day, because I have to go to work.
I'll be fine. Is there anything to eat?
Yes, let's look for some canned food!
I'll get more when I come back tonight.

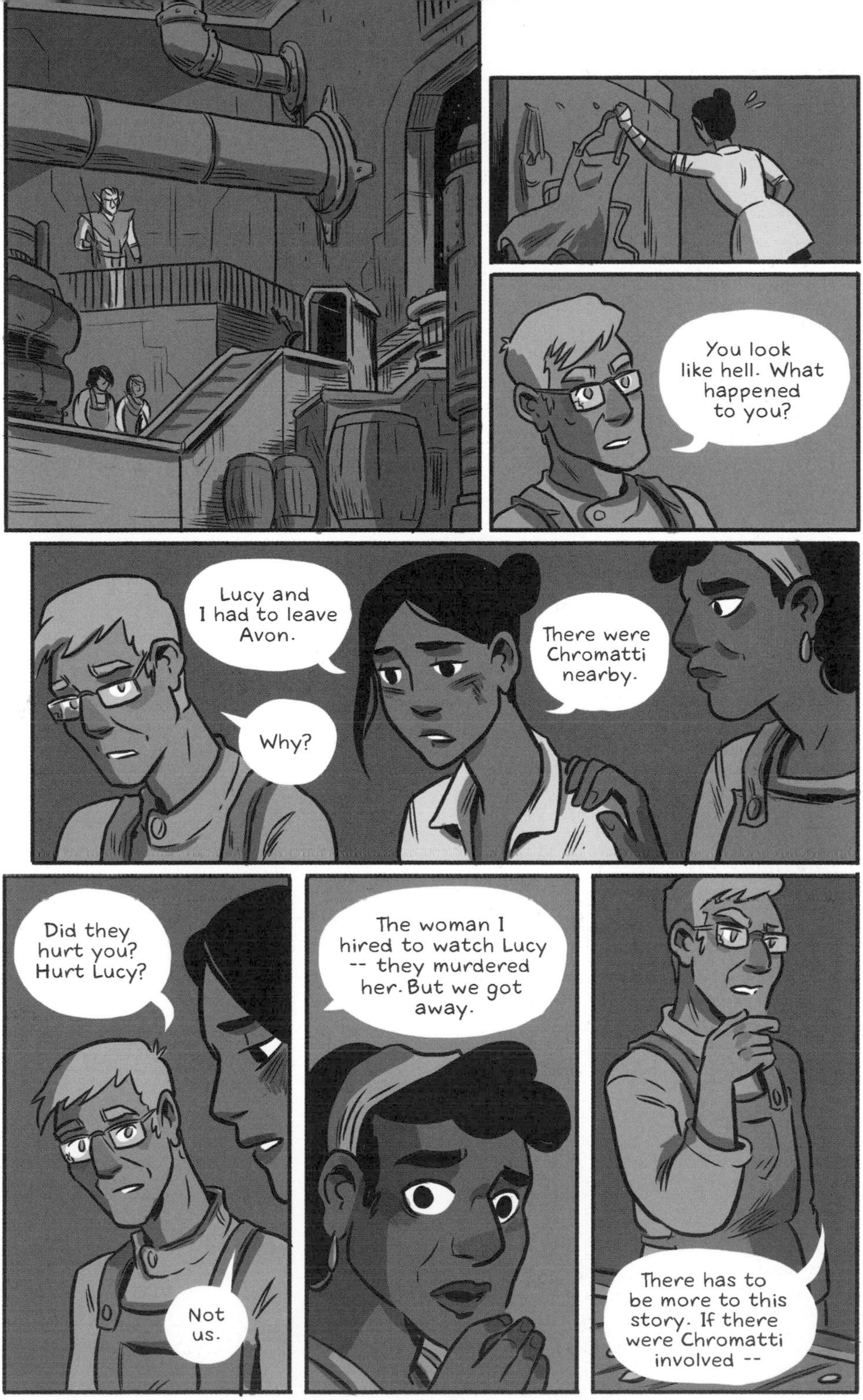

You look like hell. What happened to you?
Lucy and I had to leave Avon.
Why?
There were Chromatti nearby.
Did they hurt you? Hurt Lucy?
Not us.
The woman I hired to watch Lucy -- they murdered her. But we got away.
There has to be more to this story. If there were Chromatti involved --

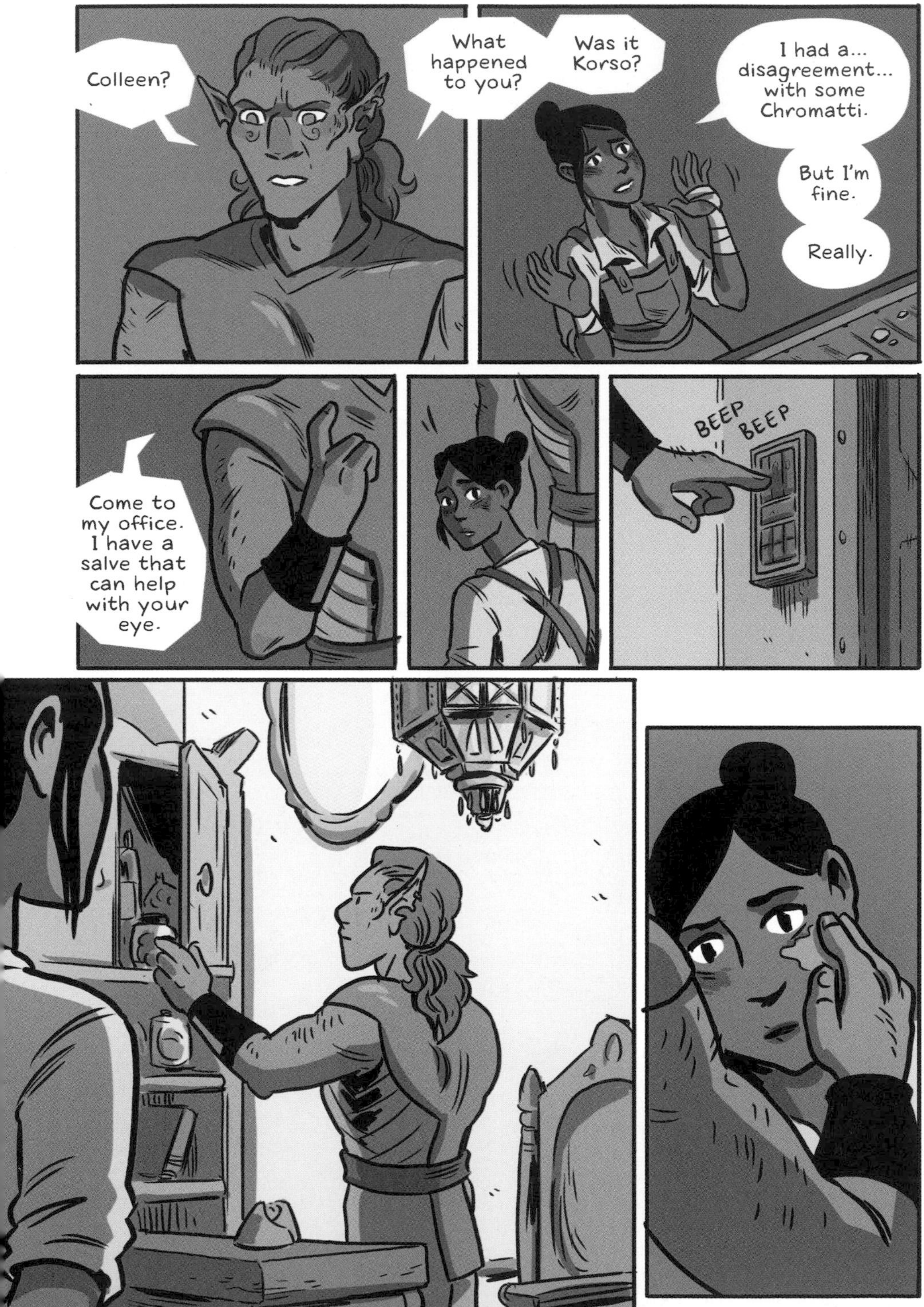
Colleen?
What happened to you?
Was it Korso?
I had a... disagreement... with some Chromatti.
But I'm fine.
Really.
Come to my office. I have a salve that can help with your eye.
BEEP BEEP

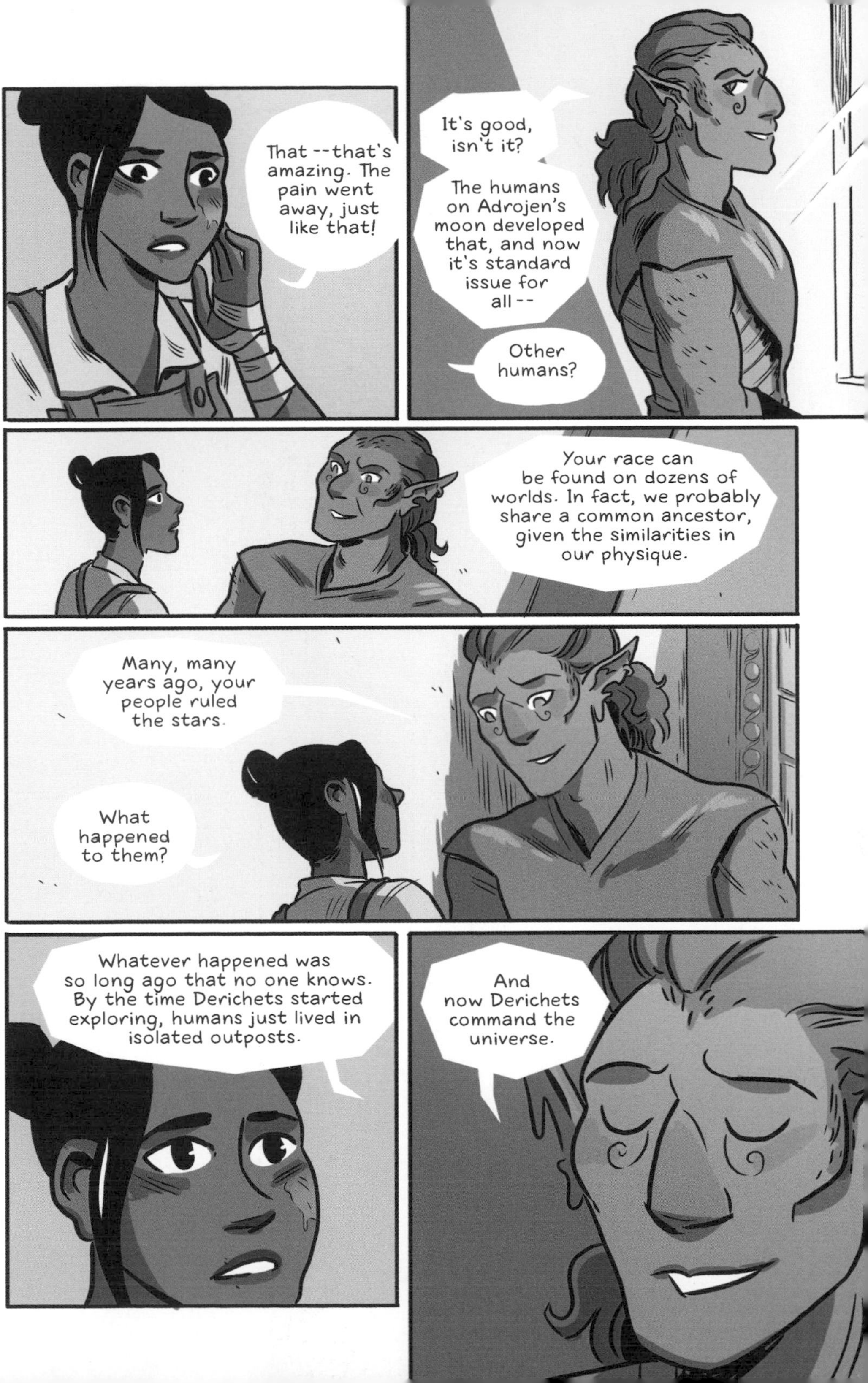
That --that's amazing. The pain went away, just like that!
It's good, isn't it?
The humans on Adrojen's moon developed that, and now it's standard issue for all --
Other humans?
Your race can be found on dozens of worlds. In fact, we probably share a common ancestor, given the similarities in our physique.
Many, many years ago, your people ruled the stars.
What happened to them?
Whatever happened was so long ago that no one knows. By the time Derichets started exploring, humans just lived in isolated outposts.
And now Derichets command the universe.

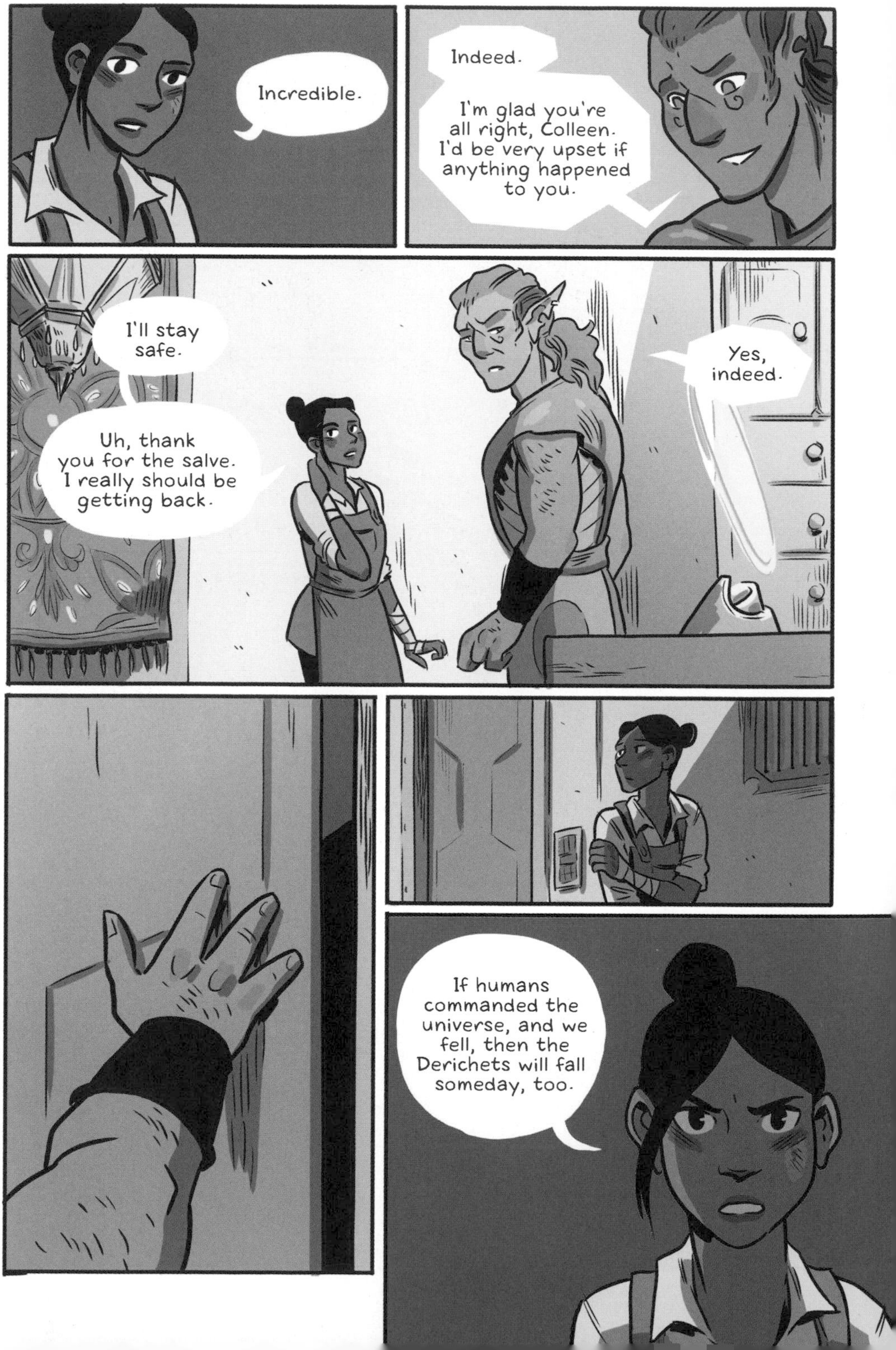
Incredible.
Indeed.
I'm glad you're all right, Colleen. I'd be very upset if anything happened to you.
I'll stay safe.
Uh, thank you for the salve. I really should be getting back.
Yes, indeed.
If humans commanded the universe, and we fell, then the Derichets will fall someday, too.

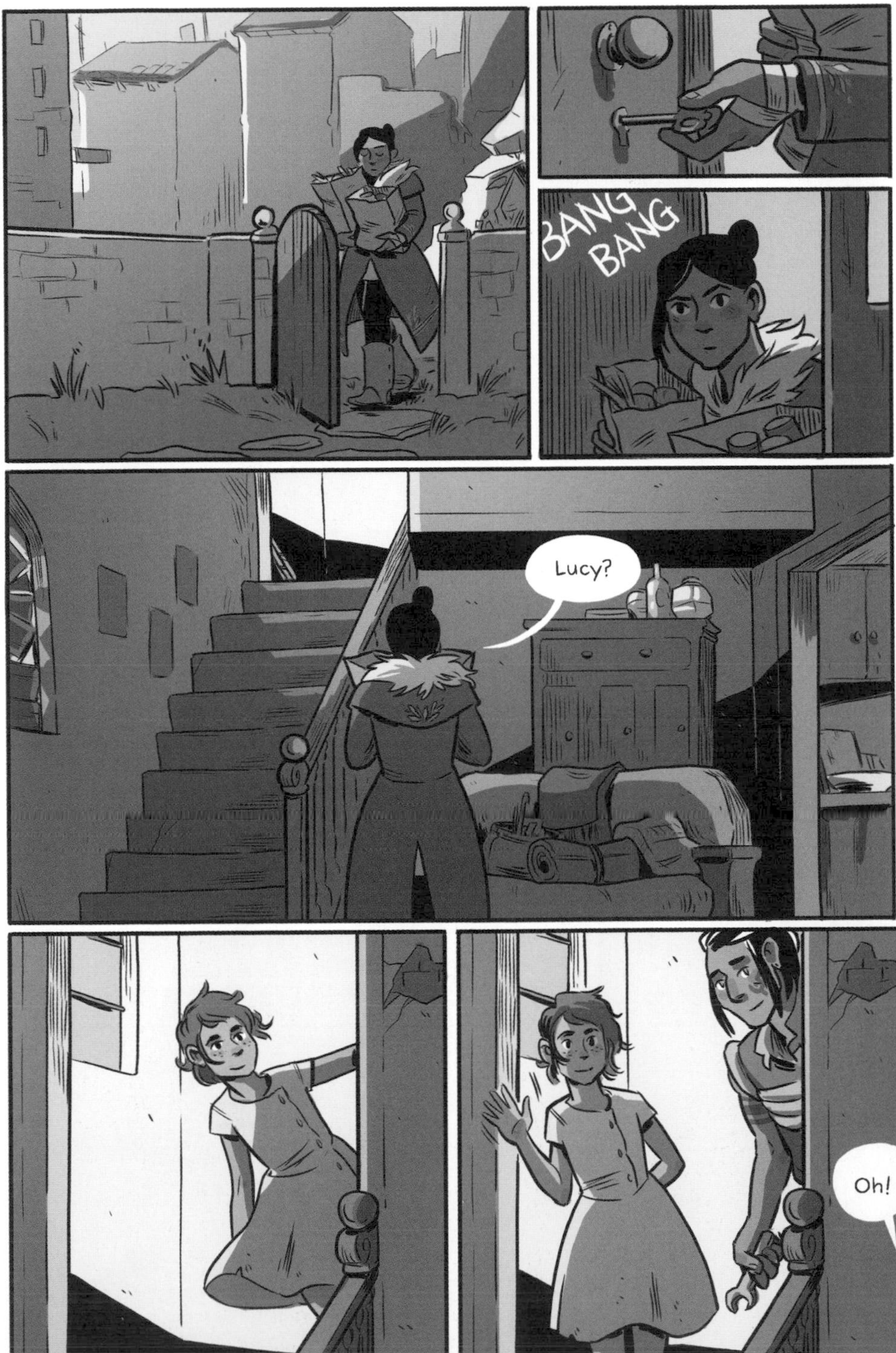
BANG
BANG
Lucy?
Oh!

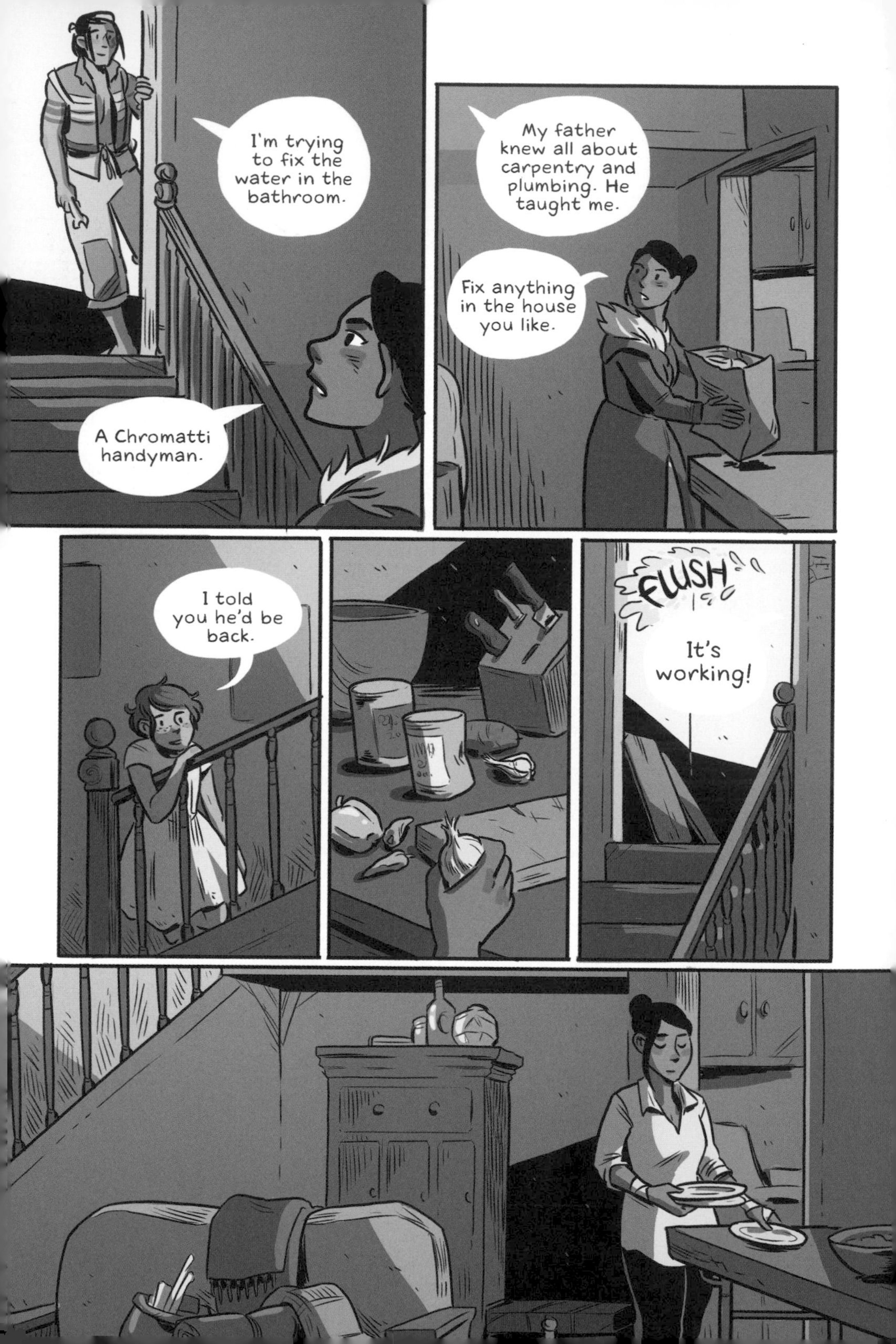
I'm trying to fix the water in the bathroom.
A Chromatti handyman.
My father knew all about carpentry and plumbing. He taught me.
Fix anything in the house you like.
I told you he'd be back.
FLUSH
It's working!

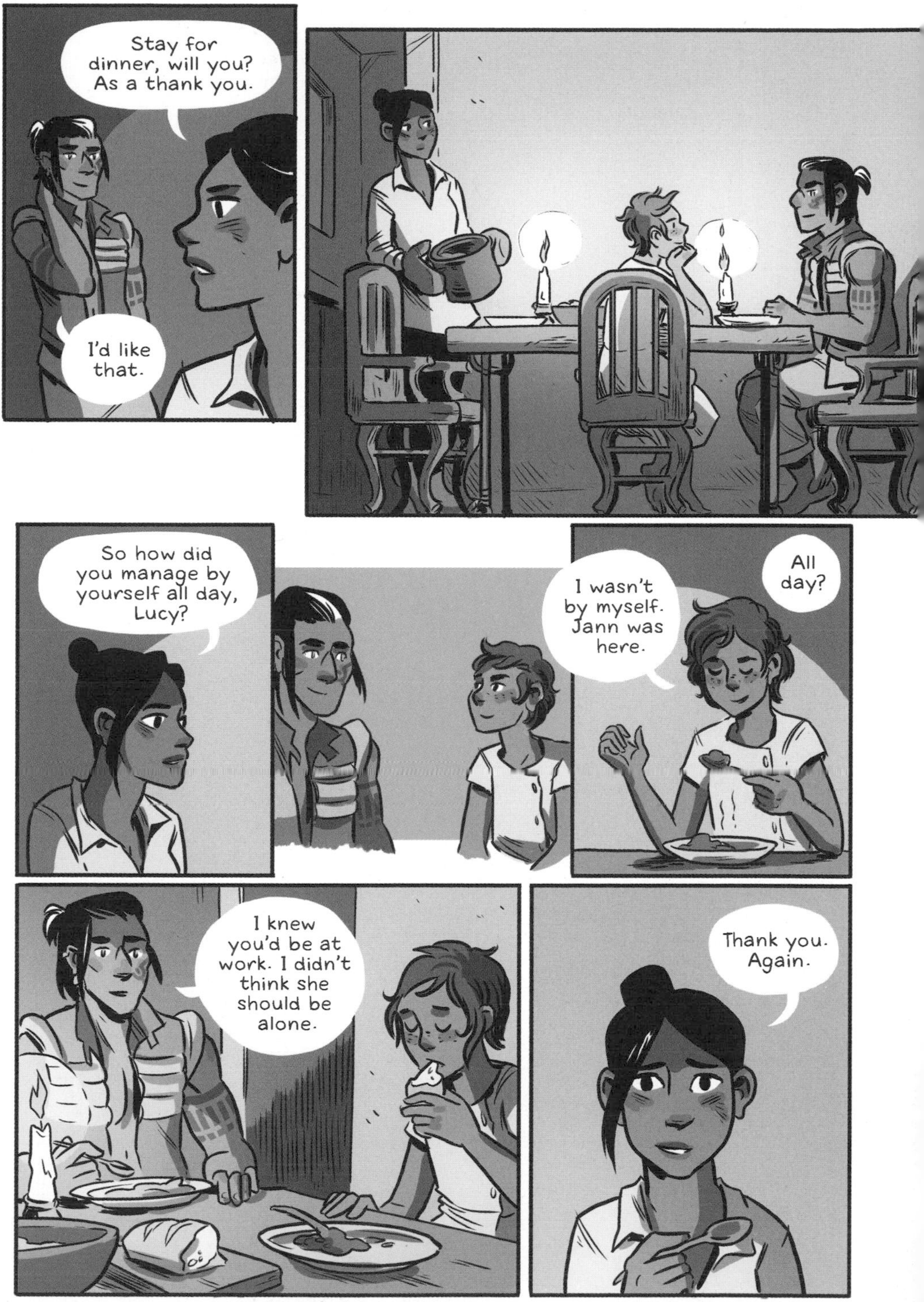
Stay for dinner, will you? As a thank you.
I'd like that.
So how did you manage by yourself all day, Lucy?
I wasn't by myself. Jann was here.
All day?
I knew you'd be at work. I didn't think she should be alone.
Thank you. Again.

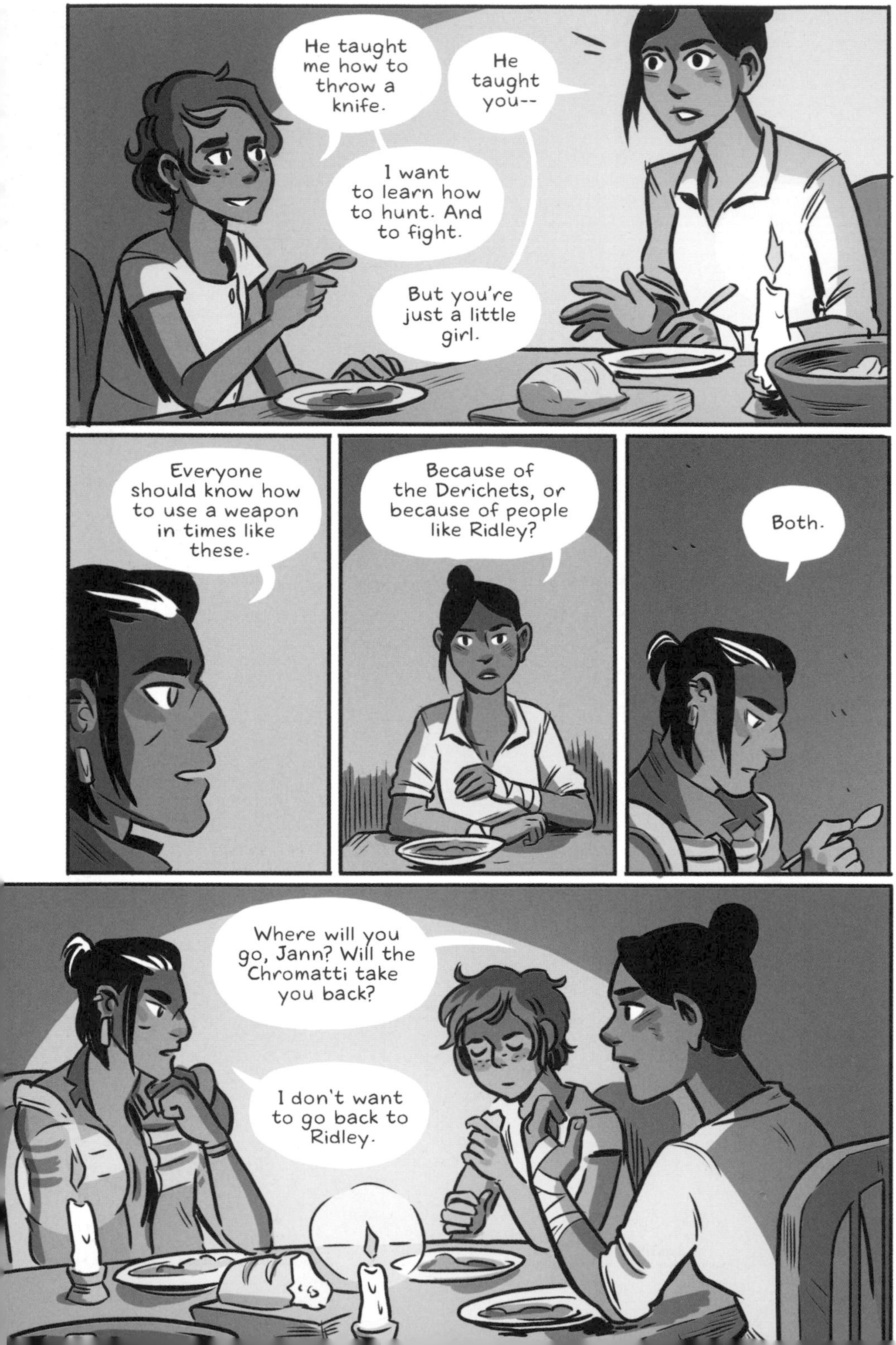
He taught me how to throw a knife.
He taught you--
I want to learn how to hunt. And to fight.
But you're just a little girl.
Everyone should know how to use a weapon in times like these.
Because of the Derichets, or because of people like Ridley?
Both.
Where will you go, Jann? Will the Chromatti take you back?
I don't want to go back to Ridley.

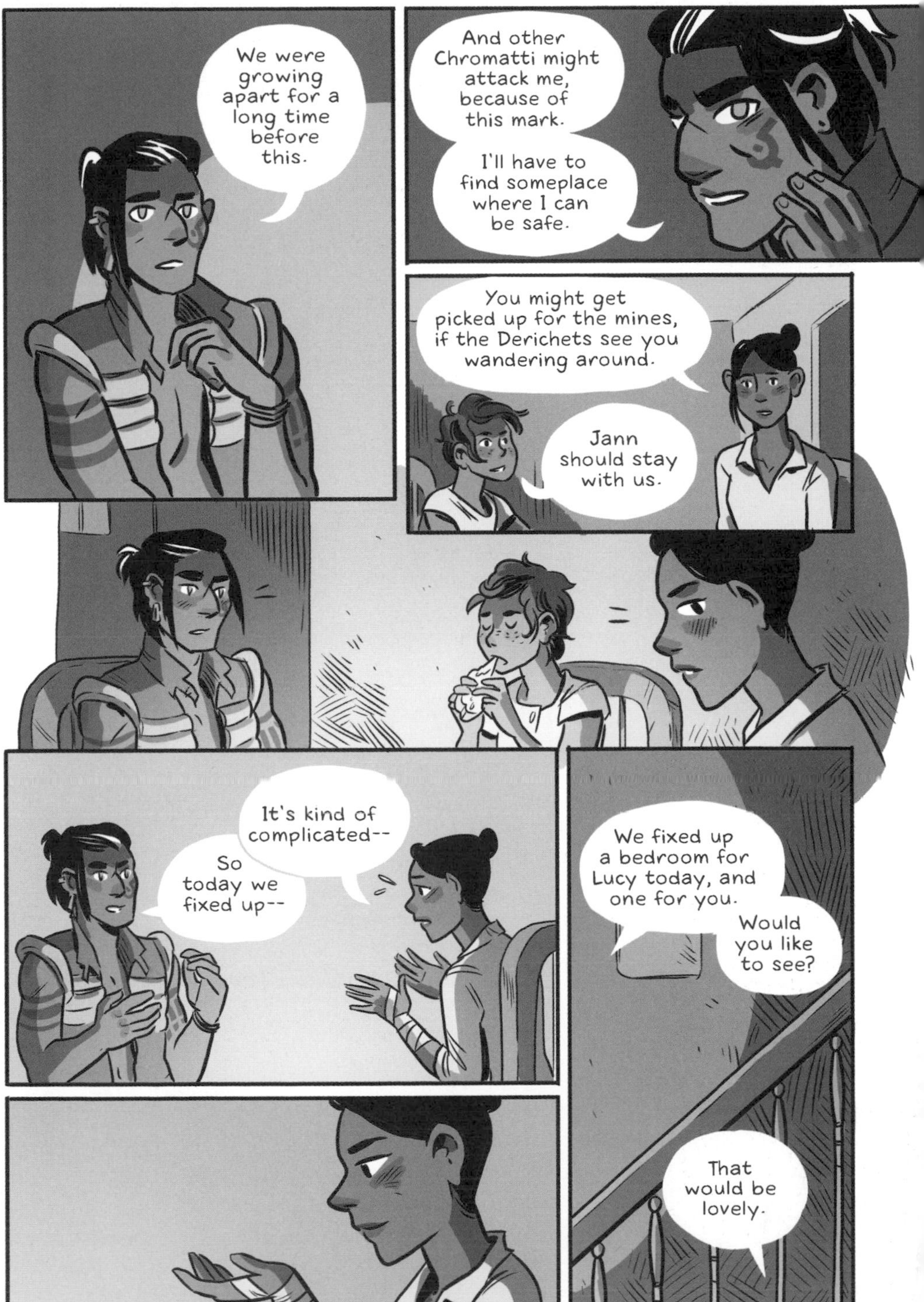
We were growing apart for a long time before this.
And other Chromatti might attack me, because of this mark.
I'll have to find someplace where I can be safe.
You might get picked up for the mines, if the Derichets see you wandering around.
Jann should stay with us.
It's kind of complicated--
So today we fixed up--
We fixed up a bedroom for Lucy today, and one for you.
Would you like to see?
That would be lovely.

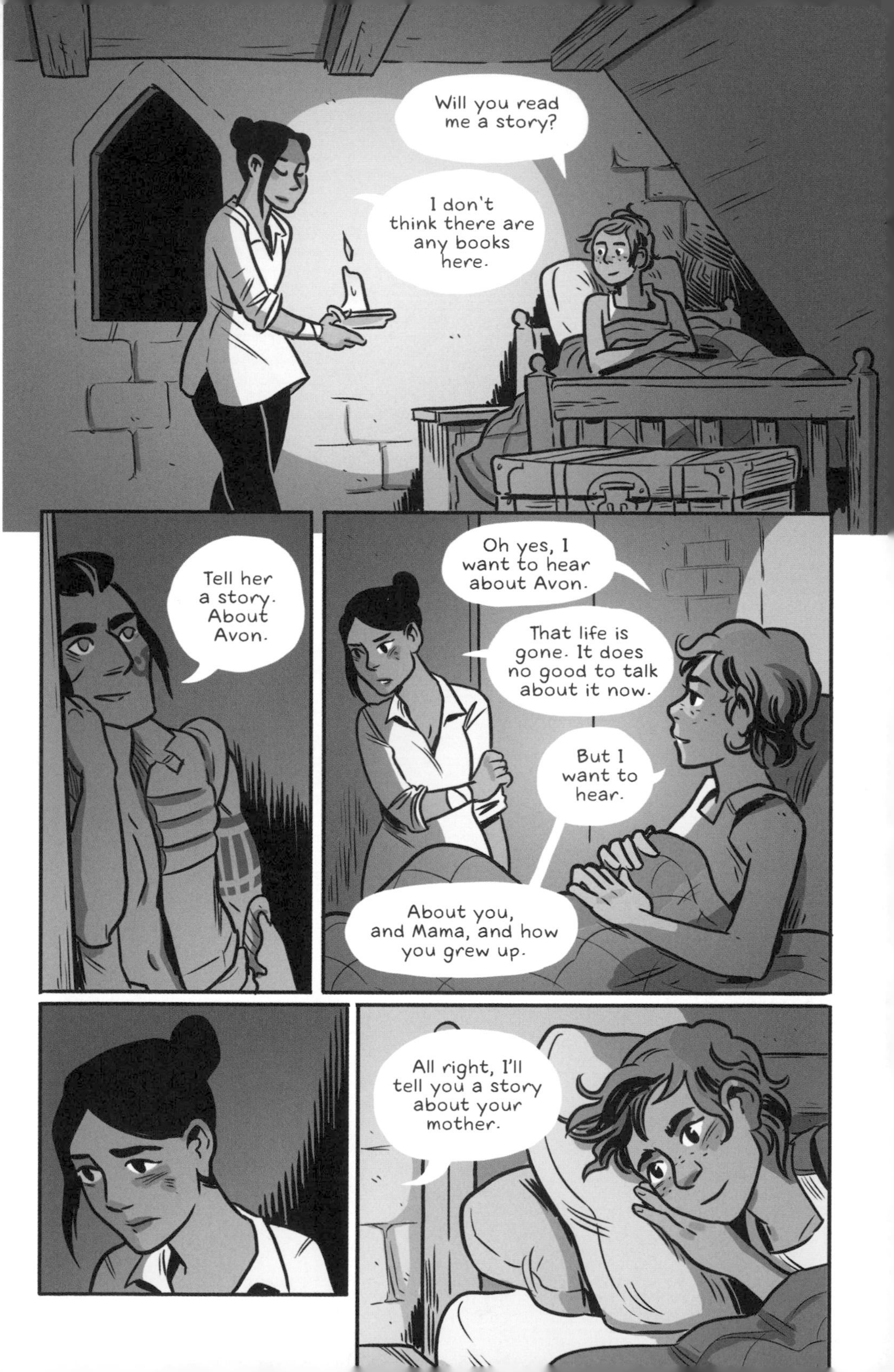
Will you read me a story?
I don't think there are any books here.
Tell her a story. About Avon.
Oh yes, I want to hear about Avon.
That life is gone. It does no good to talk about it now.
But I want to hear.
About you, and Mama, and how you grew up.
All right, I'll tell you a story about your mother.

It was winter, and we were having a party for Keighley's twelfth birthday.
Ninety-nine people sat down to dinner. There was so much food!
Keighley was wearing a beautiful dress,
I remember how soft it felt.
It was made out of feathers from a hundred doves.
And expensive.
That sounds so pretty.
Anyway, we had just started eating when one of the cooks ran in-- they could smell gas in the kitchen, there must have been a leak.
We all ran outside, but it was so cold we thought we'd freeze.

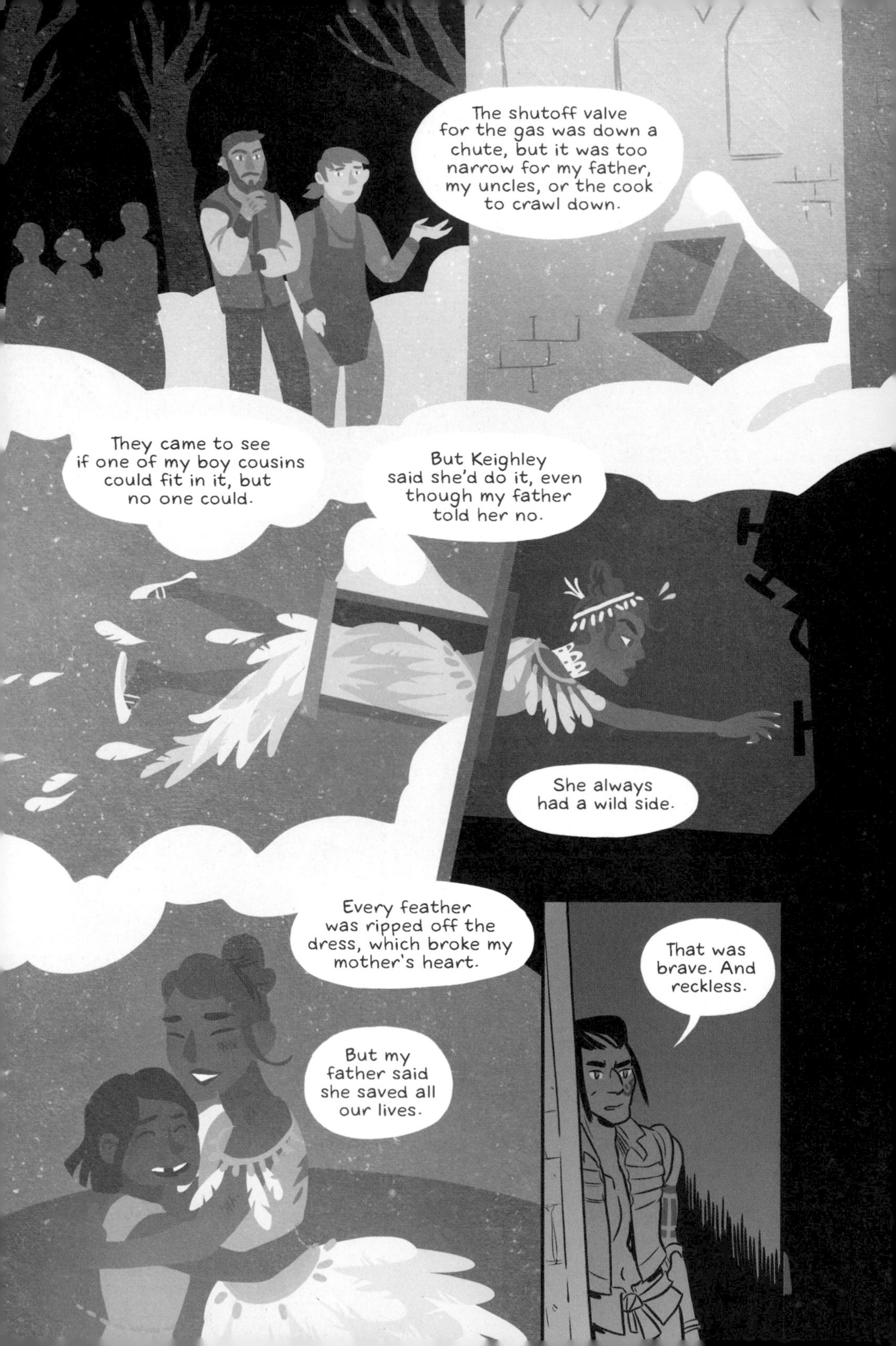
The shutoff valve for the gas was down a chute, but it was too narrow for my father, my uncles, or the cook to crawl down.
They came to see if one of my boy cousins could fit in it, but no one could.
But Keighley said she'd do it, even though my father told her no.
She always had a wild side.
Every feather was ripped off the dress, which broke my mother's heart.
But my father said she saved all our lives.
That was brave. And reckless.

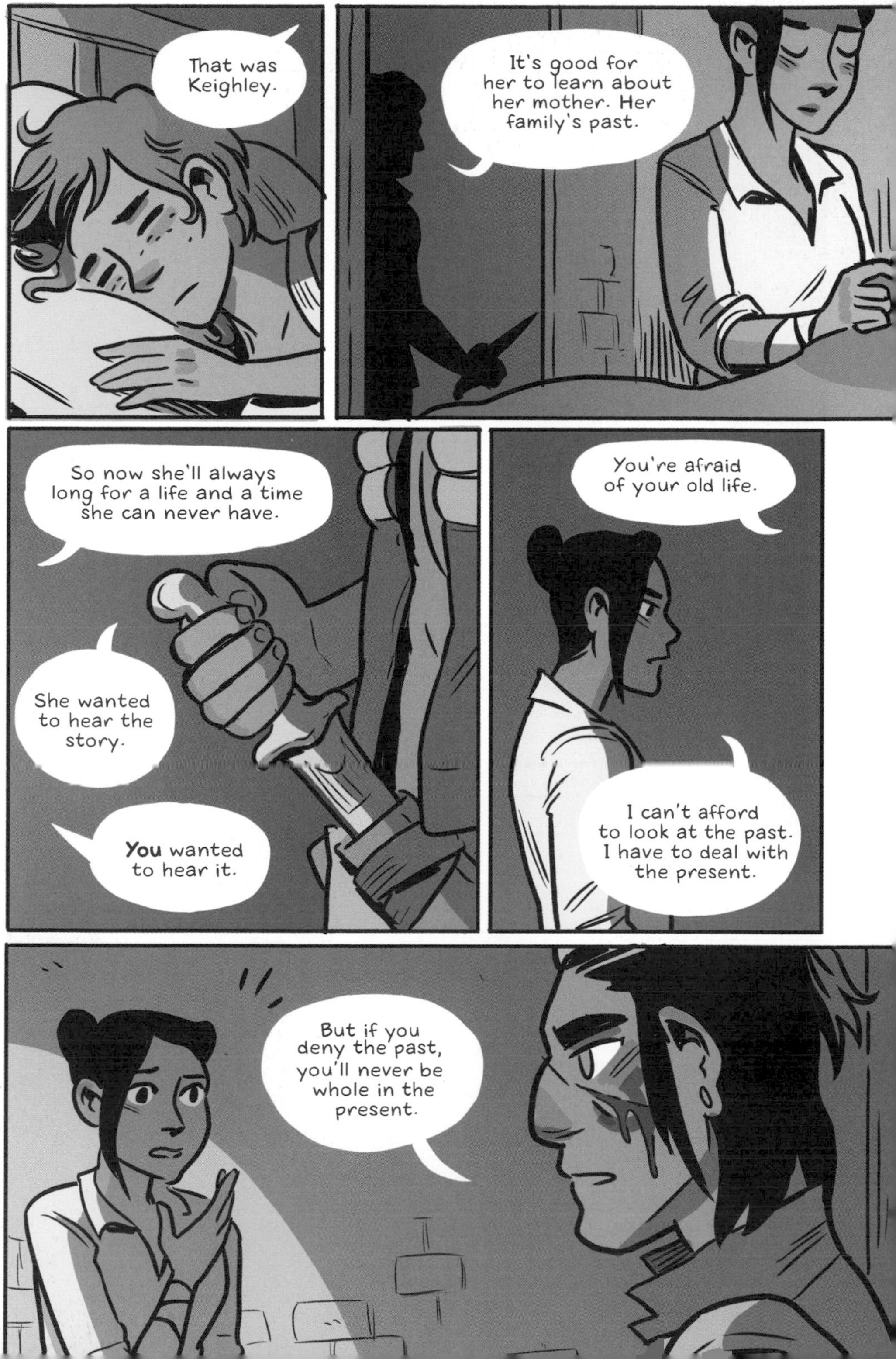
That was Keighley.
It's good for her to learn about her mother. Her family's past.
So now she'll always long for a life and a time she can never have.
She wanted to hear the story.
You wanted to hear it.
You're afraid of your old life.
I can't afford to look at the past. I have to deal with the present.
But if you deny the past, you'll never be whole in the present.

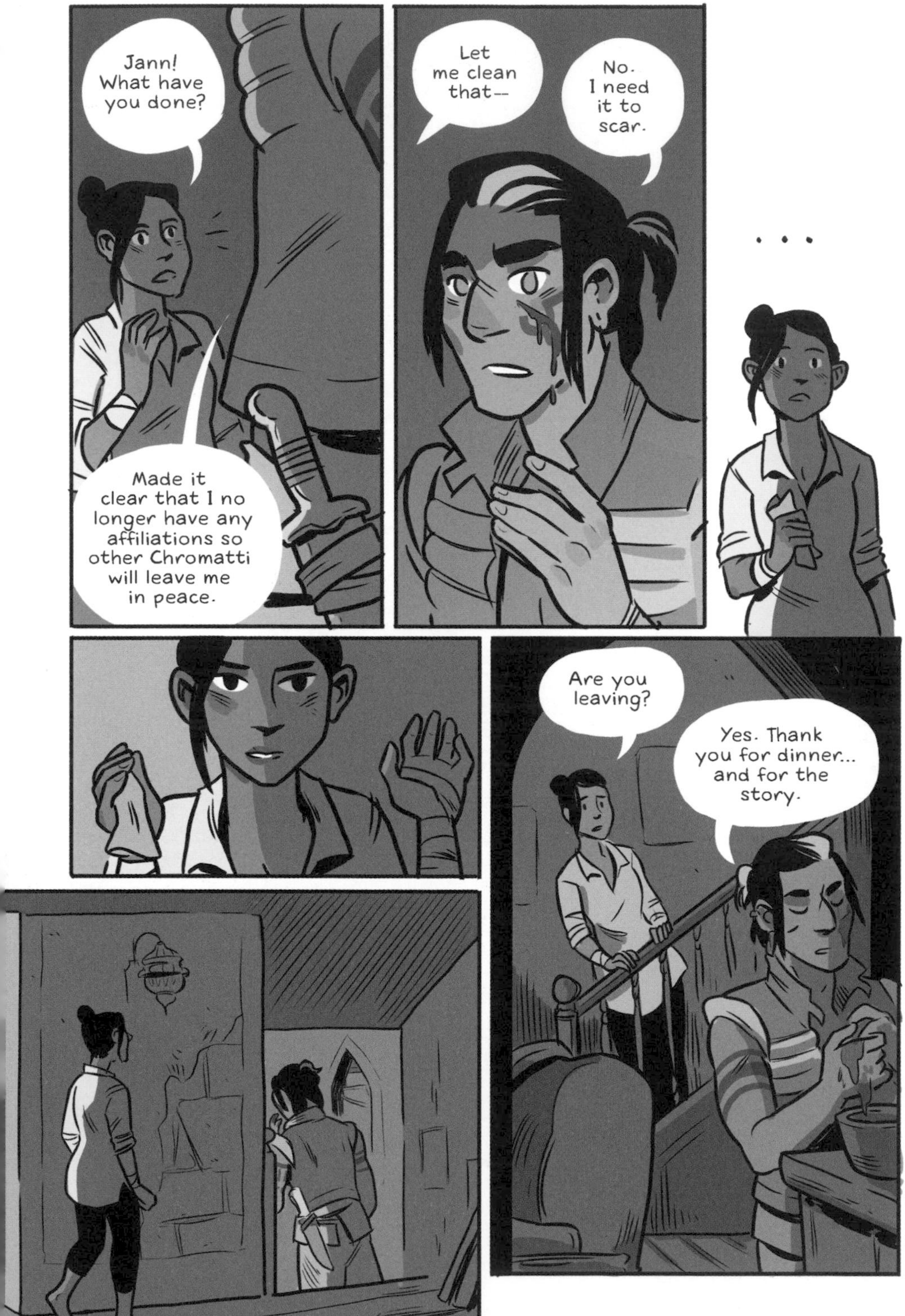
Jann! What have you done?
Made it clear that I no longer have any affiliations so other Chromatti will leave me in peace.
Let me clean that--
No. I need it to scar.
. . .
Are you leaving?
Yes. Thank you for dinner... and for the story.

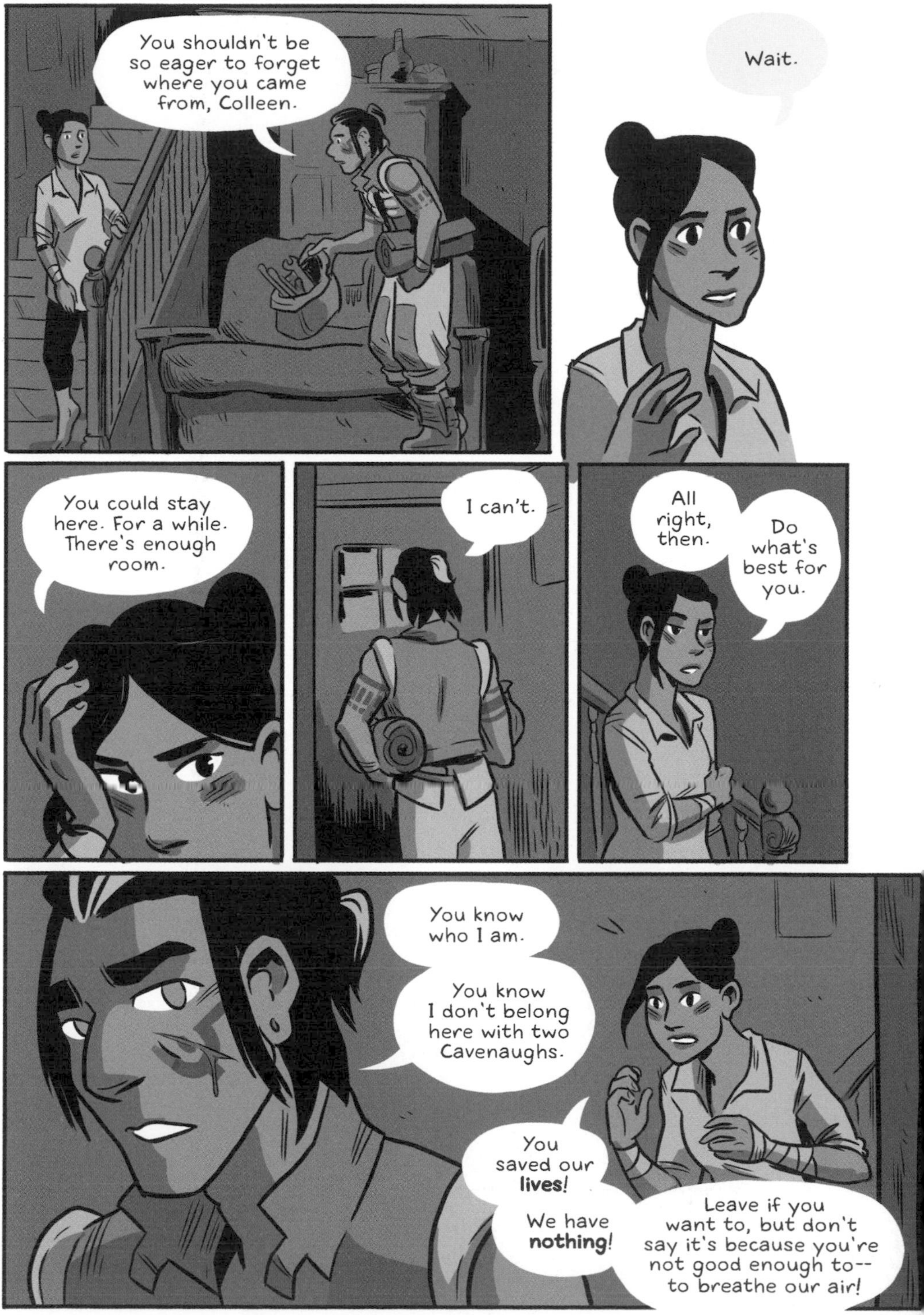
You shouldn't be so eager to forget where you came from, Colleen.
Wait.
You could stay here. For a while. There's enough room.
I can't.
All right, then.
Do what's best for you.
You know who I am.
You know I don't belong here with two Cavenaughs.
You saved our **lives**!
We have **nothing**!
Leave if you want to, but don't say it's because you're not good enough to-- to breathe our air!

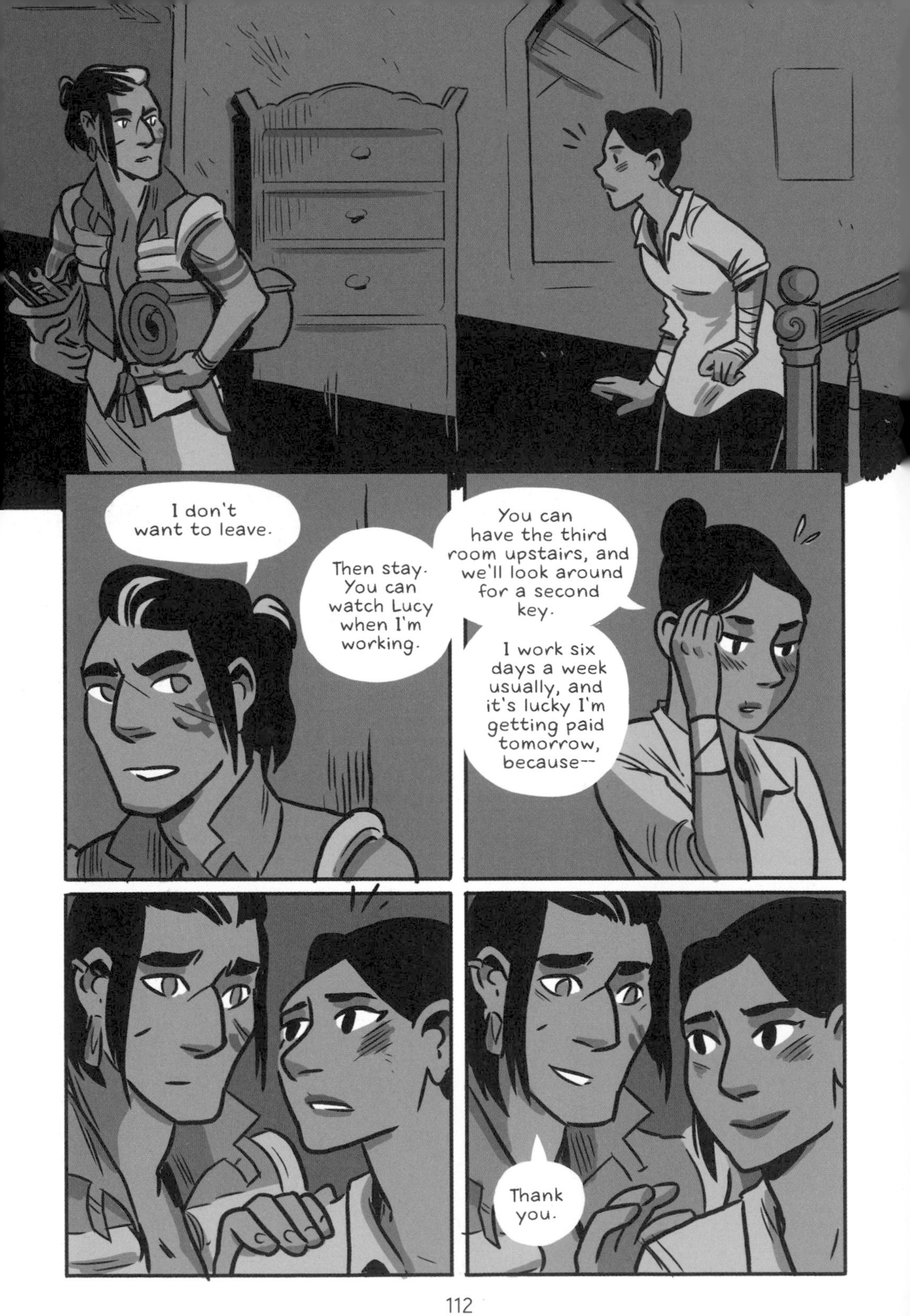
I don't want to leave.
Then stay. You can watch Lucy when I'm working.
You can have the third room upstairs, and we'll look around for a second key.
I work six days a week usually, and it's lucky I'm getting paid tomorrow, because--
Thank you.

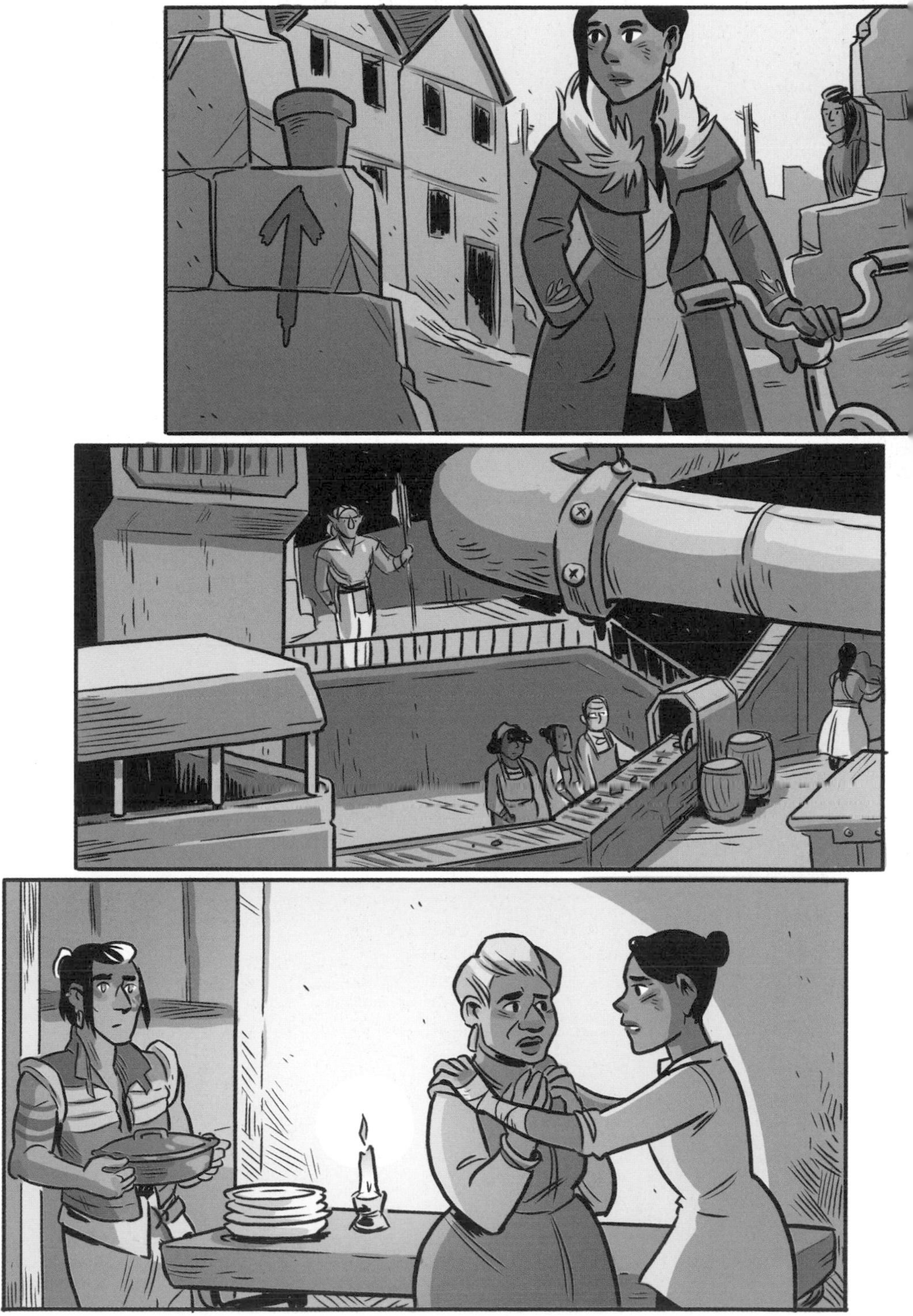

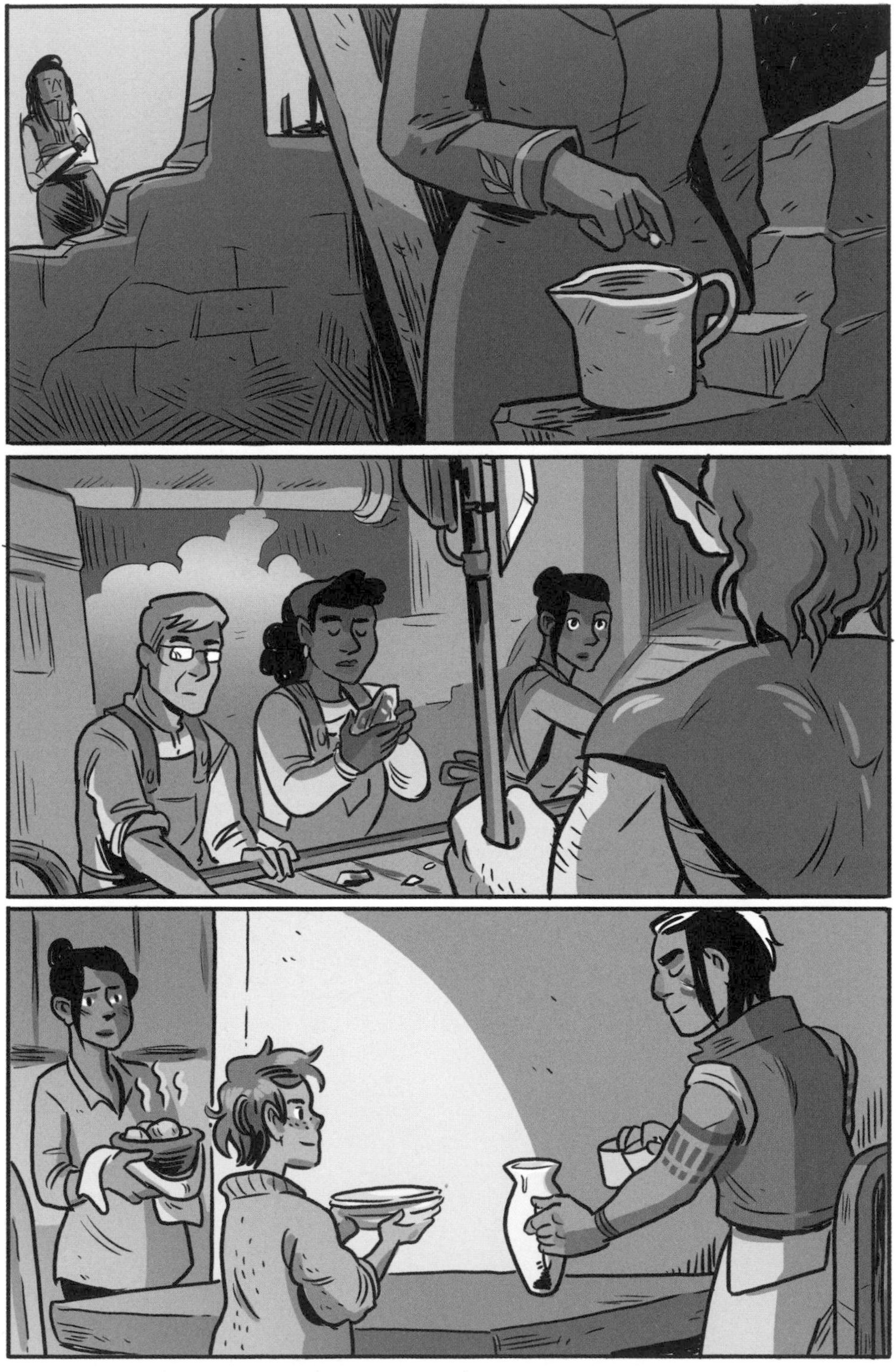

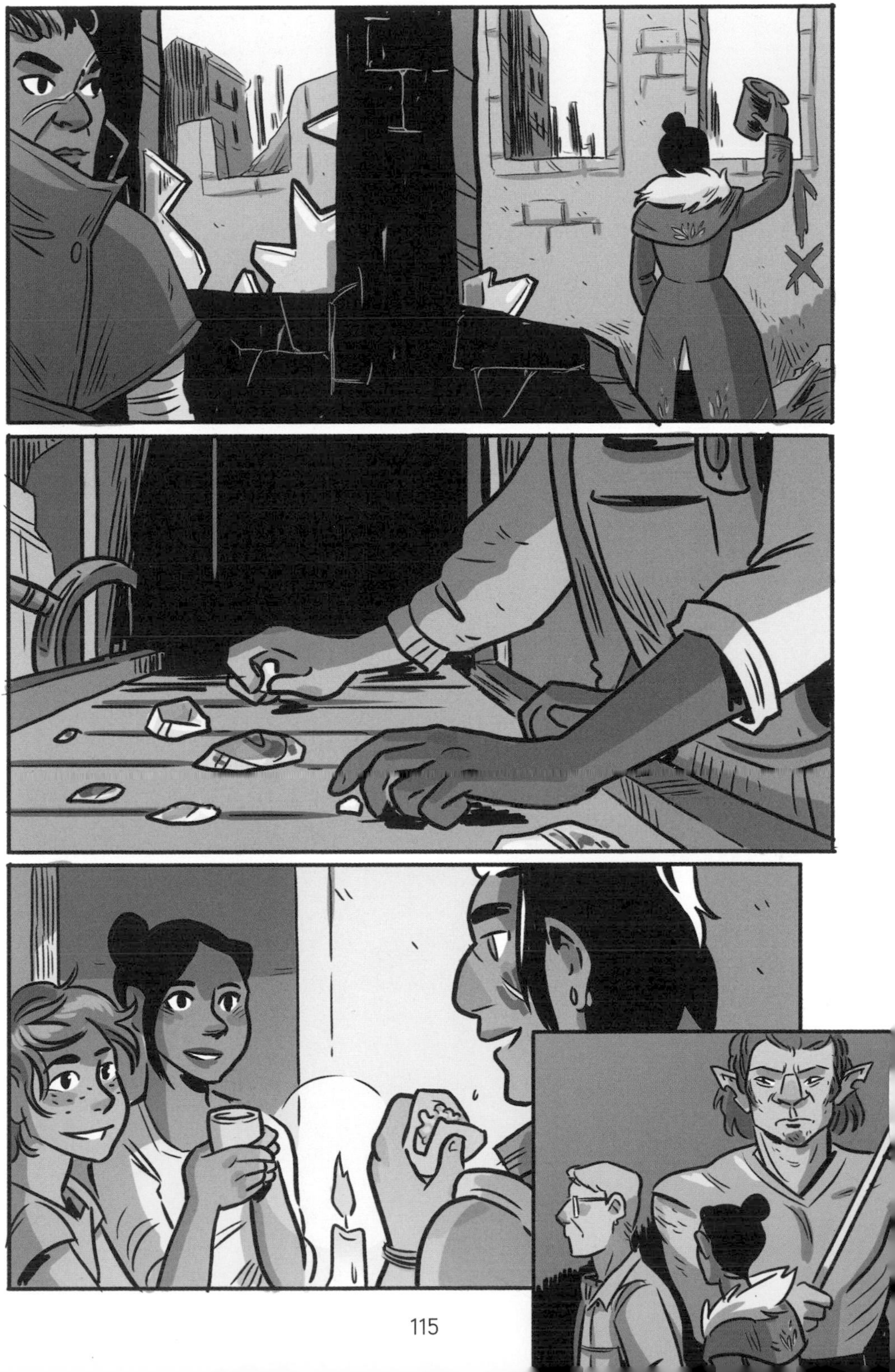

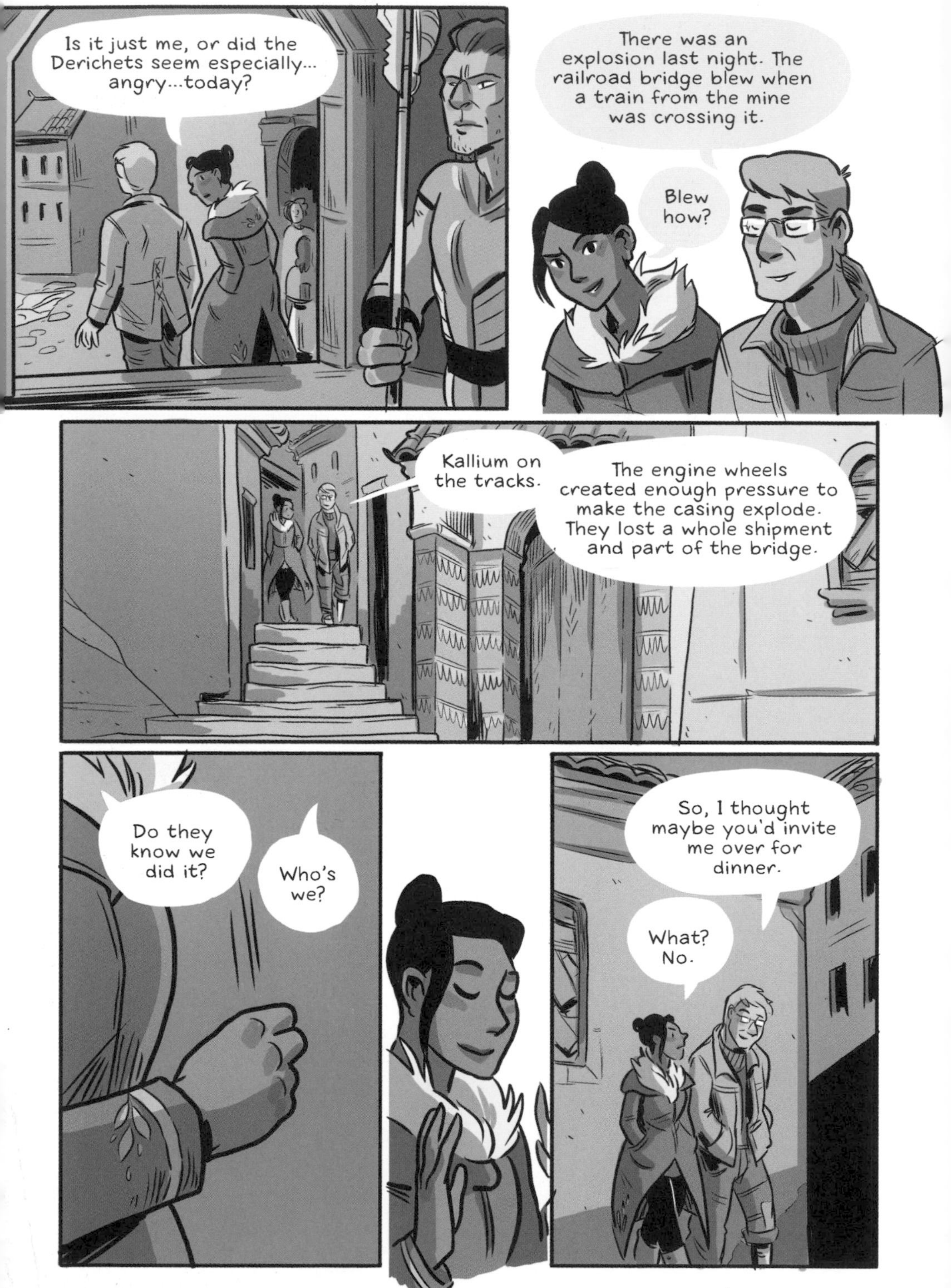
Is it just me, or did the Derichets seem especially... angry...today?
There was an explosion last night. The railroad bridge blew when a train from the mine was crossing it.
Blew how?
Kallium on the tracks.
The engine wheels created enough pressure to make the casing explode. They lost a whole shipment and part of the bridge.
Do they know we did it?
Who's we?
So, I thought maybe you'd invite me over for dinner.
What? No.

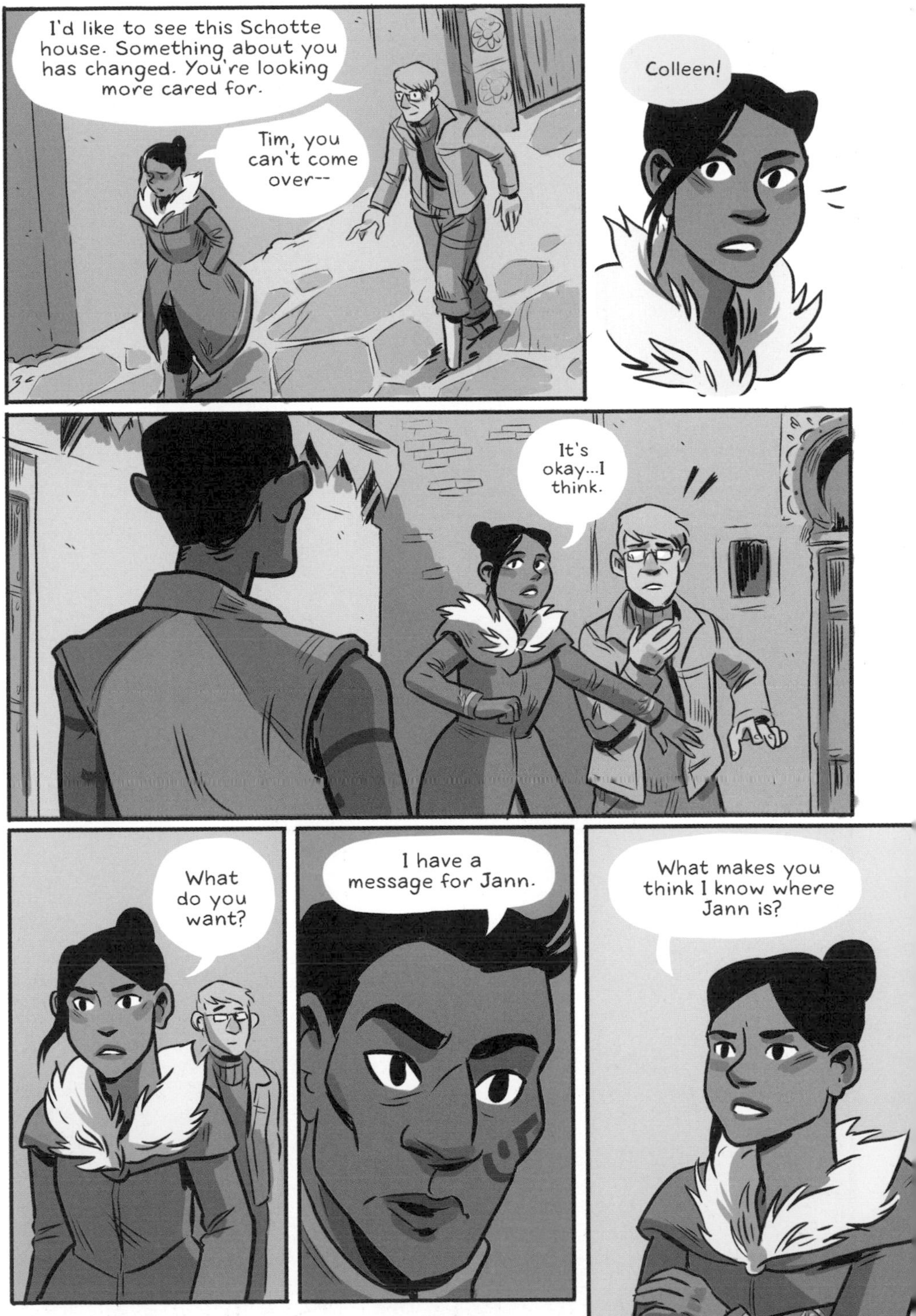
I'd like to see this Schotte house. Something about you has changed. You're looking more cared for.
Tim, you can't come over--
Colleen!
It's okay...I think.
What do you want?
I have a message for Jann.
What makes you think I know where Jann is?

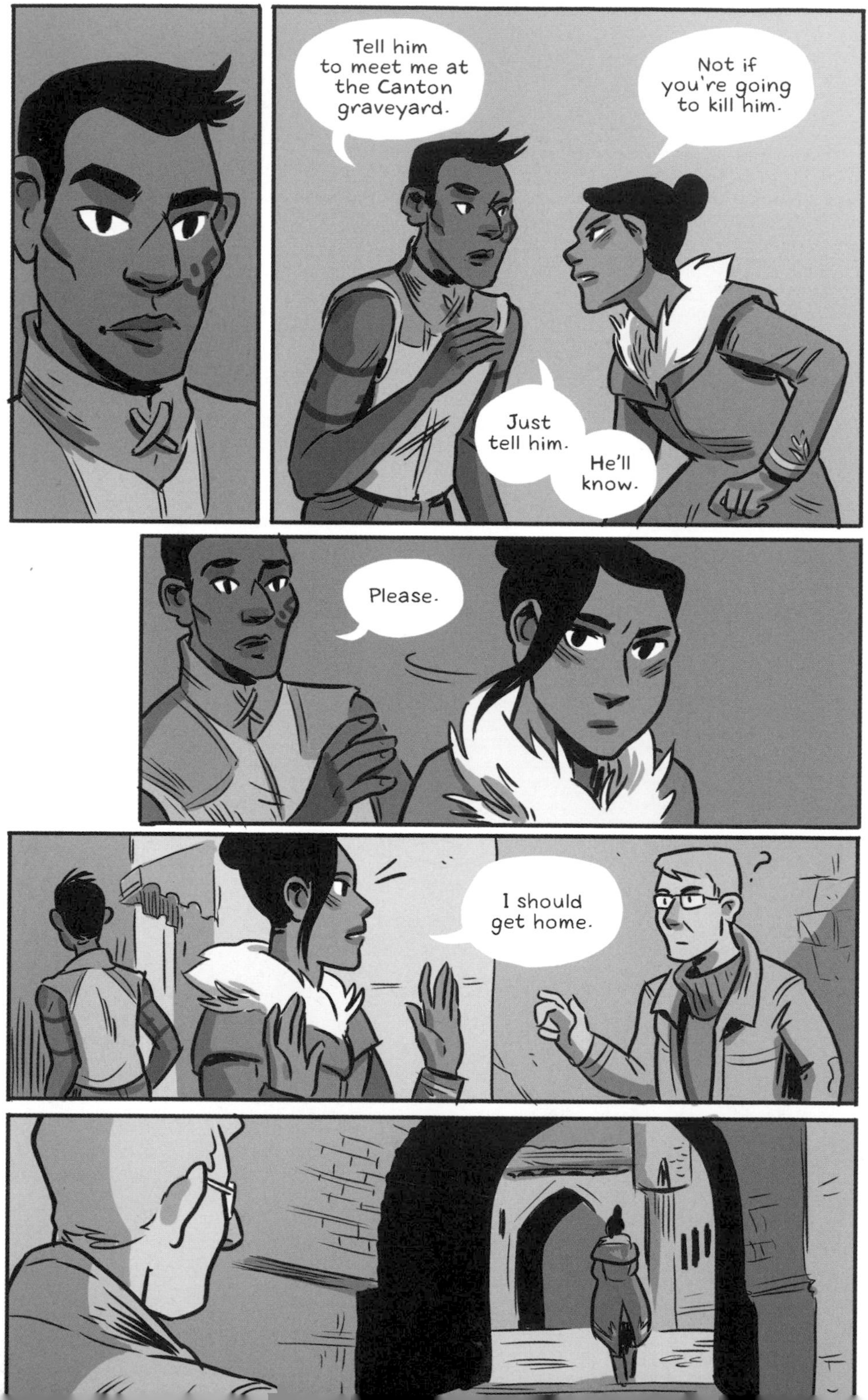
Tell him to meet me at the Canton graveyard.
Not if you're going to kill him.
Just tell him.
He'll know.
Please.
I should get home.

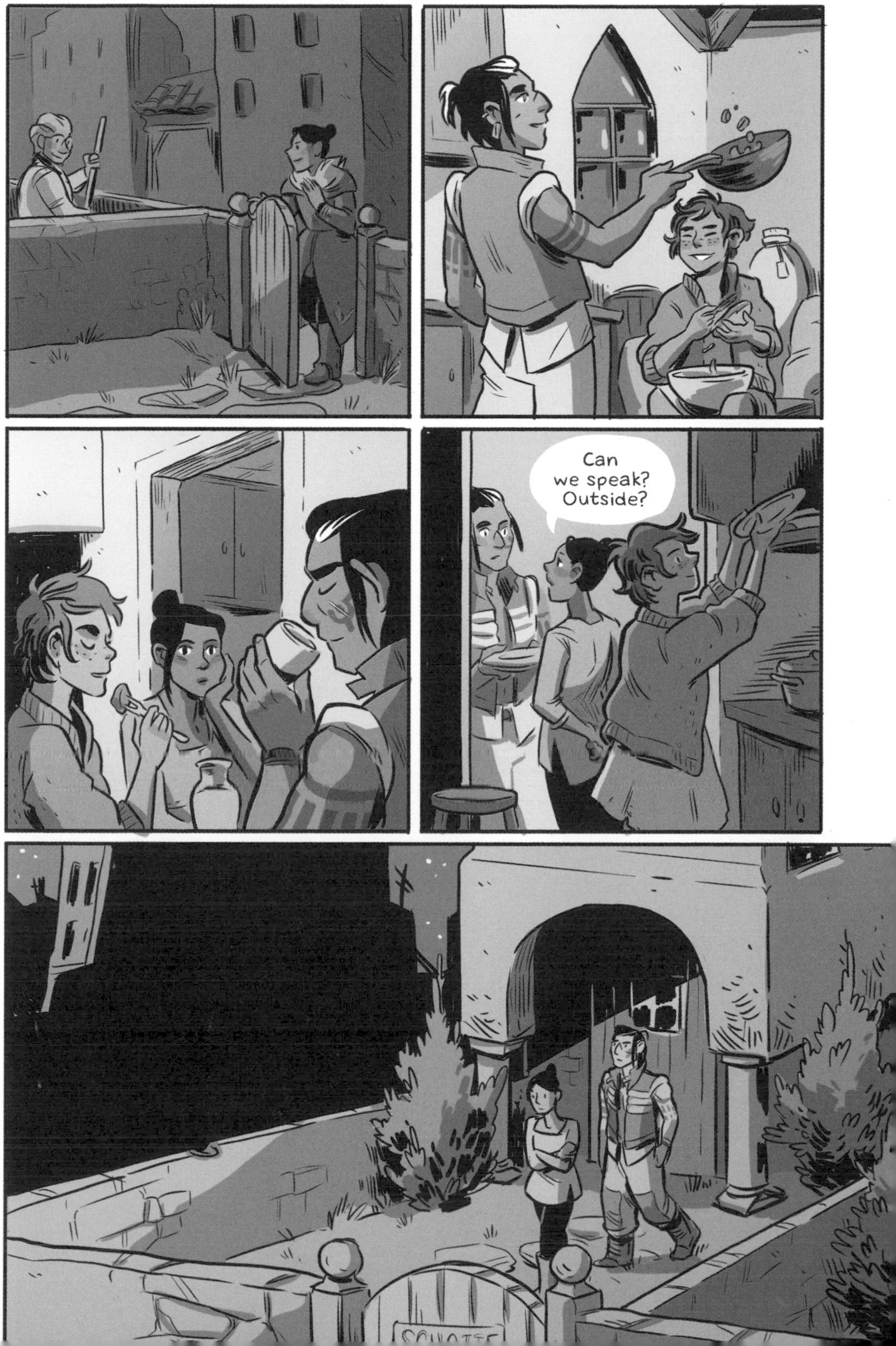
Can we speak? Outside?

Can you see it? The Shattered Warrior constellation. It's only visible for one month a year.
No. I can never see anything in the stars. Why do they call it that?
Old folk tale. My father hated it, but it was my mother's favorite story.
It's about a princess who was in love with a common soldier. The king had promised his daughter's hand in marriage to any man who could win a duel against his mortal enemy.
The warrior won the fight, but the evil lord's soldiers murdered him and hacked his body into pieces.

It was the brave warrior come back to request her hand in marriage.
The princess grieved and grieved, refusing all other suitors, and the king feared she would die. Then one day, a handsome young man came to the palace.
How could he still be alive?
That's what the princess asked him on their wedding night. And he said, "Your love was so great that it mended my body and restored my broken heart."

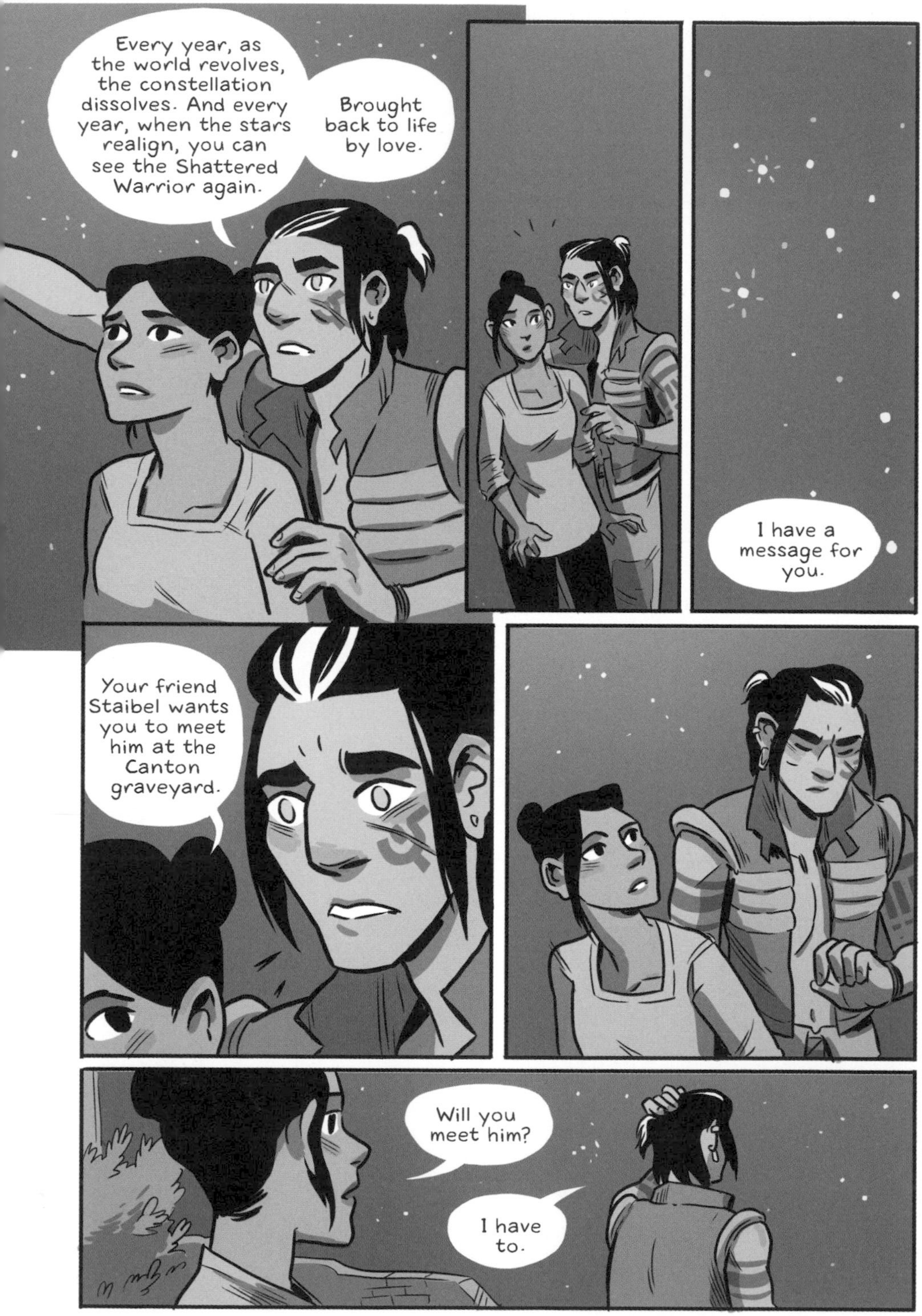
Every year, as the world revolves, the constellation dissolves. And every year, when the stars realign, you can see the Shattered Warrior again.
Brought back to life by love.
I have a message for you.
Your friend Staibel wants you to meet him at the Canton graveyard.
Will you meet him?
I have to.

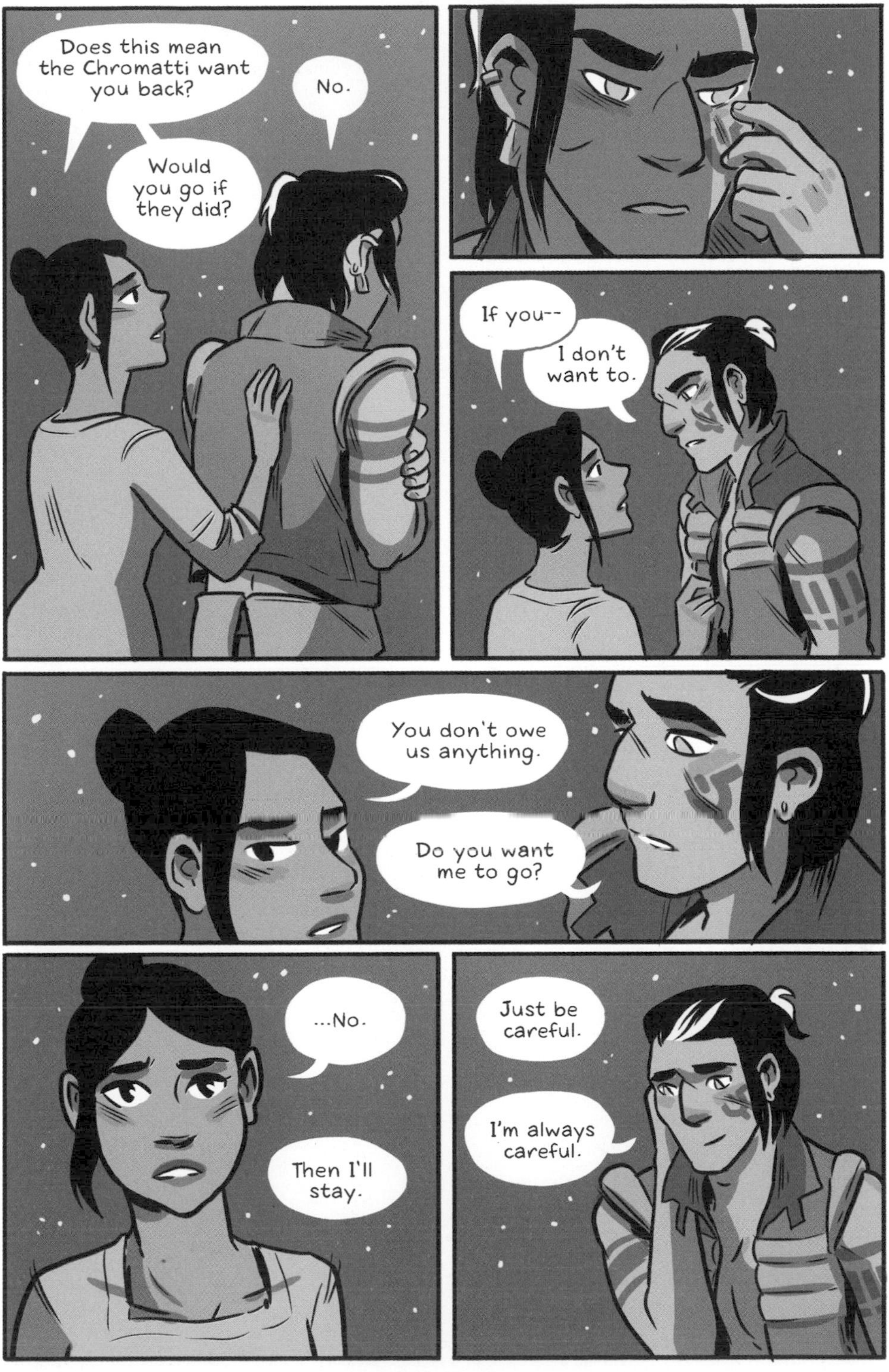
Does this mean the Chromatti want you back?
No.
Would you go if they did?
If you--
I don't want to.
You don't owe us anything.
Do you want me to go?
...No.
Then I'll stay.
Just be careful.
I'm always careful.

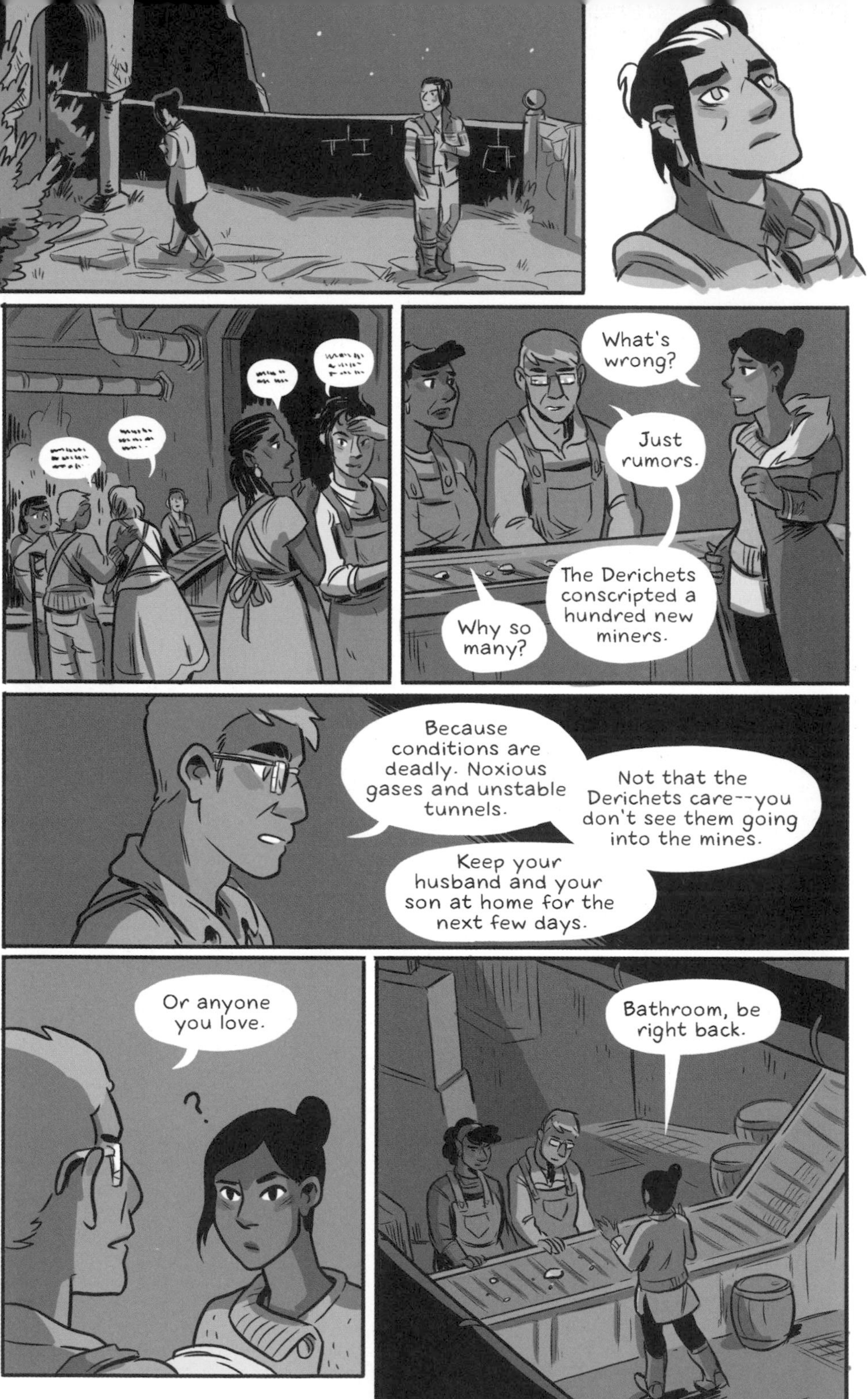
What's wrong?
Just rumors.
The Derichets conscripted a hundred new miners.
Why so many?
Because conditions are deadly. Noxious gases and unstable tunnels.
Not that the Derichets care--you don't see them going into the mines.
Keep your husband and your son at home for the next few days.
Or anyone you love.
?
Bathroom, be right back.

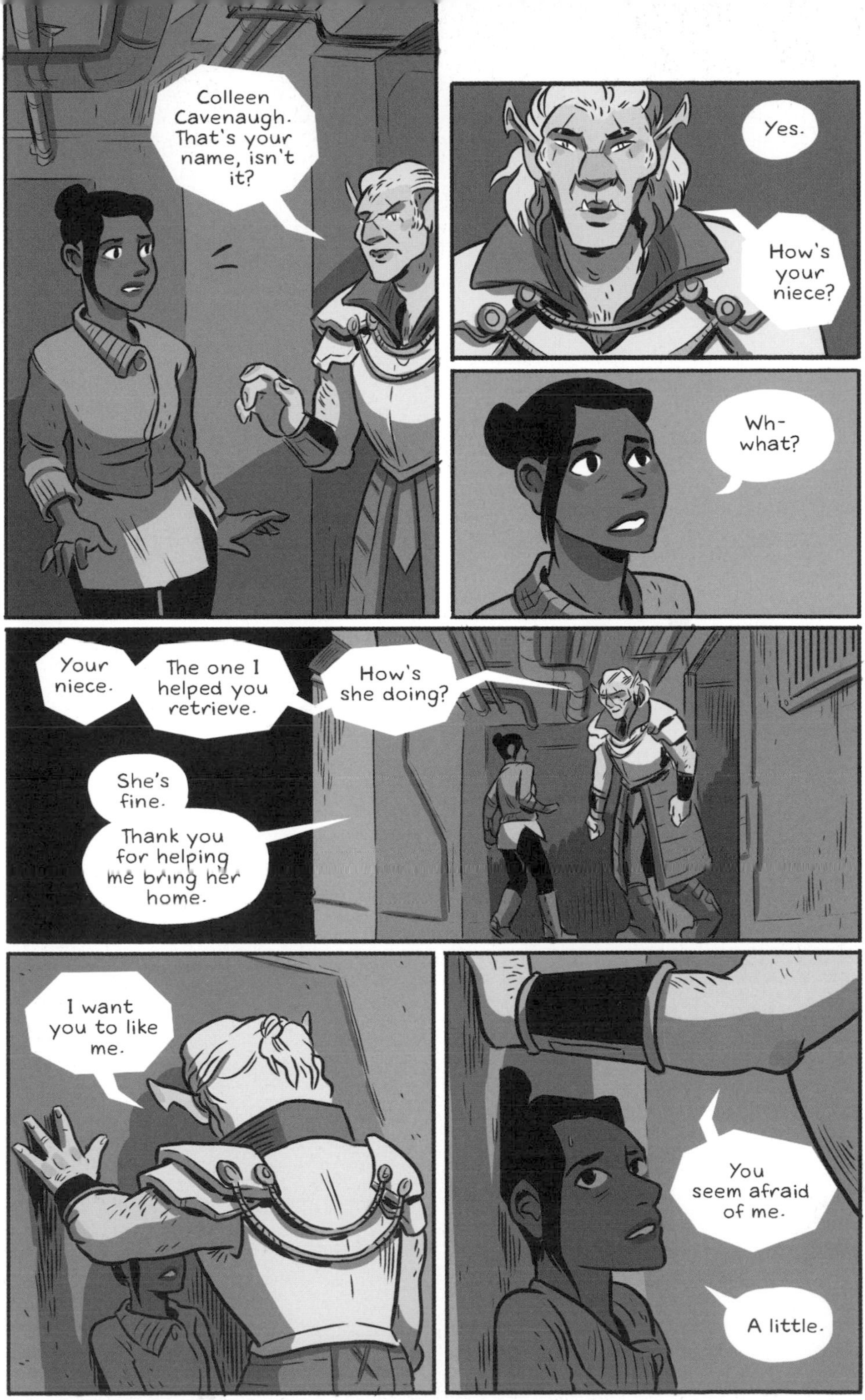
Colleen Cavenaugh. That's your name, isn't it?
Yes.
How's your niece?
Wh- what?
Your niece.
The one I helped you retrieve.
How's she doing?
She's fine.
Thank you for helping me bring her home.
I want you to like me.
You seem afraid of me.
A little.

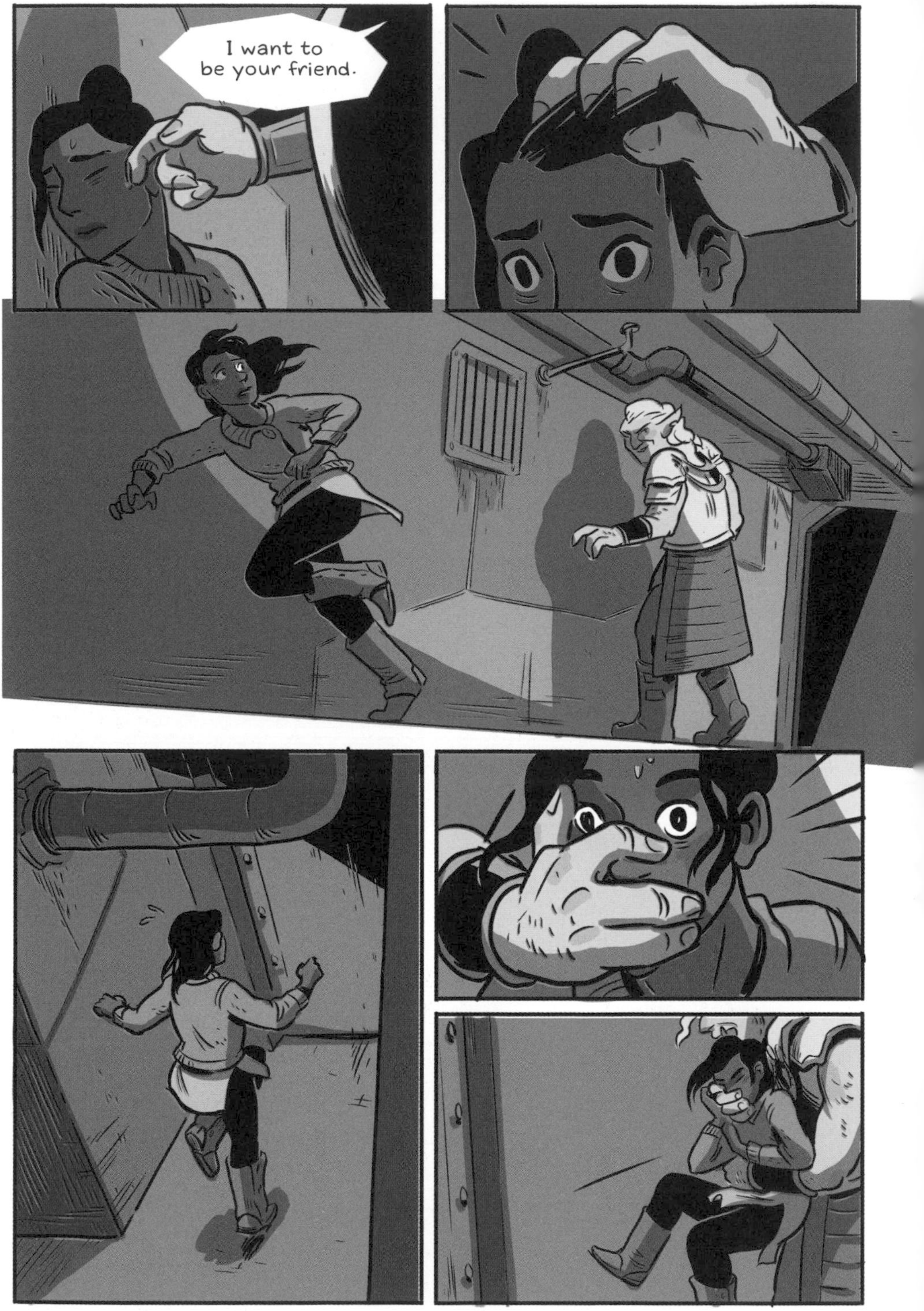
I want to be your friend.

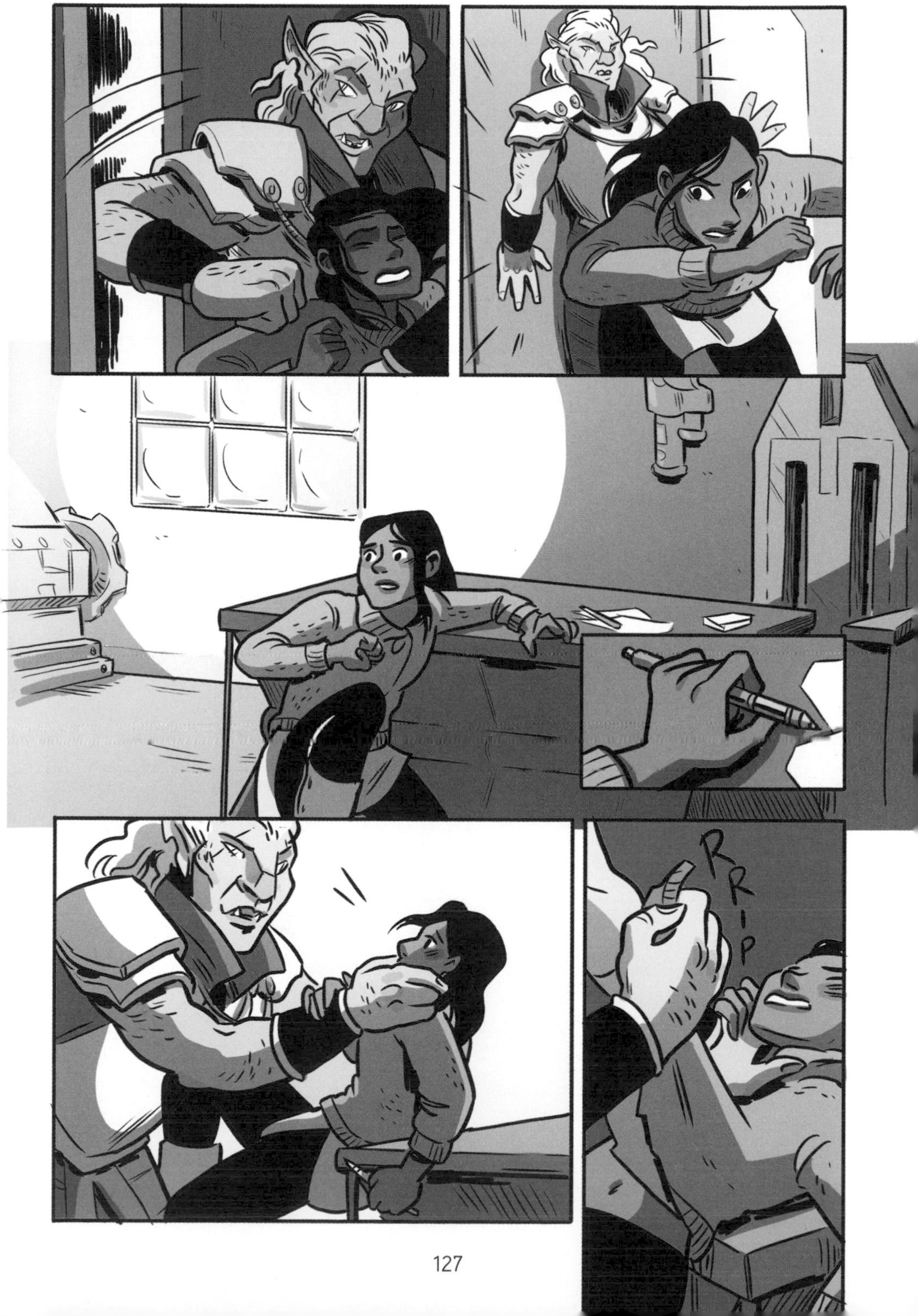
RRIP

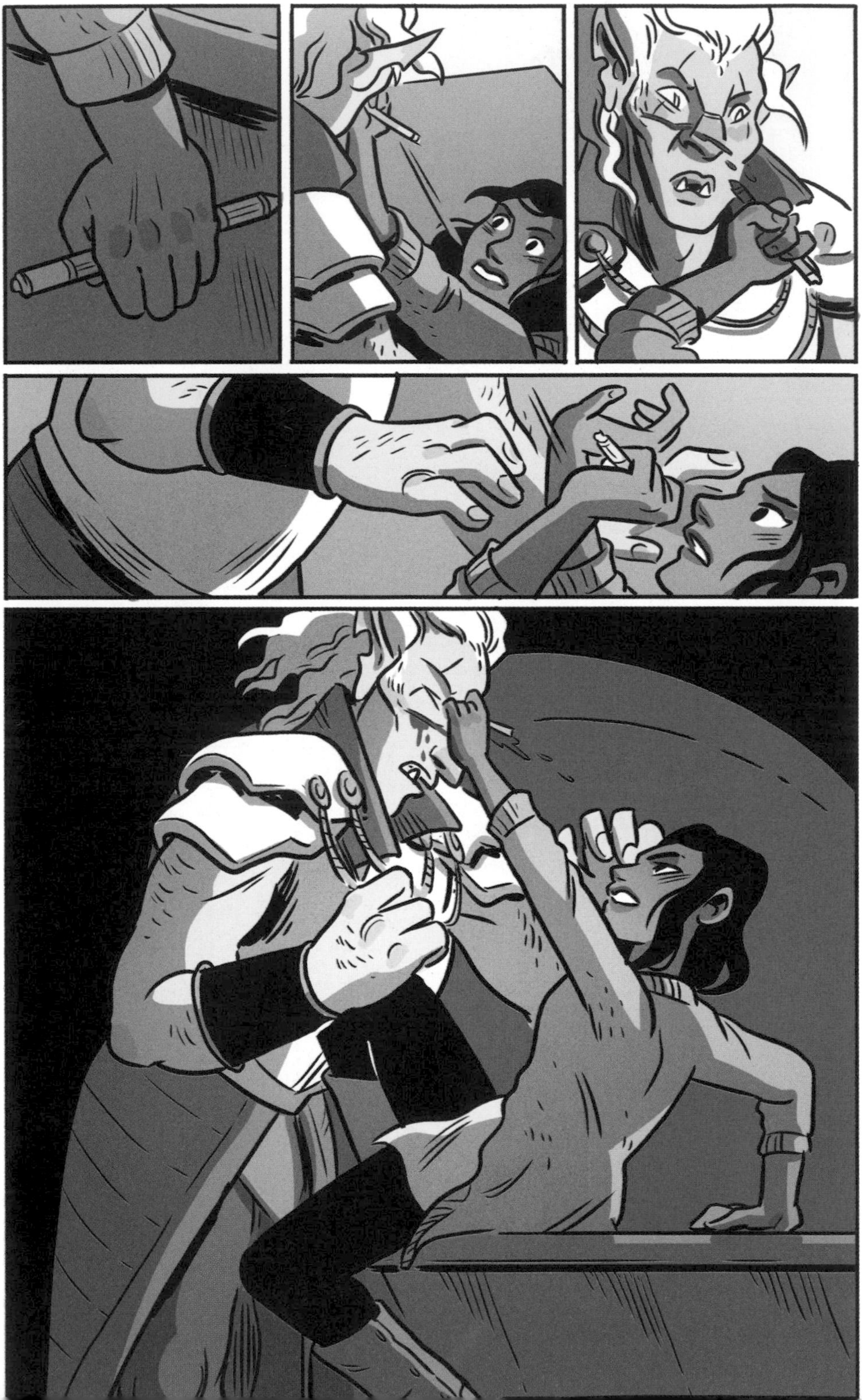

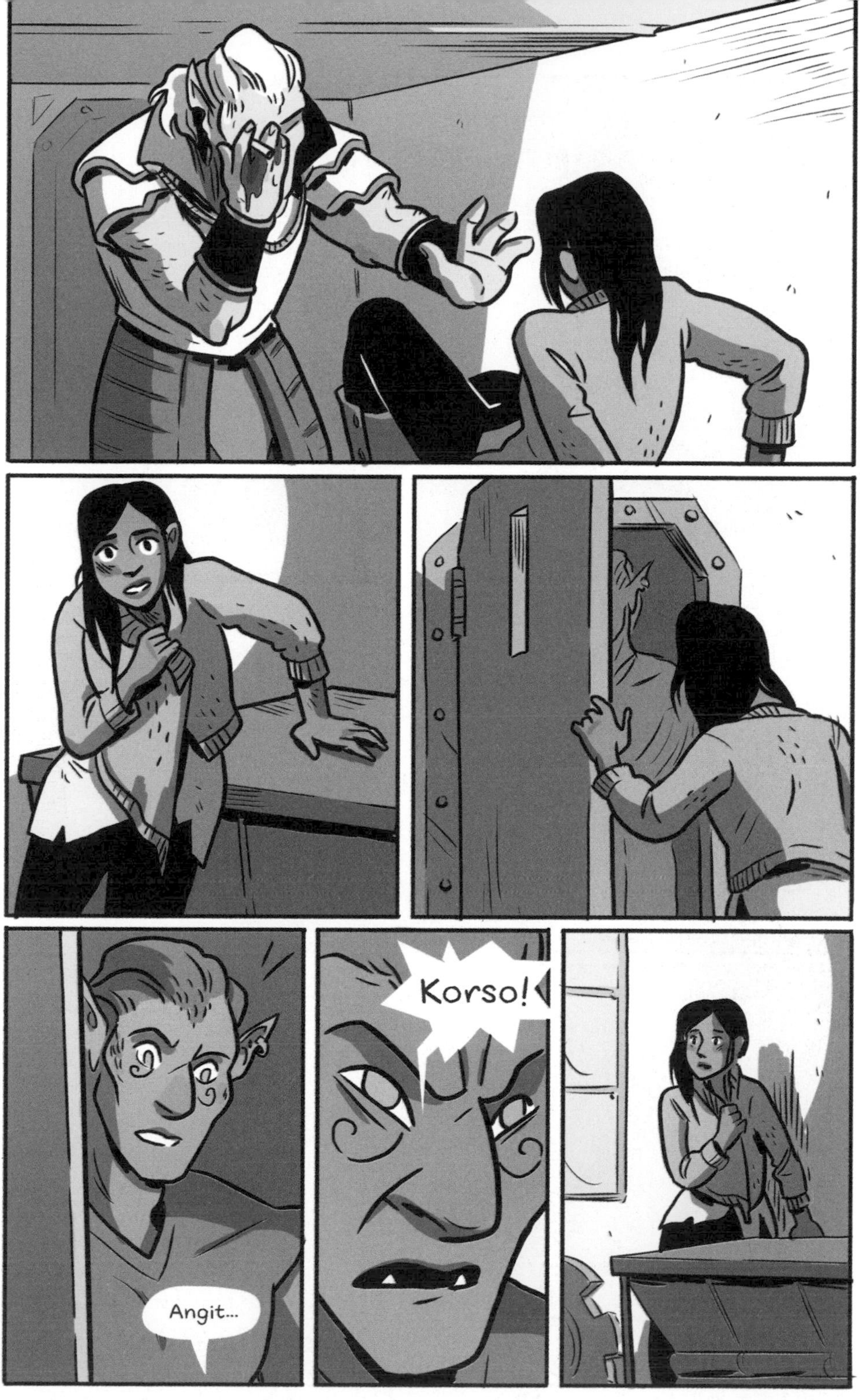
Angit...
Korso!

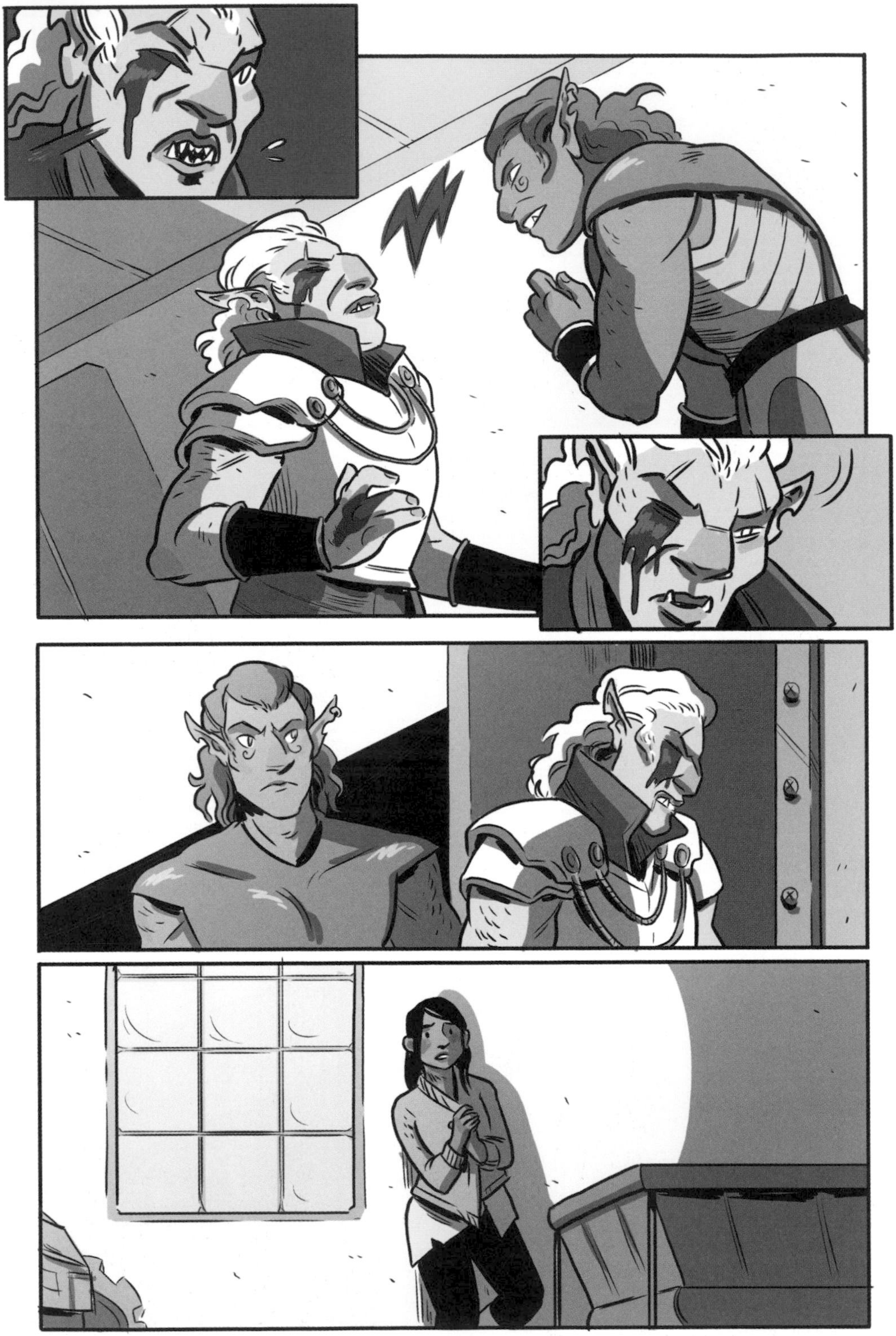

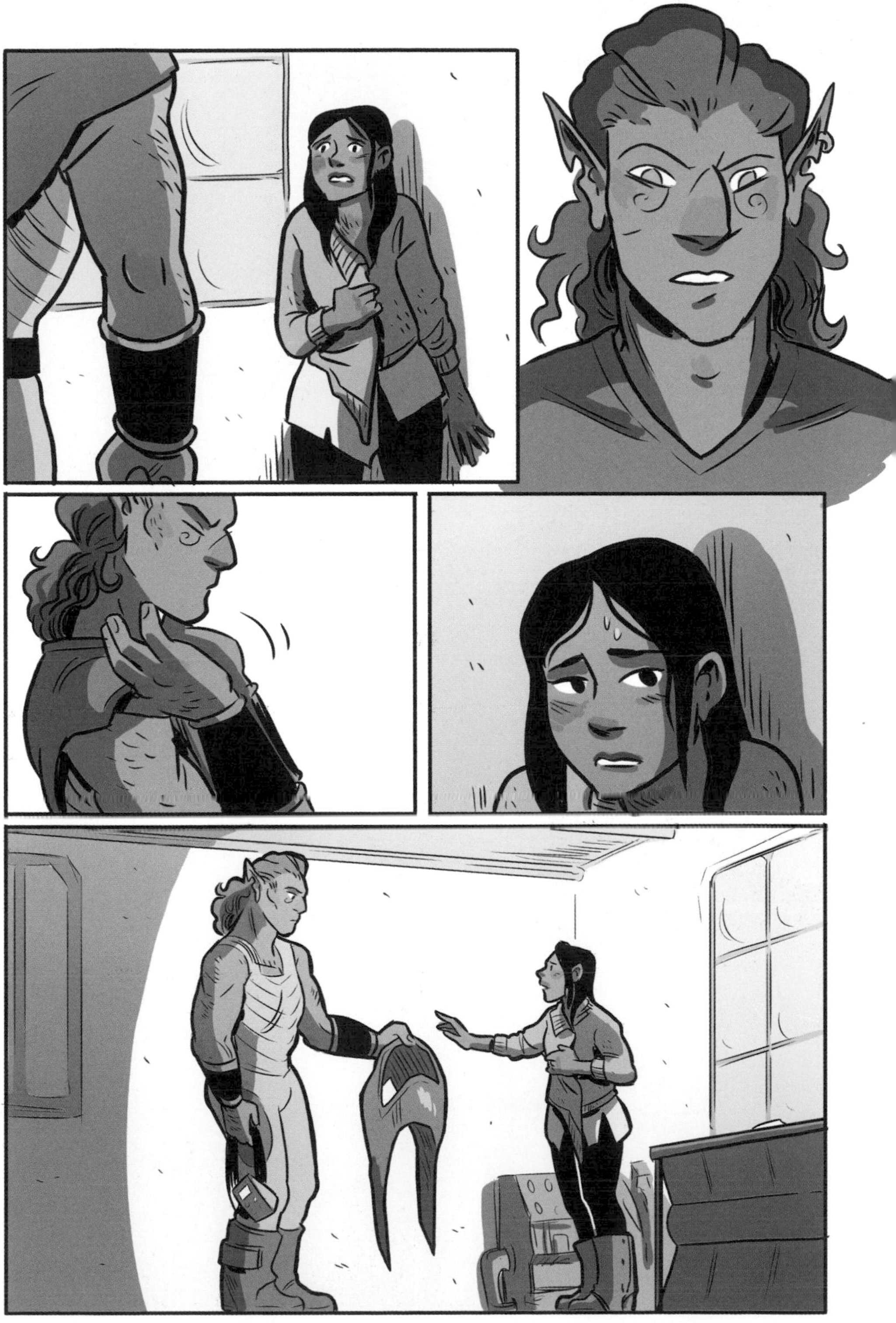

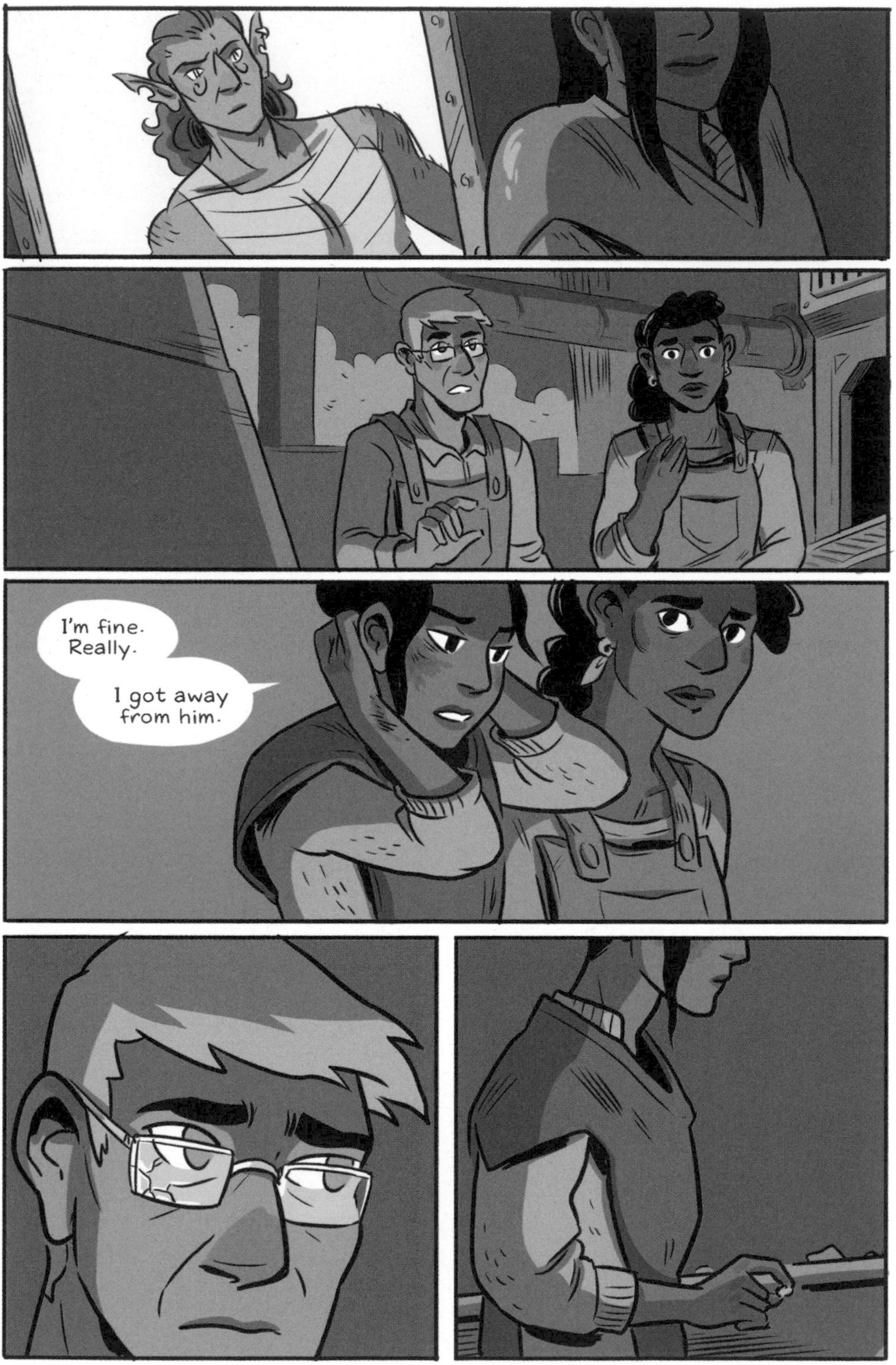
I'm fine. Really.
I got away from him.

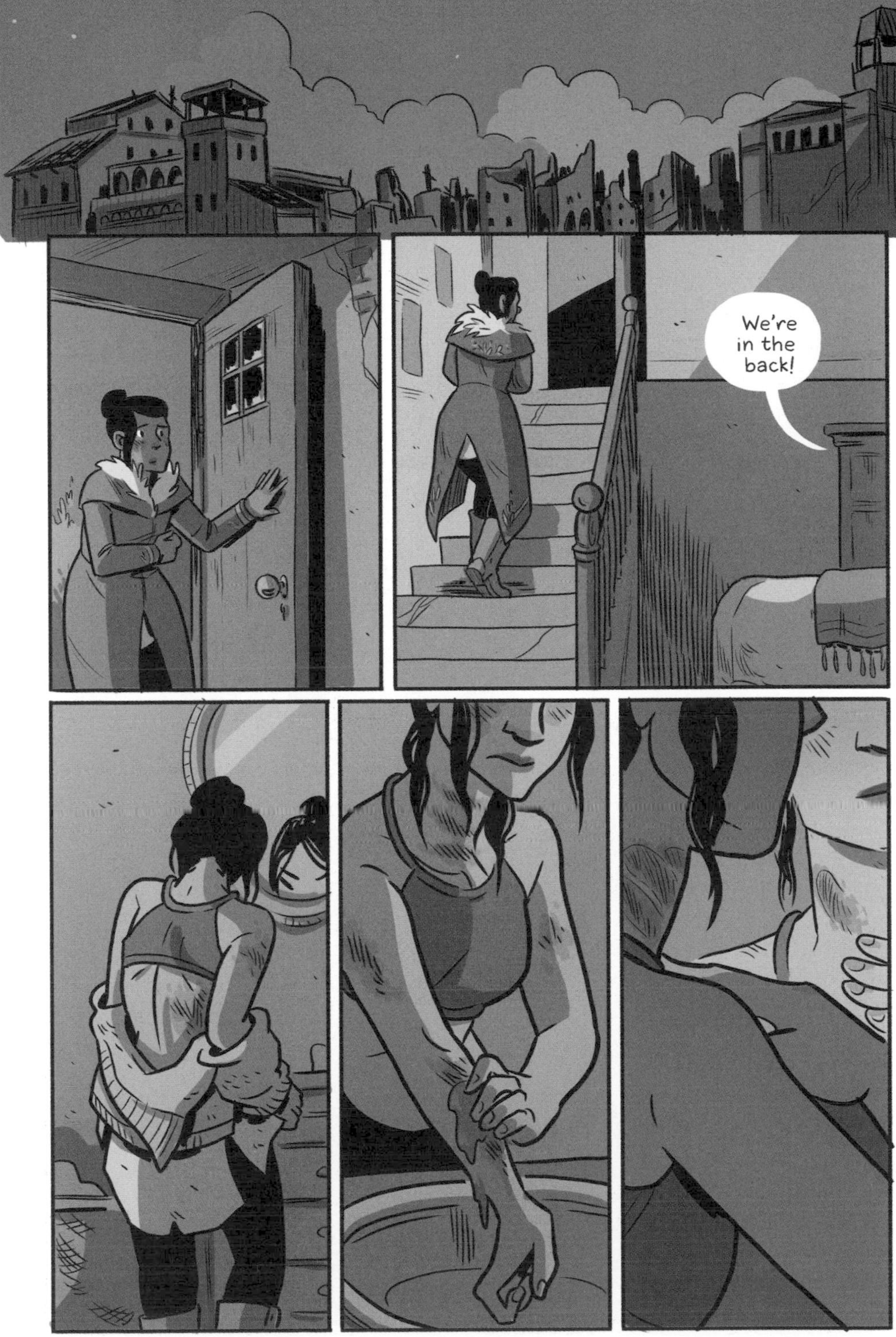
We're in the back!

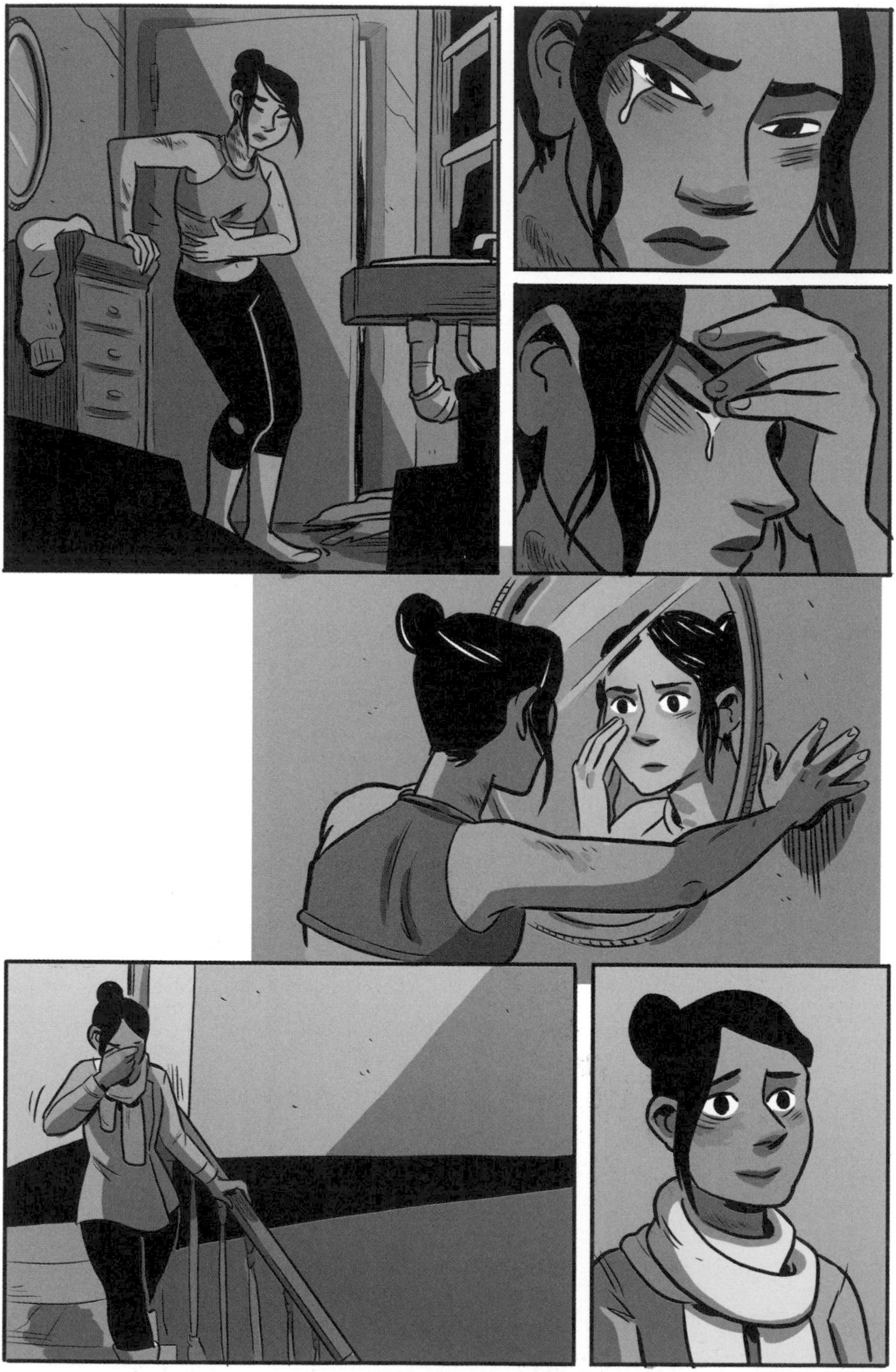

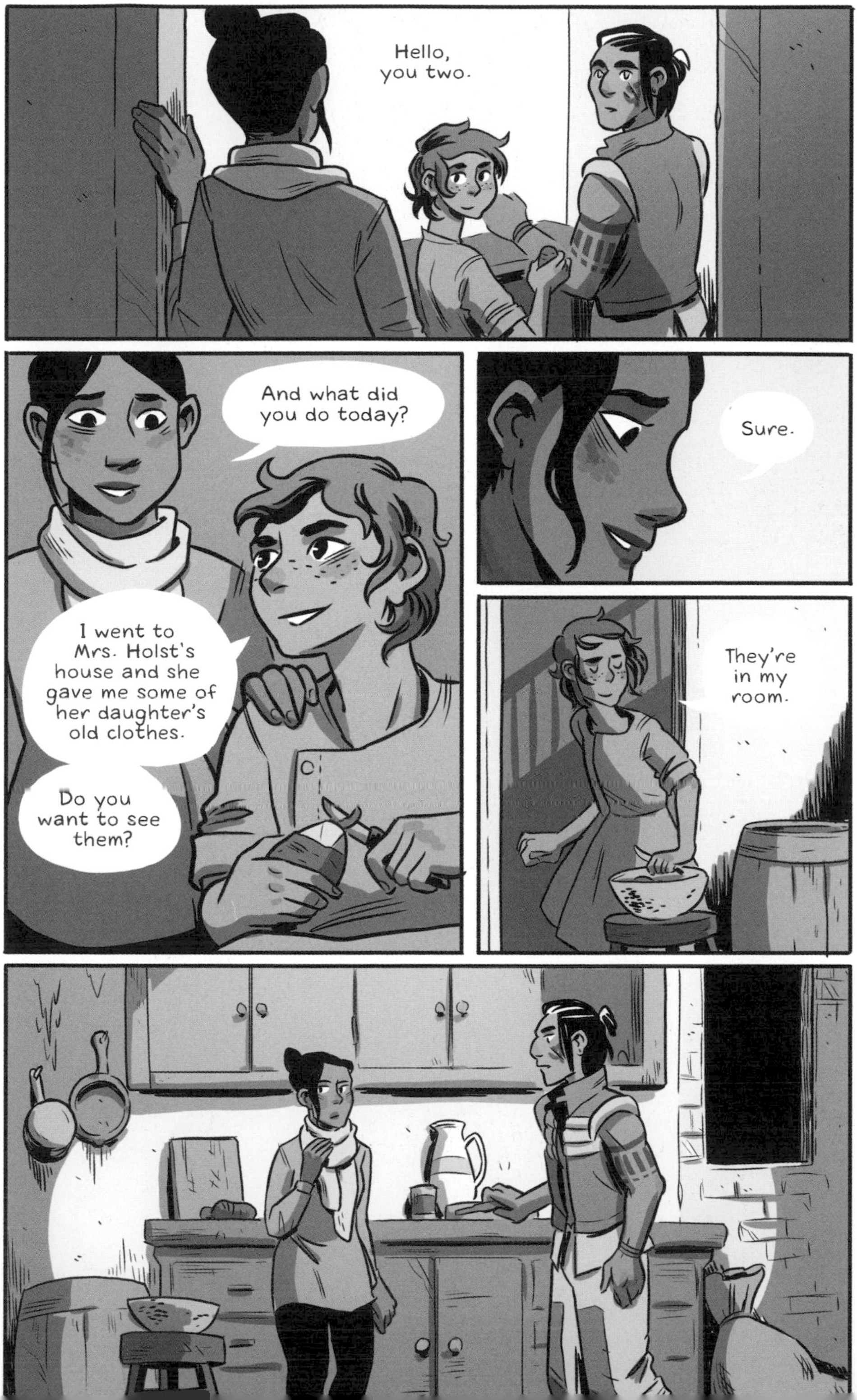

Hello, you two.
And what did you do today?
I went to Mrs. Holst's house and she gave me some of her daughter's old clothes.
Do you want to see them?
Sure.
They're in my room.

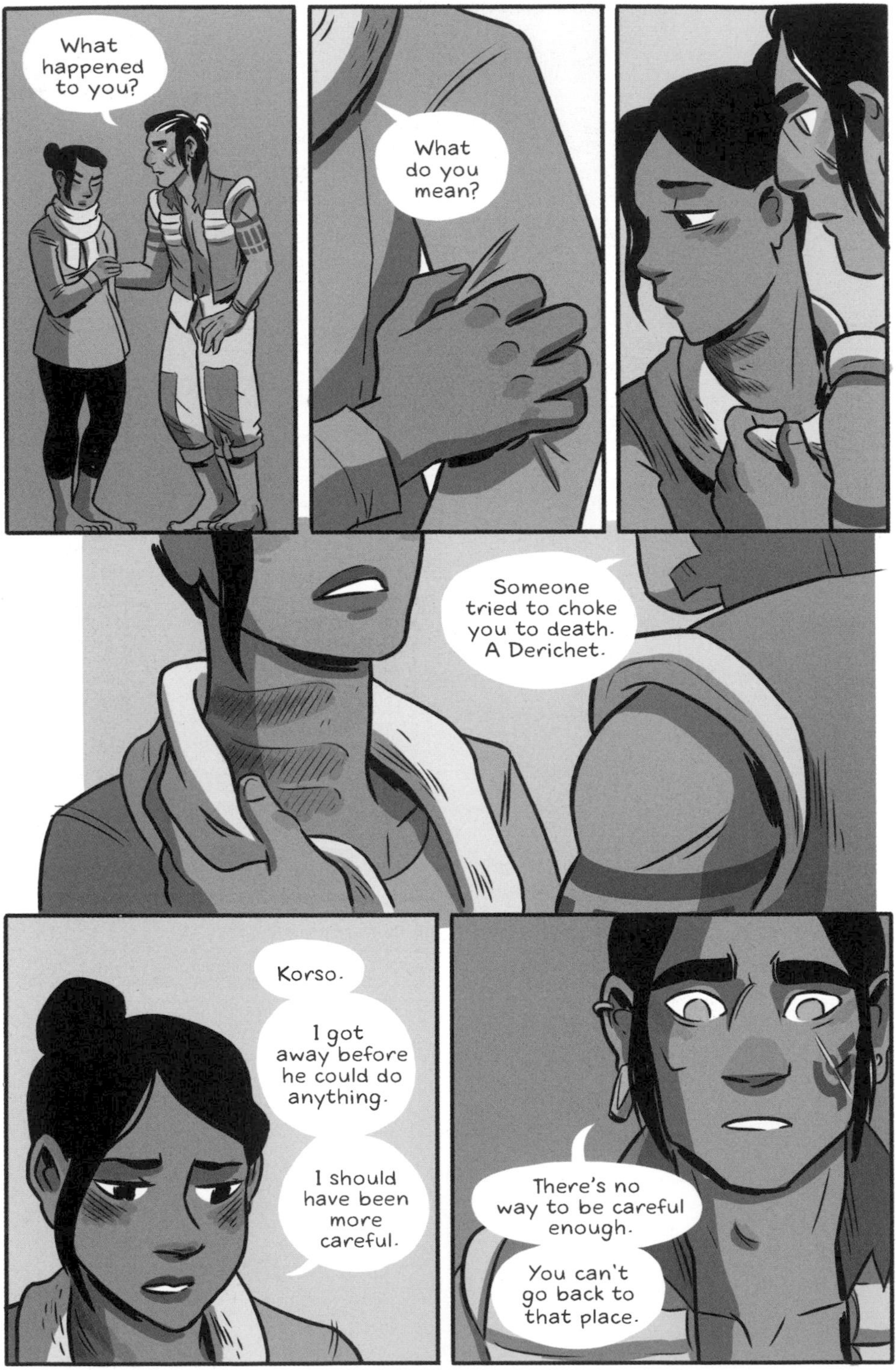
What happened to you?
What do you mean?
Someone tried to choke you to death. A Derichet.
Korso.
I got away before he could do anything.
I should have been more careful.
There's no way to be careful enough.
You can't go back to that place.

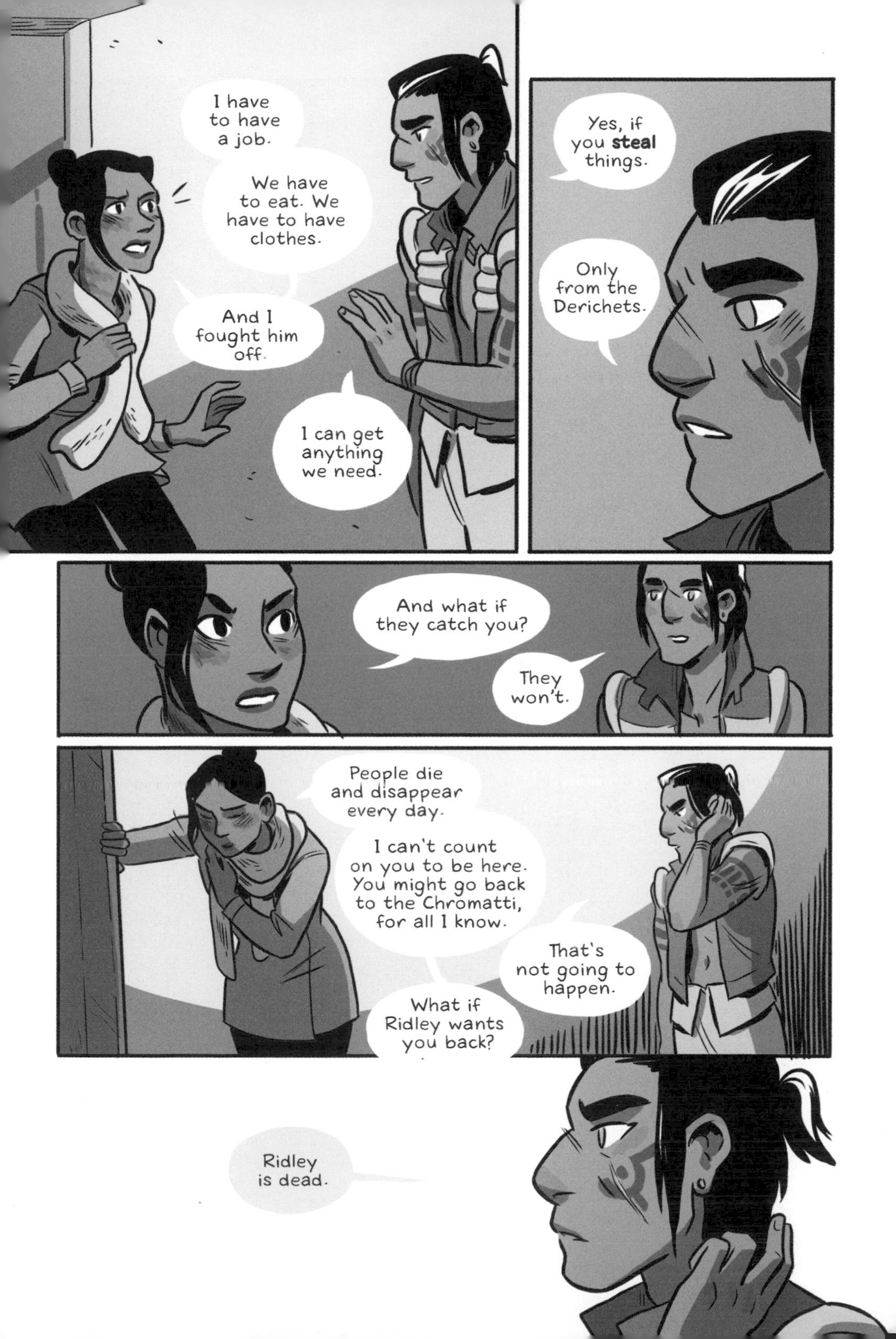
I have to have a job.
We have to eat. We have to have clothes.
And I fought him off.
I can get anything we need.
Yes, if you **steal** things.
Only from the Derichets.
And what if they catch you?
They won't.
People die and disappear every day.
I can't count on you to be here. You might go back to the Chromatti, for all I know.
That's not going to happen.
What if Ridley wants you back?
Ridley is dead.

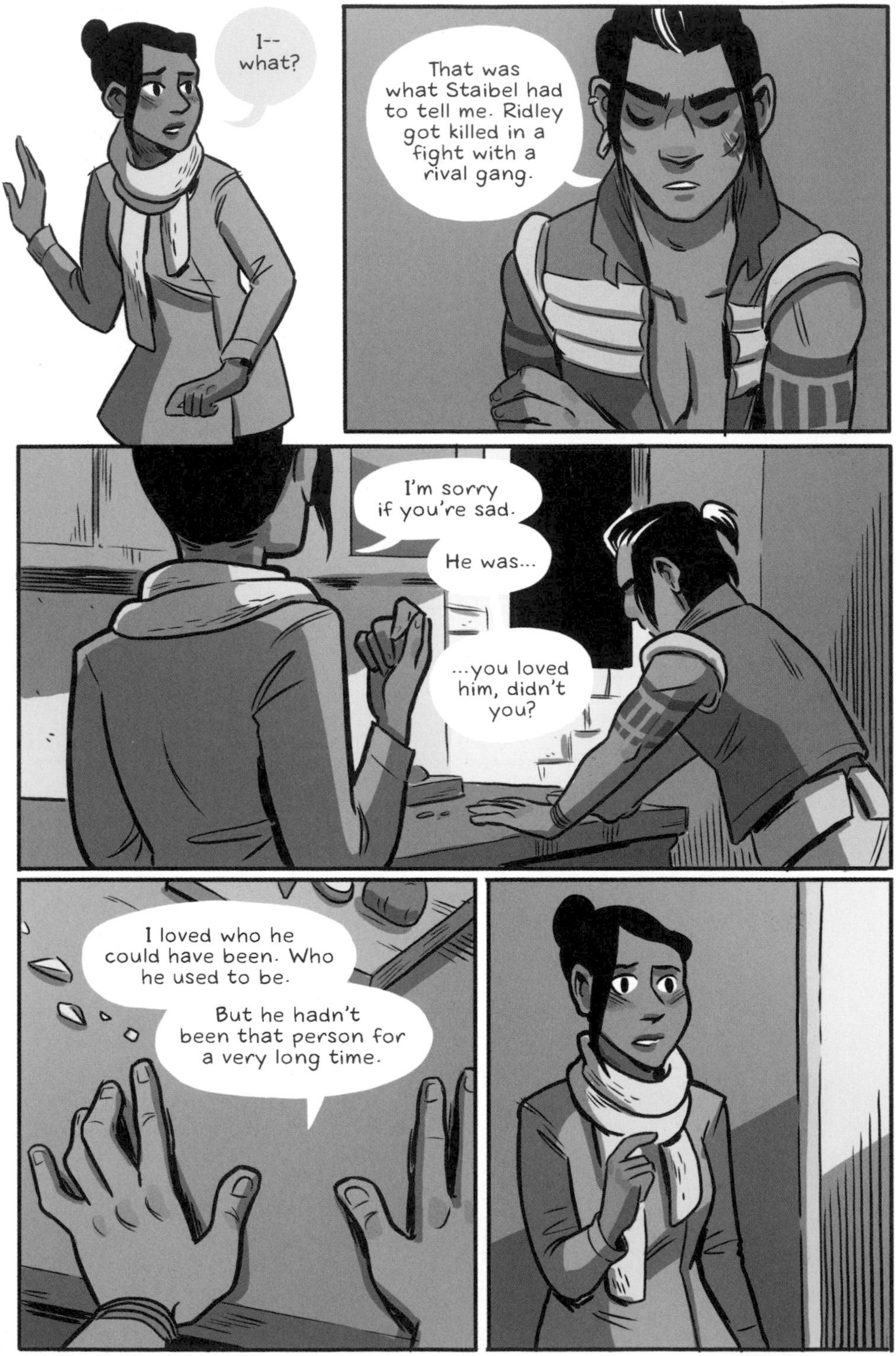

I-- what?
That was what Staibel had to tell me. Ridley got killed in a fight with a rival gang.
I'm sorry if you're sad.
He was...
...you loved him, didn't you?
I loved who he could have been. Who he used to be.
But he hadn't been that person for a very long time.

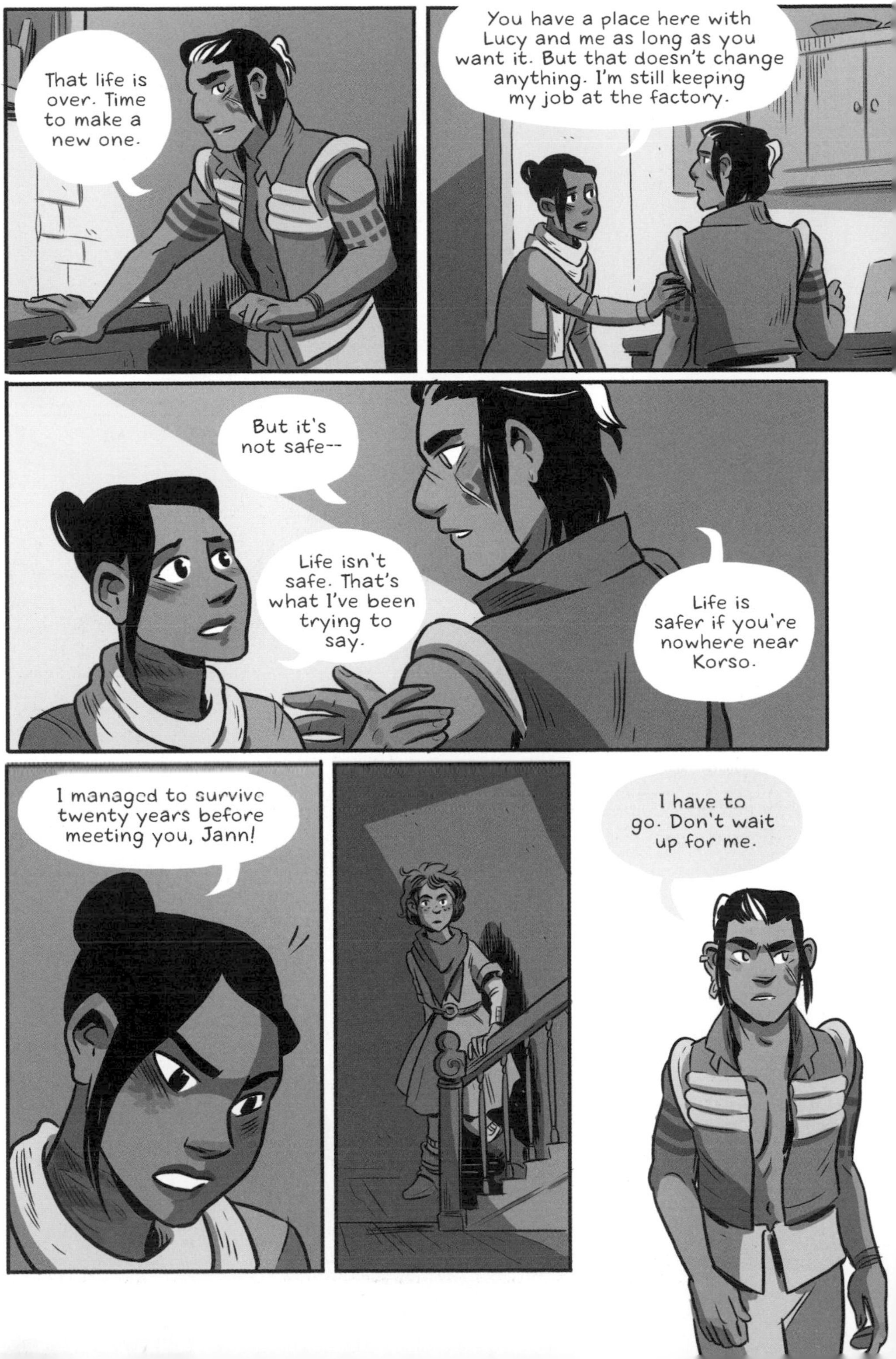
That life is over. Time to make a new one.
You have a place here with Lucy and me as long as you want it. But that doesn't change anything. I'm still keeping my job at the factory.
But it's not safe--
Life isn't safe. That's what I've been trying to say.
Life is safer if you're nowhere near Korso.
I managed to survive twenty years before meeting you, Jann!
I have to go. Don't wait up for me.

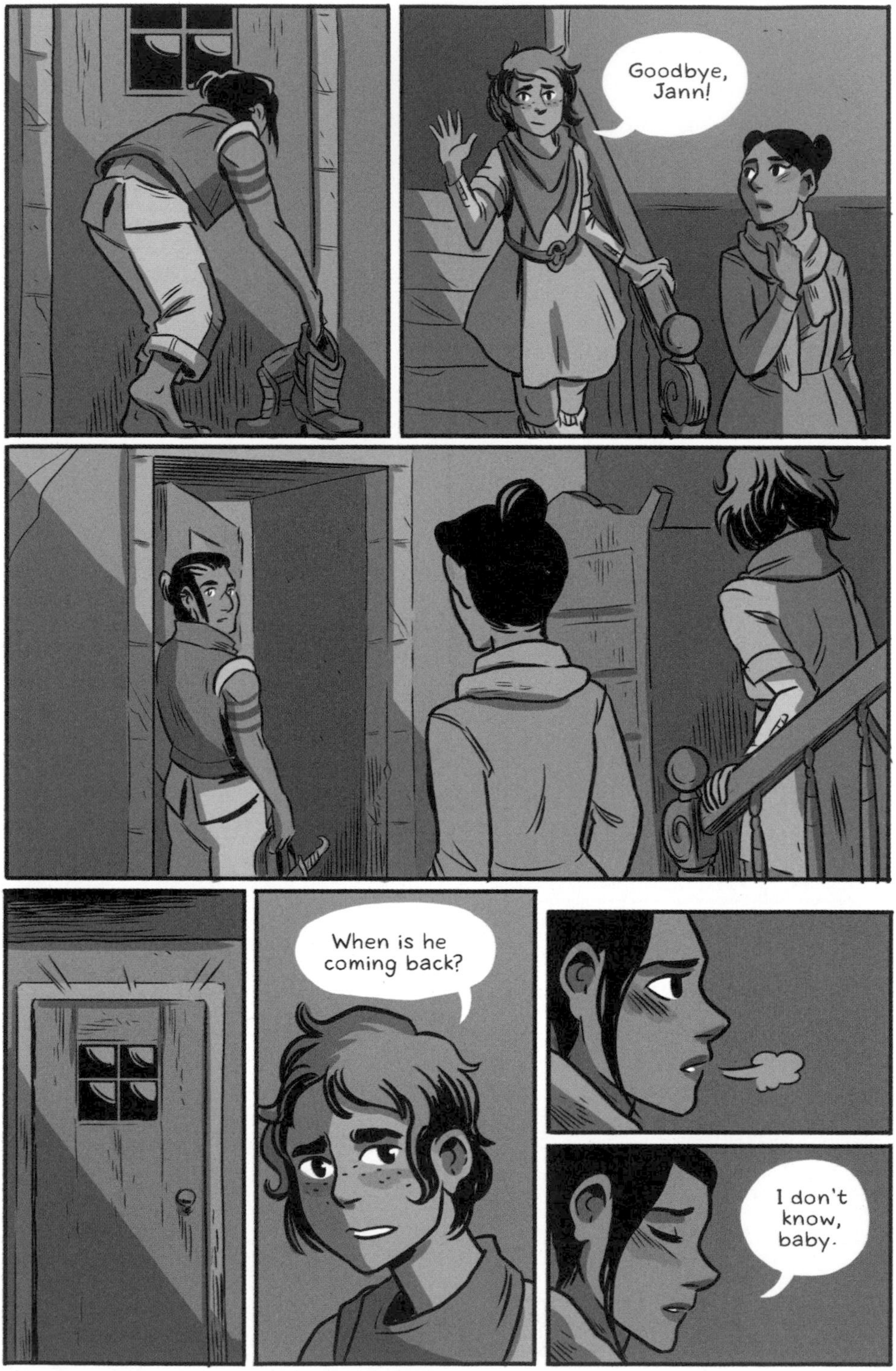
Goodbye, Jann!
When is he coming back?
I don't know, baby.

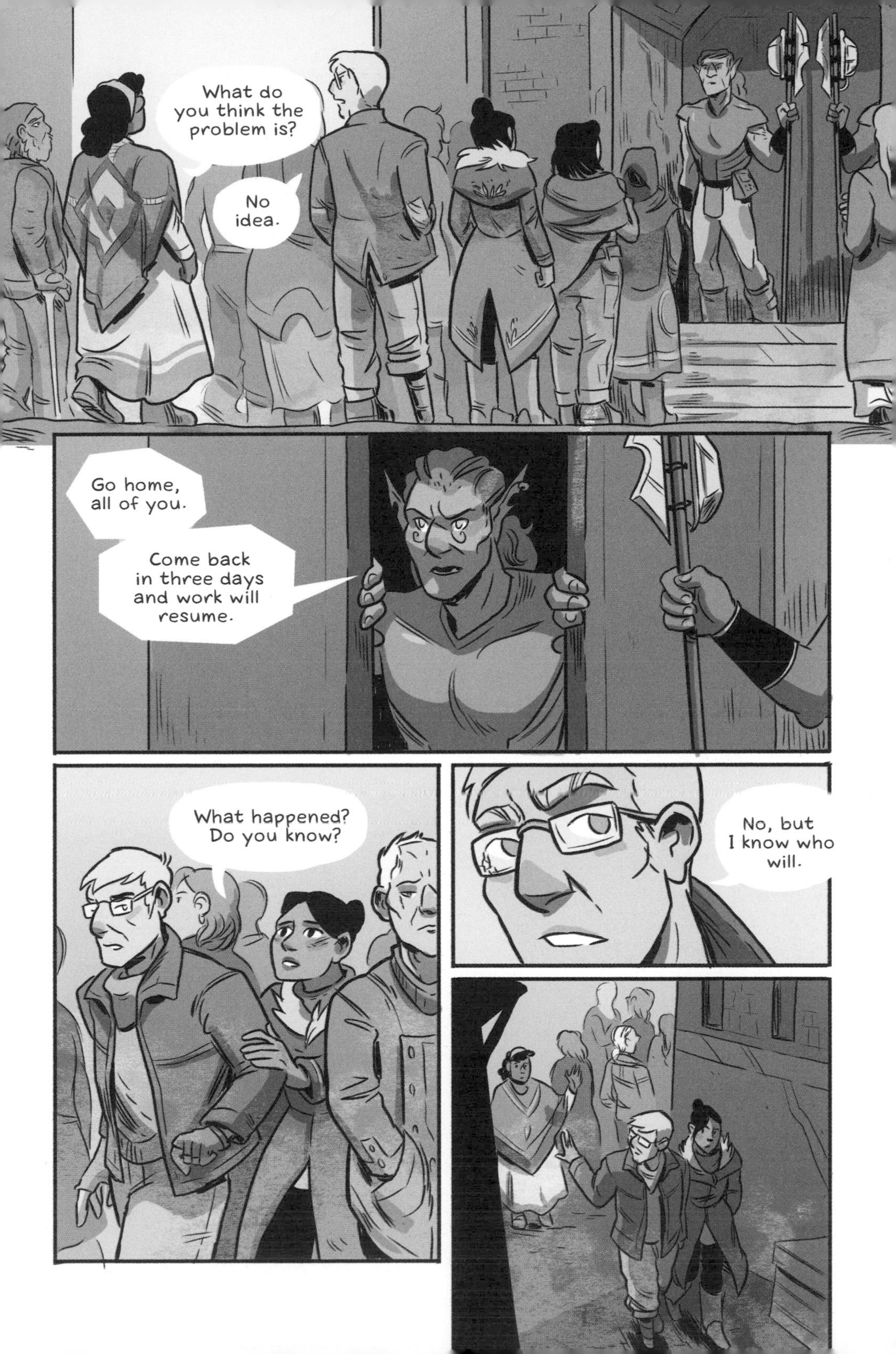
What do you think the problem is?
No idea.
Go home, all of you.
Come back in three days and work will resume.
What happened? Do you know?
No, but I know who will.

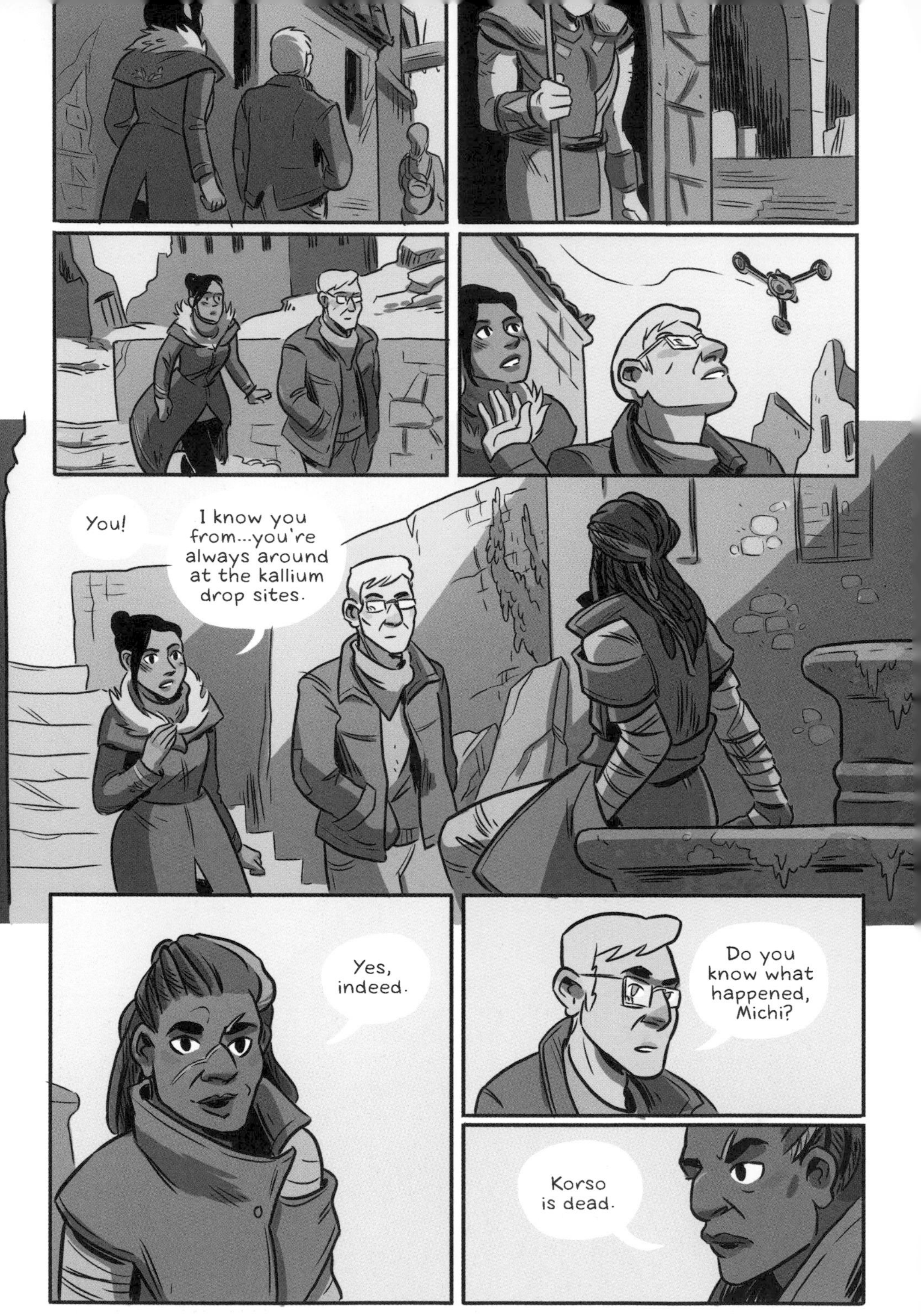
You!
I know you from...you're always around at the kallium drop sites.
Yes, indeed.
Do you know what happened, Michi?
Korso is dead.

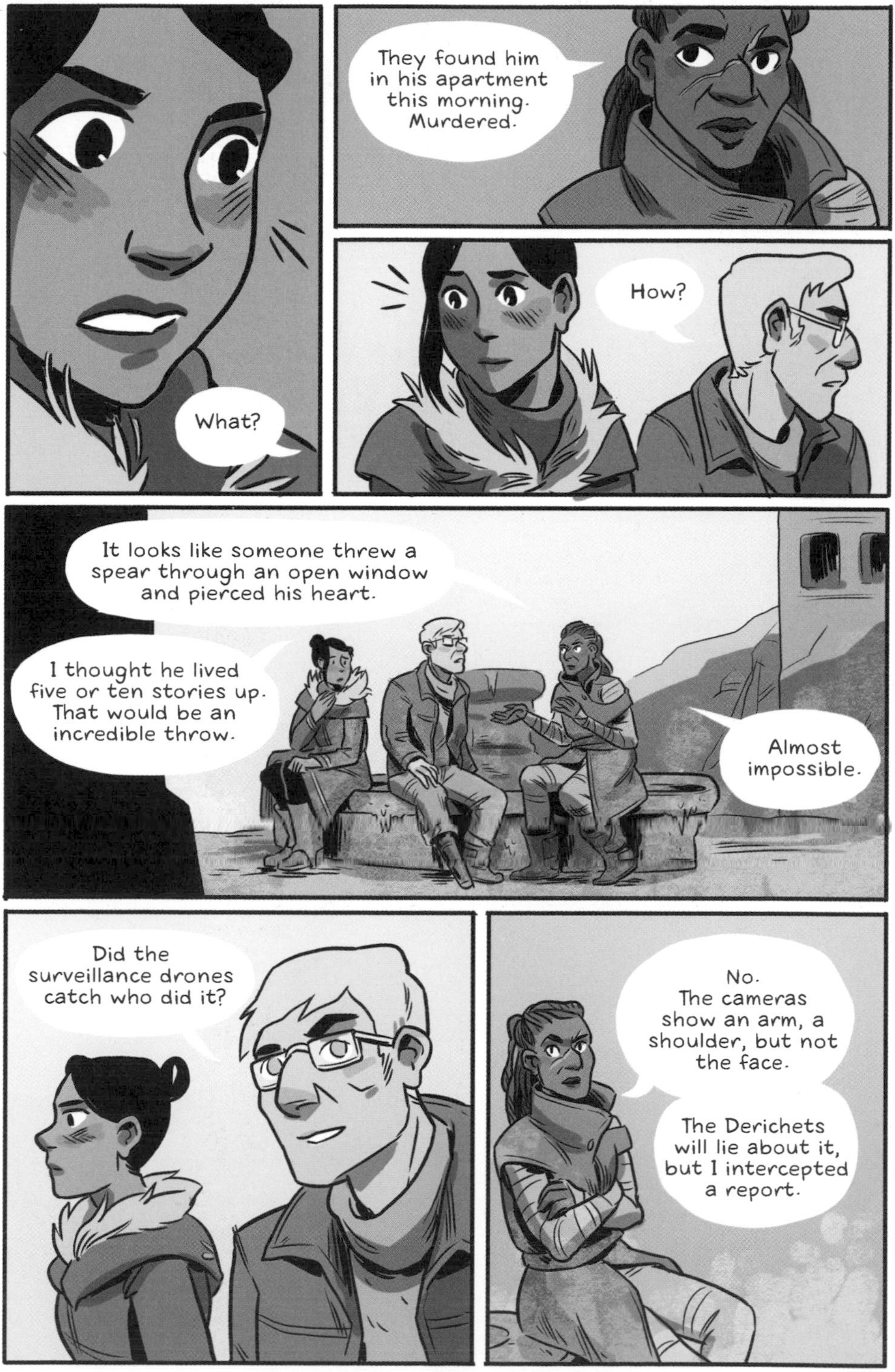
What?
They found him in his apartment this morning. Murdered.
How?
It looks like someone threw a spear through an open window and pierced his heart.
I thought he lived five or ten stories up. That would be an incredible throw.
Almost impossible.
Did the surveillance drones catch who did it?
No. The cameras show an arm, a shoulder, but not the face.
The Derichets will lie about it, but I intercepted a report.

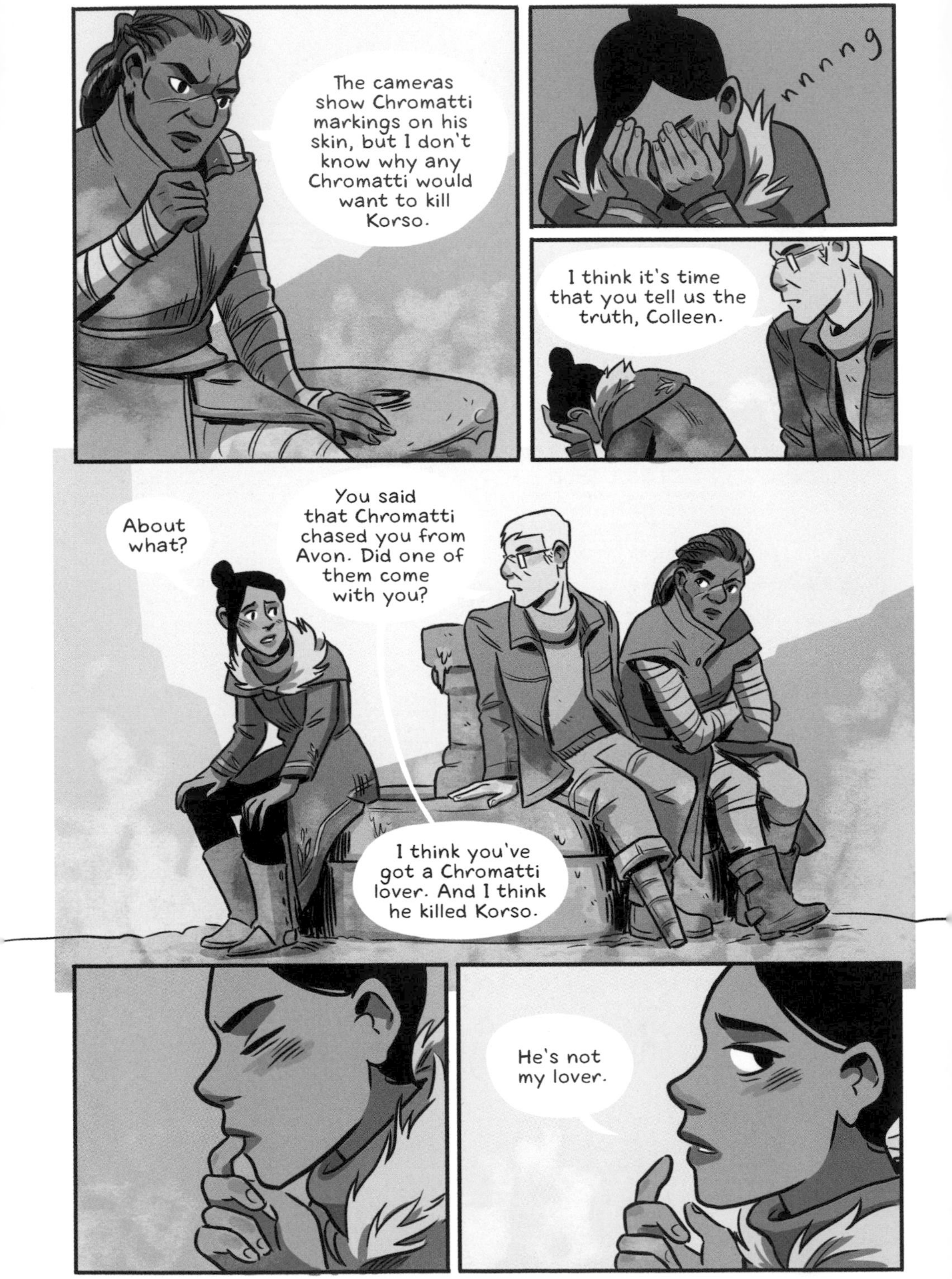
The cameras show Chromatti markings on his skin, but I don't know why any Chromatti would want to kill Korso.
nnnng
I think it's time that you tell us the truth, Colleen.
About what?
You said that Chromatti chased you from Avon. Did one of them come with you?
I think you've got a Chromatti lover. And I think he killed Korso.
He's not my lover.

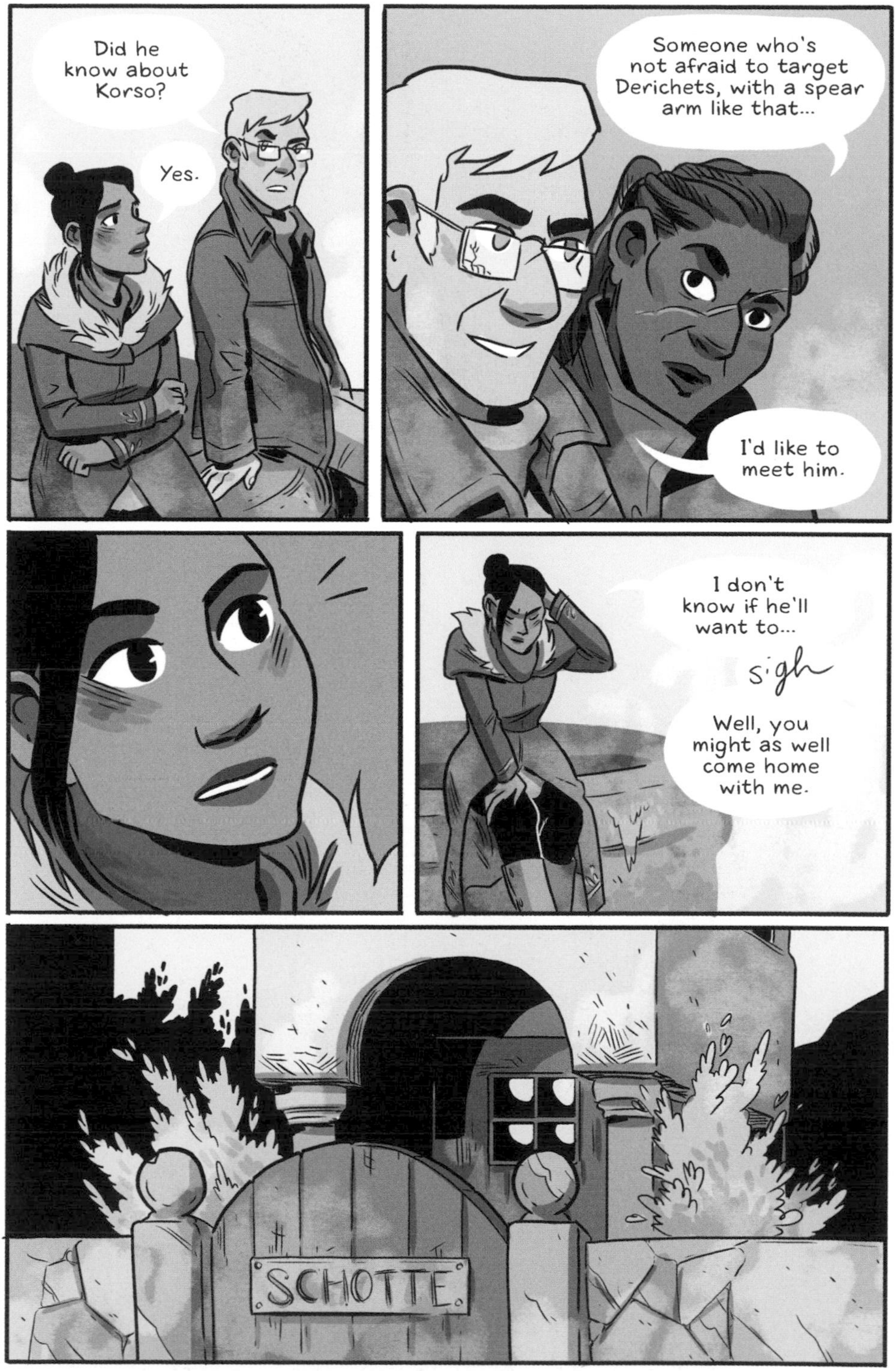
Did he know about Korso?
Yes.
Someone who's not afraid to target Derichets, with a spear arm like that...
I'd like to meet him.
I don't know if he'll want to...
sigh
Well, you might as well come home with me.
SCHOTTE

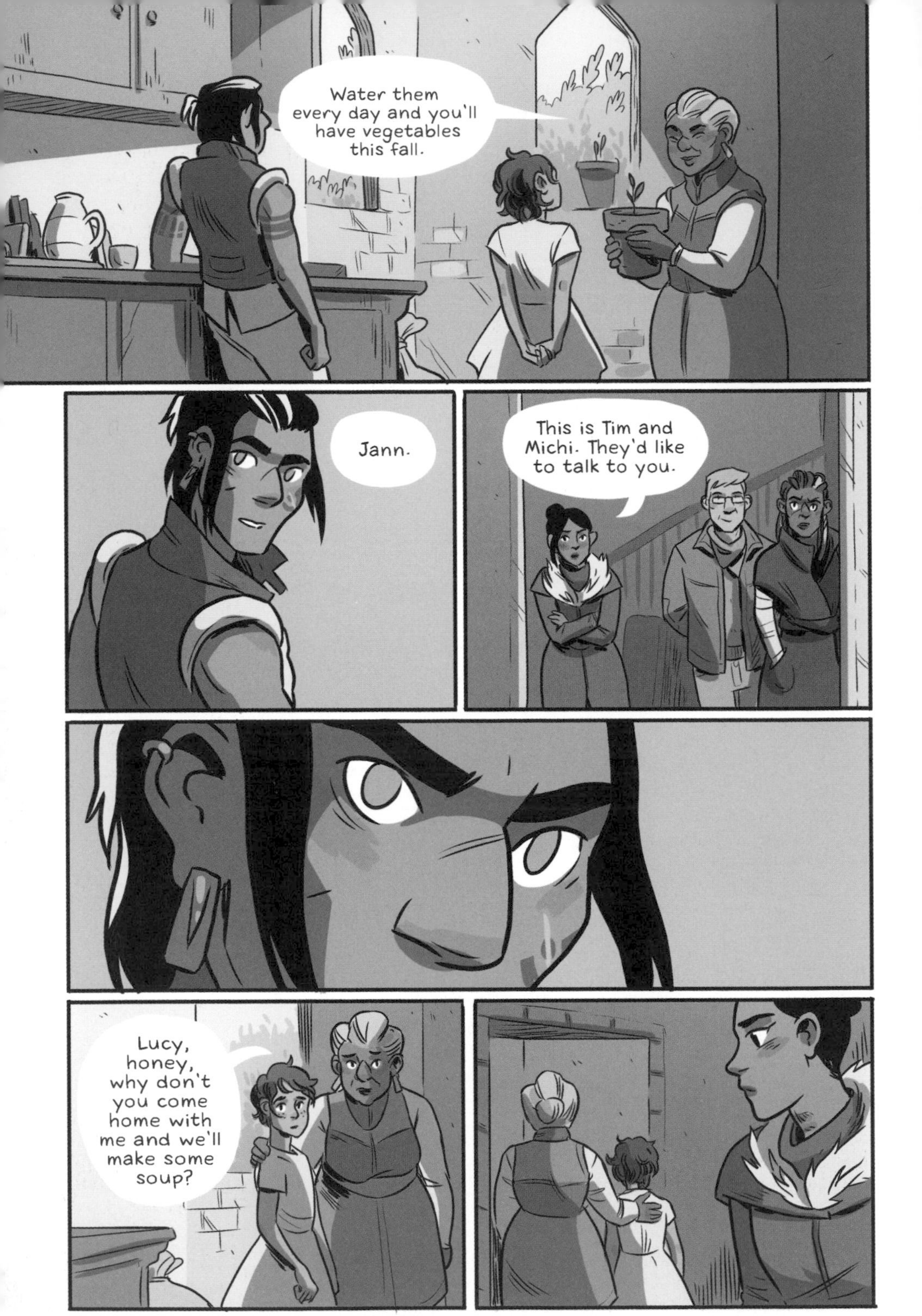
Water them every day and you'll have vegetables this fall.
Jann.
This is Tim and Michi. They'd like to talk to you.
Lucy, honey, why don't you come home with me and we'll make some soup?

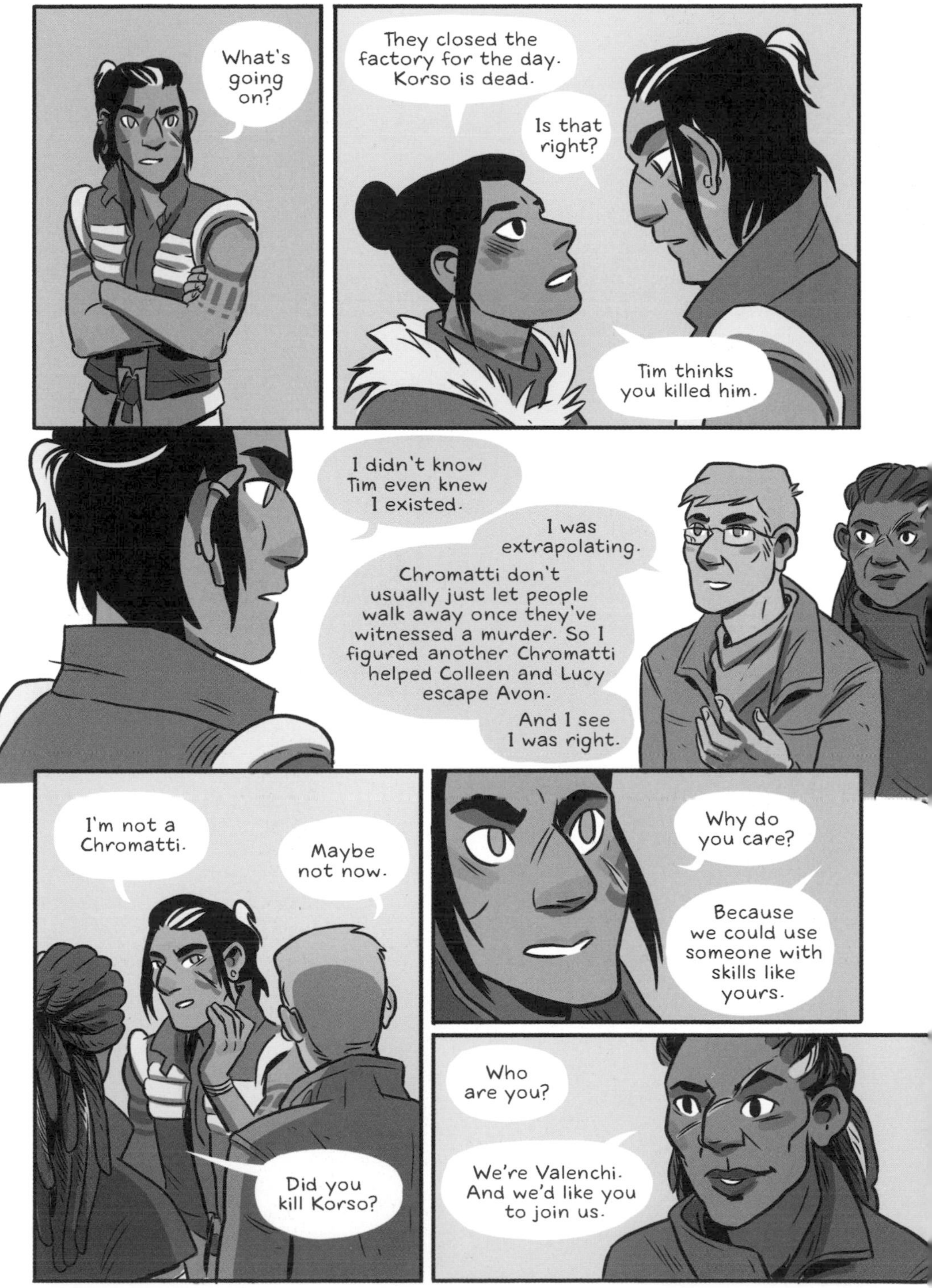
What's going on?
They closed the factory for the day. Korso is dead.
Is that right?
Tim thinks you killed him.
I didn't know Tim even knew I existed.
I was extrapolating.
Chromatti don't usually just let people walk away once they've witnessed a murder. So I figured another Chromatti helped Colleen and Lucy escape Avon.
And I see I was right.
I'm not a Chromatti.
Maybe not now.
Did you kill Korso?
Why do you care?
Because we could use someone with skills like yours.
Who are you?
We're Valenchi. And we'd like you to join us.

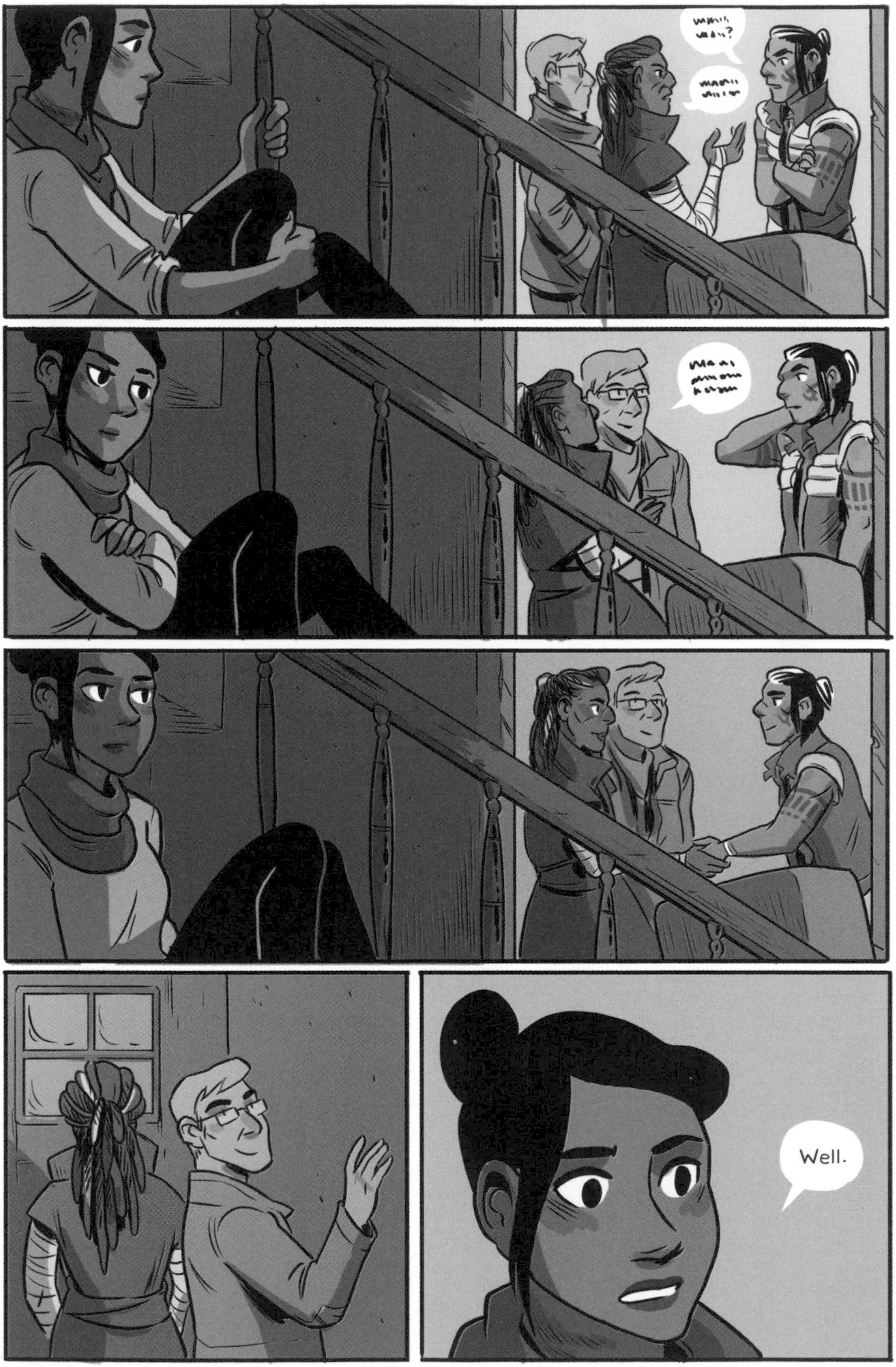
Well.

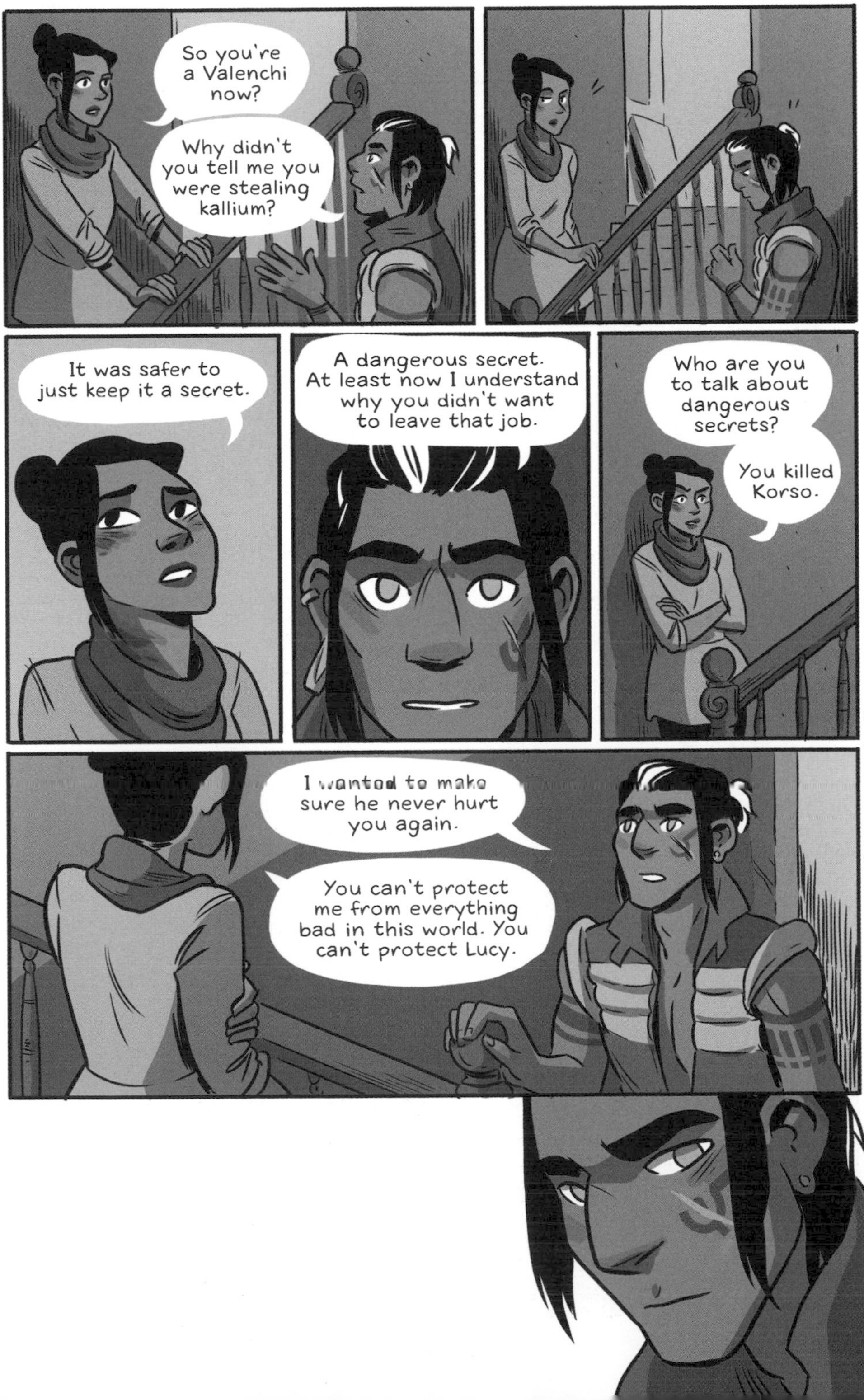

So you're a Valenchi now?
Why didn't you tell me you were stealing kallium?
It was safer to just keep it a secret.
A dangerous secret. At least now I understand why you didn't want to leave that job.
Who are you to talk about dangerous secrets?
You killed Korso.
I wanted to make sure he never hurt you again.
You can't protect me from everything bad in this world. You can't protect Lucy.

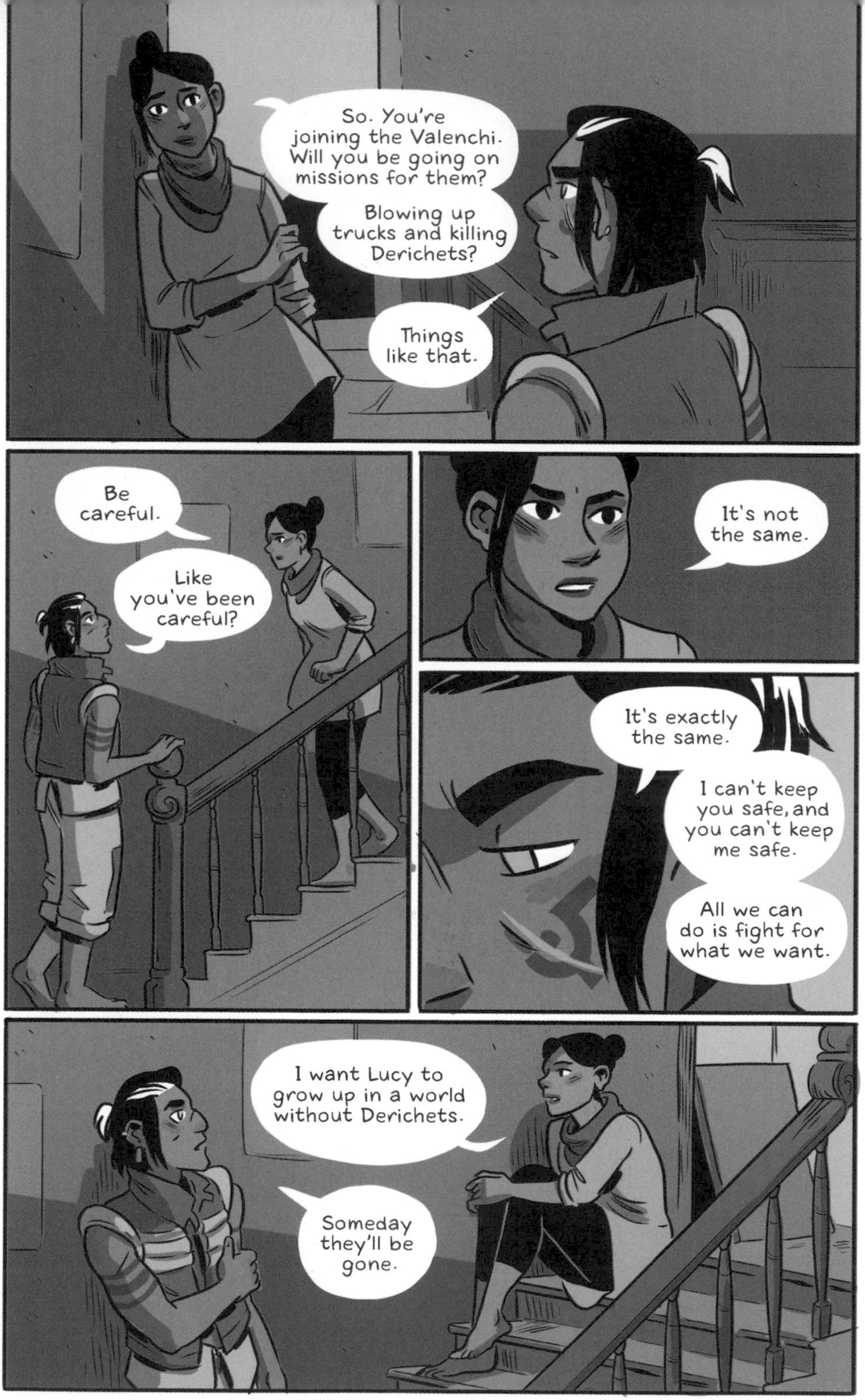
So. You're joining the Valenchi. Will you be going on missions for them?
Blowing up trucks and killing Derichets?
Things like that.
Be careful.
Like you've been careful?
It's not the same.
It's exactly the same.
I can't keep you safe, and you can't keep me safe.
All we can do is fight for what we want.
I want Lucy to grow up in a world without Derichets.
Someday they'll be gone.

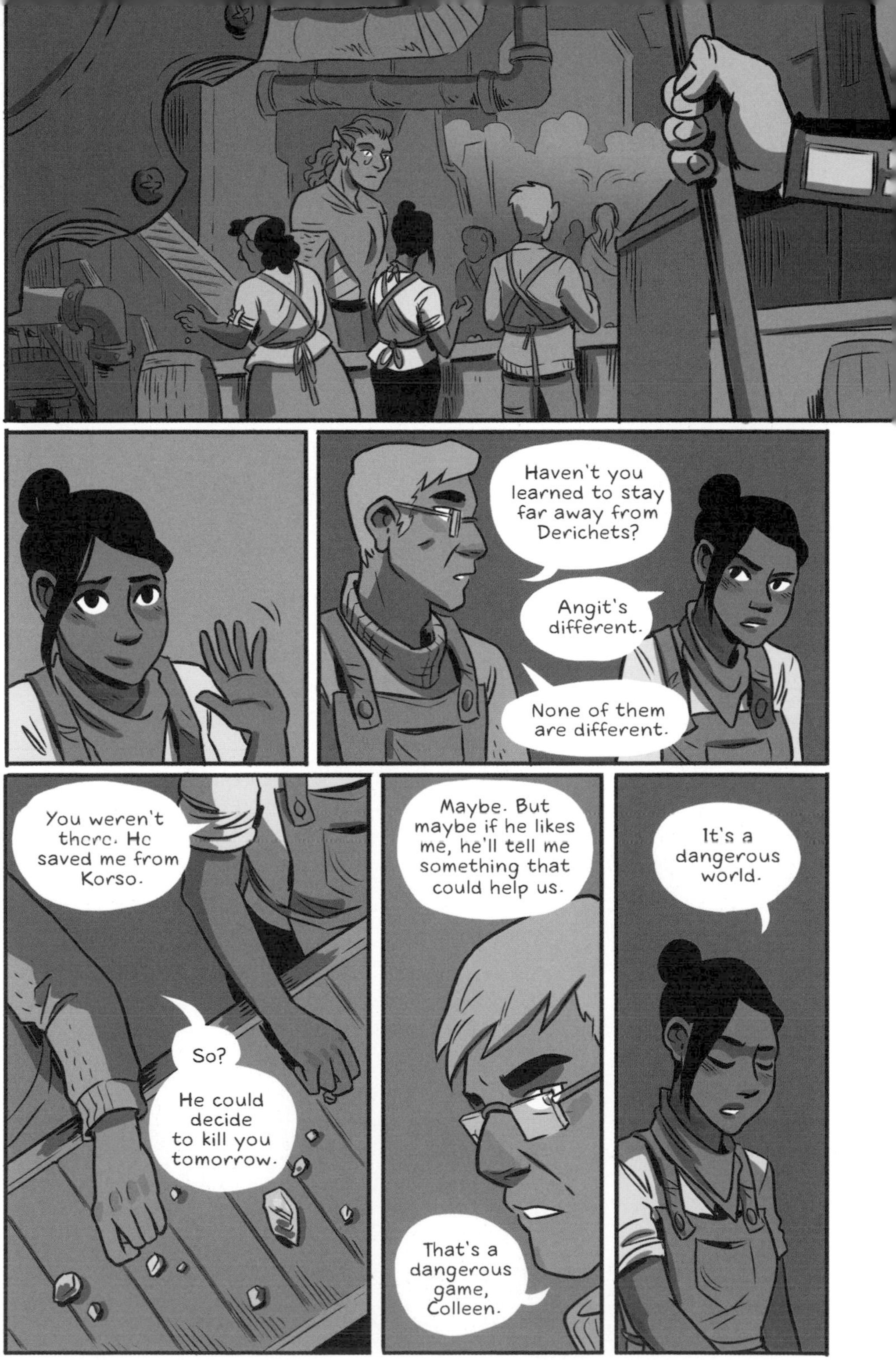
Haven't you learned to stay far away from Derichets?
Angit's different.
None of them are different.
You weren't there. He saved me from Korso.
So?
He could decide to kill you tomorrow.
Maybe. But maybe if he likes me, he'll tell me something that could help us.
That's a dangerous game, Colleen.
It's a dangerous world.

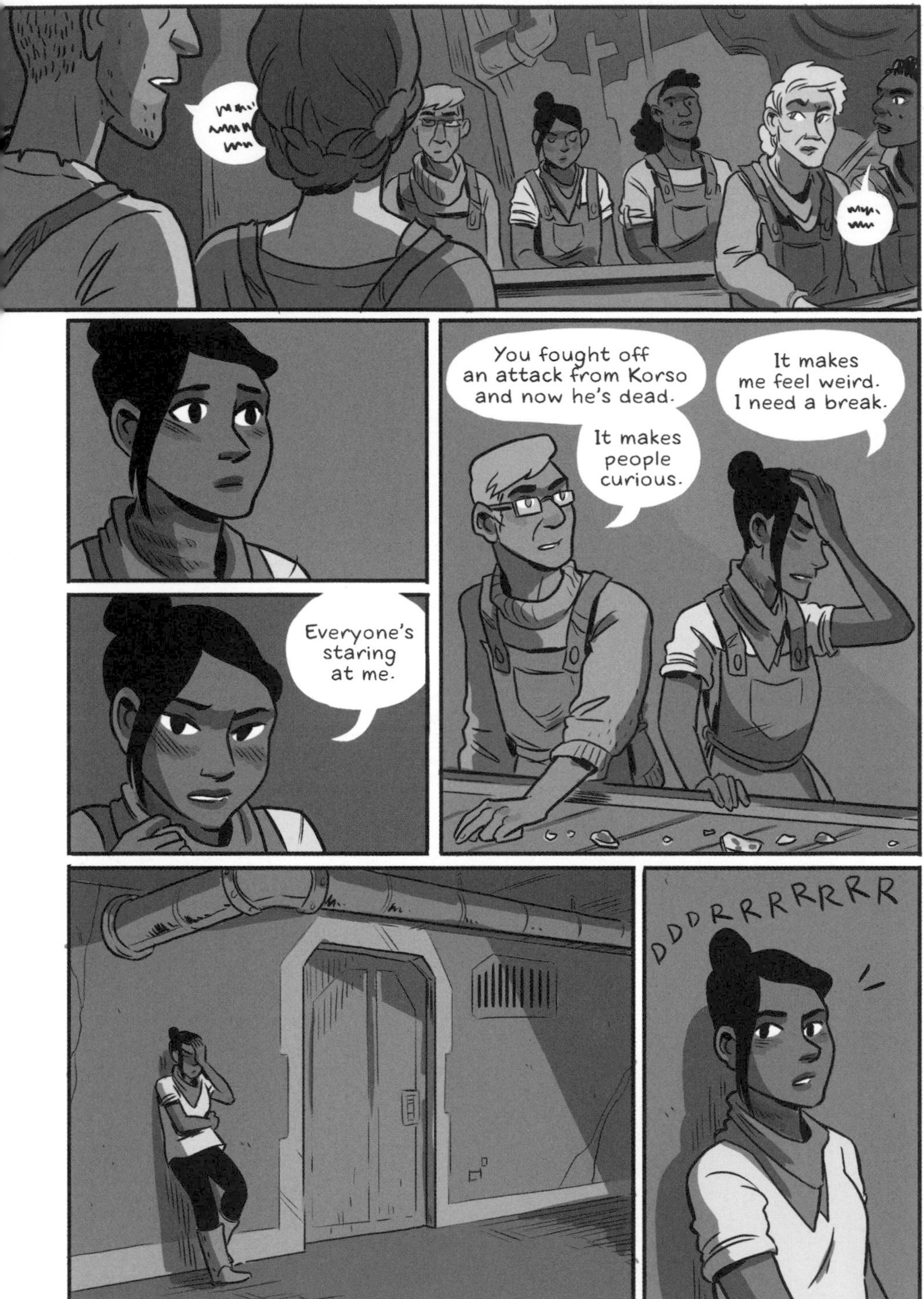
You fought off an attack from Korso and now he's dead.
It makes people curious.
It makes me feel weird. I need a break.
Everyone's staring at me.
DDDRRRRRRRR

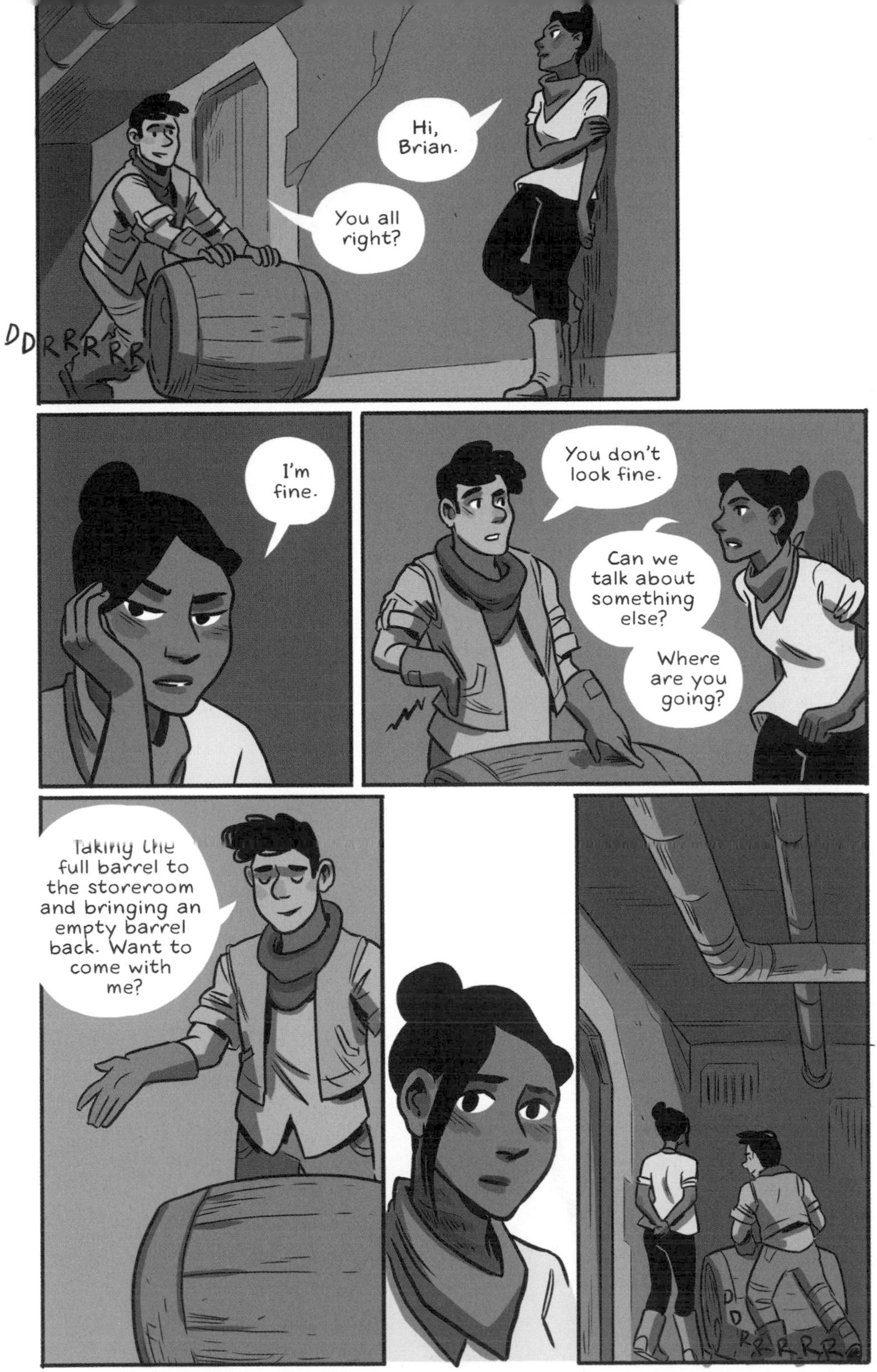
Hi, Brian.
You all right?
DDRRRRR
I'm fine.
You don't look fine.
Can we talk about something else?
Where are you going?
Taking the full barrel to the storeroom and bringing an empty barrel back. Want to come with me?
DDRRRRR

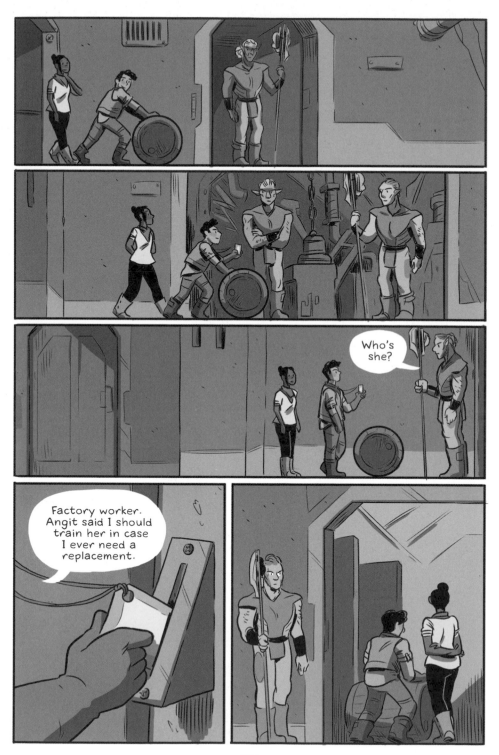

Who's she?

Factory worker. Angit said I should train her in case I ever need a replacement.

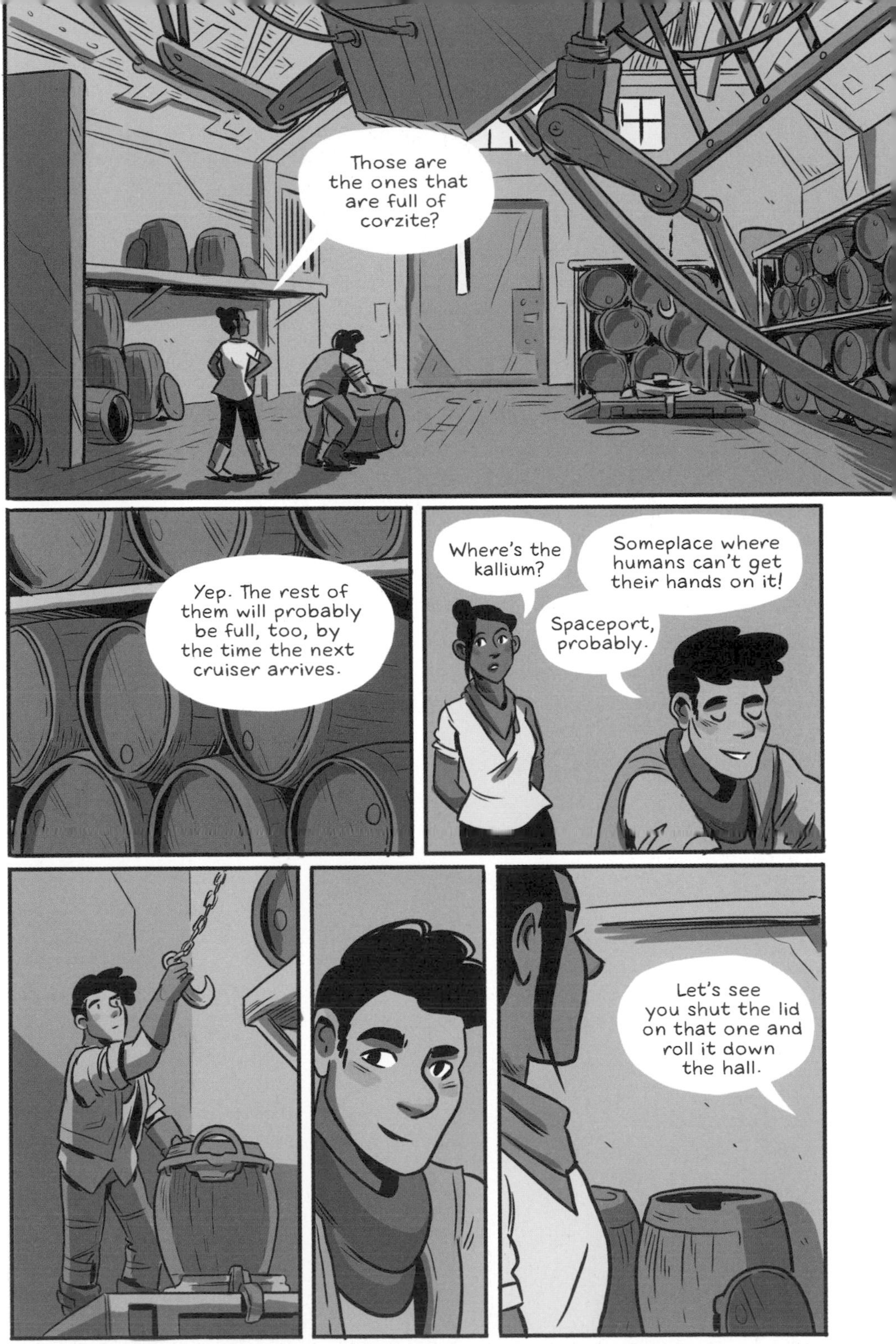
Those are the ones that are full of corzite?
Yep. The rest of them will probably be full, too, by the time the next cruiser arrives.
Where's the kallium?
Someplace where humans can't get their hands on it!
Spaceport, probably.
Let's see you shut the lid on that one and roll it down the hall.

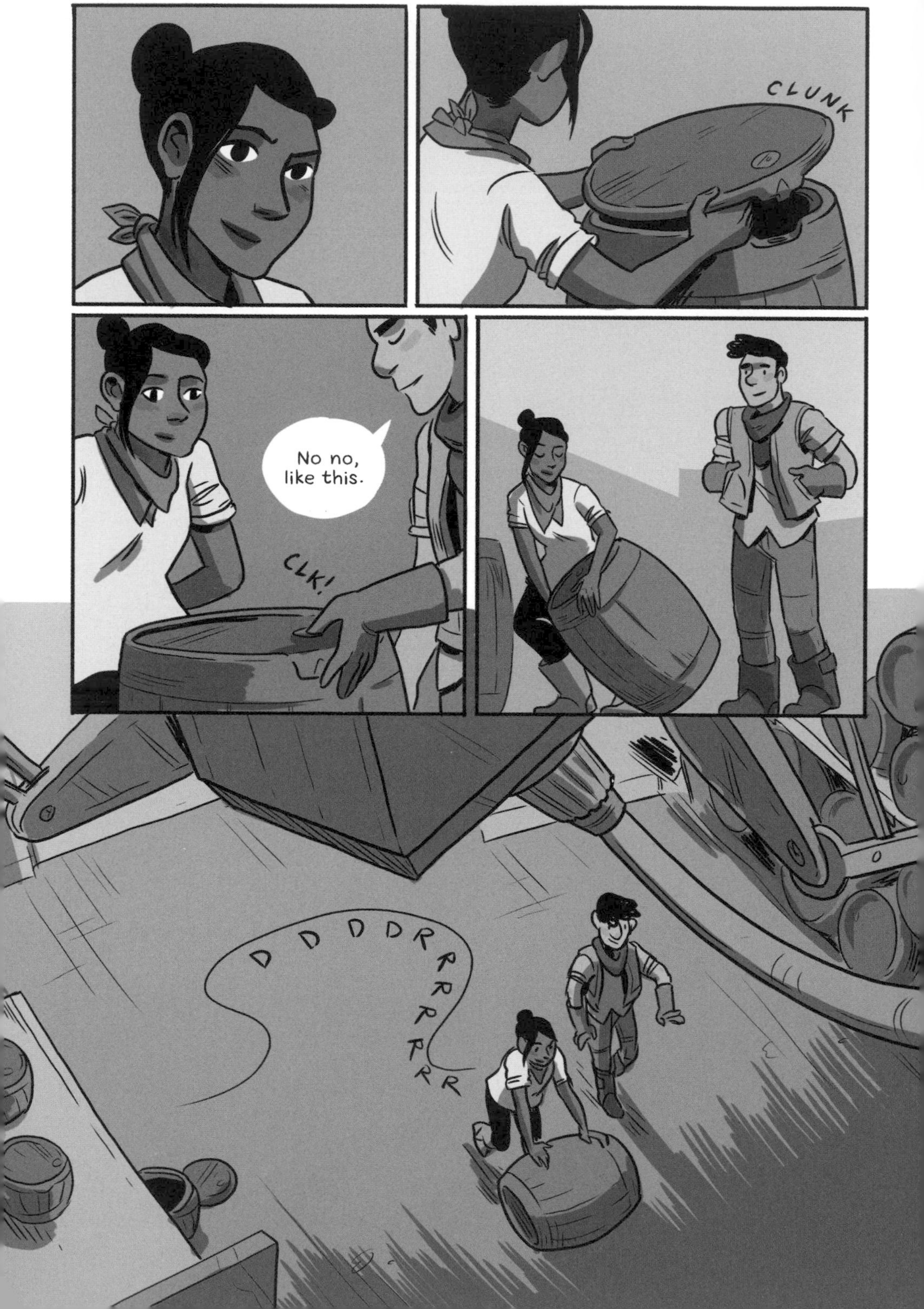
CLUNK
No no, like this.
CLK!
DDDDRRRRRRRRR

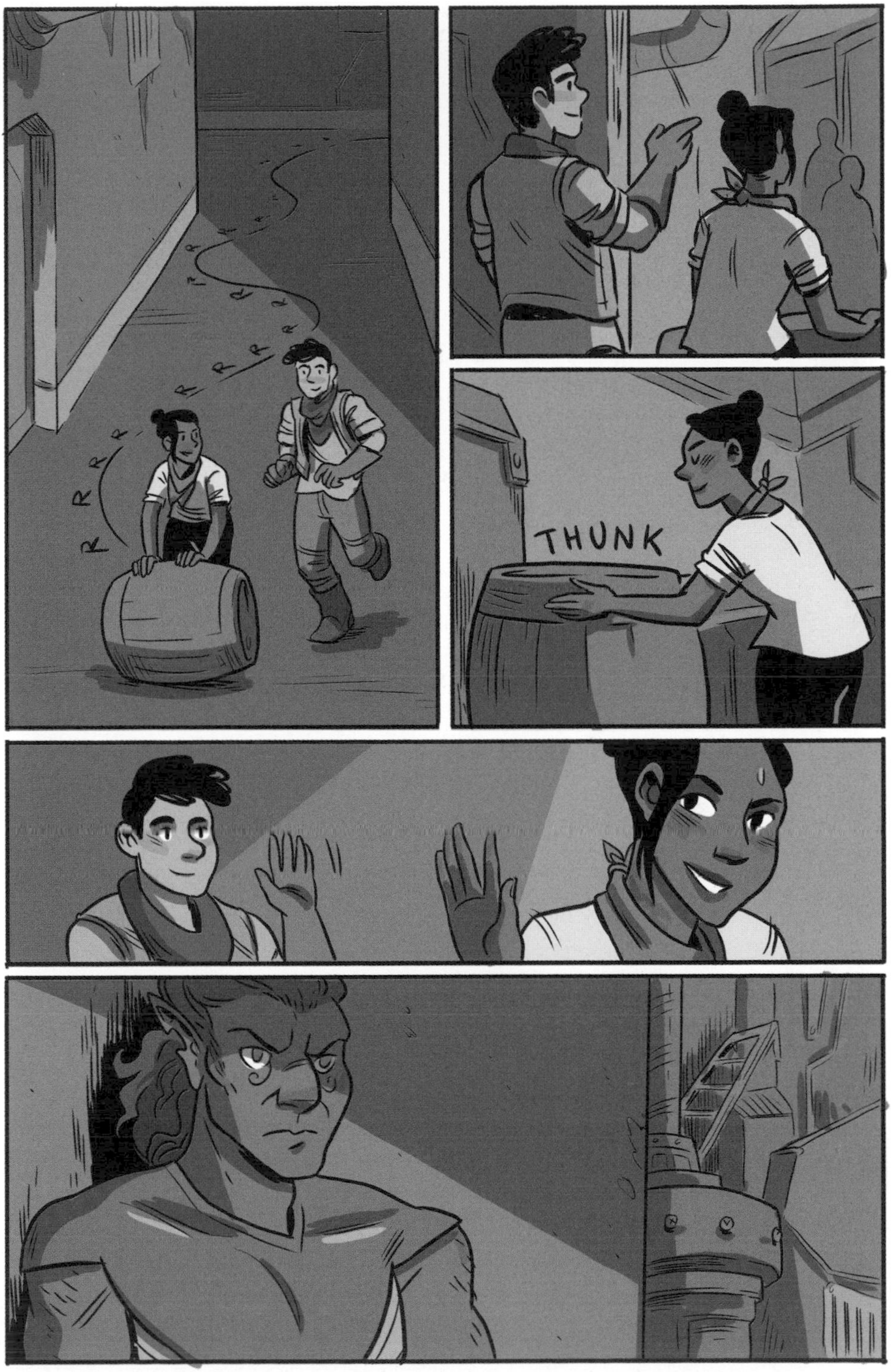
THUNK

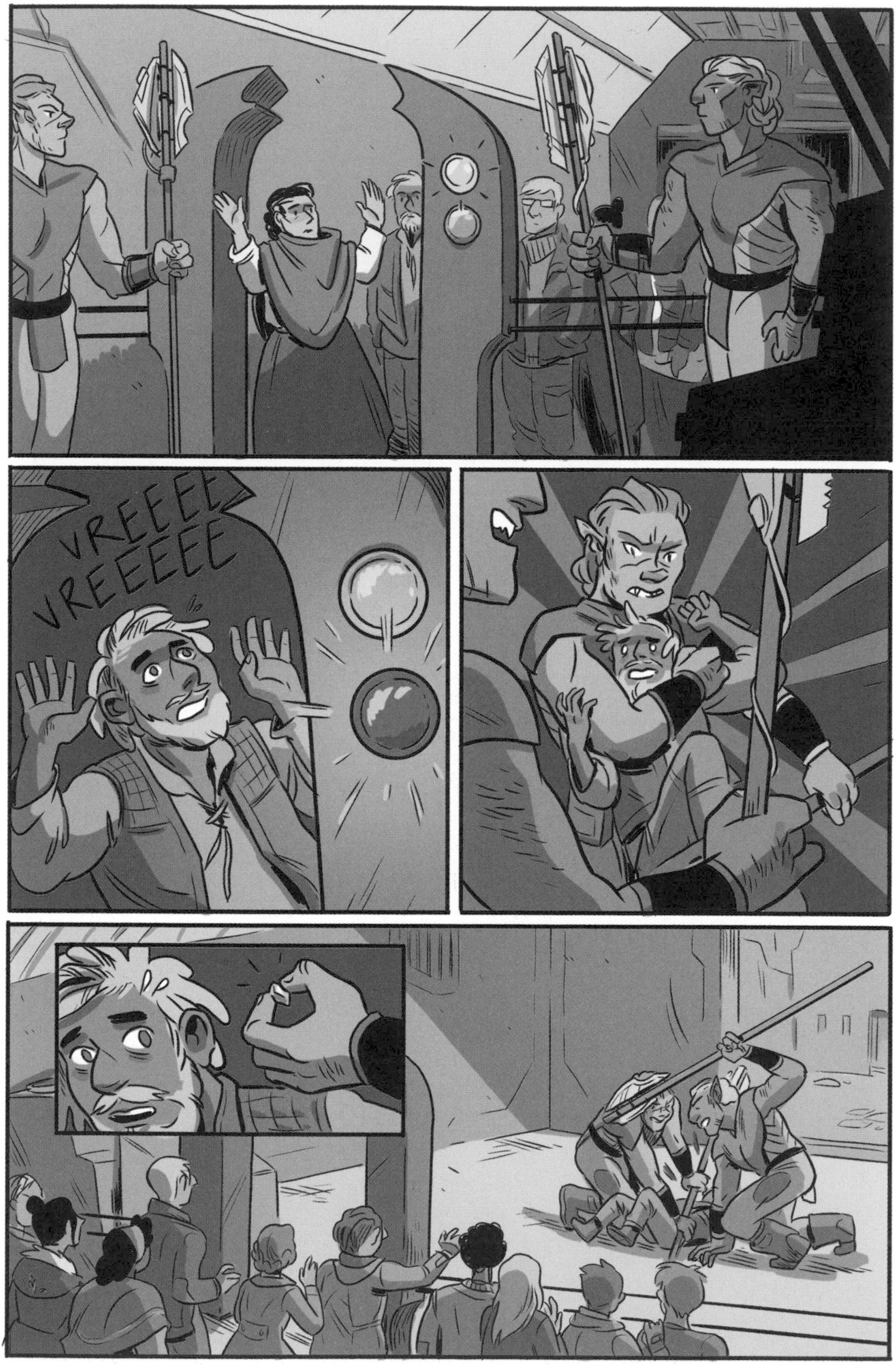
VREEEE
VREEEEE

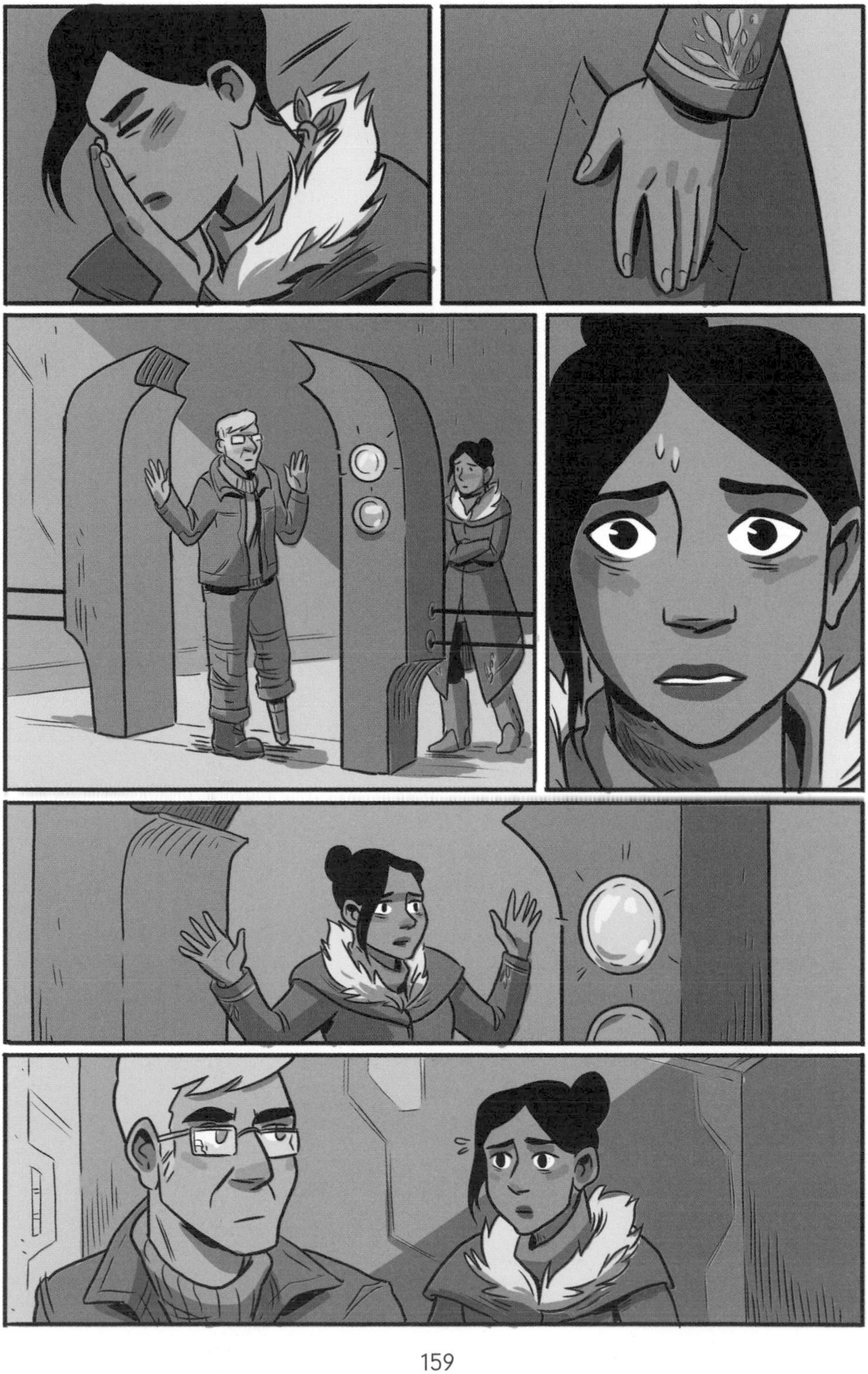

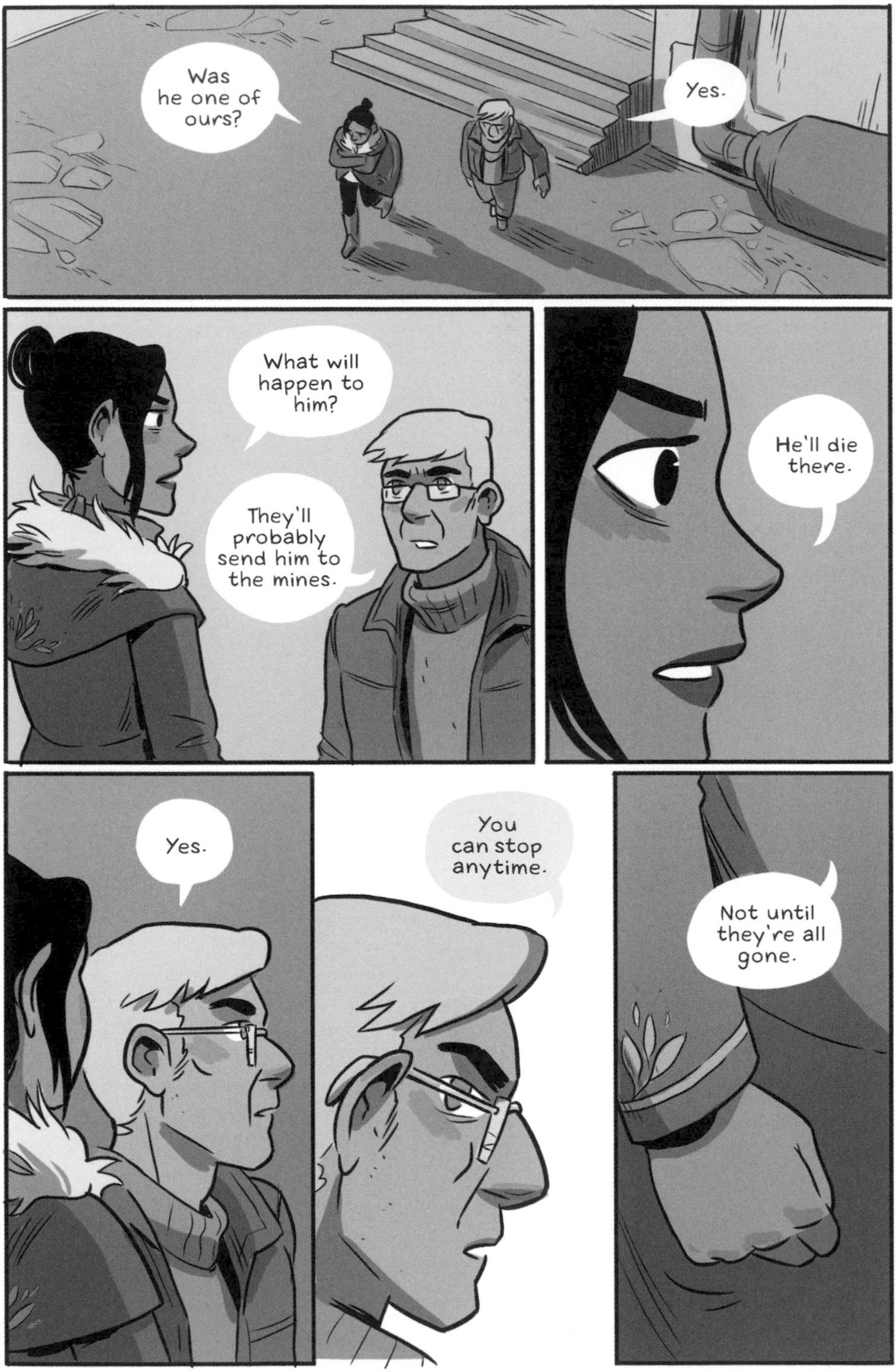
Was he one of ours?
Yes.
What will happen to him?
They'll probably send him to the mines.
He'll die there.
Yes.
You can stop anytime.
Not until they're all gone.

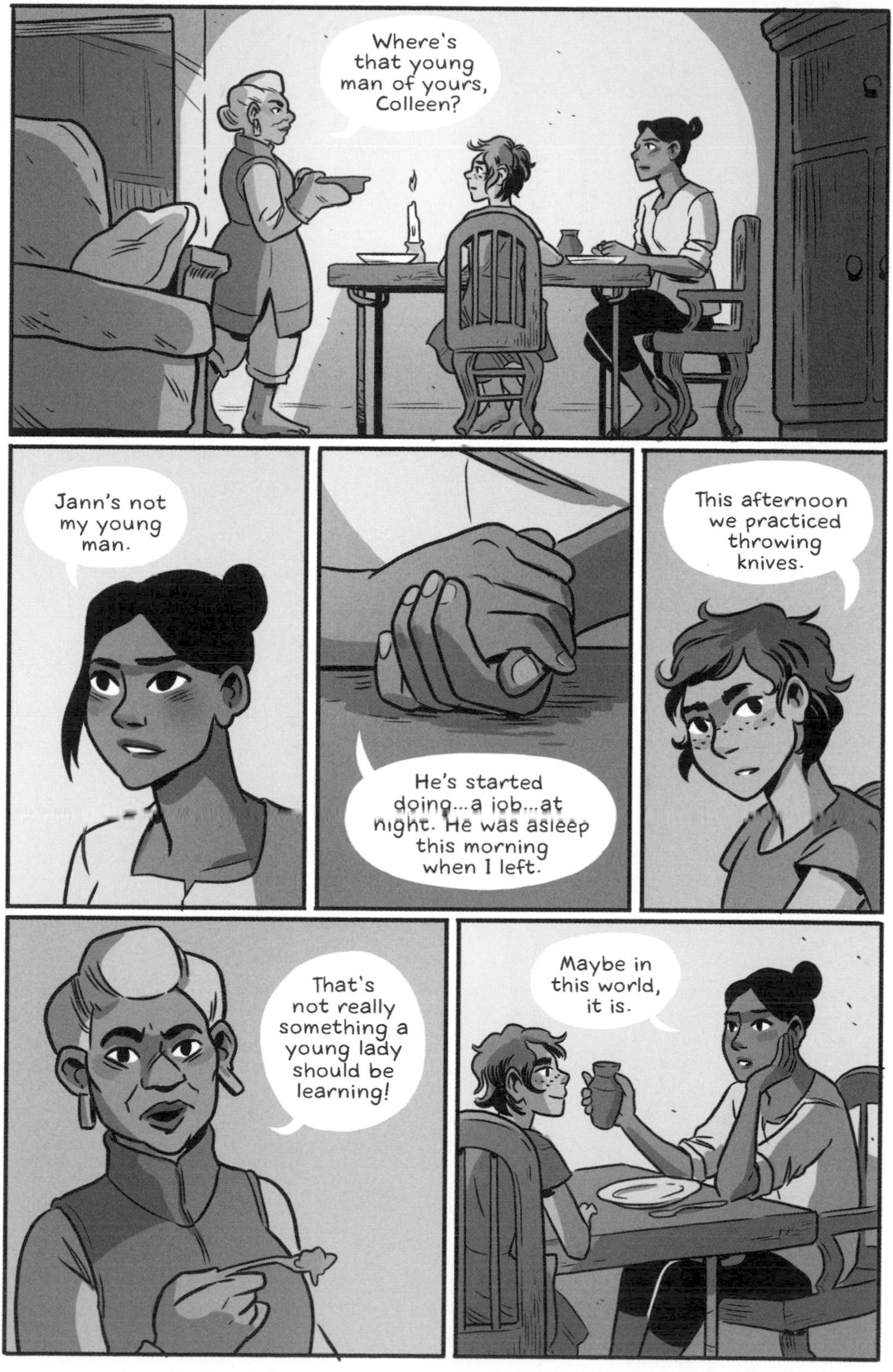
Where's that young man of yours, Colleen?
Jann's not my young man.
He's started doing...a job...at night. He was asleep this morning when I left.
This afternoon we practiced throwing knives.
That's not really something a young lady should be learning!
Maybe in this world, it is.

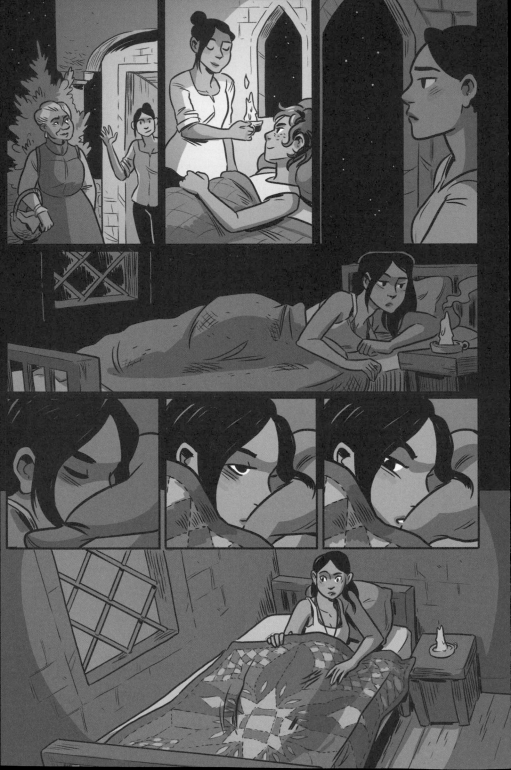

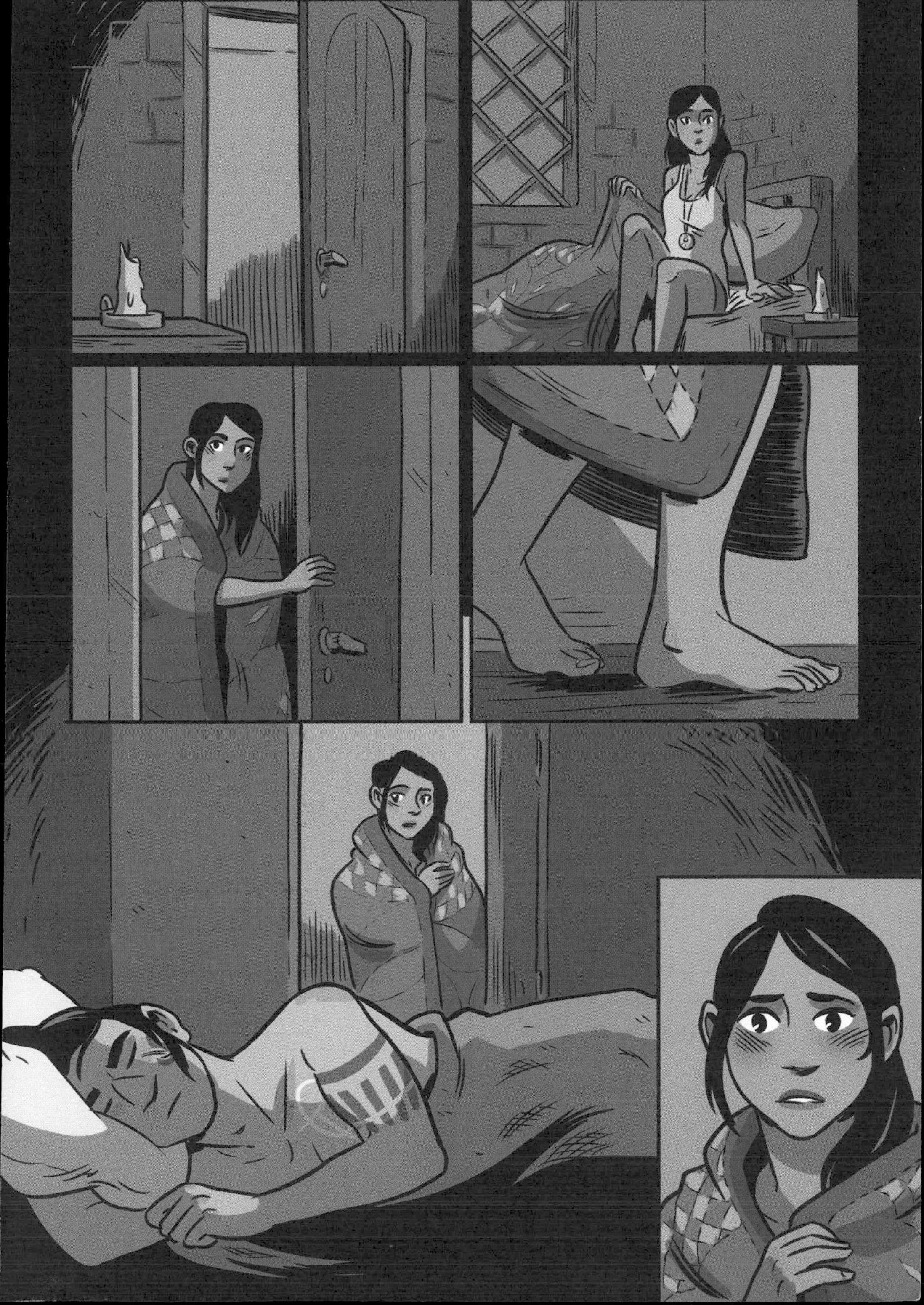

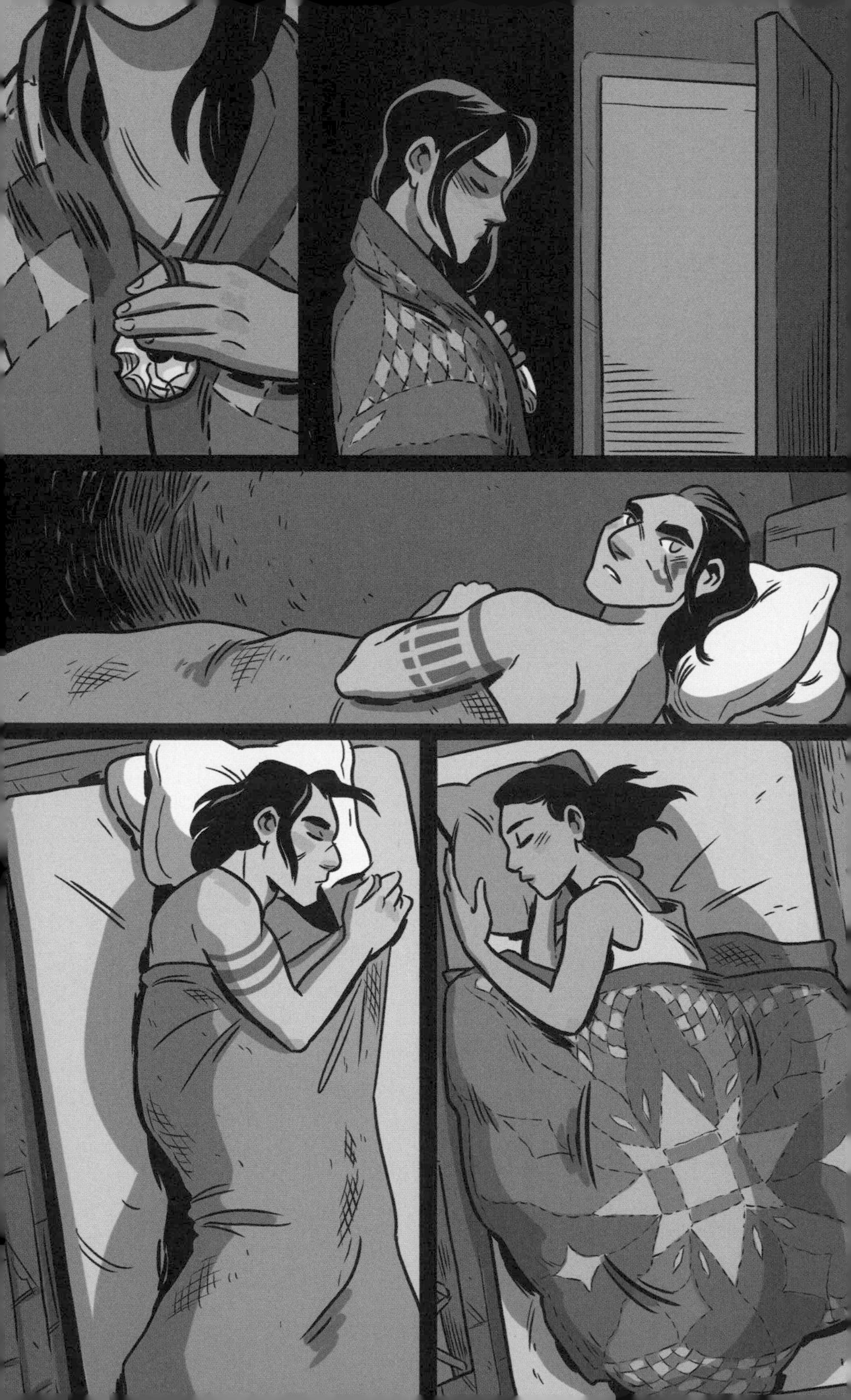

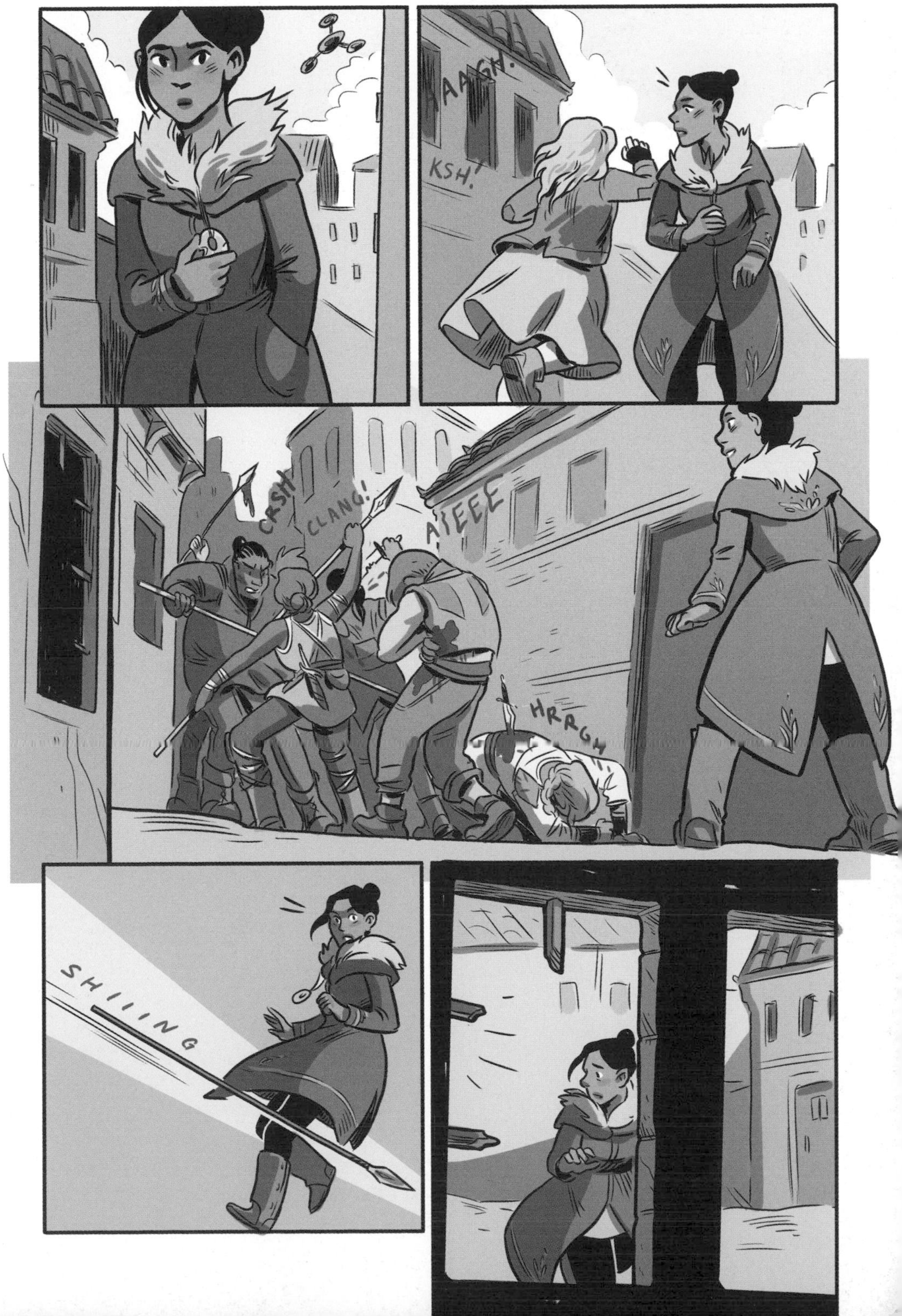
AAAGH.
KSH!
CRSH
CLANG!
AIEEE
HRRGH
SHIIING

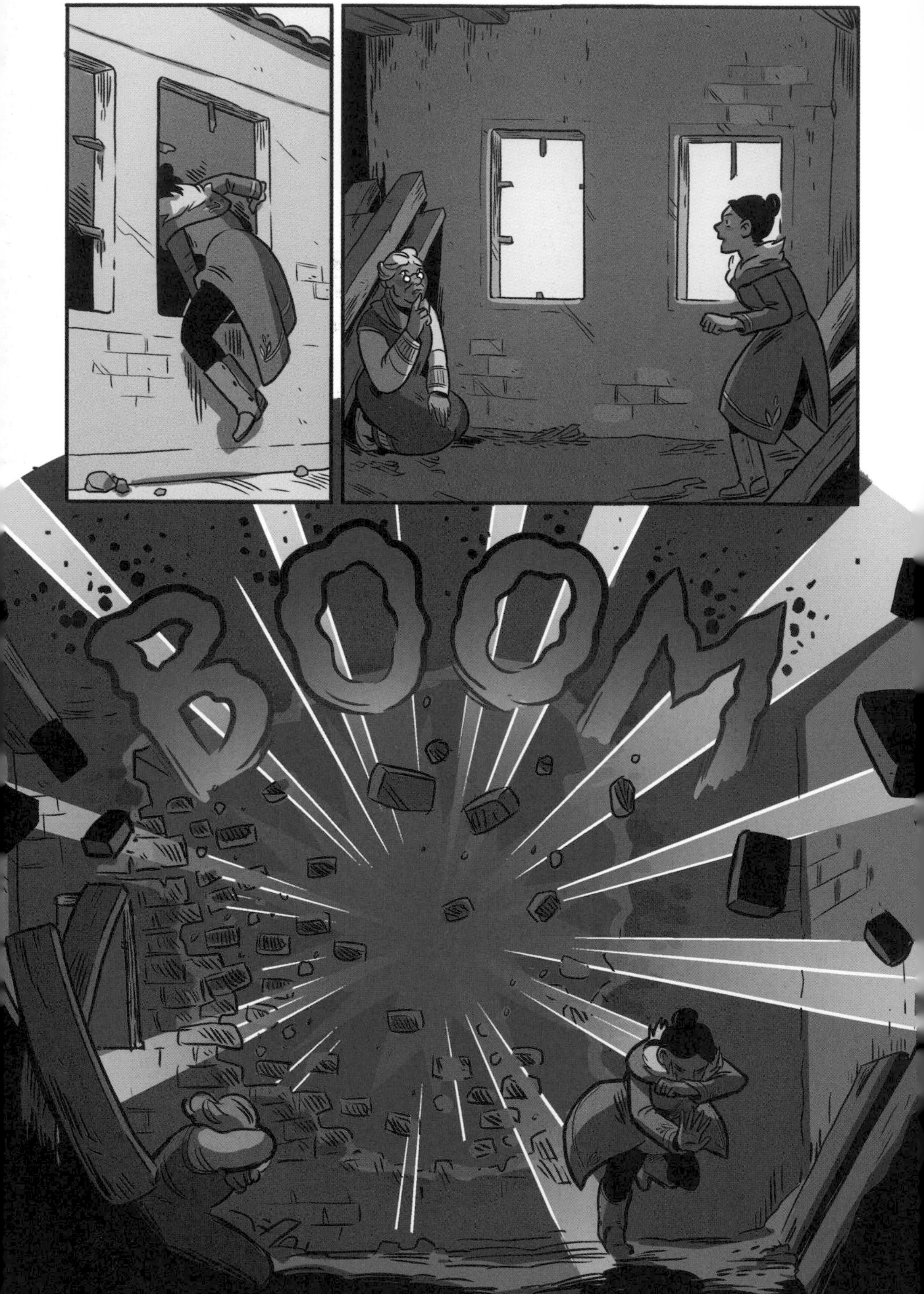
BOOM

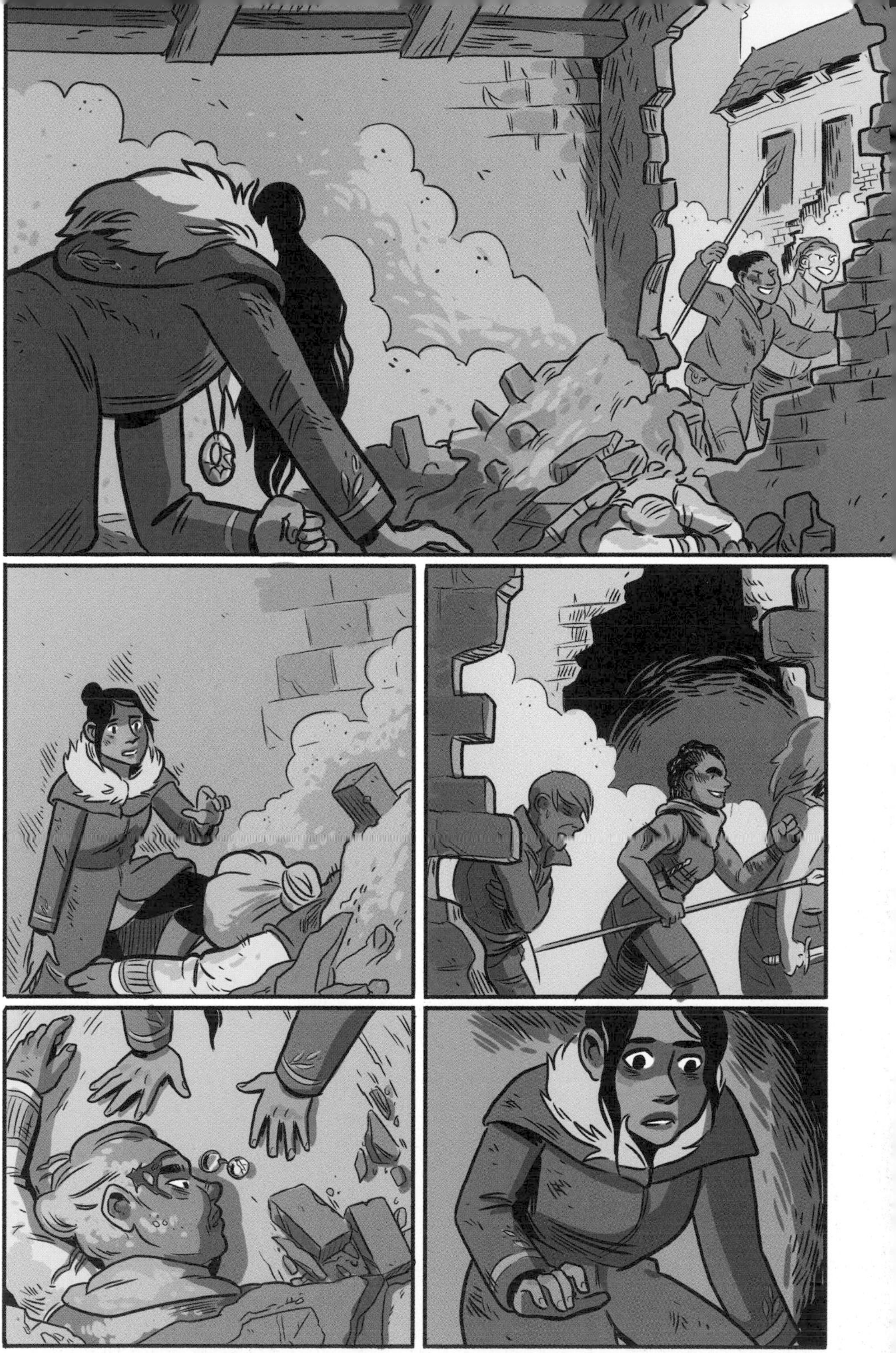

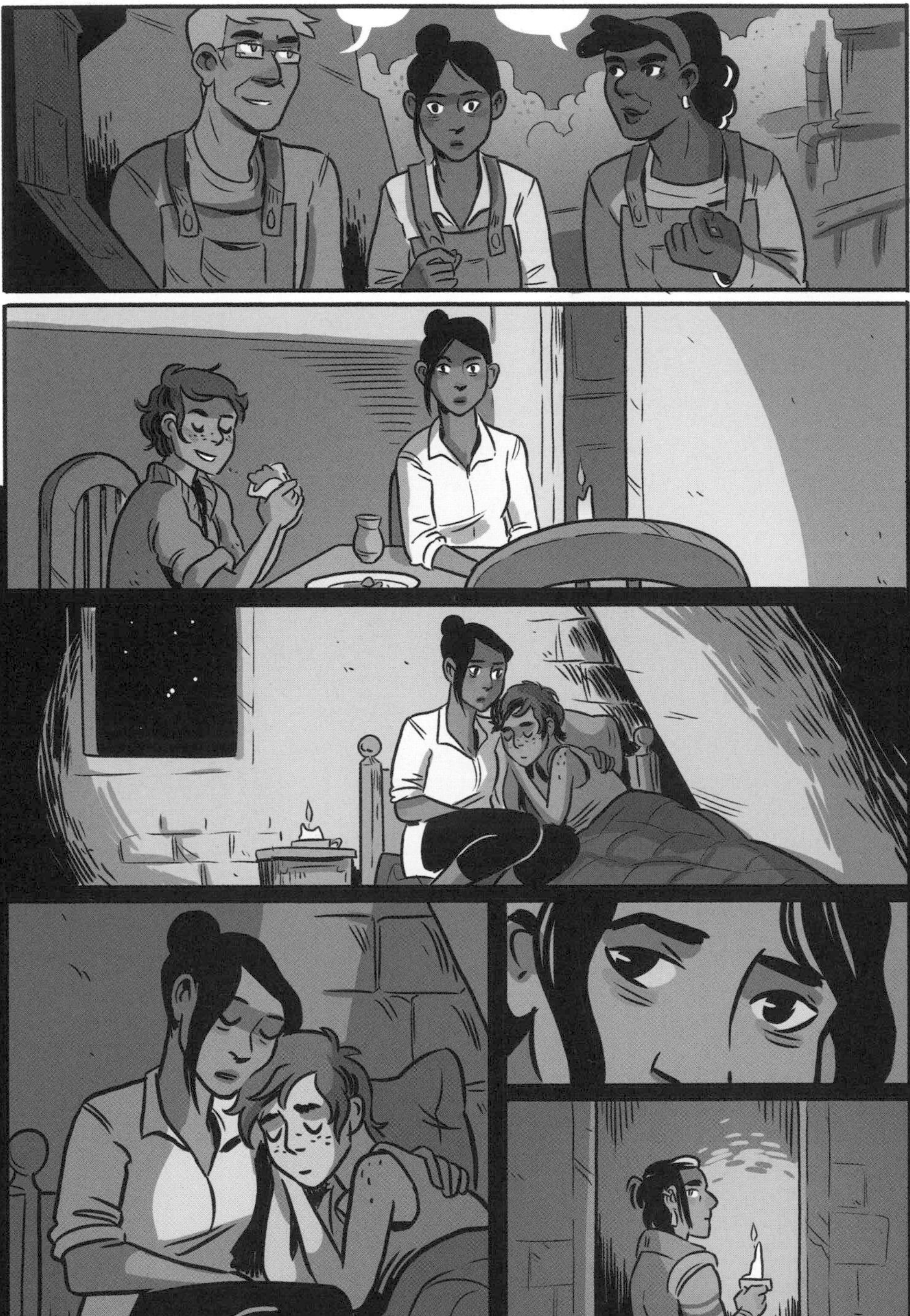

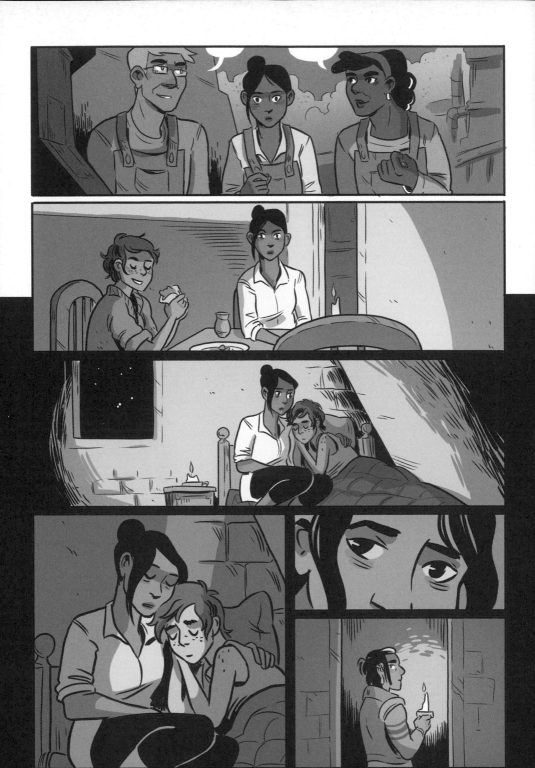

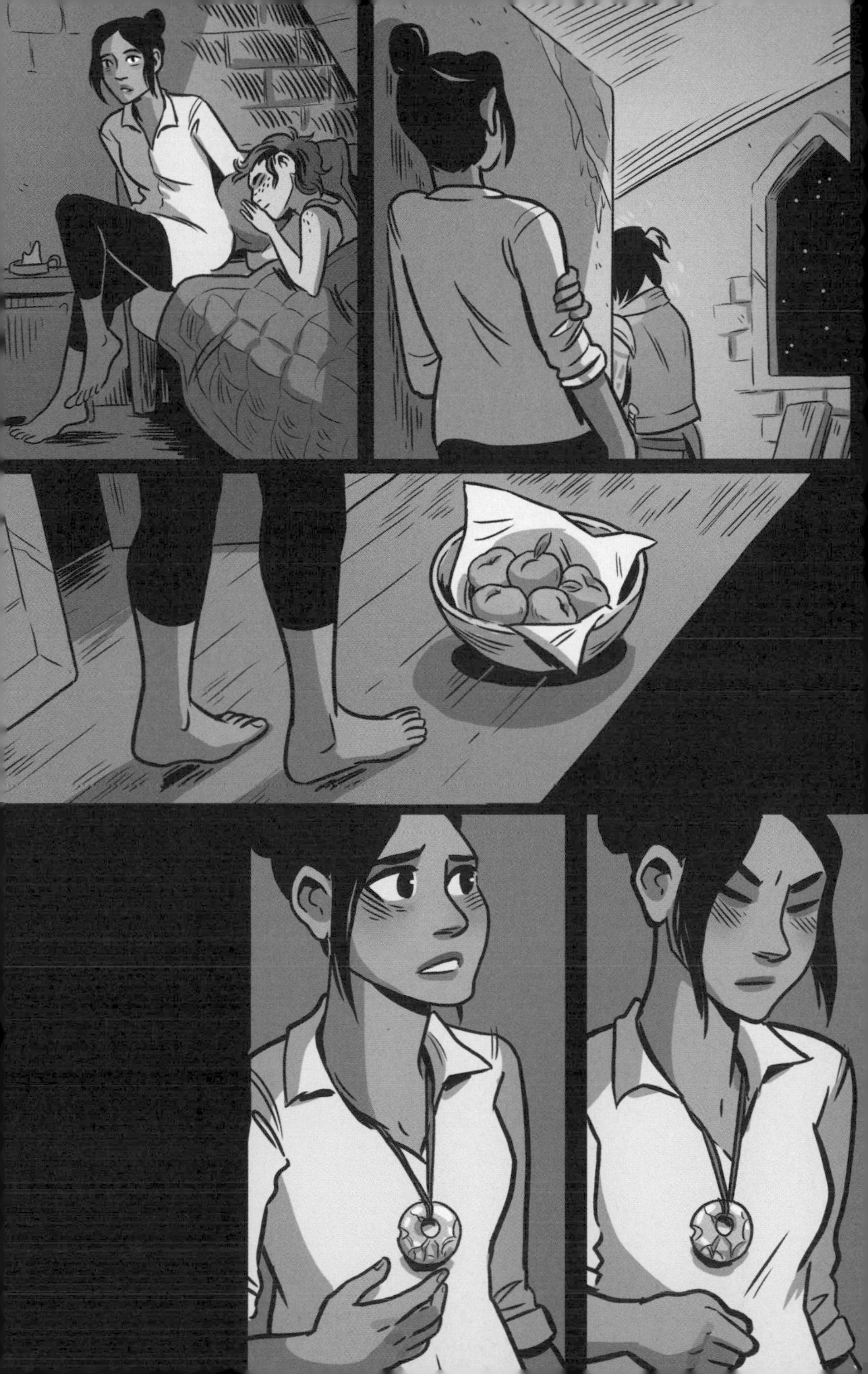

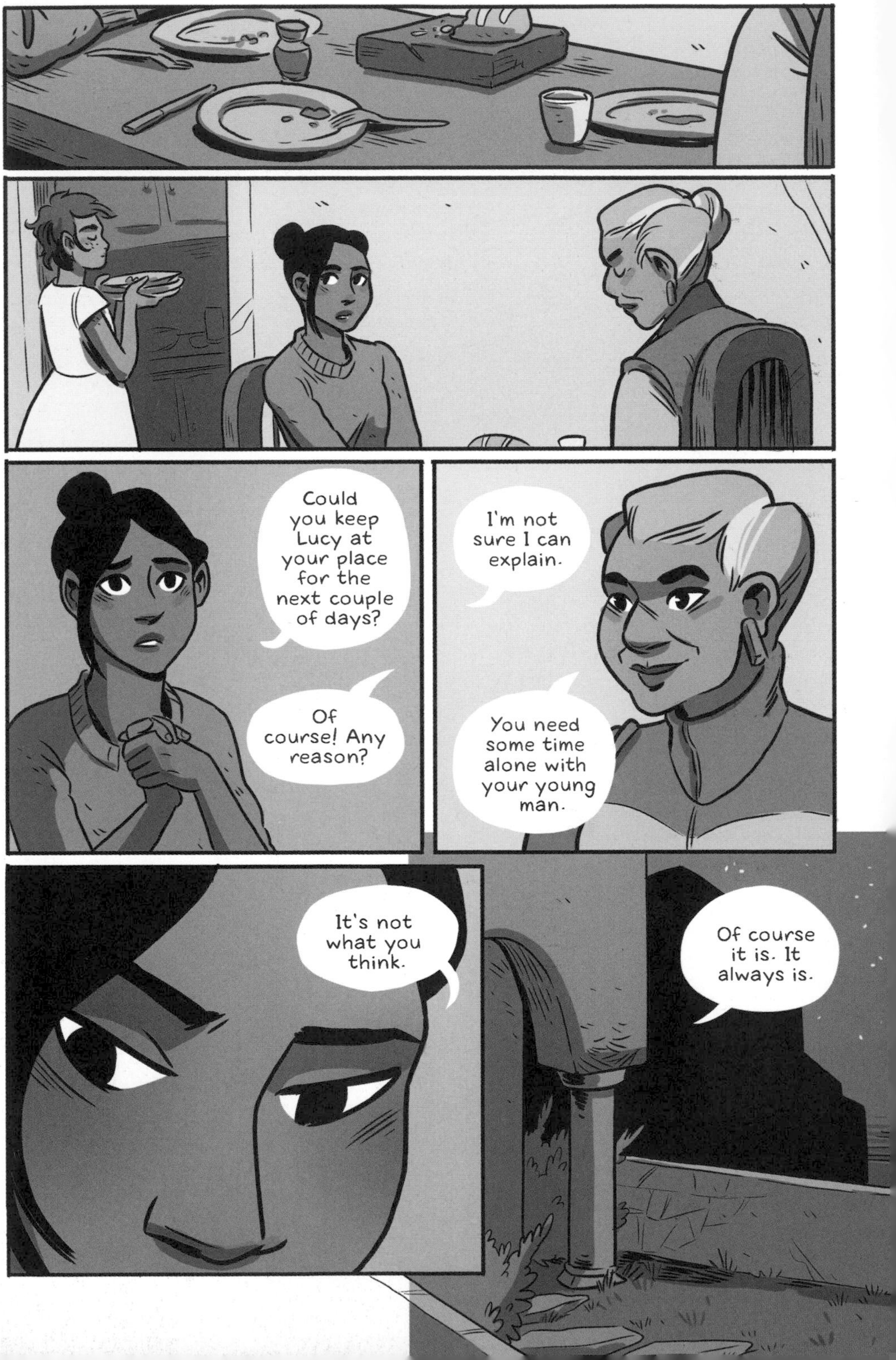
Could you keep Lucy at your place for the next couple of days?
Of course! Any reason?
I'm not sure I can explain.
You need some time alone with your young man.
It's not what you think.
Of course it is. It always is.

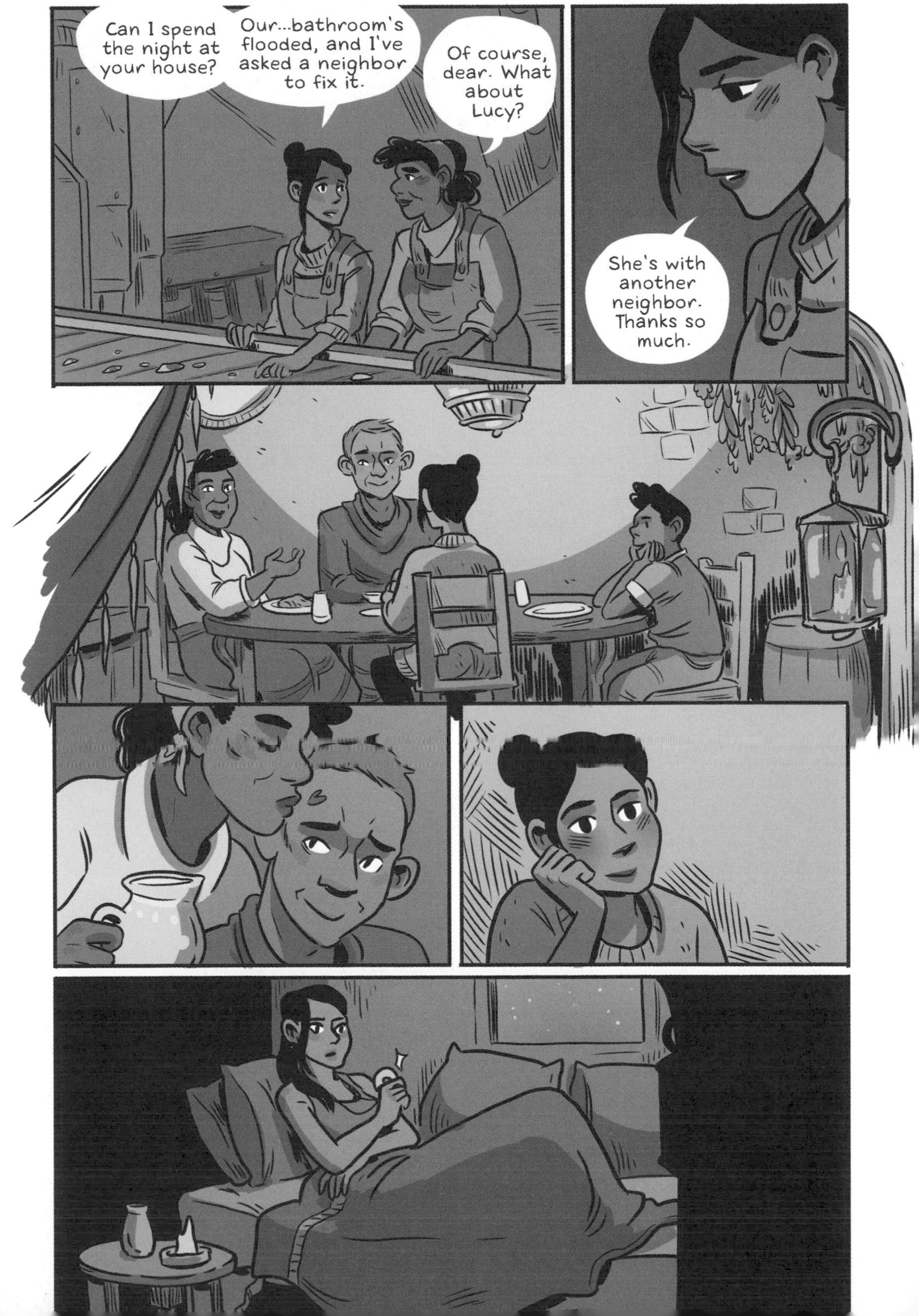
Can I spend the night at your house?
Our...bathroom's flooded, and I've asked a neighbor to fix it.
Of course, dear. What about Lucy?
She's with another neighbor. Thanks so much.

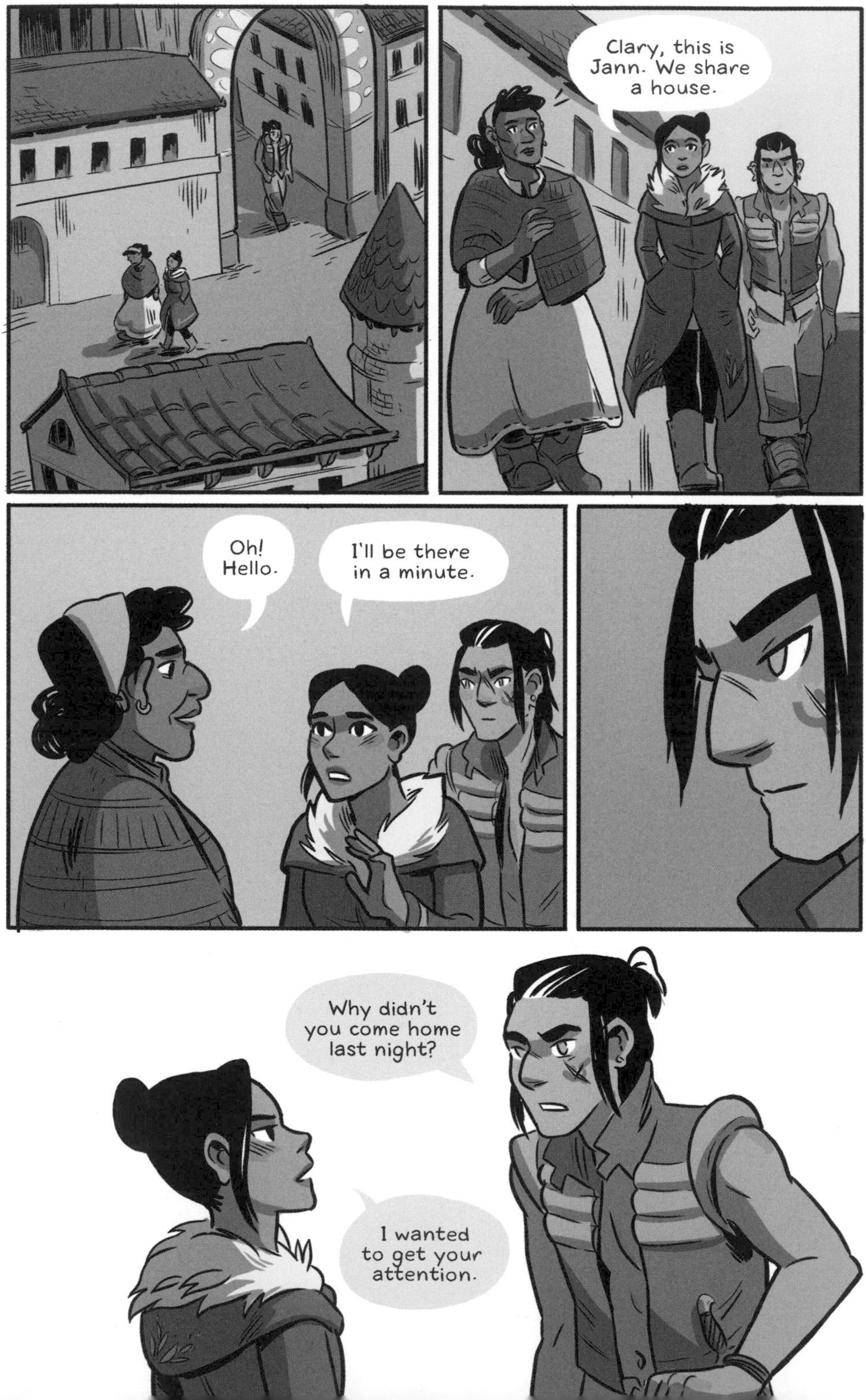
Clary, this is Jann. We share a house.
Oh! Hello.
I'll be there in a minute.
Why didn't you come home last night?
I wanted to get your attention.

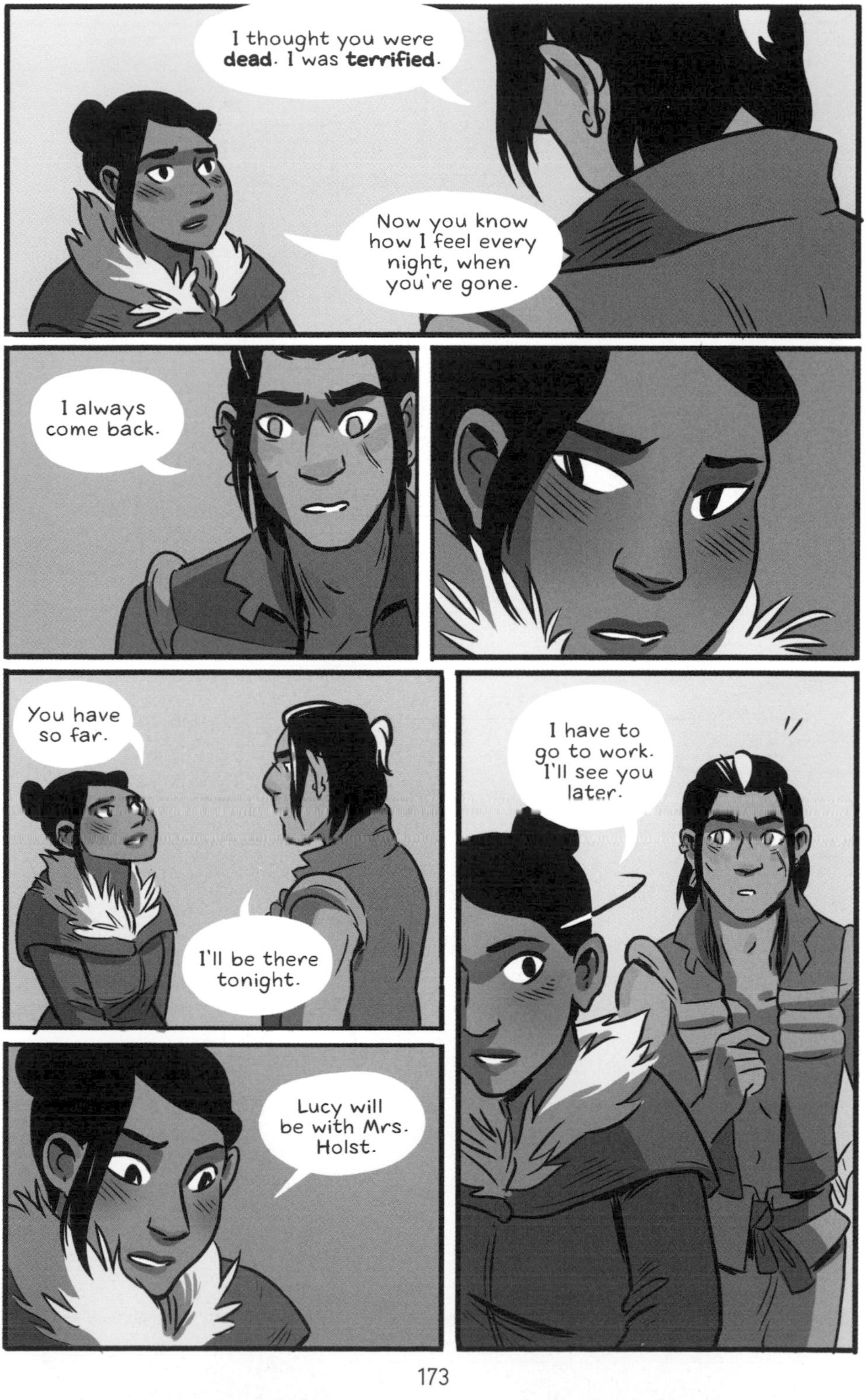
I thought you were **dead**. I was **terrified**.
Now you know how I feel every night, when you're gone.
I always come back.
You have so far.
I'll be there tonight.
Lucy will be with Mrs. Holst.
I have to go to work. I'll see you later.

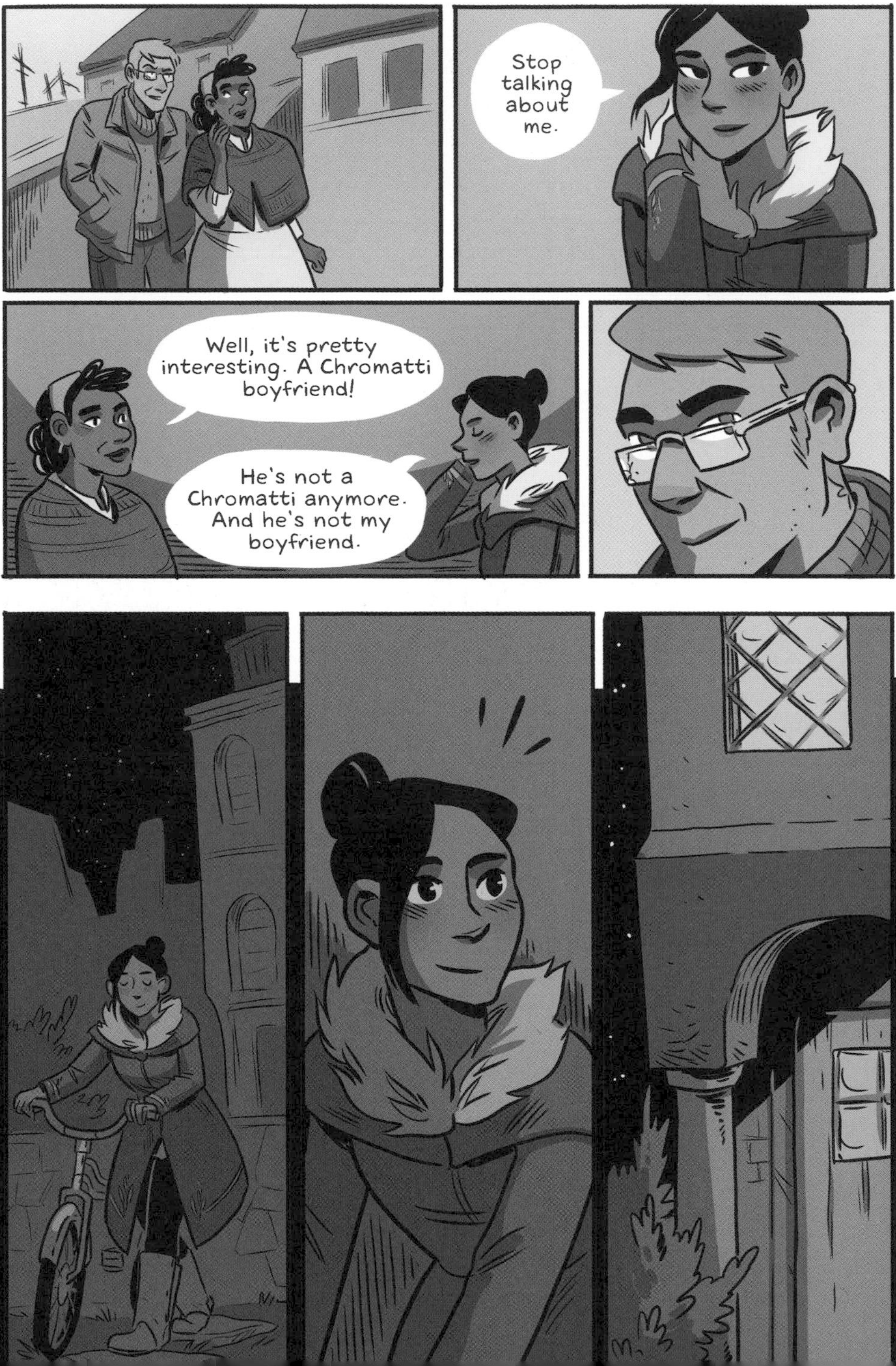
Stop talking about me.
Well, it's pretty interesting. A Chromatti boyfriend!
He's not a Chromatti anymore. And he's not my boyfriend.

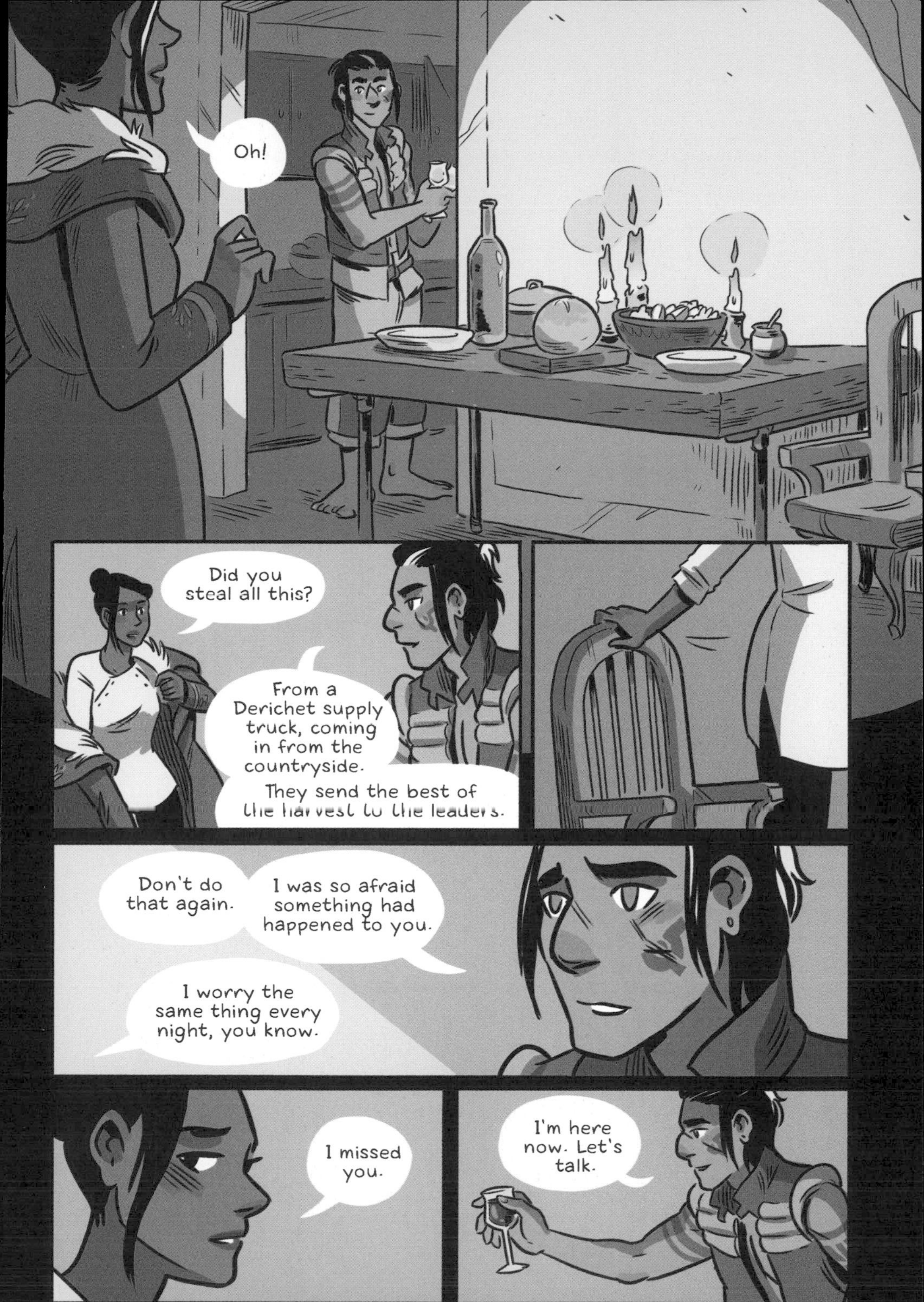
Oh!
Did you steal all this?
From a Derichet supply truck, coming in from the countryside.
They send the best of the harvest to the leaders.
Don't do that again.
I was so afraid something had happened to you.
I worry the same thing every night, you know.
I missed you.
I'm here now. Let's talk.

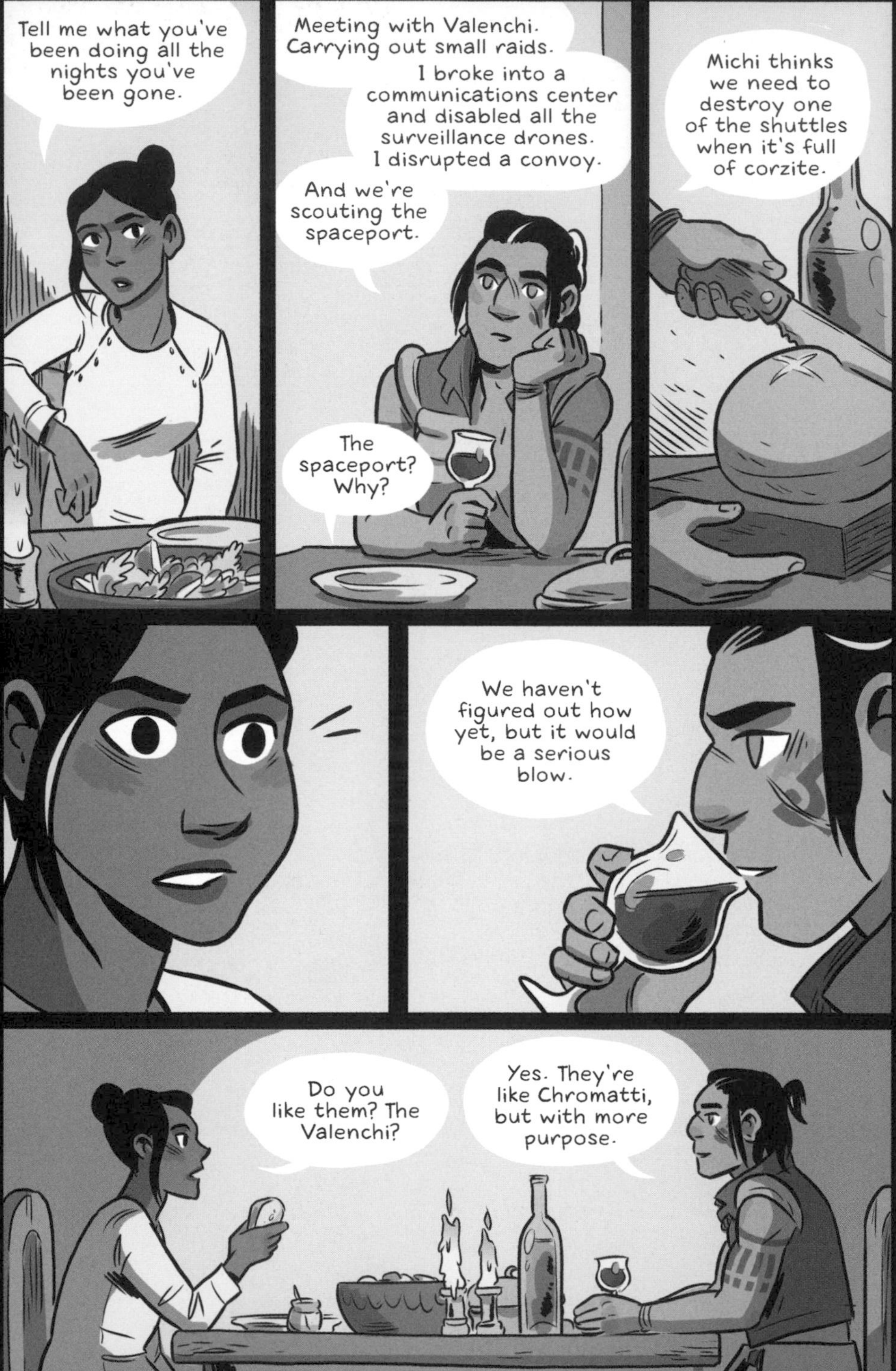
Tell me what you've been doing all the nights you've been gone.
Meeting with Valenchi. Carrying out small raids.
I broke into a communications center and disabled all the surveillance drones. I disrupted a convoy.
And we're scouting the spaceport.
The spaceport? Why?
Michi thinks we need to destroy one of the shuttles when it's full of corzite.
We haven't figured out how yet, but it would be a serious blow.
Do you like them? The Valenchi?
Yes. They're like Chromatti, but with more purpose.

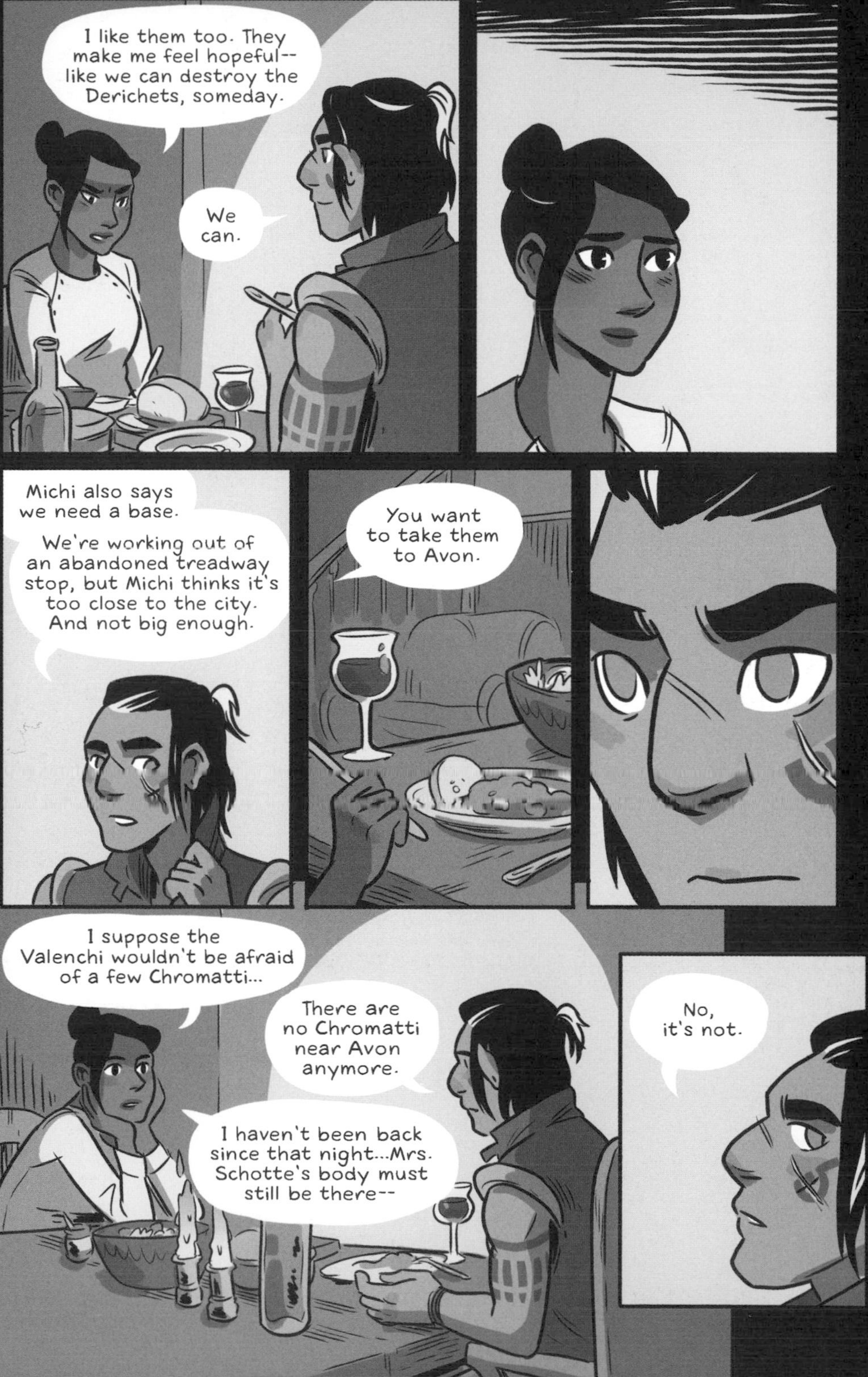
I like them too. They make me feel hopeful-- like we can destroy the Derichets, someday.
We can.
Michi also says we need a base.
We're working out of an abandoned treadway stop, but Michi thinks it's too close to the city. And not big enough.
You want to take them to Avon.
I suppose the Valenchi wouldn't be afraid of a few Chromatti...
There are no Chromatti near Avon anymore.
I haven't been back since that night...Mrs. Schotte's body must still be there--
No, it's not.

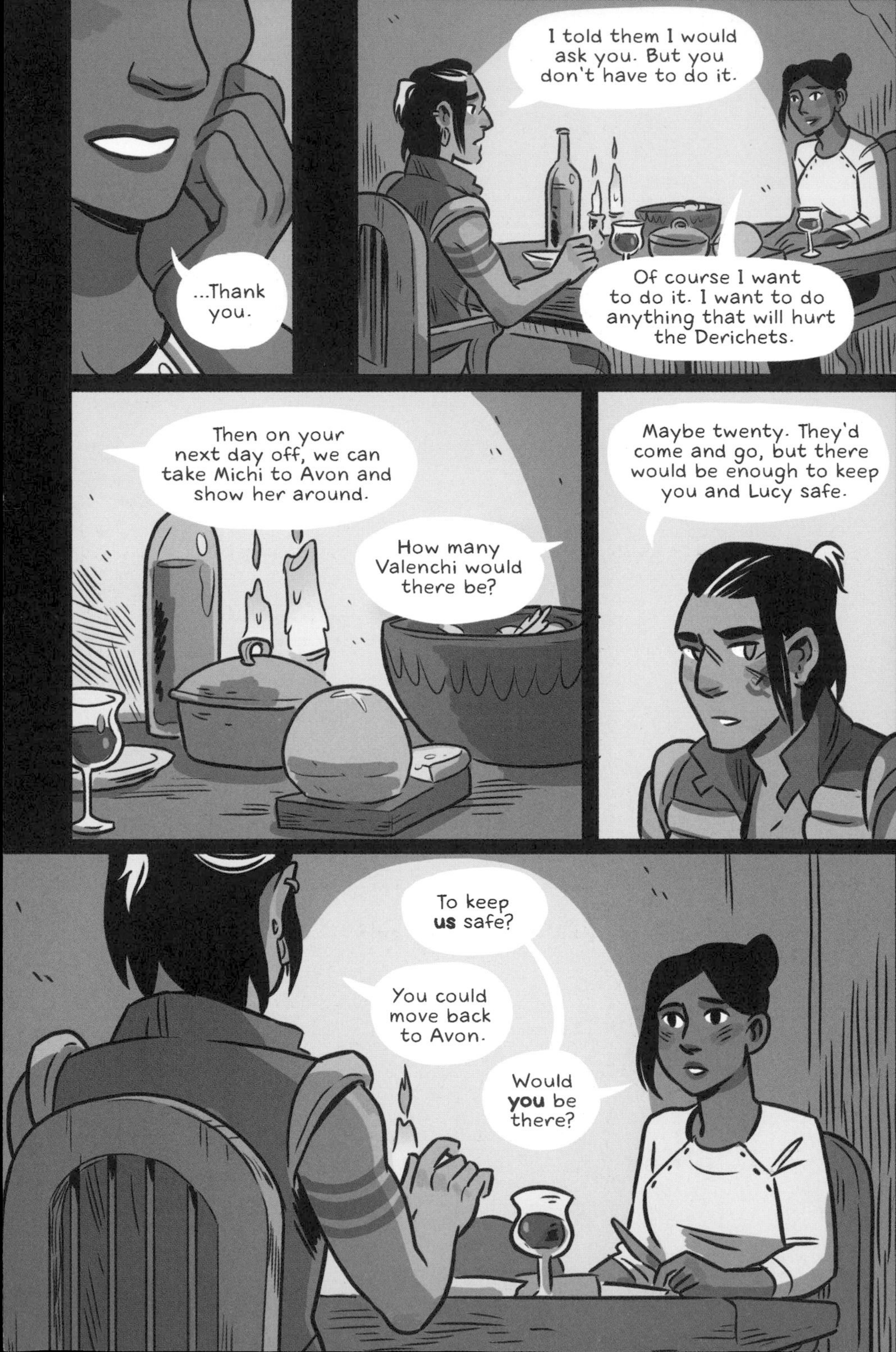

...Thank you.
I told them I would ask you. But you don't have to do it.
Of course I want to do it. I want to do anything that will hurt the Derichets.
Then on your next day off, we can take Michi to Avon and show her around.
How many Valenchi would there be?
Maybe twenty. They'd come and go, but there would be enough to keep you and Lucy safe.
To keep **us** safe?
You could move back to Avon.
Would **you** be there?

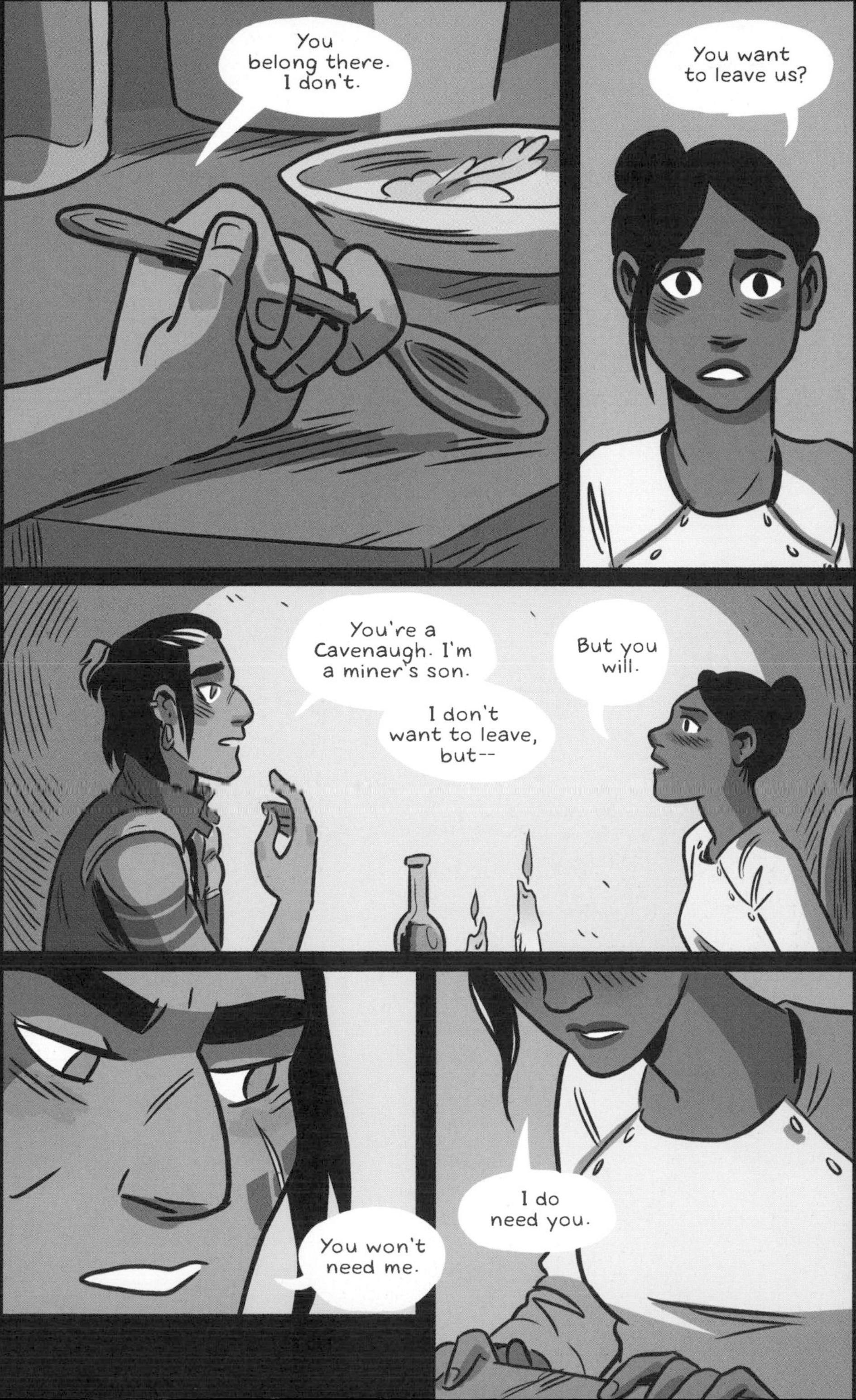
You belong there. I don't.
You want to leave us?
You're a Cavenaugh. I'm a miner's son.
I don't want to leave, but--
But you will.
You won't need me.
I do need you.

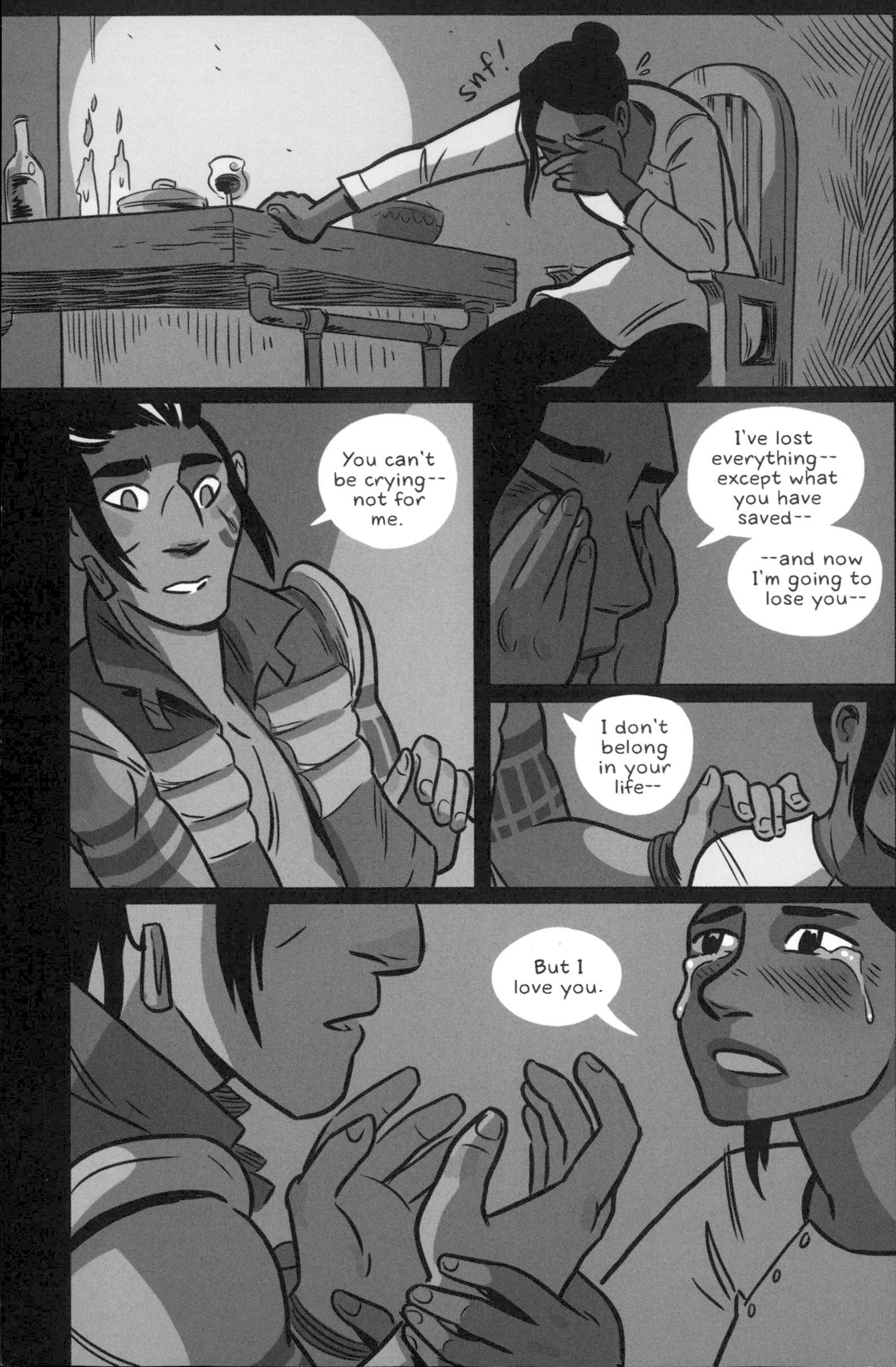
snf!
You can't be crying-- not for me.
I've lost everything-- except what you have saved--
--and now I'm going to lose you--
I don't belong in your life--
But I love you.

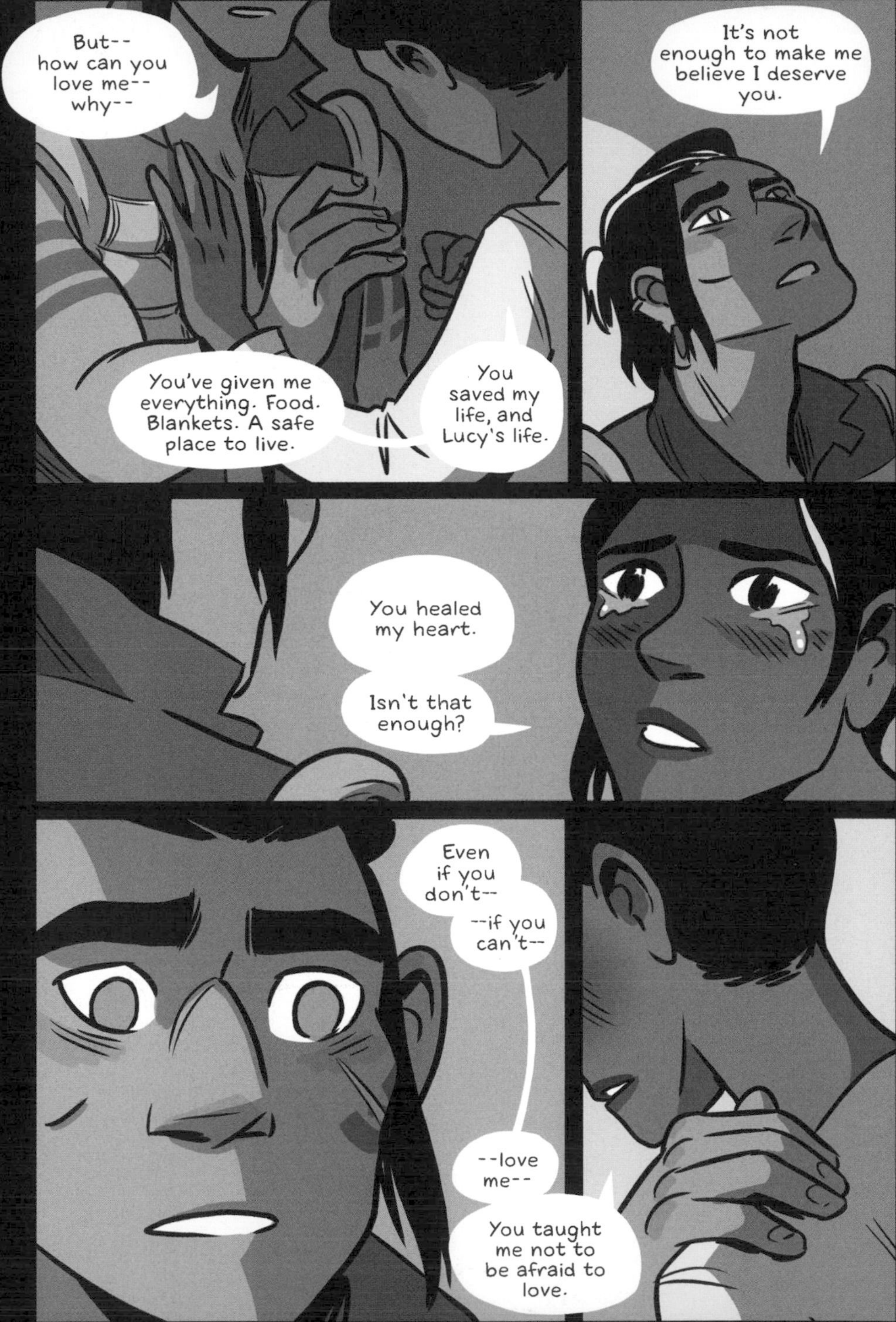
But-- how can you love me-- why--
You've given me everything. Food. Blankets. A safe place to live.
You saved my life, and Lucy's life.
It's not enough to make me believe I deserve you.
You healed my heart.
Isn't that enough?
Even if you don't--
--if you can't--
--love me--
You taught me not to be afraid to love.

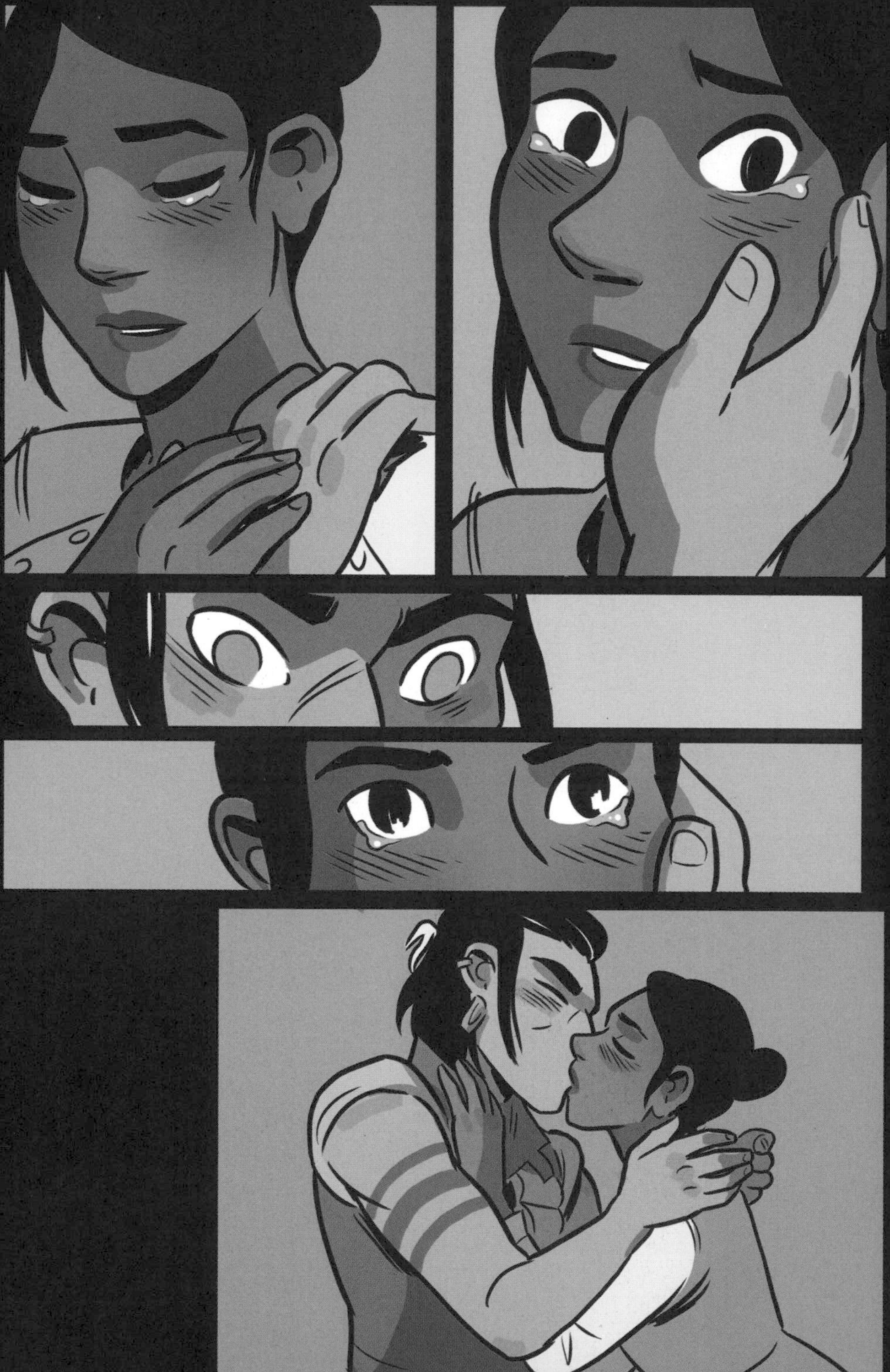

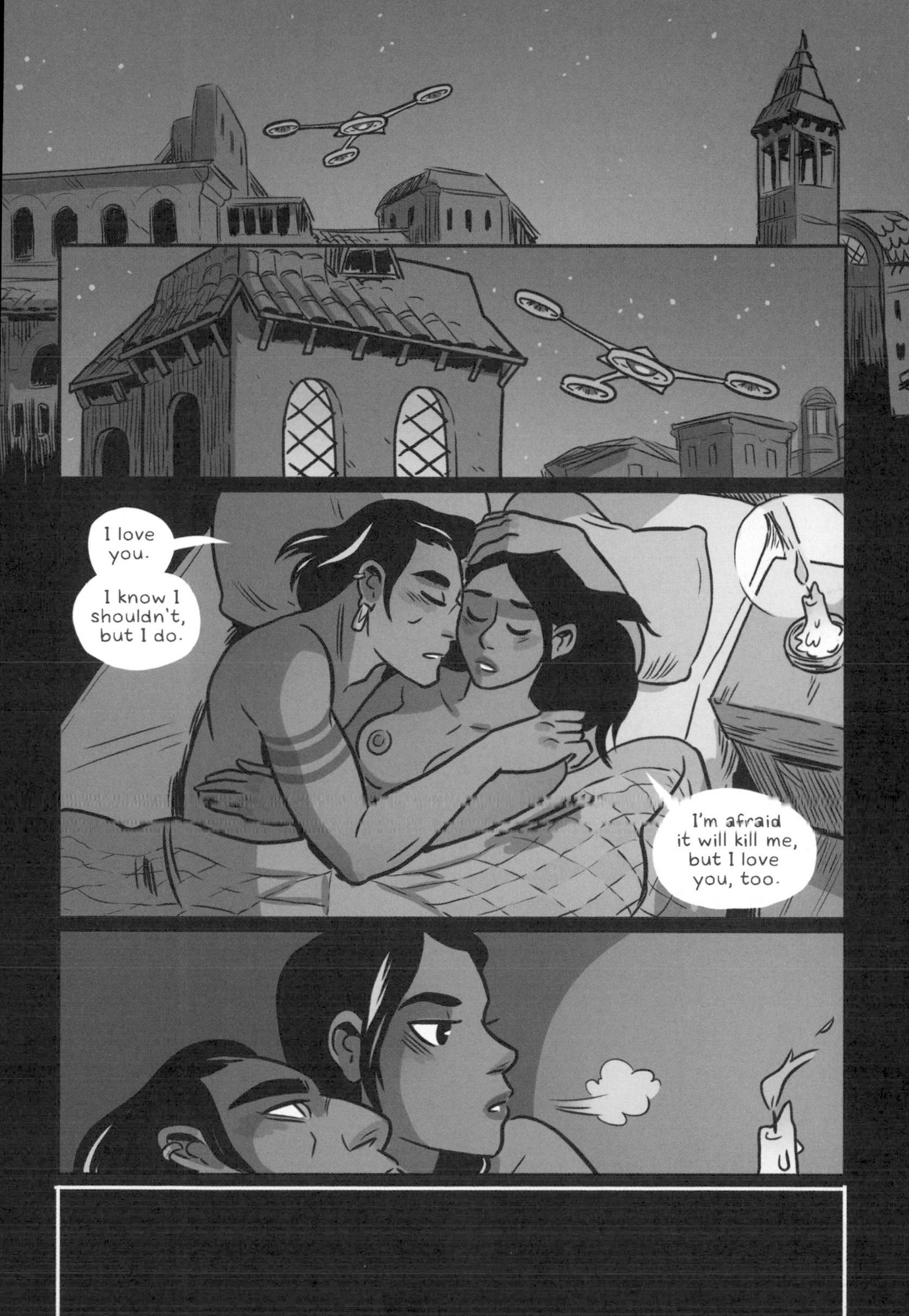
I love you.
I know I shouldn't, but I do.
I'm afraid it will kill me, but I love you, too.

part 3

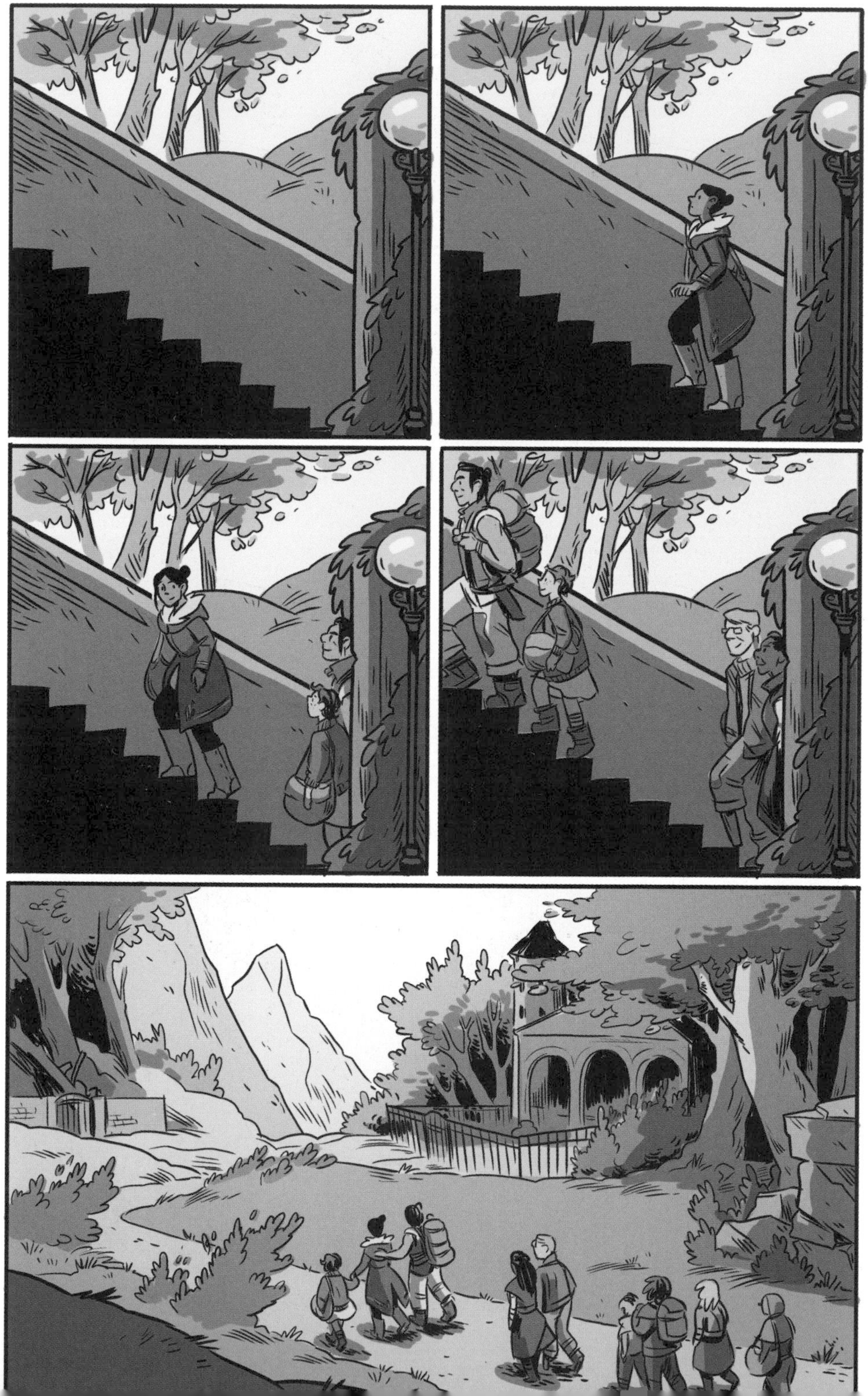

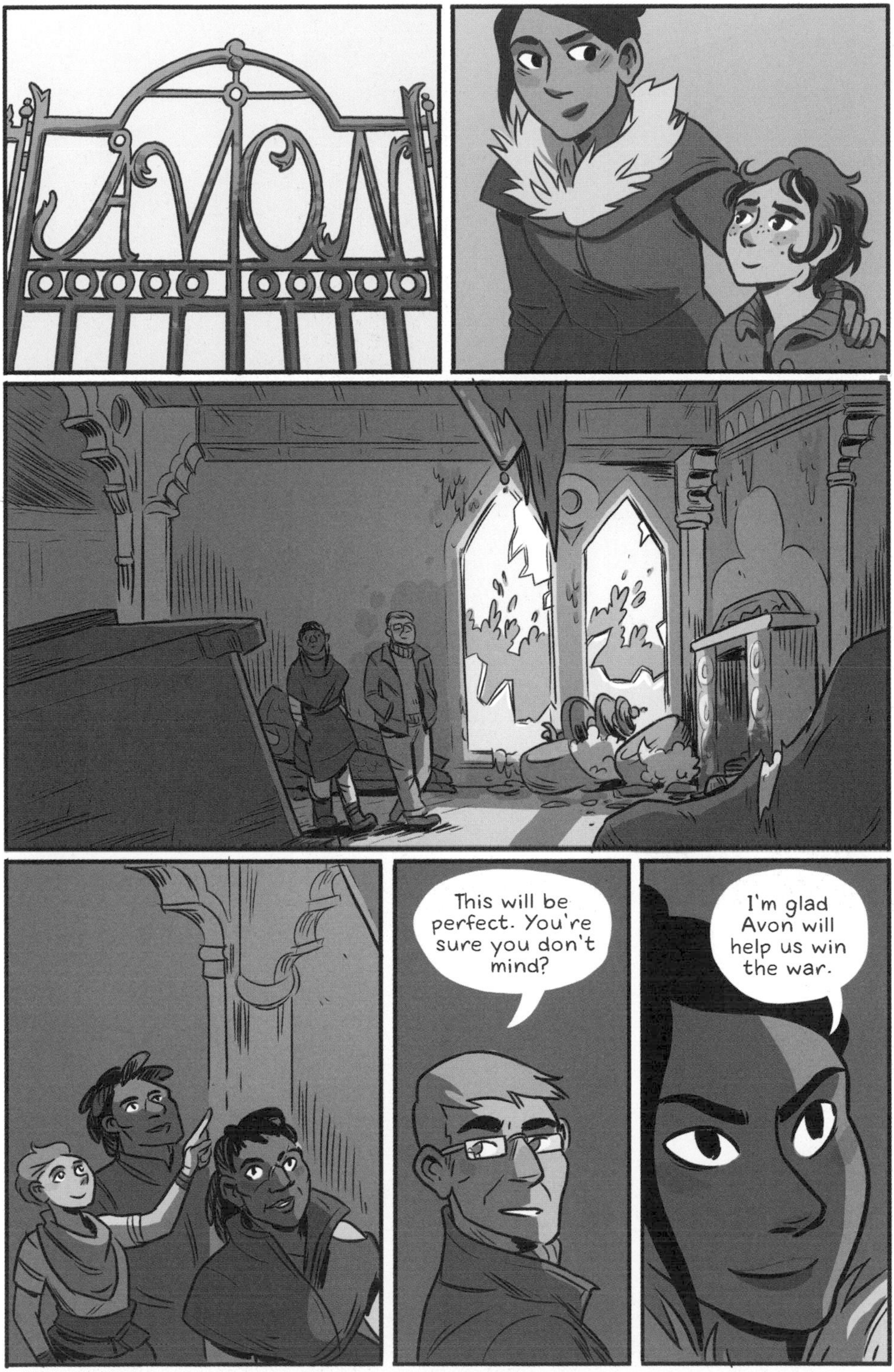
AVON
This will be perfect. You're sure you don't mind?
I'm glad Avon will help us win the war.

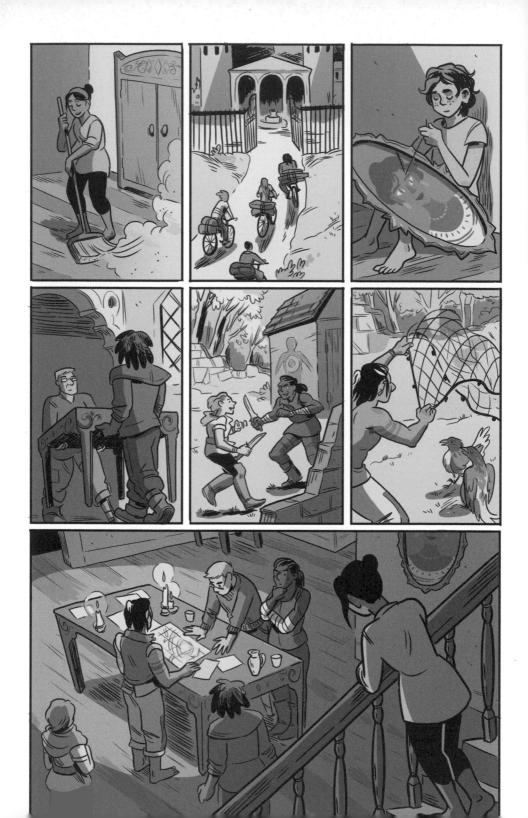

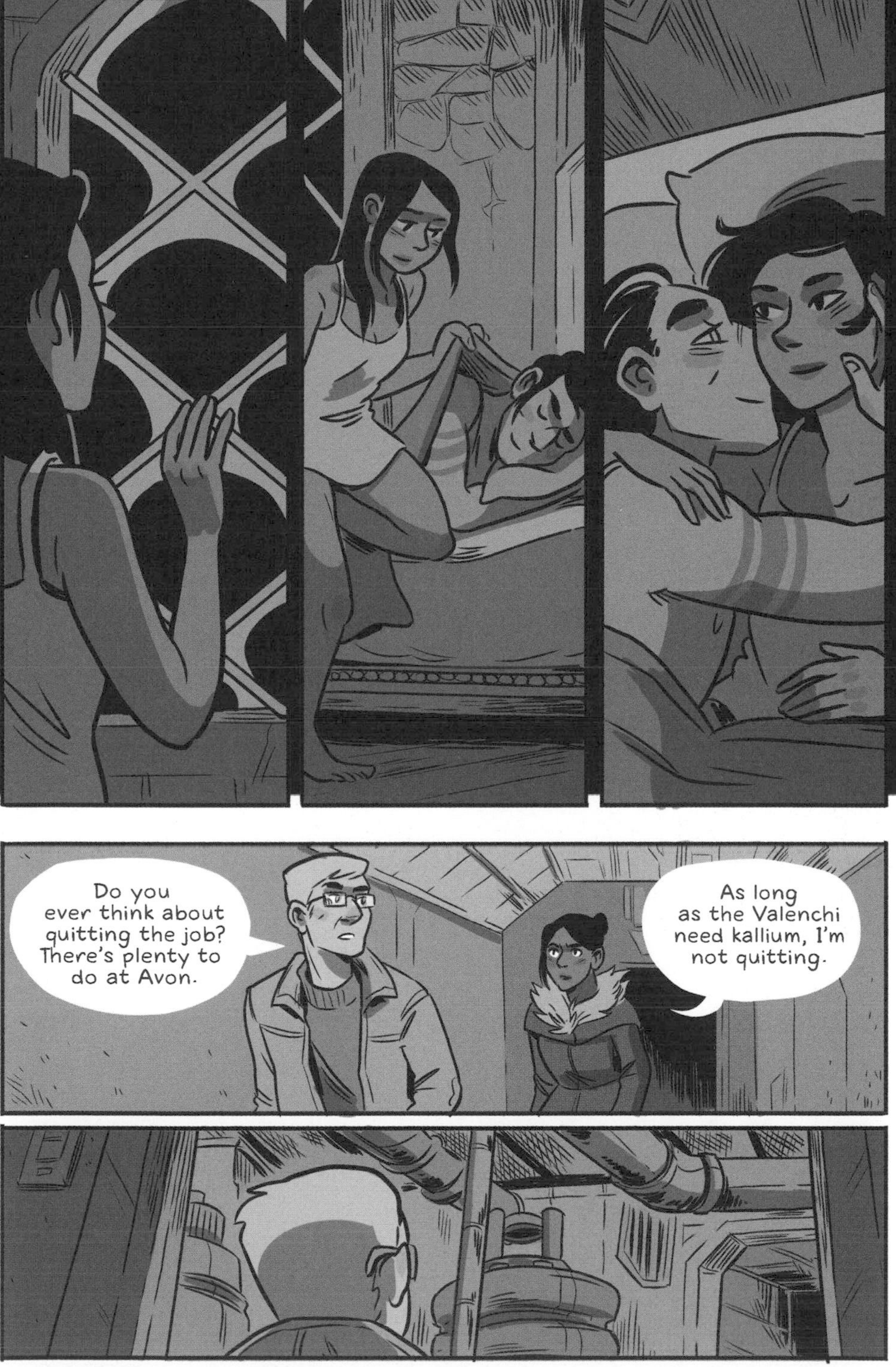
Do you ever think about quitting the job? There's plenty to do at Avon.
As long as the Valenchi need kallium, I'm not quitting.

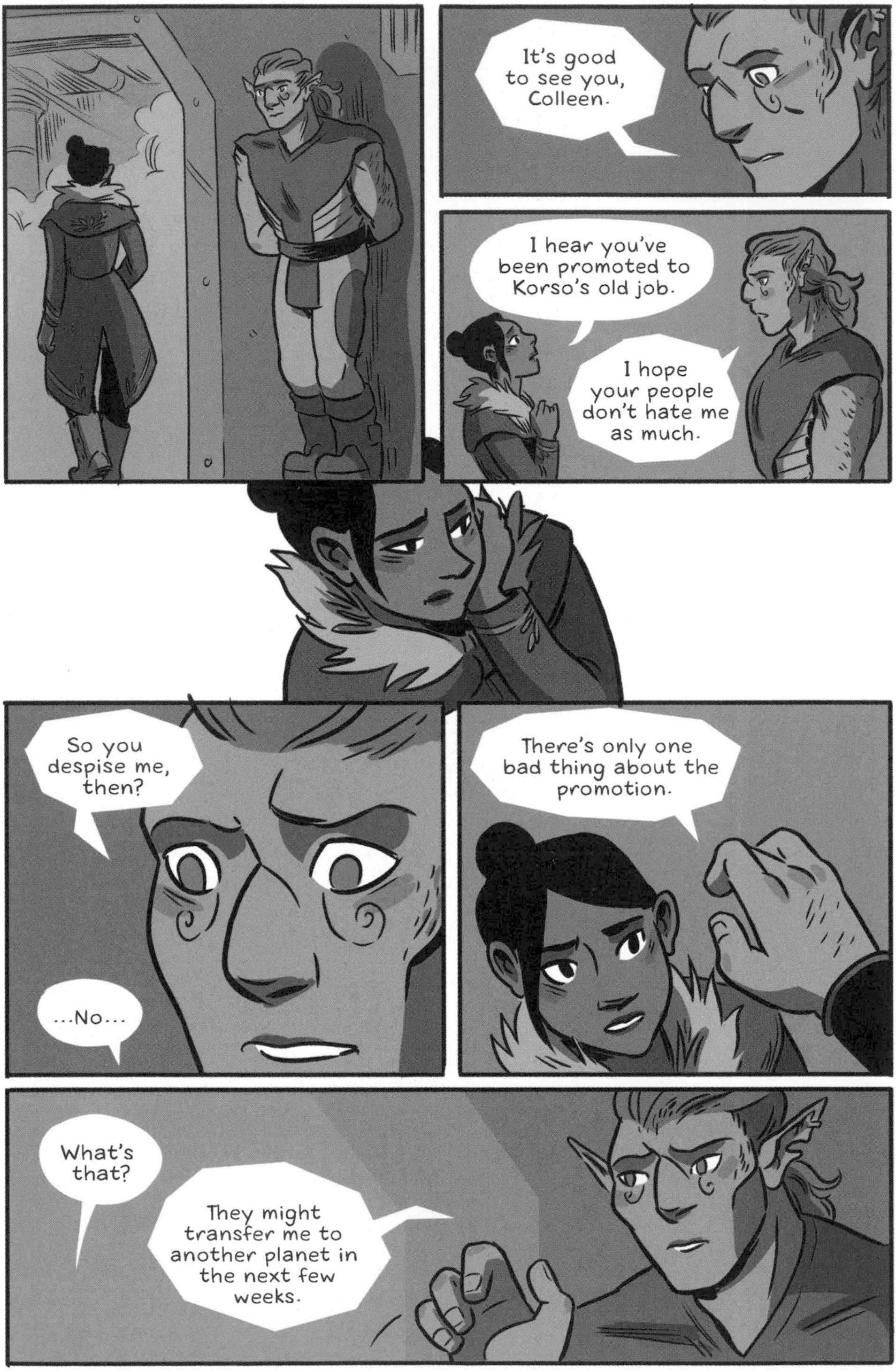
It's good to see you, Colleen.
I hear you've been promoted to Korso's old job.
I hope your people don't hate me as much.
So you despise me, then?
...No...
There's only one bad thing about the promotion.
What's that?
They might transfer me to another planet in the next few weeks.

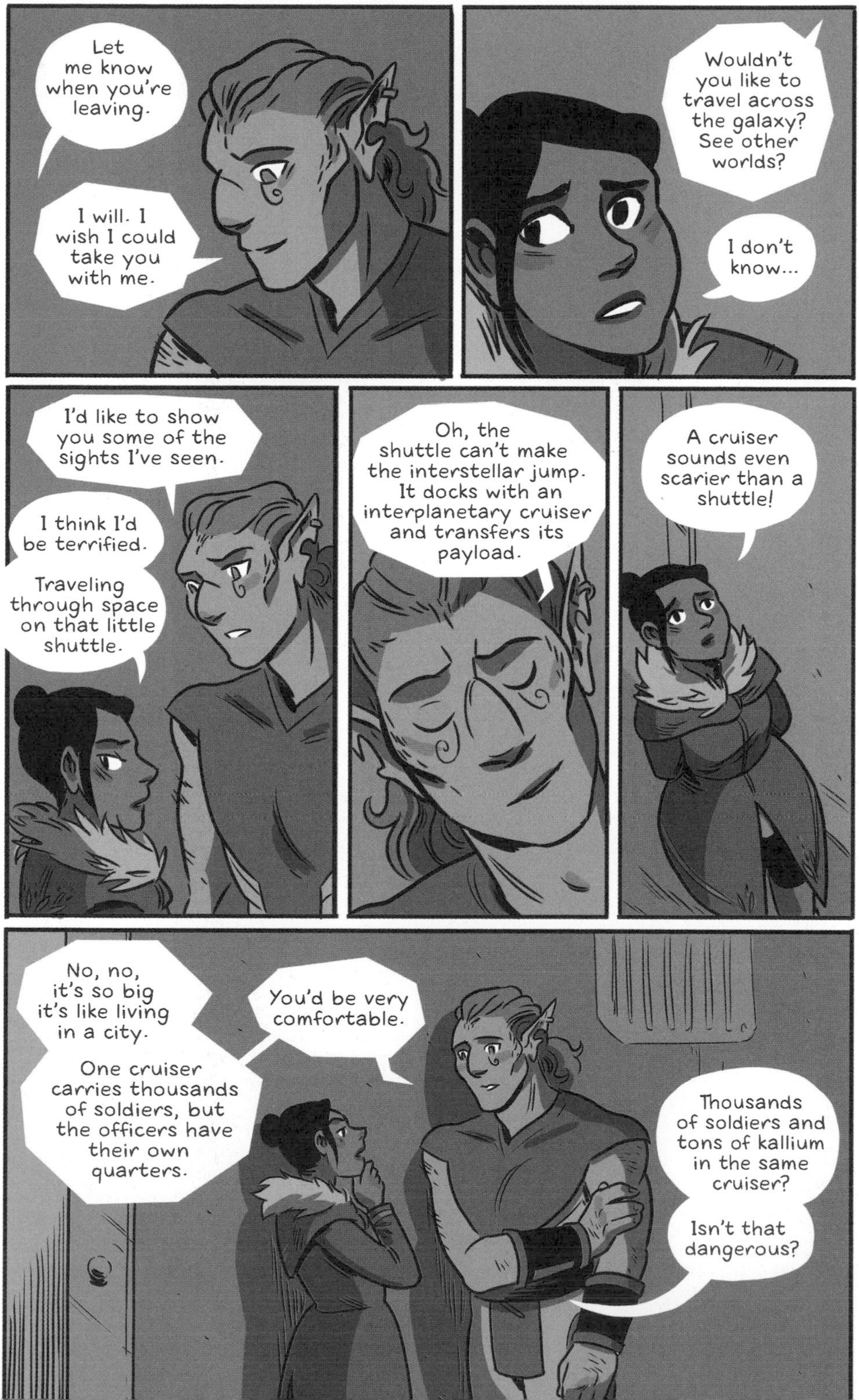
Let me know when you're leaving.
I will. I wish I could take you with me.
Wouldn't you like to travel across the galaxy? See other worlds?
I don't know...
I'd like to show you some of the sights I've seen.
I think I'd be terrified.
Traveling through space on that little shuttle.
Oh, the shuttle can't make the interstellar jump. It docks with an interplanetary cruiser and transfers its payload.
A cruiser sounds even scarier than a shuttle!
No, no, it's so big it's like living in a city.
One cruiser carries thousands of soldiers, but the officers have their own quarters.
You'd be very comfortable.
Thousands of soldiers and tons of kallium in the same cruiser?
Isn't that dangerous?

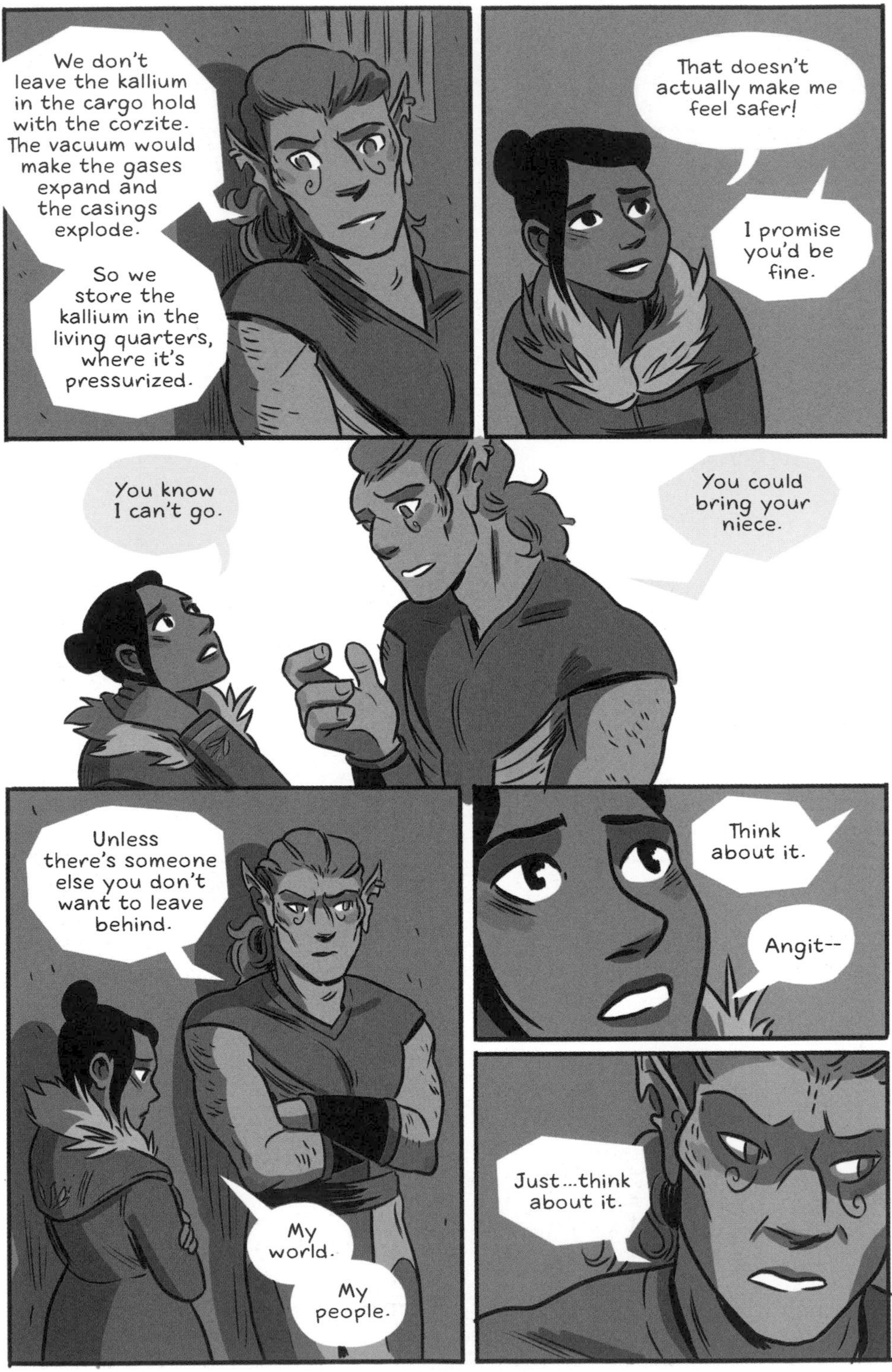
We don't leave the kallium in the cargo hold with the corzite. The vacuum would make the gases expand and the casings explode.
So we store the kallium in the living quarters, where it's pressurized.
That doesn't actually make me feel safer!
I promise you'd be fine.
You know I can't go.
You could bring your niece.
Unless there's someone else you don't want to leave behind.
My world.
My people.
Think about it.
Angit--
Just...think about it.

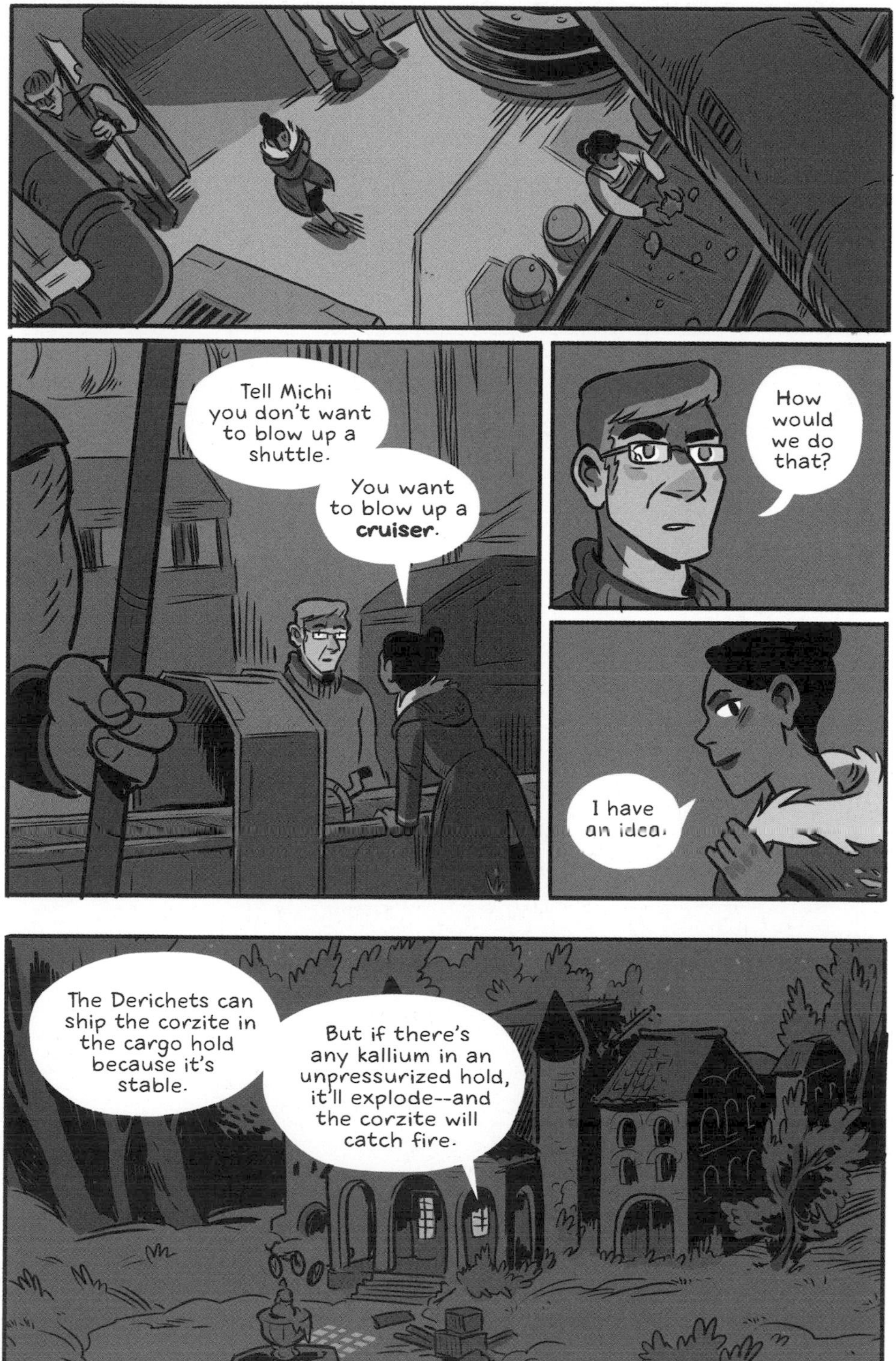
Tell Michi you don't want to blow up a shuttle.
You want to blow up a **cruiser**.
How would we do that?
I have an idea.
The Derichets can ship the corzite in the cargo hold because it's stable.
But if there's any kallium in an unpressurized hold, it'll explode--and the corzite will catch fire.

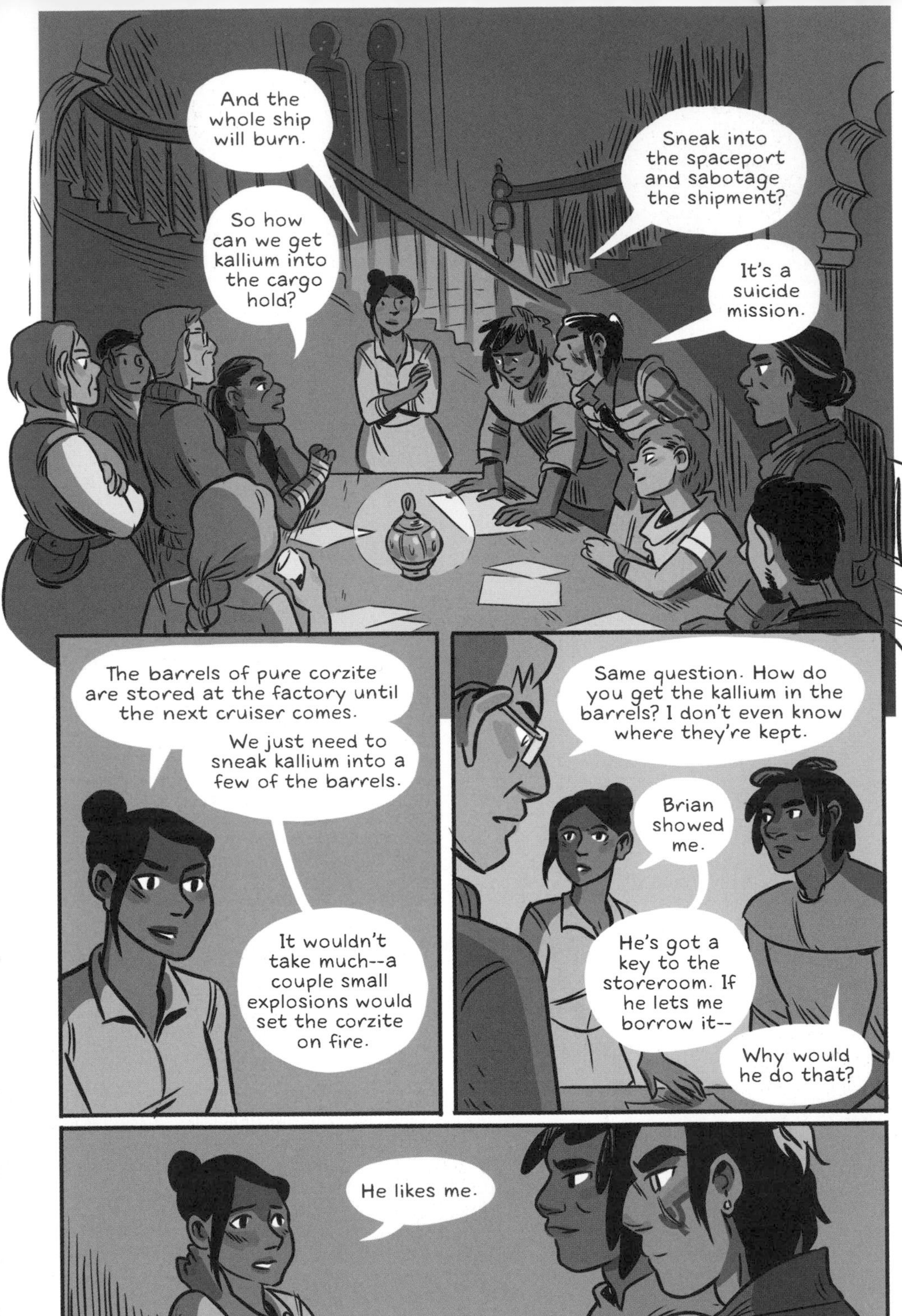

And the whole ship will burn.
So how can we get kallium into the cargo hold?
Sneak into the spaceport and sabotage the shipment?
It's a suicide mission.
The barrels of pure corzite are stored at the factory until the next cruiser comes.
We just need to sneak kallium into a few of the barrels.
It wouldn't take much--a couple small explosions would set the corzite on fire.
Same question. How do you get the kallium in the barrels? I don't even know where they're kept.
Brian showed me.
He's got a key to the storeroom. If he lets me borrow it--
Why would he do that?
He likes me.

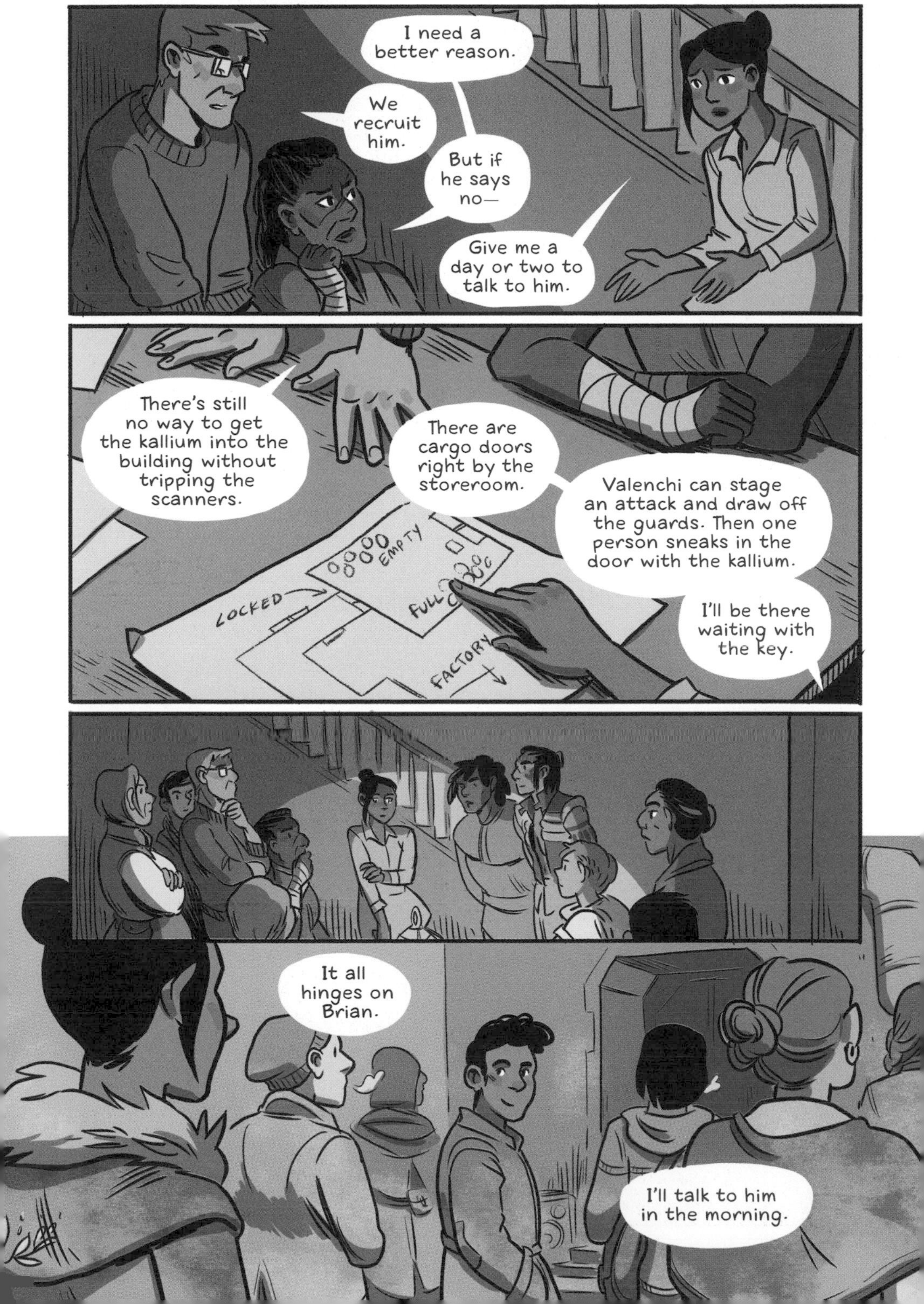
I need a better reason.
We recruit him.
But if he says no—
Give me a day or two to talk to him.
There's still no way to get the kallium into the building without tripping the scanners.
There are cargo doors right by the storeroom.
EMPTY
LOCKED
FULL
FACTORY
Valenchi can stage an attack and draw off the guards. Then one person sneaks in the door with the kallium.
I'll be there waiting with the key.
It all hinges on Brian.
I'll talk to him in the morning.

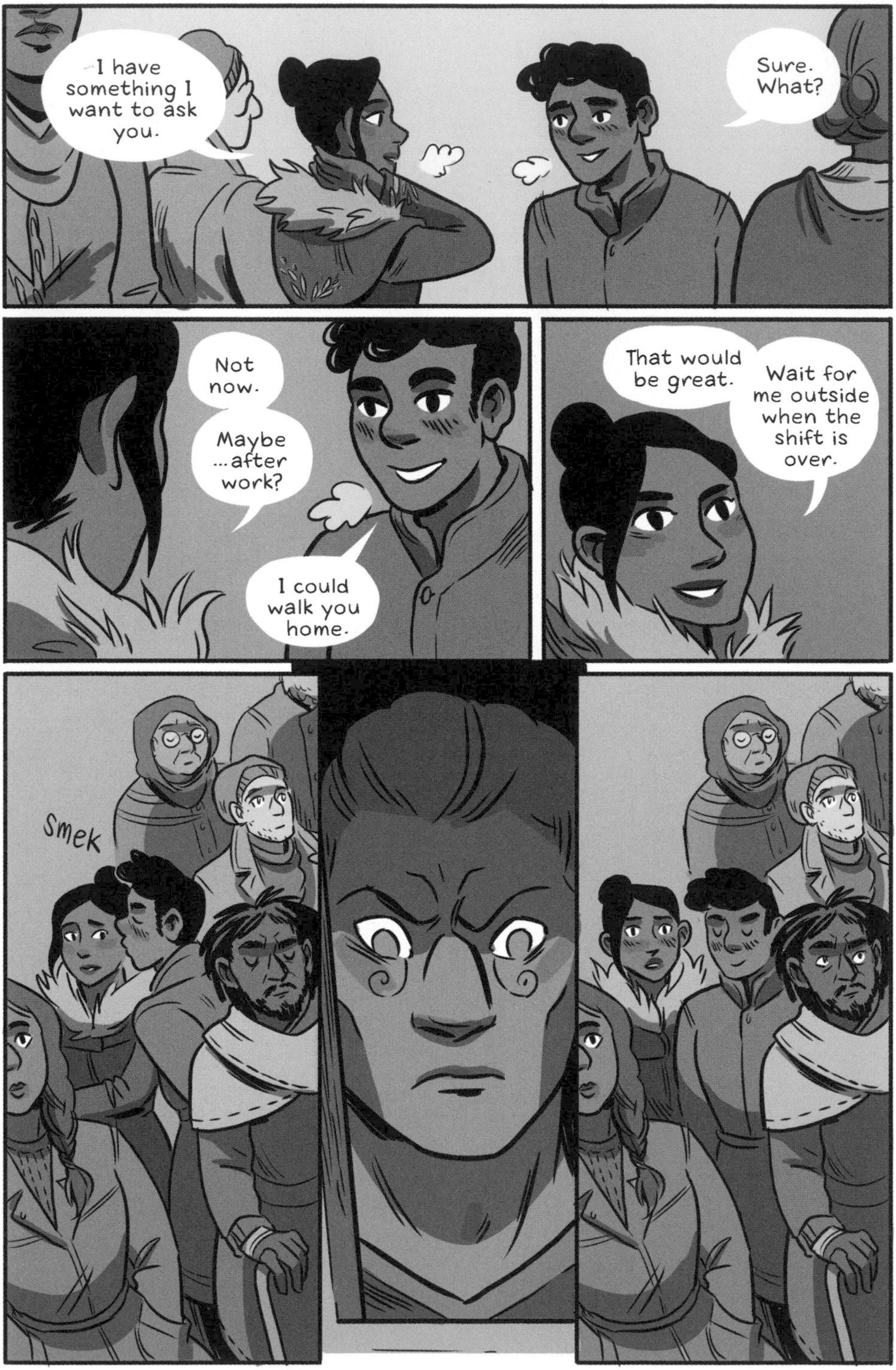
I have something I want to ask you.
Sure. What?
Not now.
Maybe ...after work?
I could walk you home.
That would be great.
Wait for me outside when the shift is over.
Smek

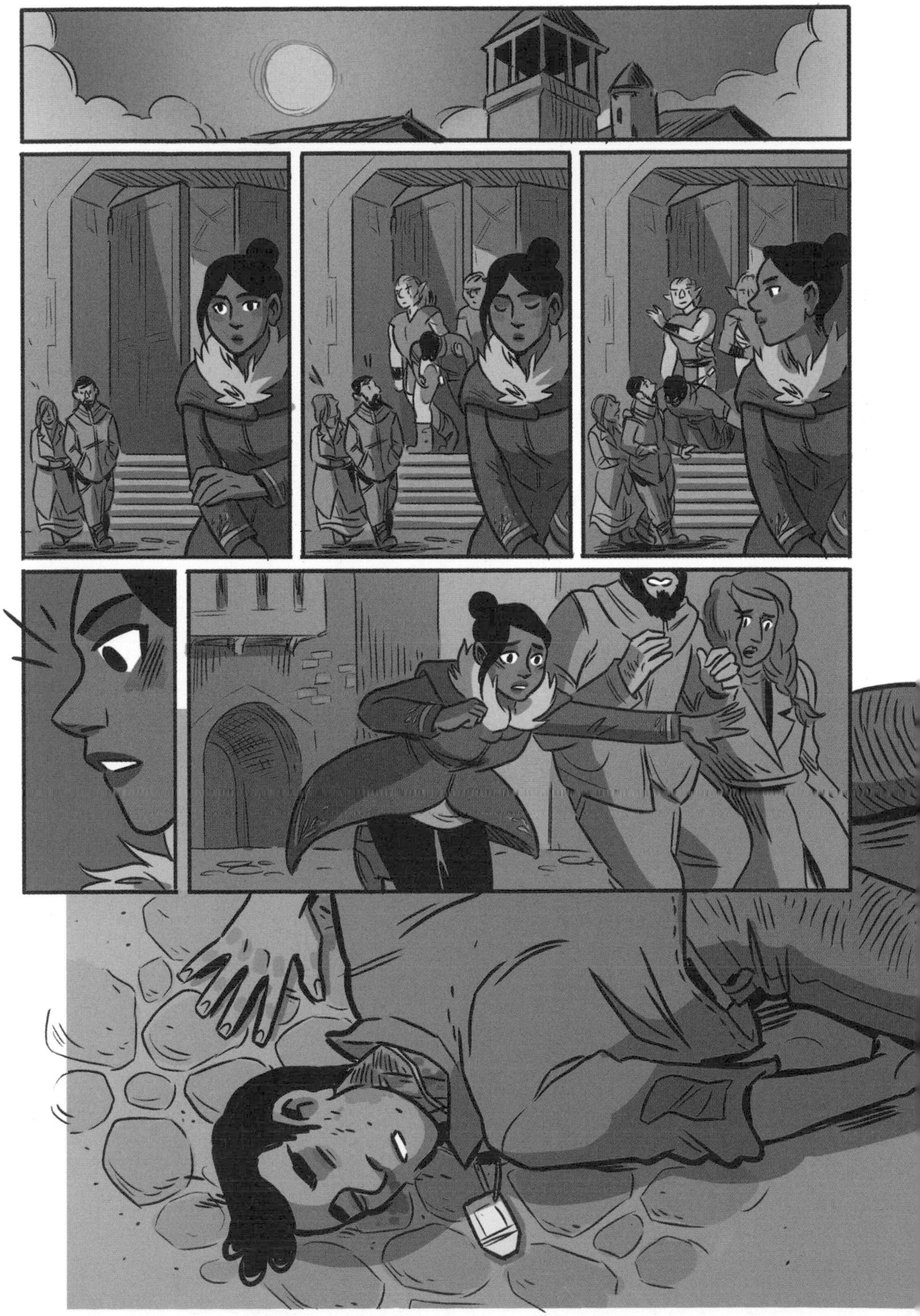

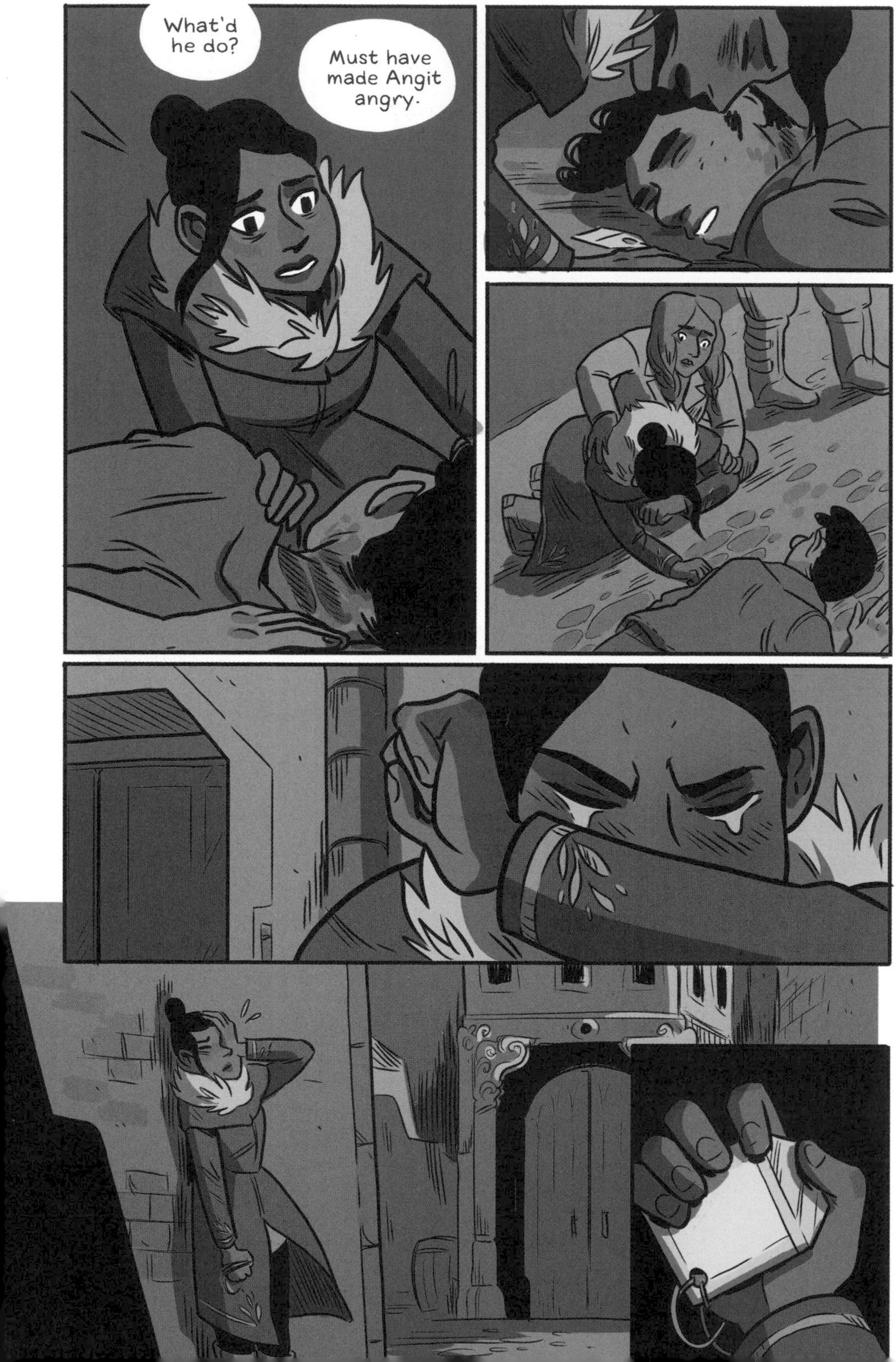
What'd he do?
Must have made Angit angry.

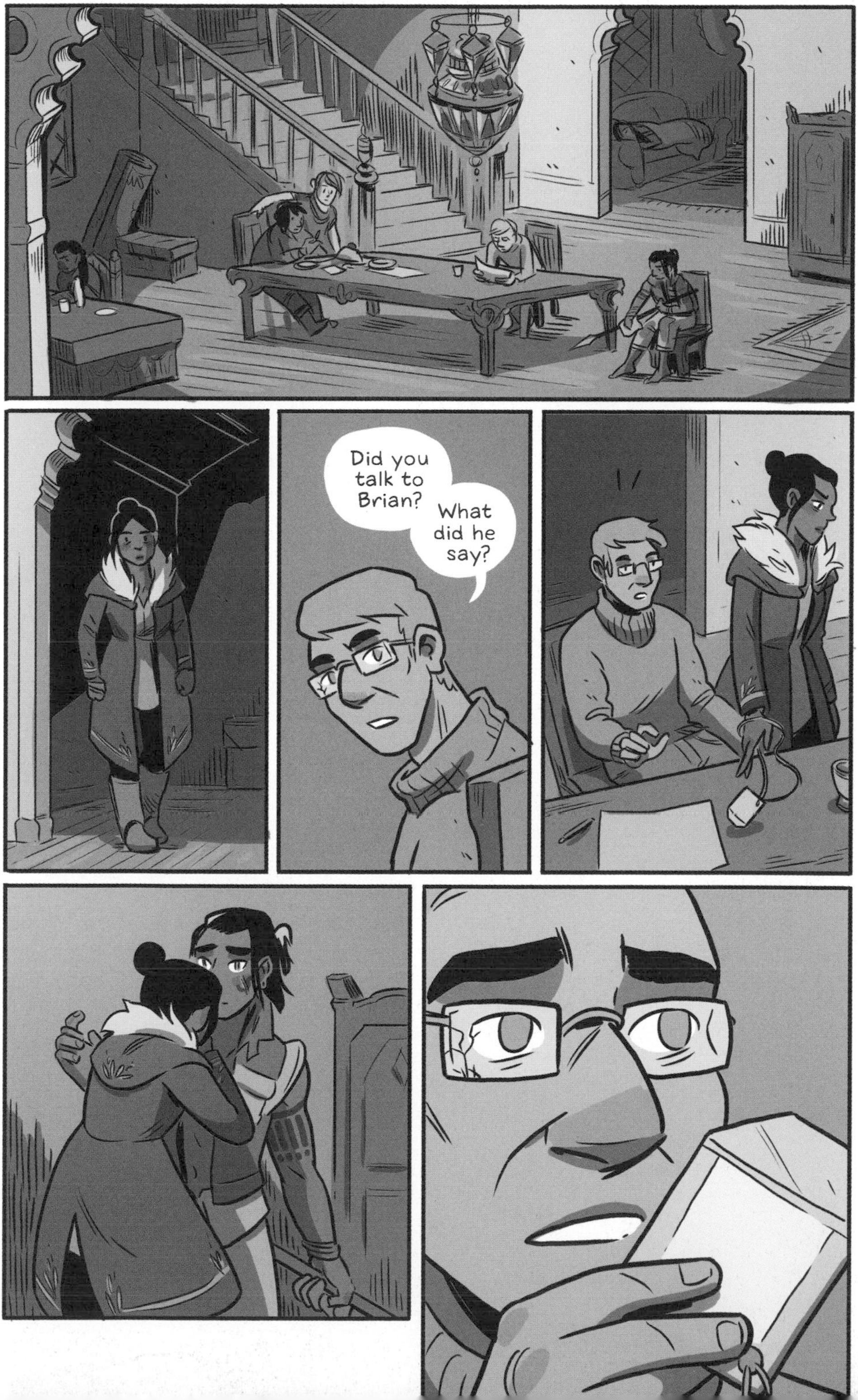
Did you talk to Brian?
What did he say?

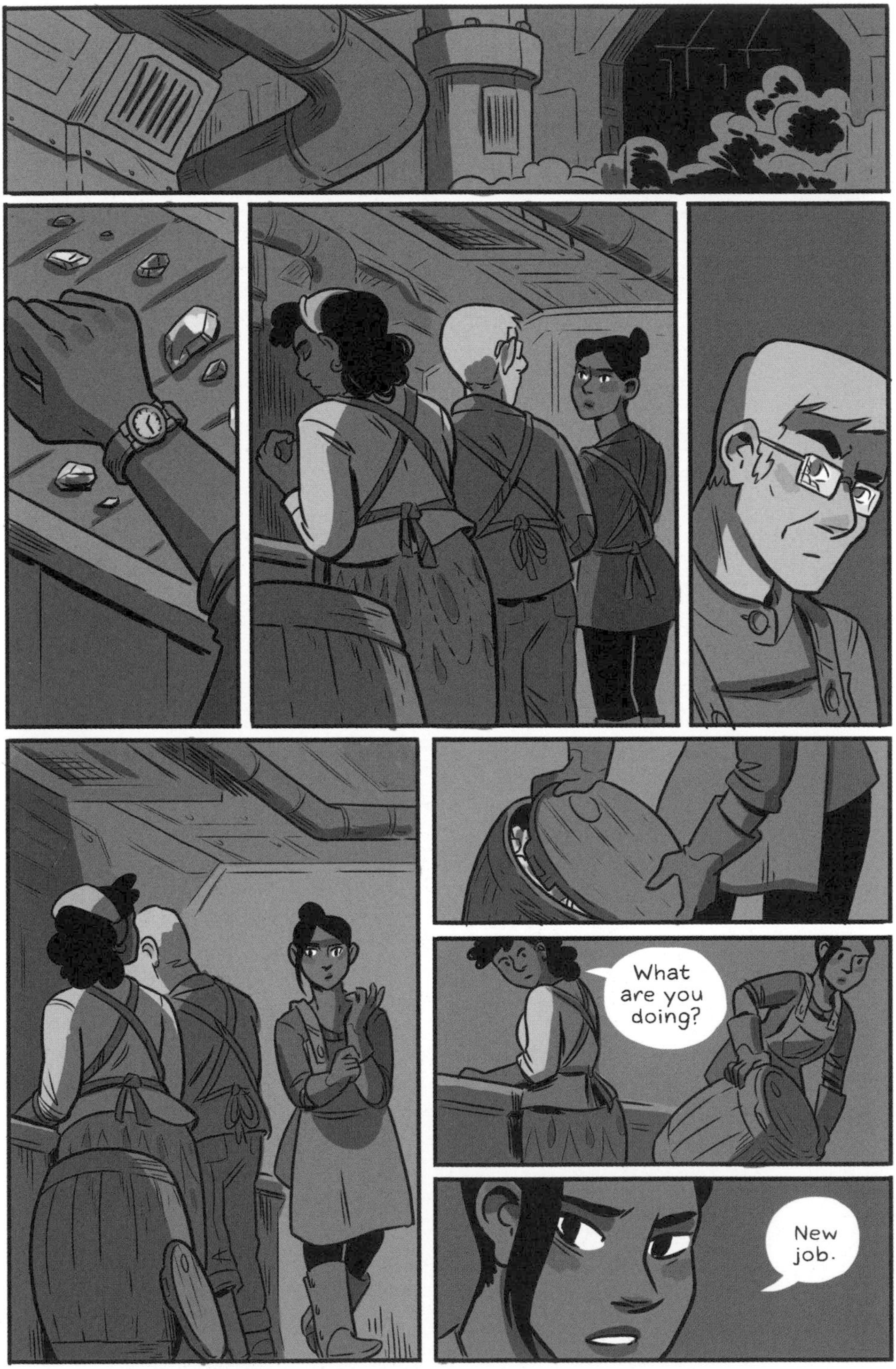
What are you doing?
New job.

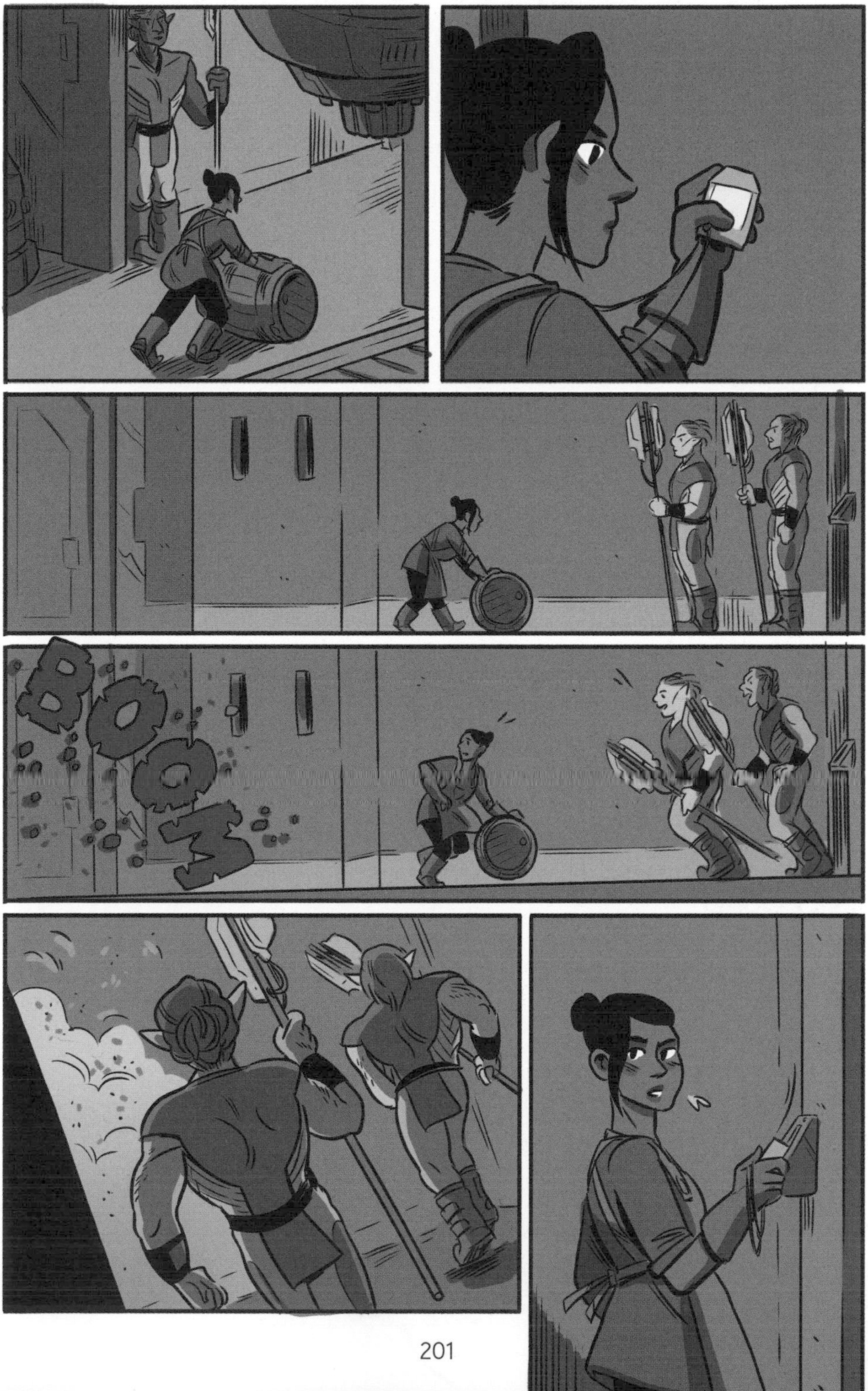
BOOM

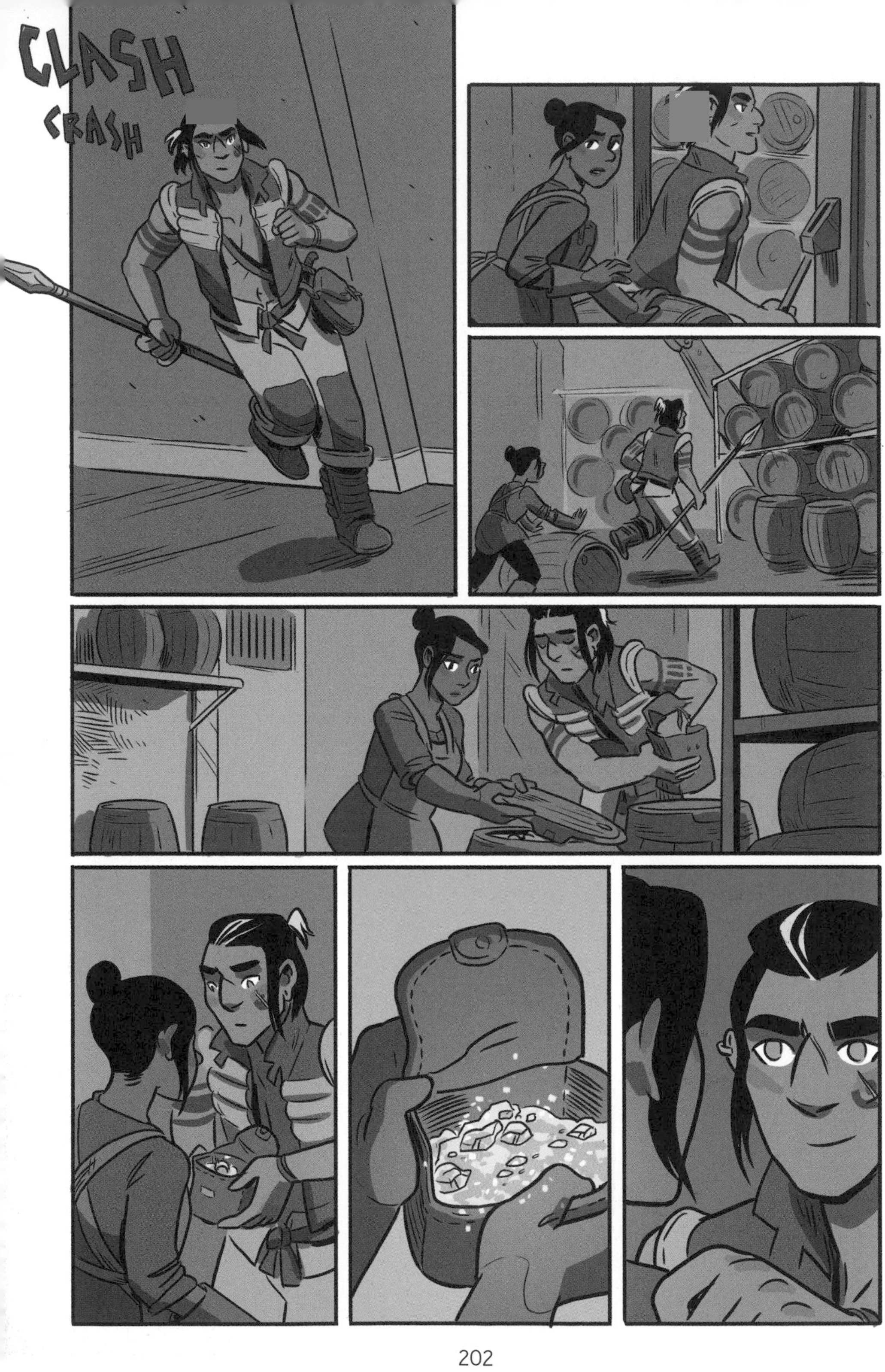
CLASH
CRASH

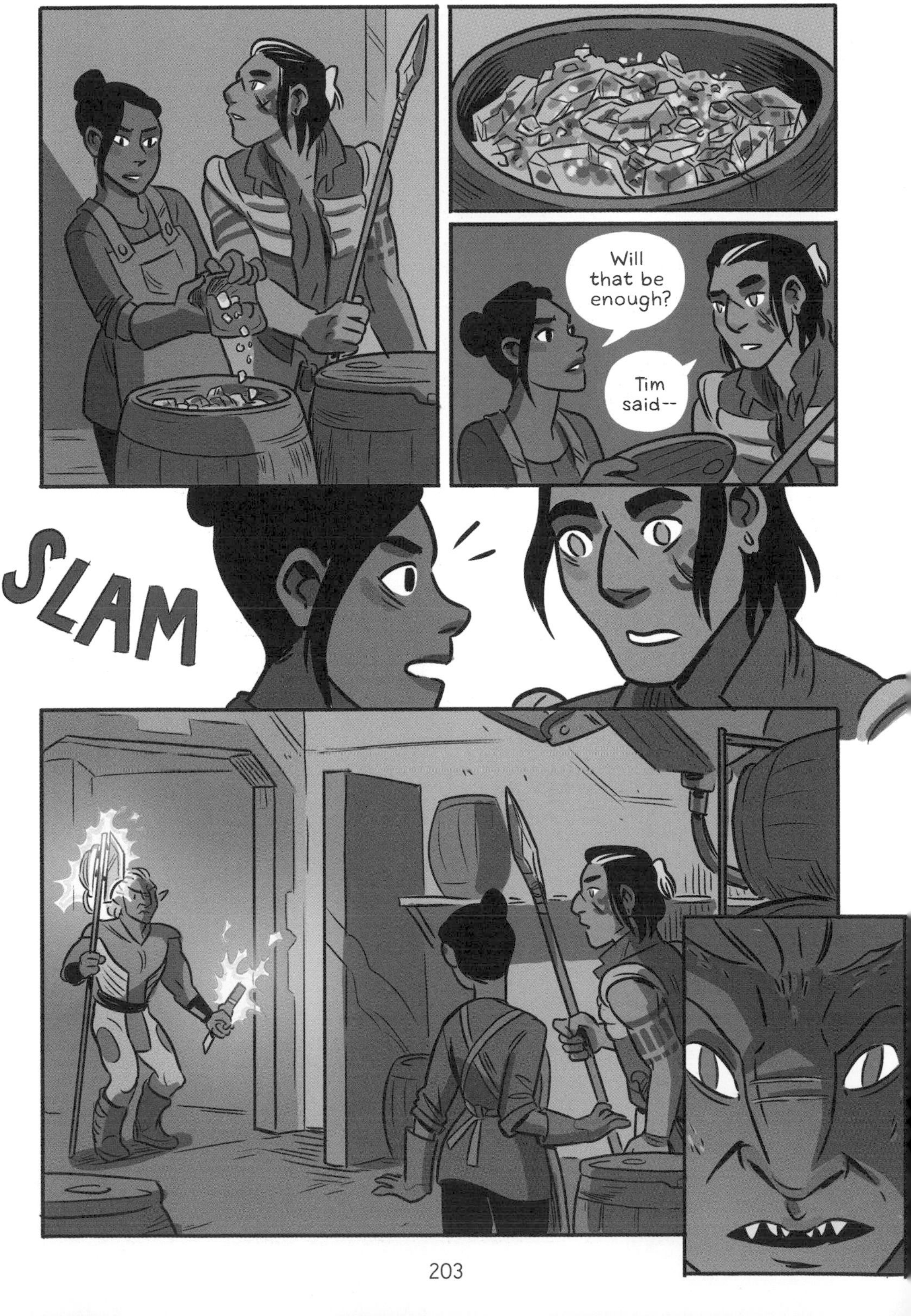
Will that be enough?
Tim said--
SLAM

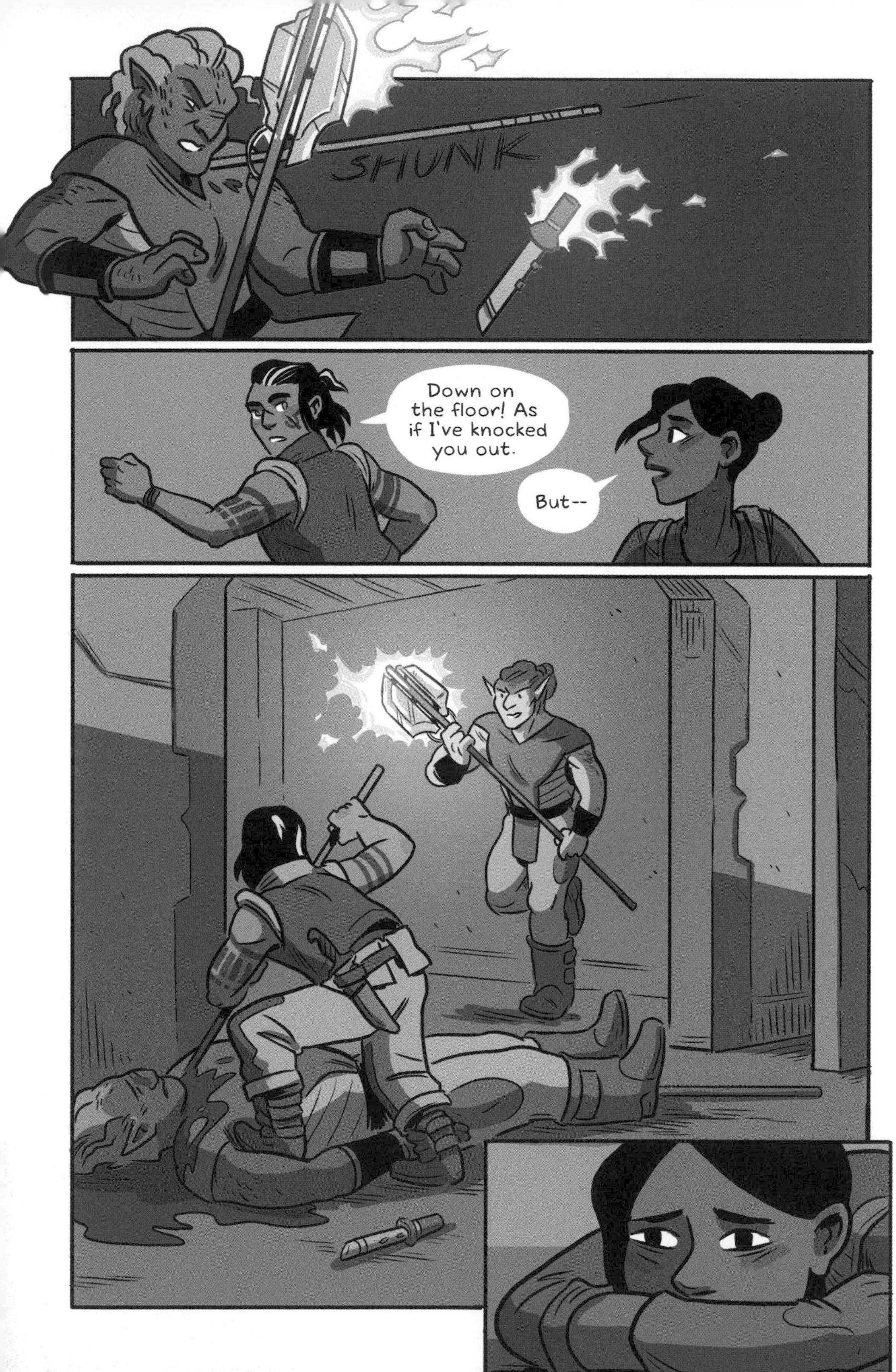
SHUNK
Down on the floor! As if I've knocked you out.
But--

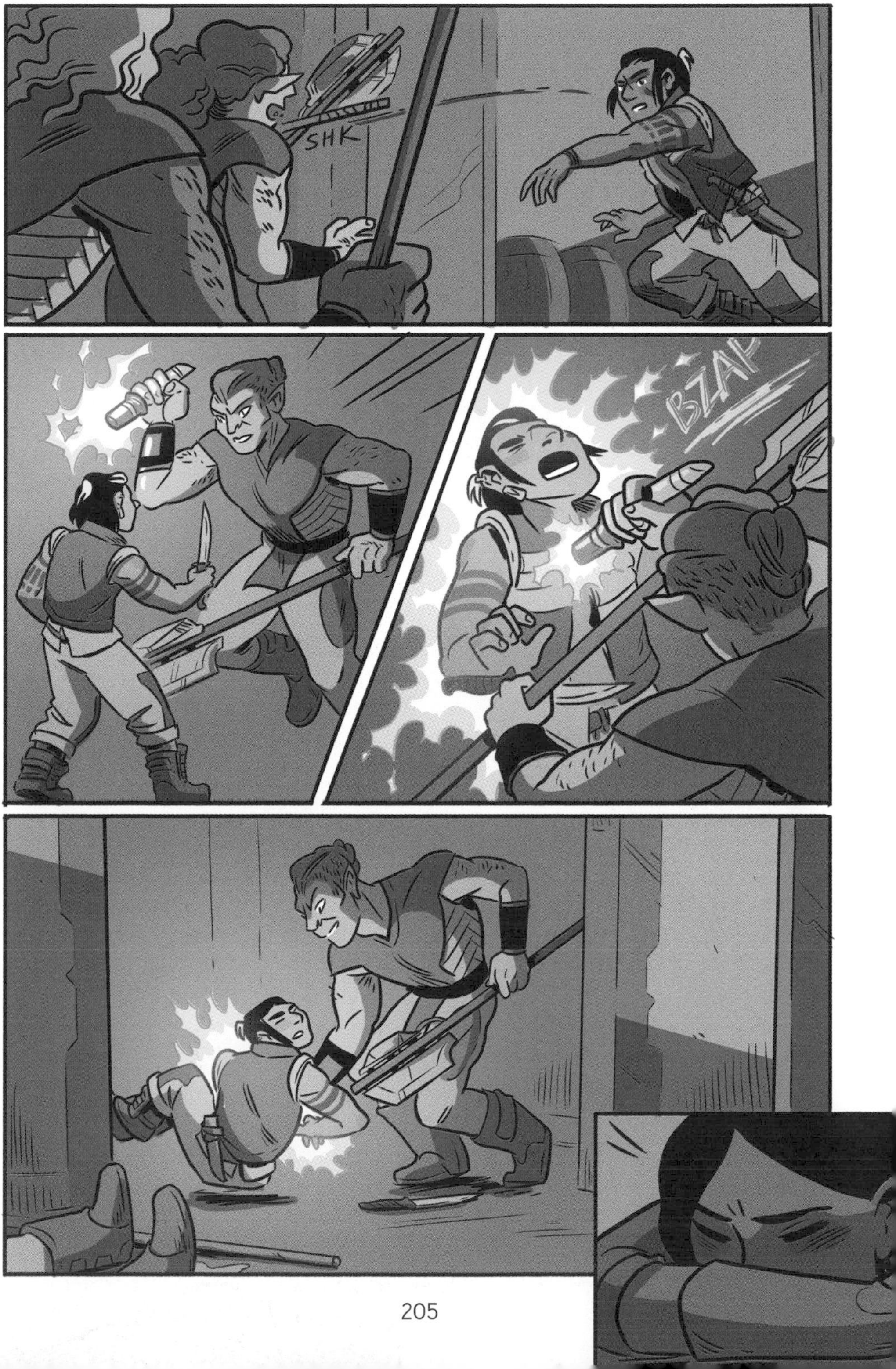
SHK
BZAP

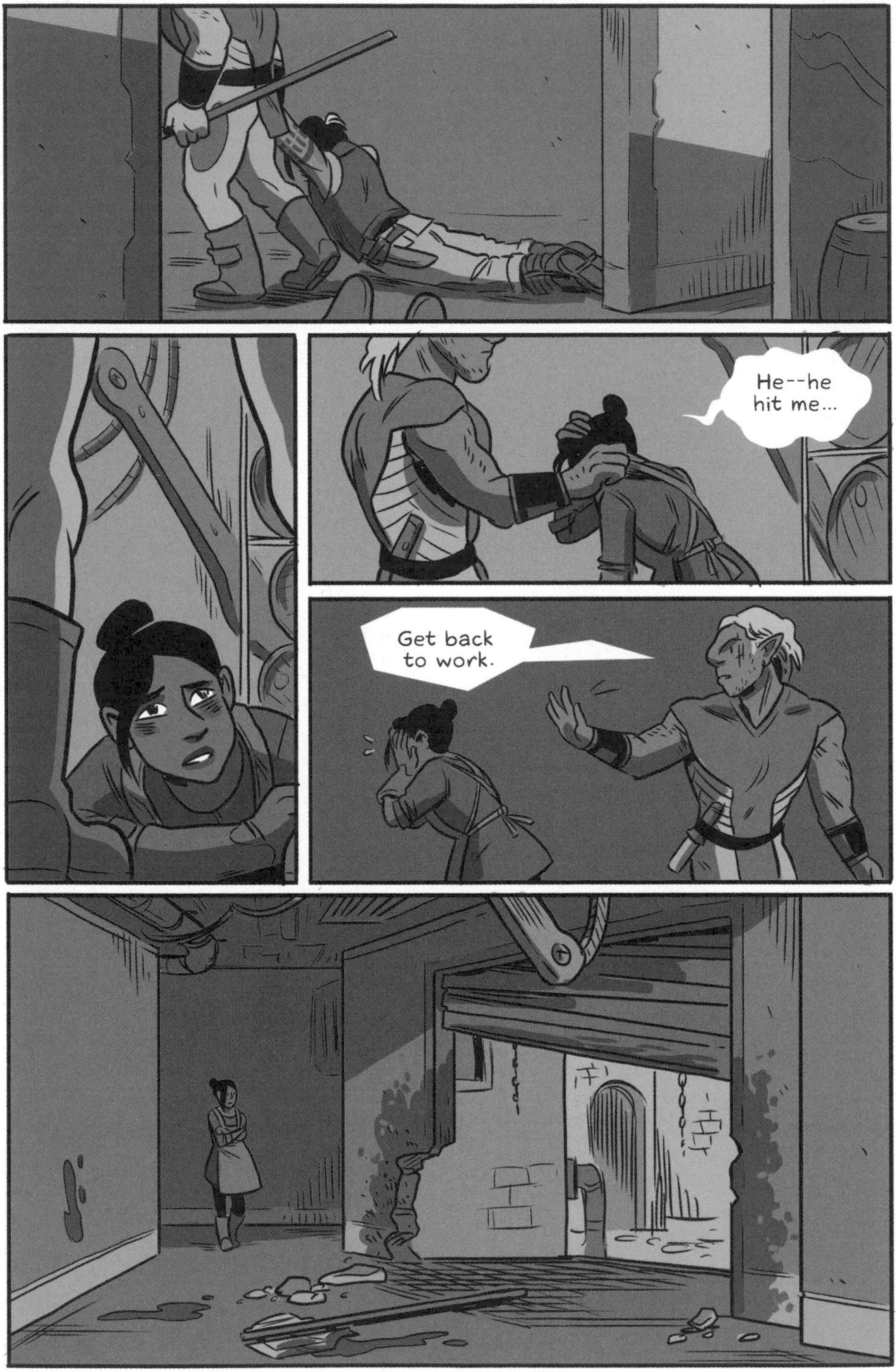
He--he
hit me...
Get back
to work.

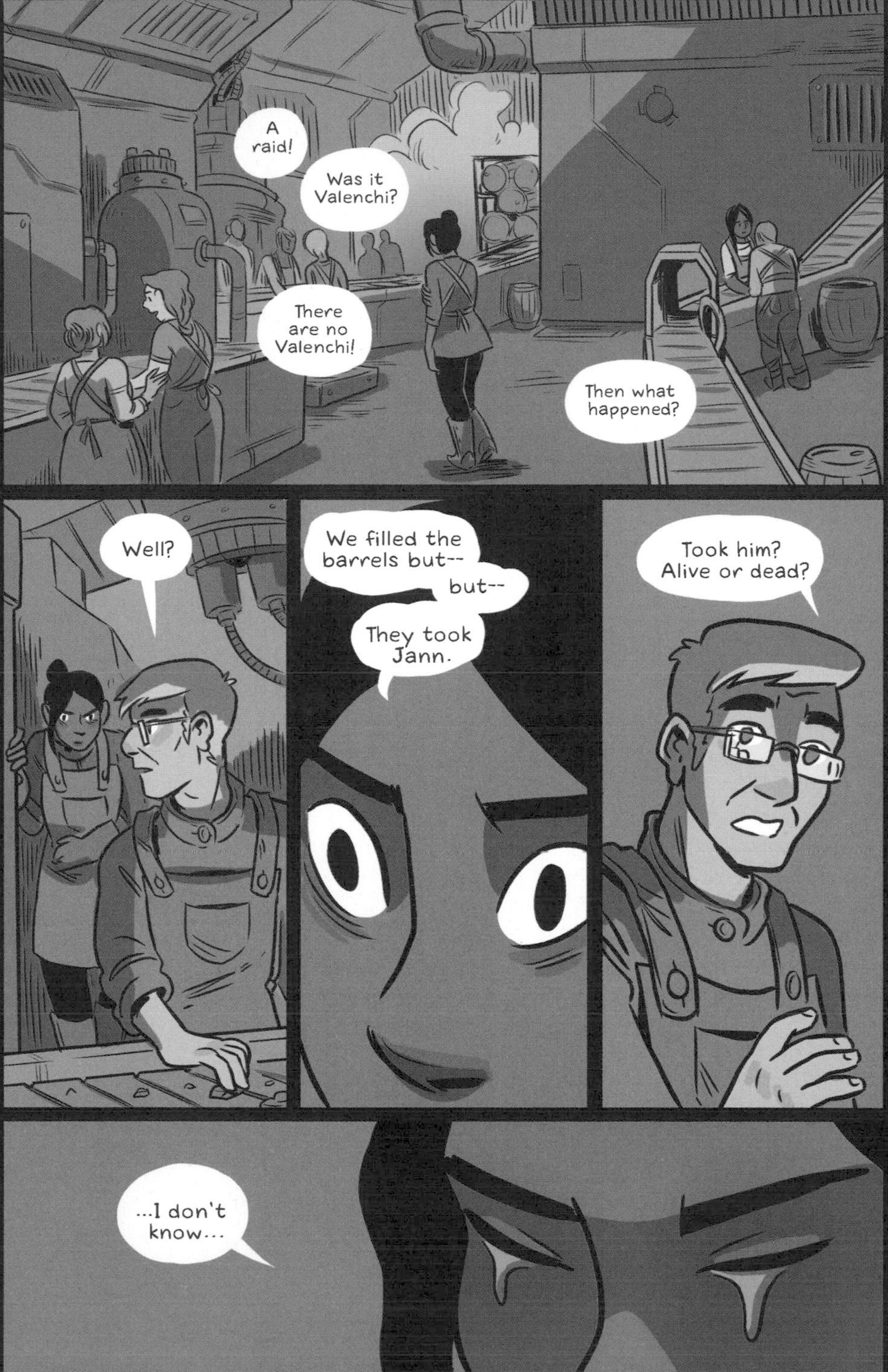
A raid!
Was it Valenchi?
There are no Valenchi!
Then what happened?
Well?
We filled the barrels but--
but--
They took Jann.
Took him? Alive or dead?
...I don't know...

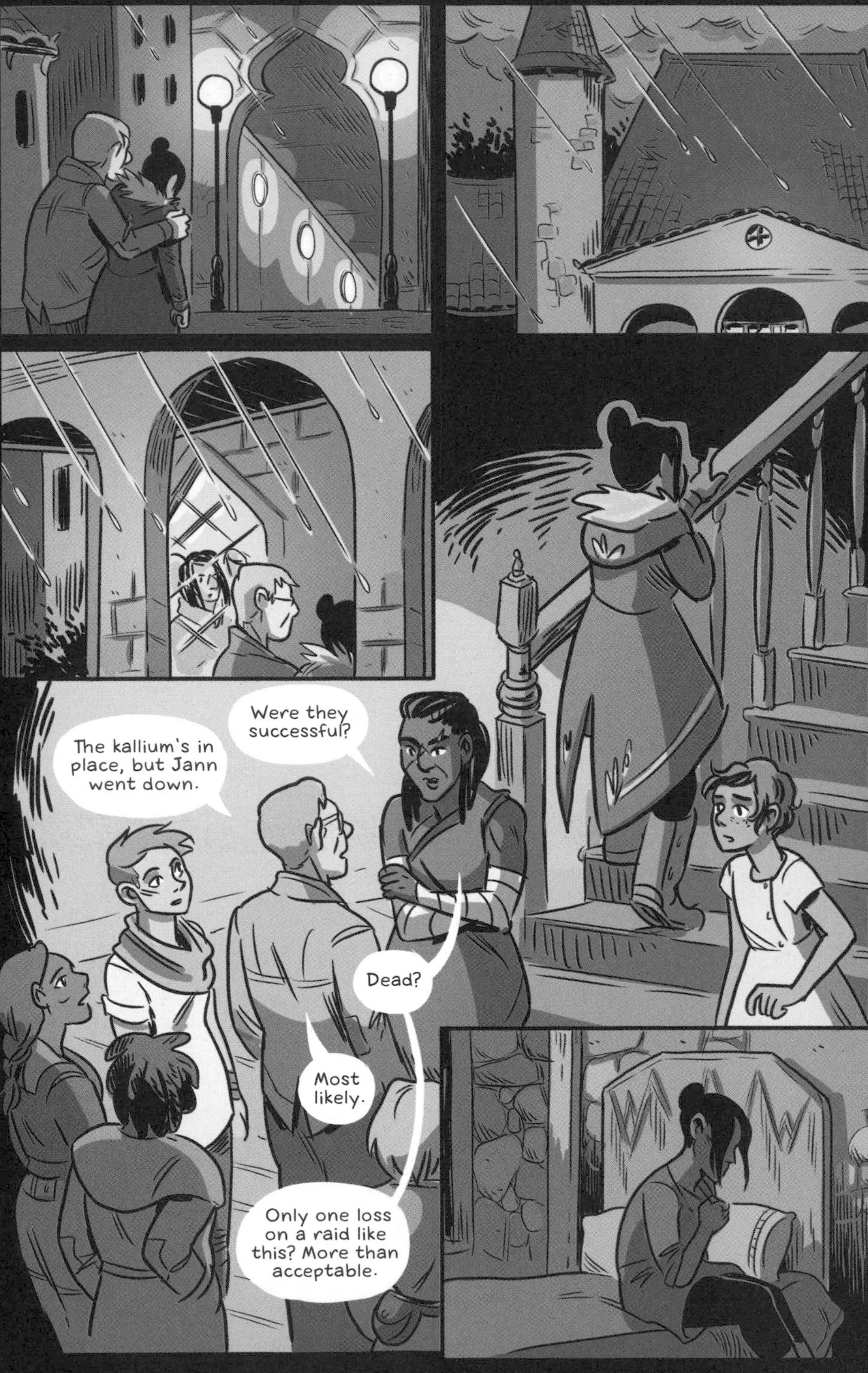
The kallium's in place, but Jann went down.
Were they successful?
Dead?
Most likely.
Only one loss on a raid like this? More than acceptable.

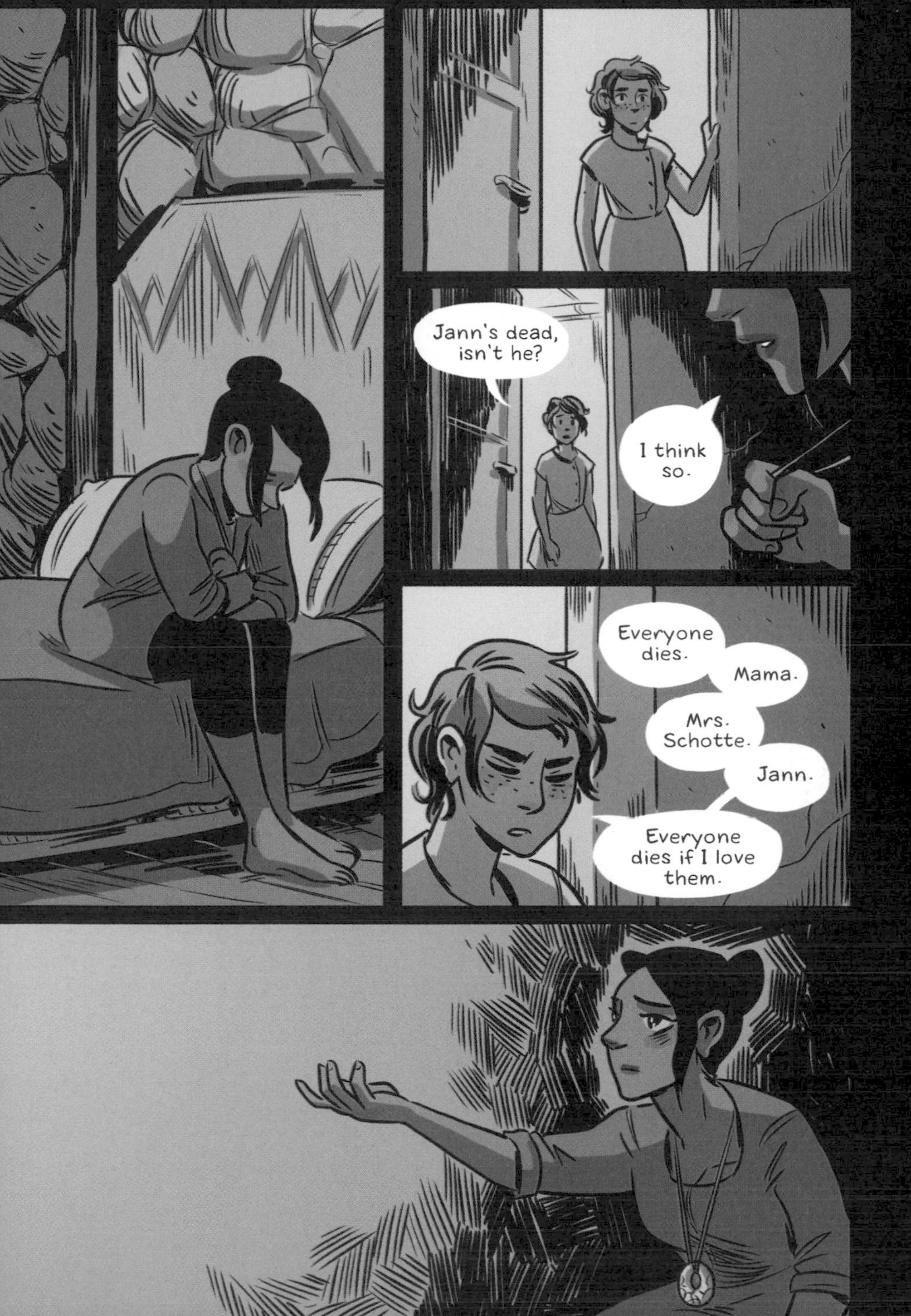
Jann's dead, isn't he?
I think so.
Everyone dies.
Mama.
Mrs. Schotte.
Jann.
Everyone dies if I love them.

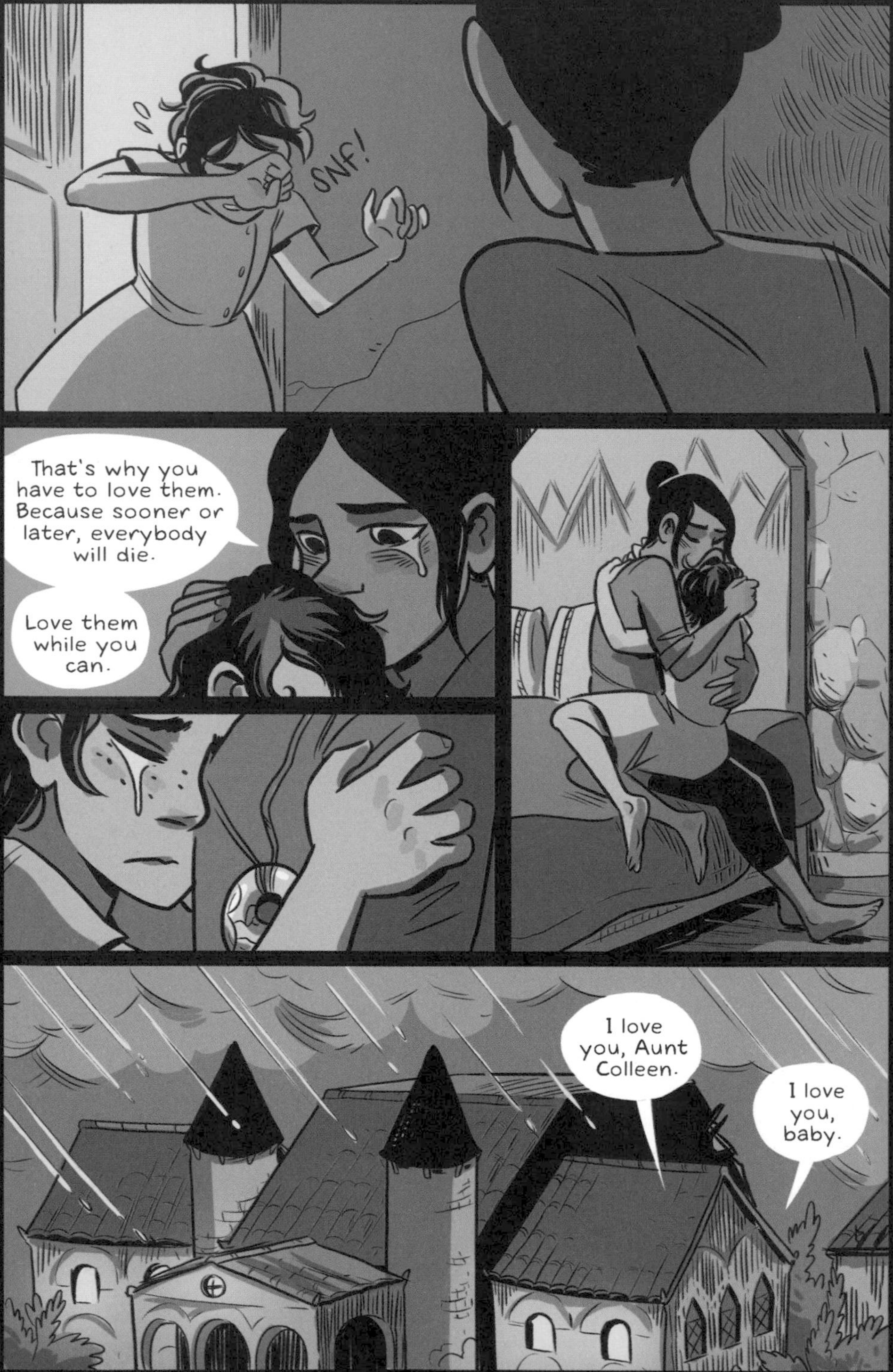
SNF!
That's why you have to love them. Because sooner or later, everybody will die.
Love them while you can.
I love you, Aunt Colleen.
I love you, baby.

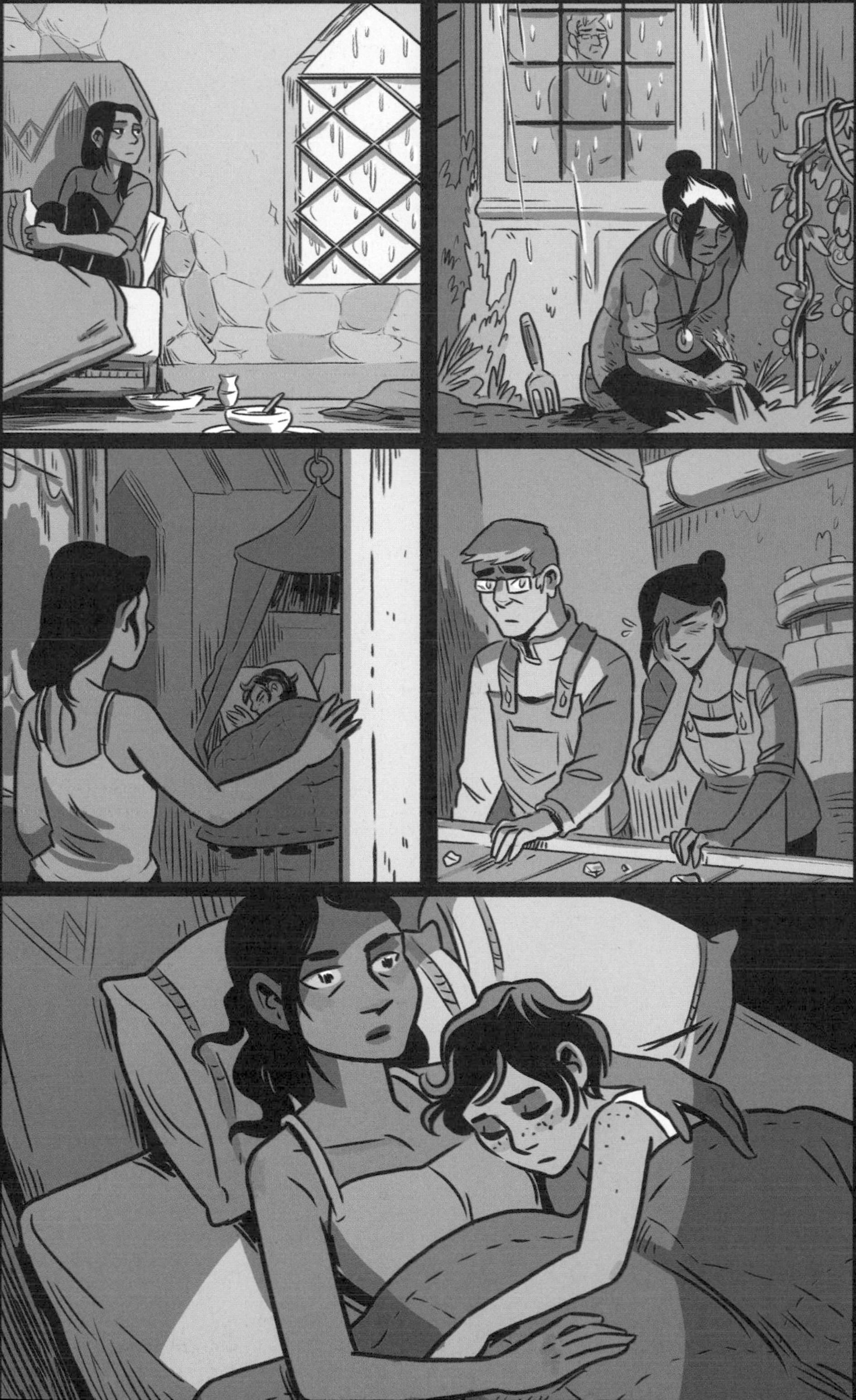

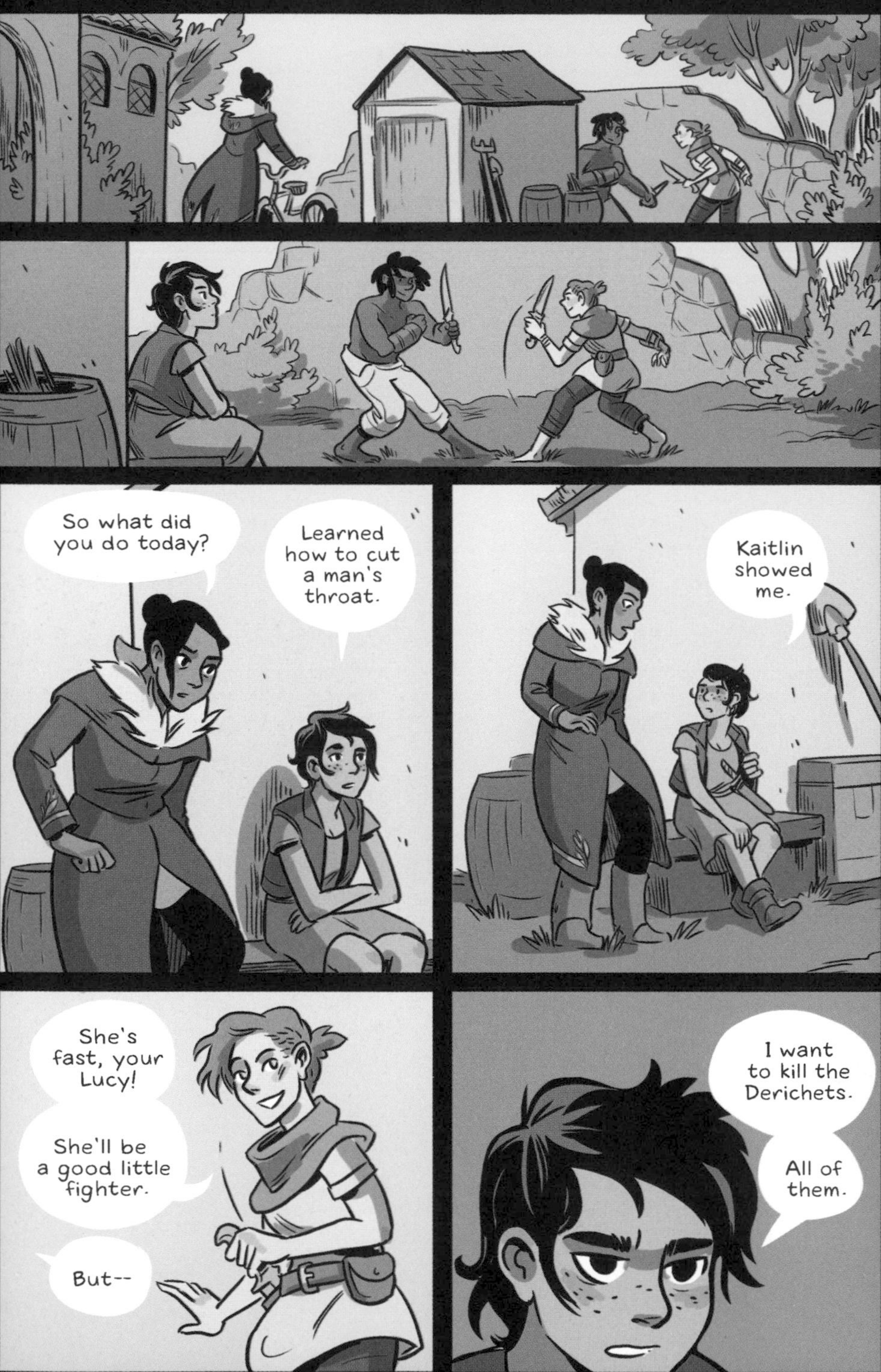

So what did you do today?
Learned how to cut a man's throat.
Kaitlin showed me.
She's fast, your Lucy!
She'll be a good little fighter.
But--
I want to kill the Derichets.
All of them.

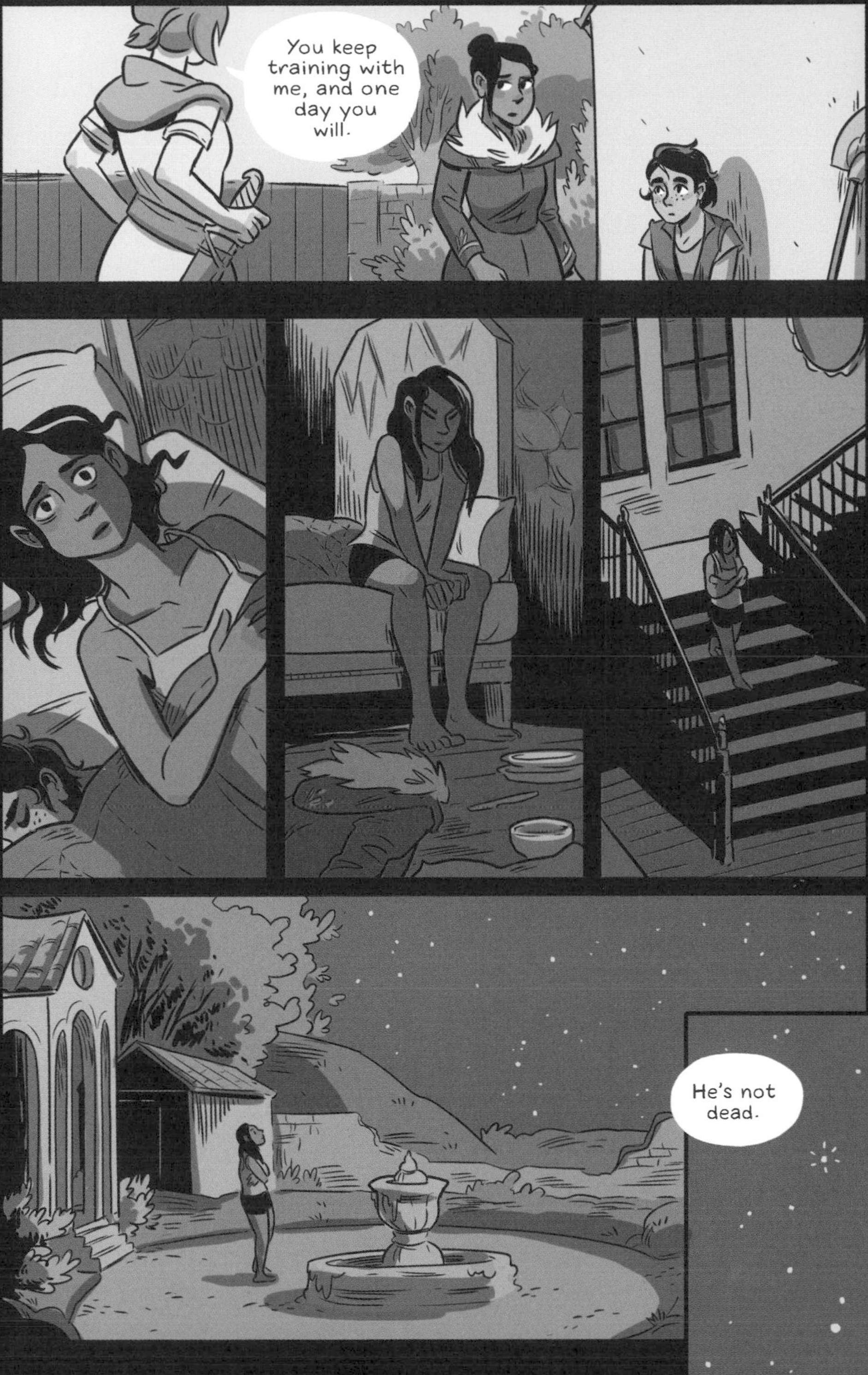
You keep training with me, and one day you will.
He's not dead.

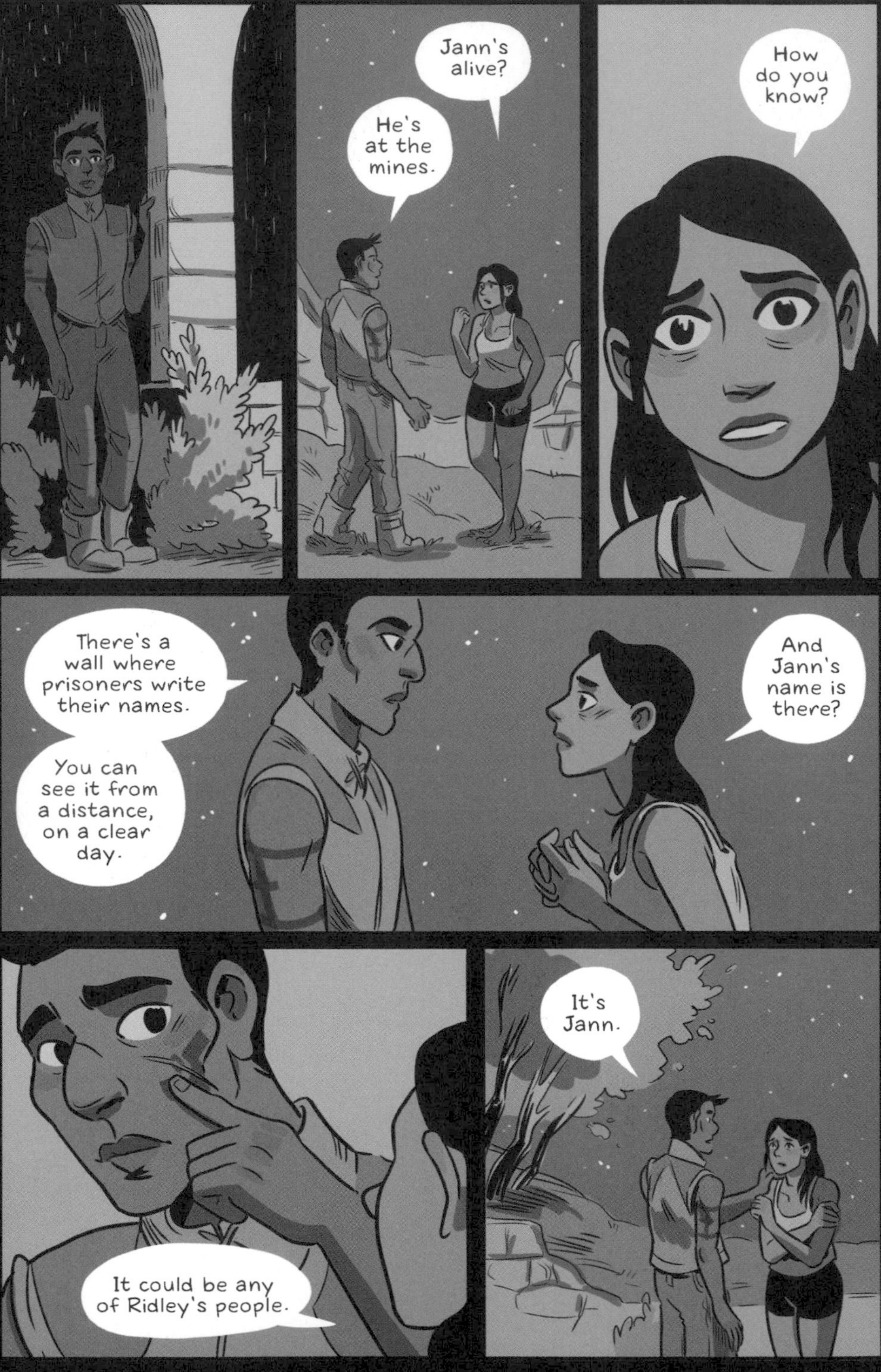
Jann's alive?
He's at the mines.
How do you know?
There's a wall where prisoners write their names.
You can see it from a distance, on a clear day.
And Jann's name is there?
It could be any of Ridley's people.
It's Jann.

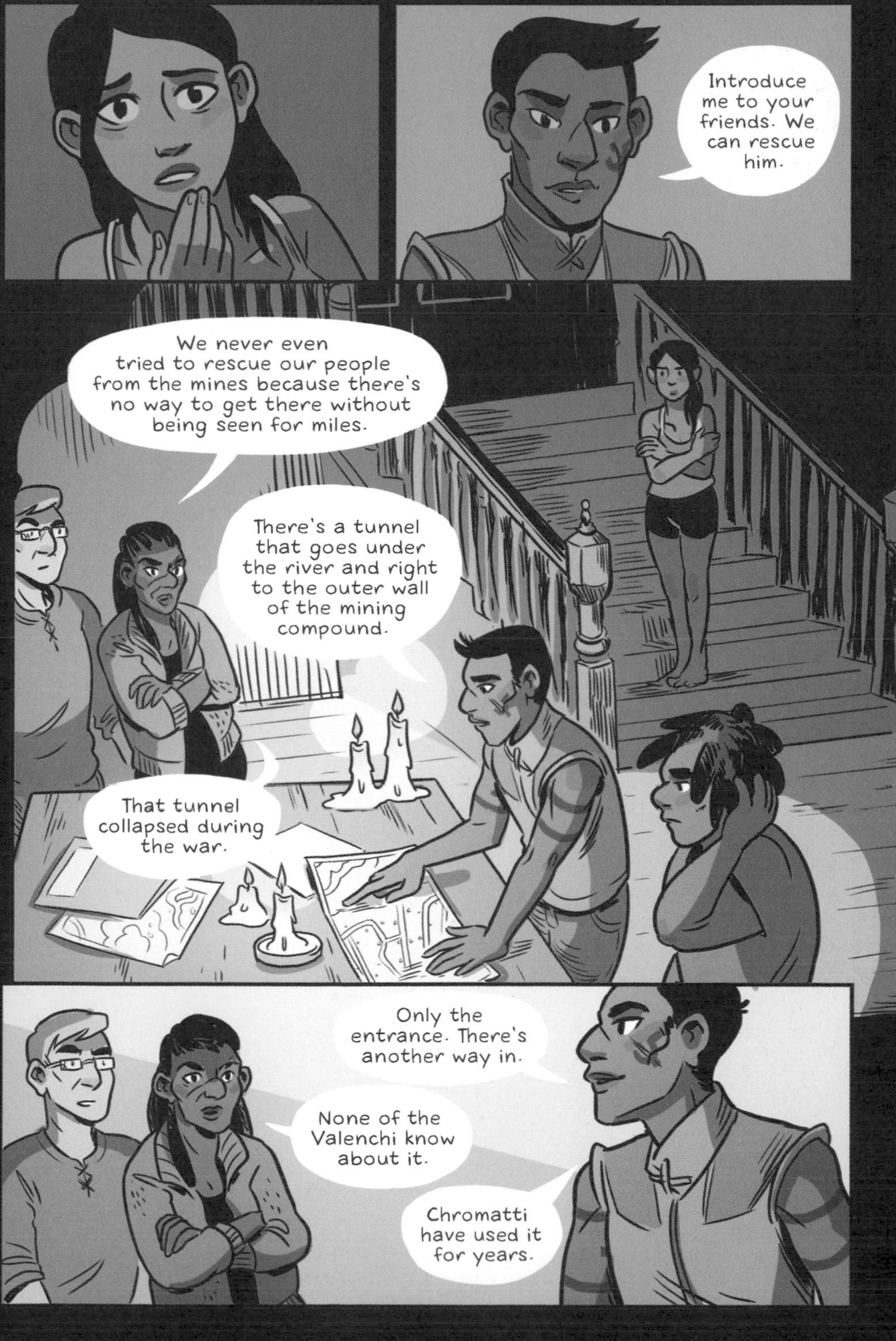
Introduce me to your friends. We can rescue him.
We never even tried to rescue our people from the mines because there's no way to get there without being seen for miles.
There's a tunnel that goes under the river and right to the outer wall of the mining compound.
That tunnel collapsed during the war.
Only the entrance. There's another way in.
None of the Valenchi know about it.
Chromatti have used it for years.

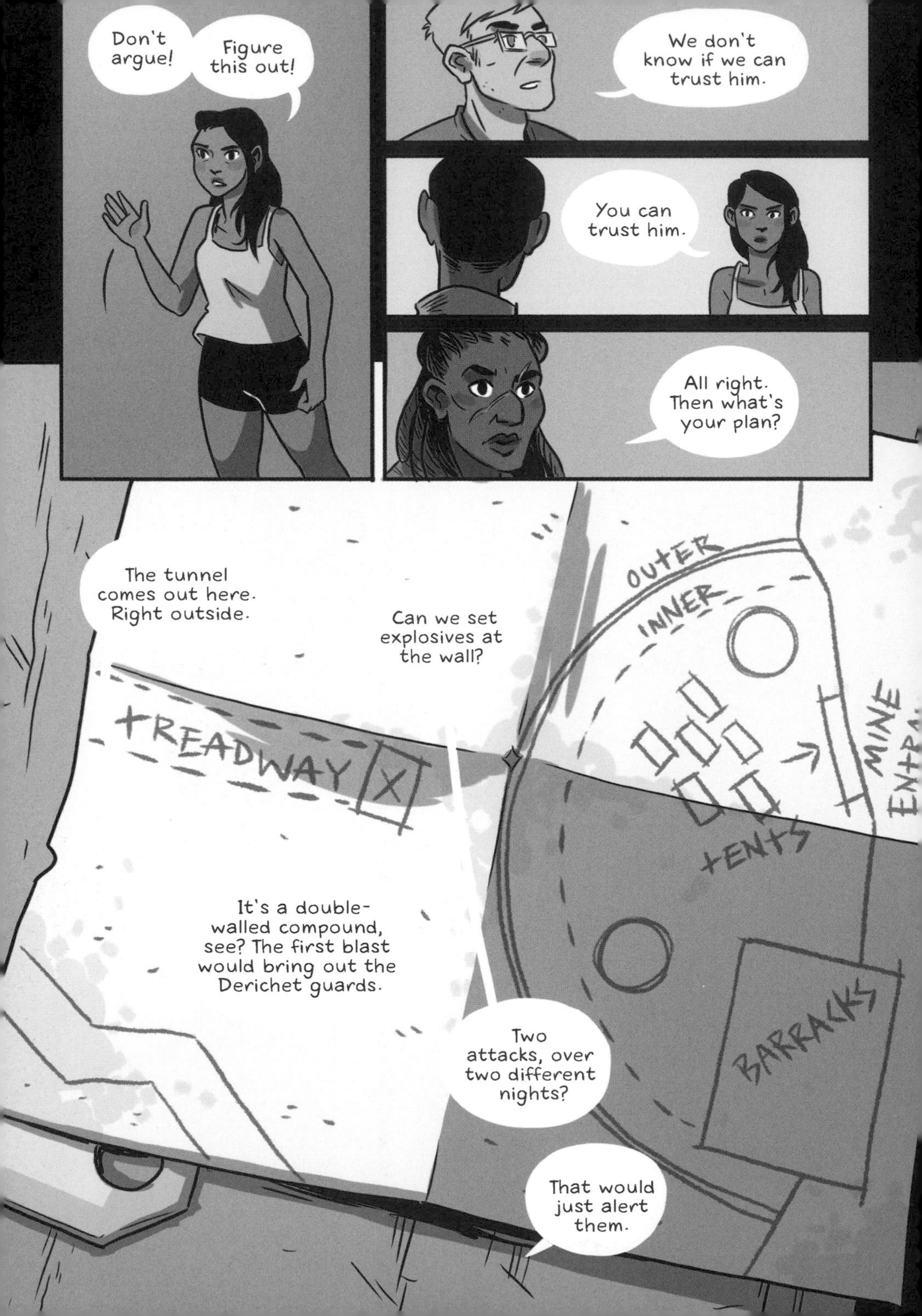

Don't argue!
Figure this out!
We don't know if we can trust him.
You can trust him.
All right. Then what's your plan?
The tunnel comes out here. Right outside.
Can we set explosives at the wall?
OUTER
INNER
TREADWAY
X
MINE ENTRA
TENTS
It's a double-walled compound, see? The first blast would bring out the Derichet guards.
BARRACKS
Two attacks, over two different nights?
That would just alert them.

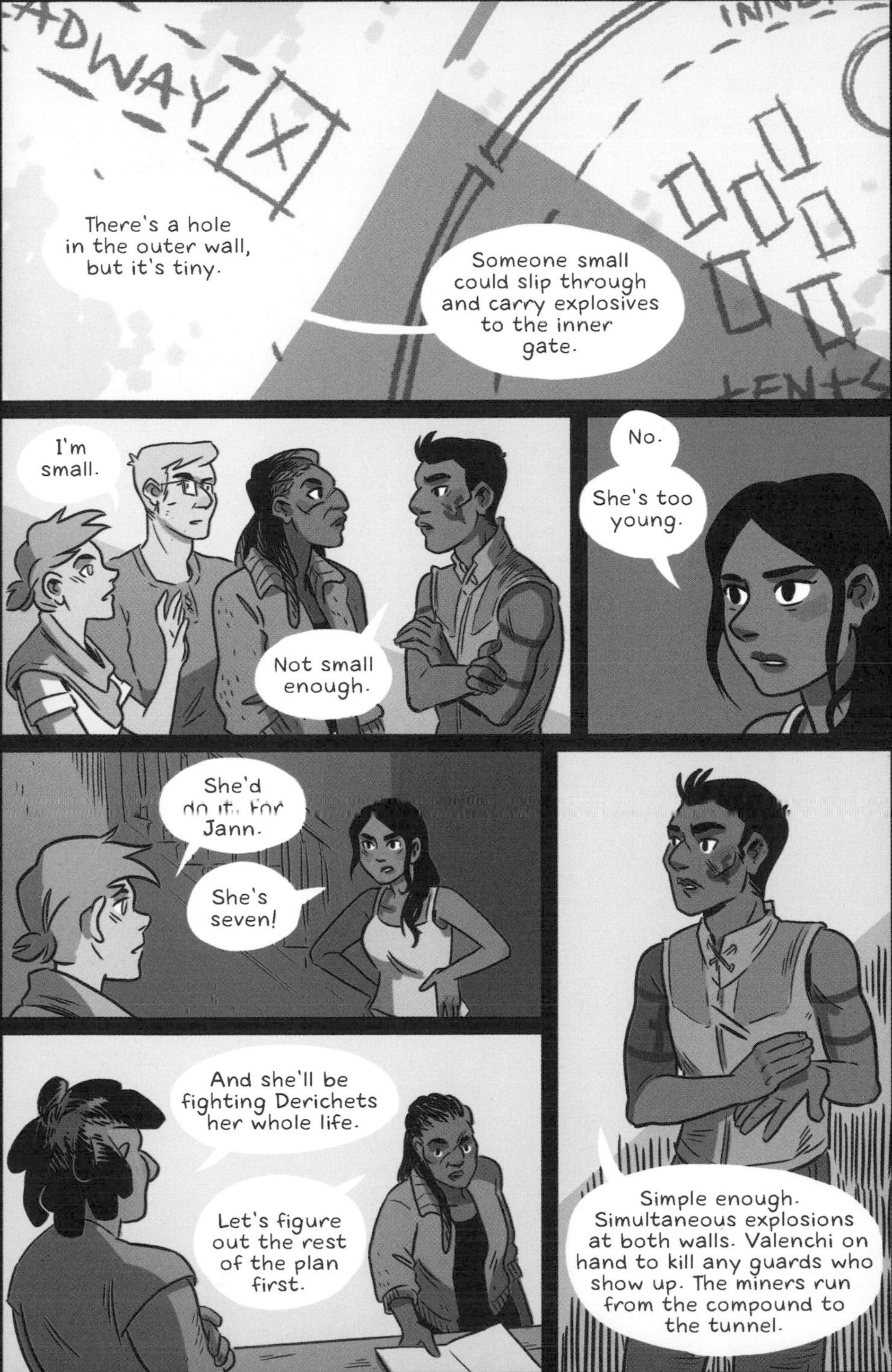
There's a hole in the outer wall, but it's tiny.
Someone small could slip through and carry explosives to the inner gate.
I'm small.
Not small enough.
No.
She's too young.
She'd do it for Jann.
She's seven!
And she'll be fighting Derichets her whole life.
Let's figure out the rest of the plan first.
Simple enough. Simultaneous explosions at both walls. Valenchi on hand to kill any guards who show up. The miners run from the compound to the tunnel.

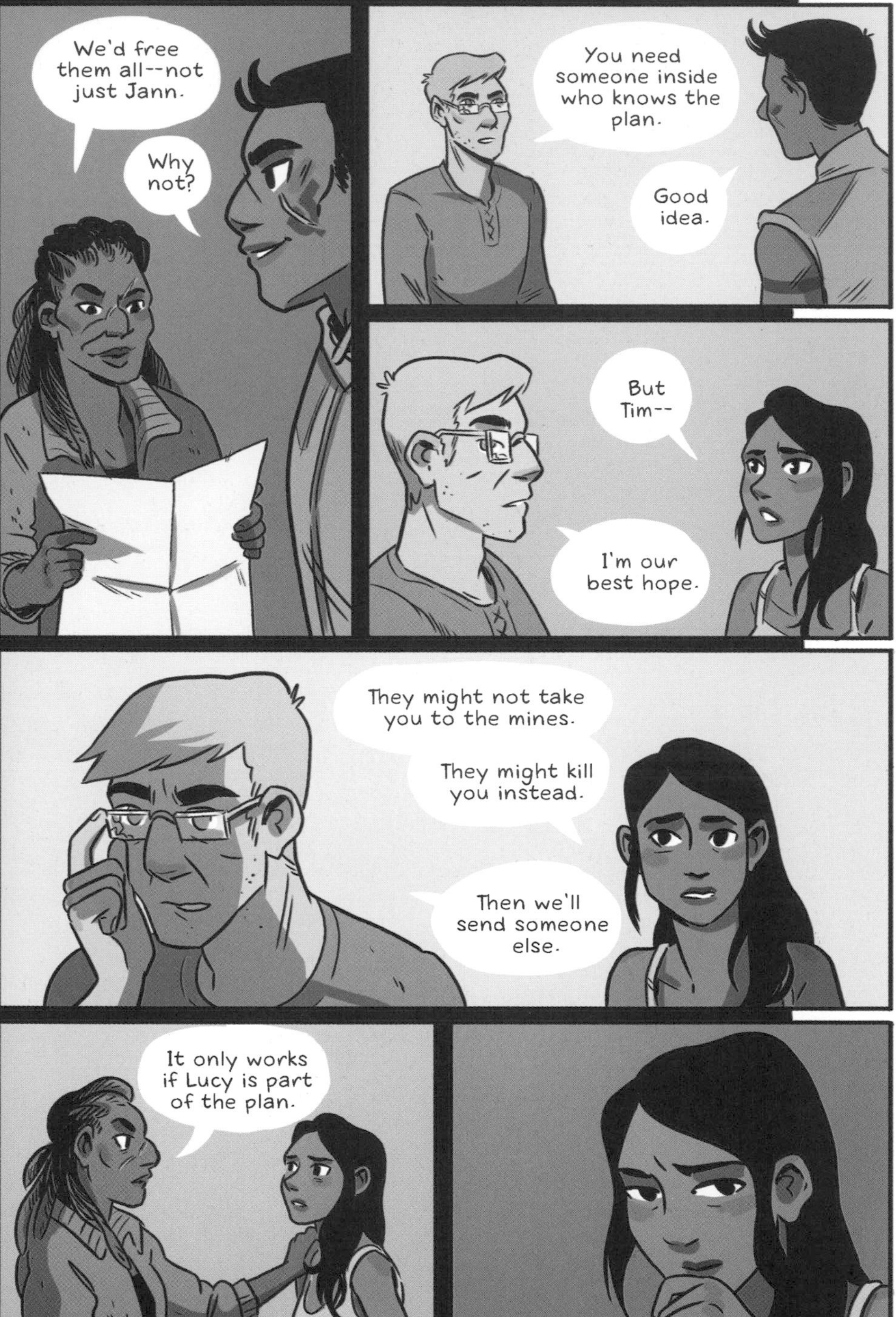
We'd free them all--not just Jann.
Why not?
You need someone inside who knows the plan.
Good idea.
But Tim--
I'm our best hope.
They might not take you to the mines.
They might kill you instead.
Then we'll send someone else.
It only works if Lucy is part of the plan.

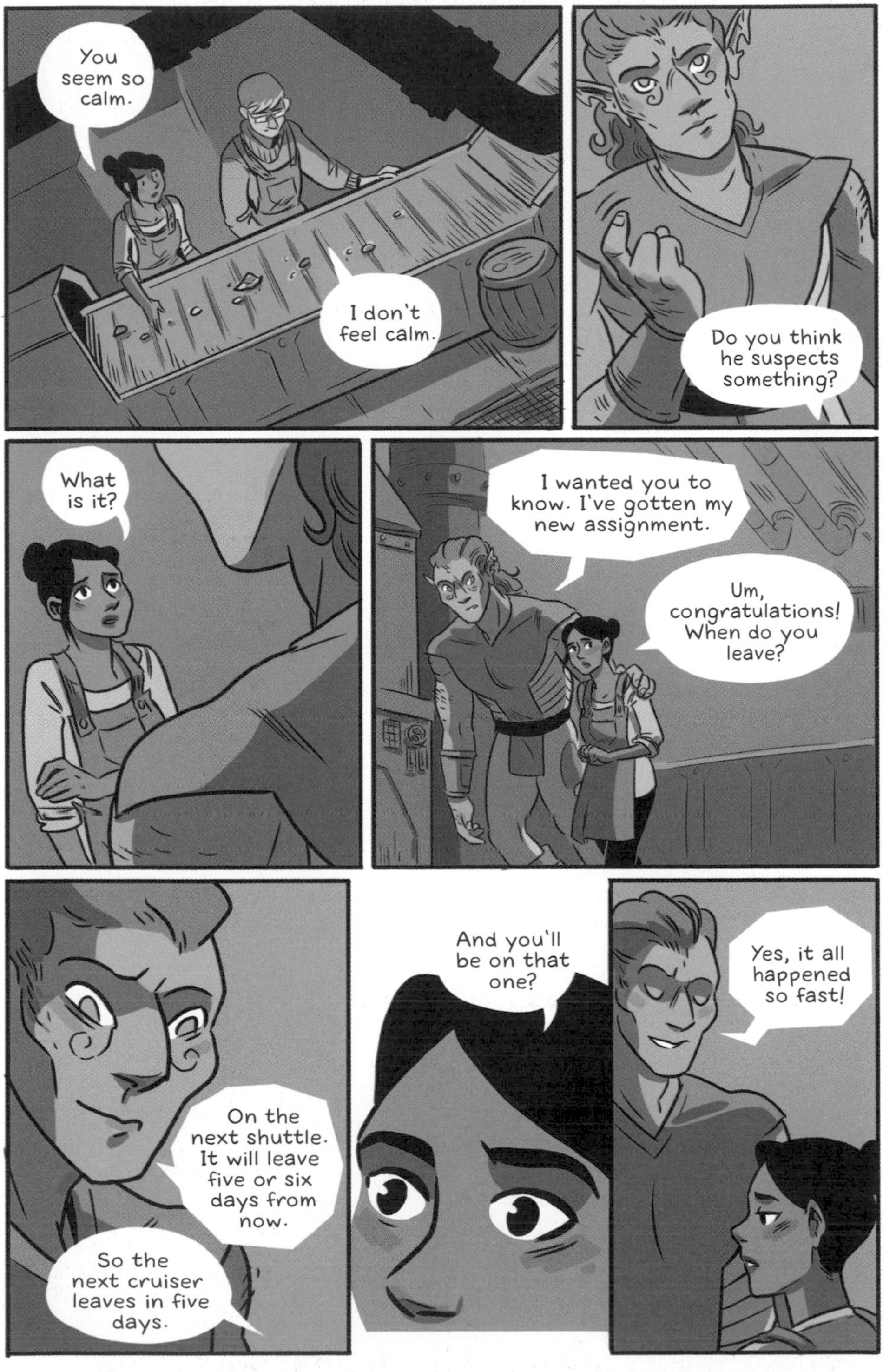
You seem so calm.
I don't feel calm.
Do you think he suspects something?
What is it?
I wanted you to know. I've gotten my new assignment.
Um, congratulations! When do you leave?
On the next shuttle. It will leave five or six days from now.
So the next cruiser leaves in five days.
And you'll be on that one?
Yes, it all happened so fast!

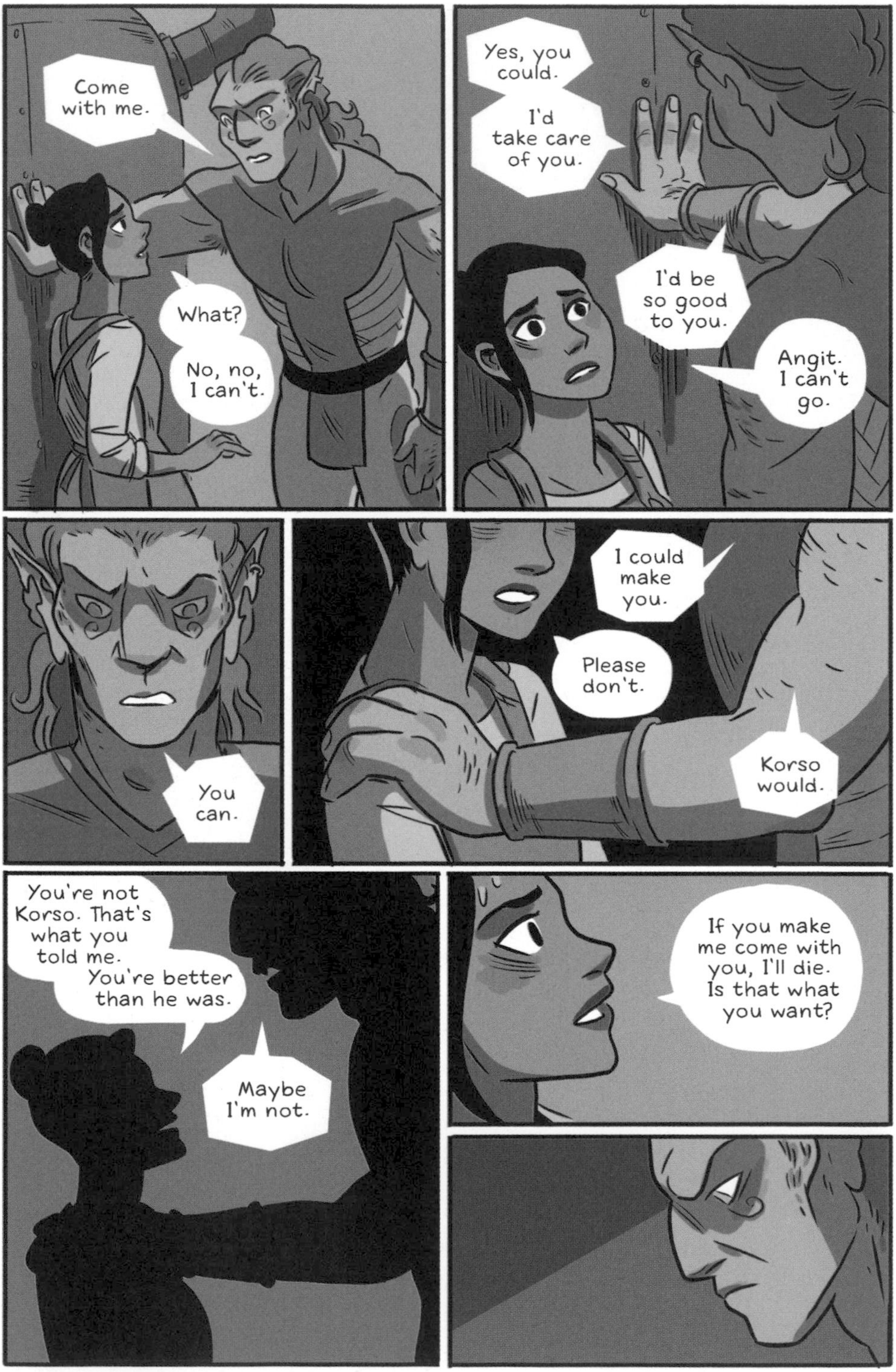
Come with me.
What?
No, no, I can't.
Yes, you could.
I'd take care of you.
I'd be so good to you.
Angit. I can't go.
You can.
I could make you.
Please don't.
Korso would.
You're not Korso. That's what you told me.
You're better than he was.
Maybe I'm not.
If you make me come with you, I'll die. Is that what you want?

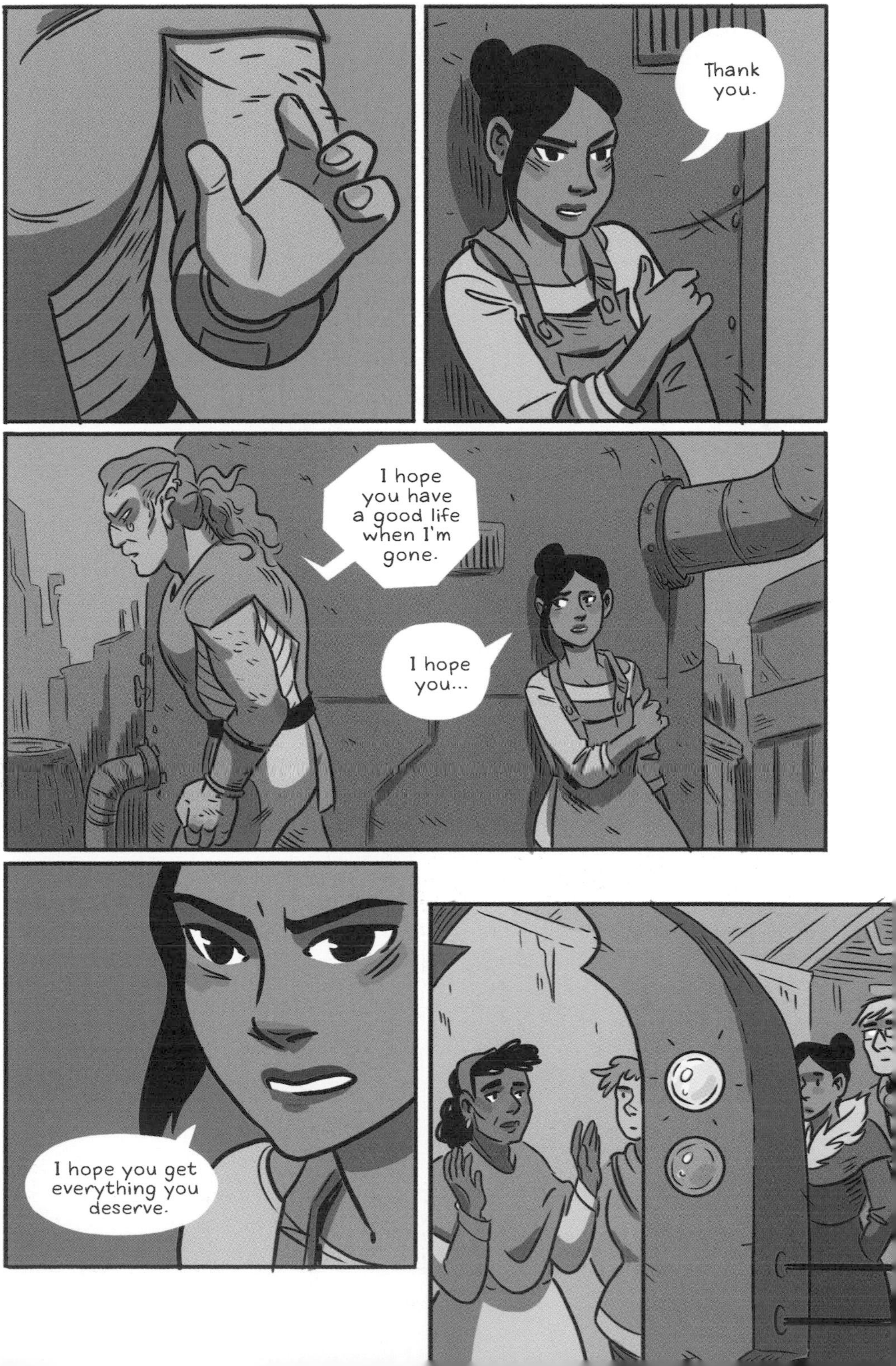
Thank you.
I hope you have a good life when I'm gone.
I hope you...
I hope you get everything you deserve.

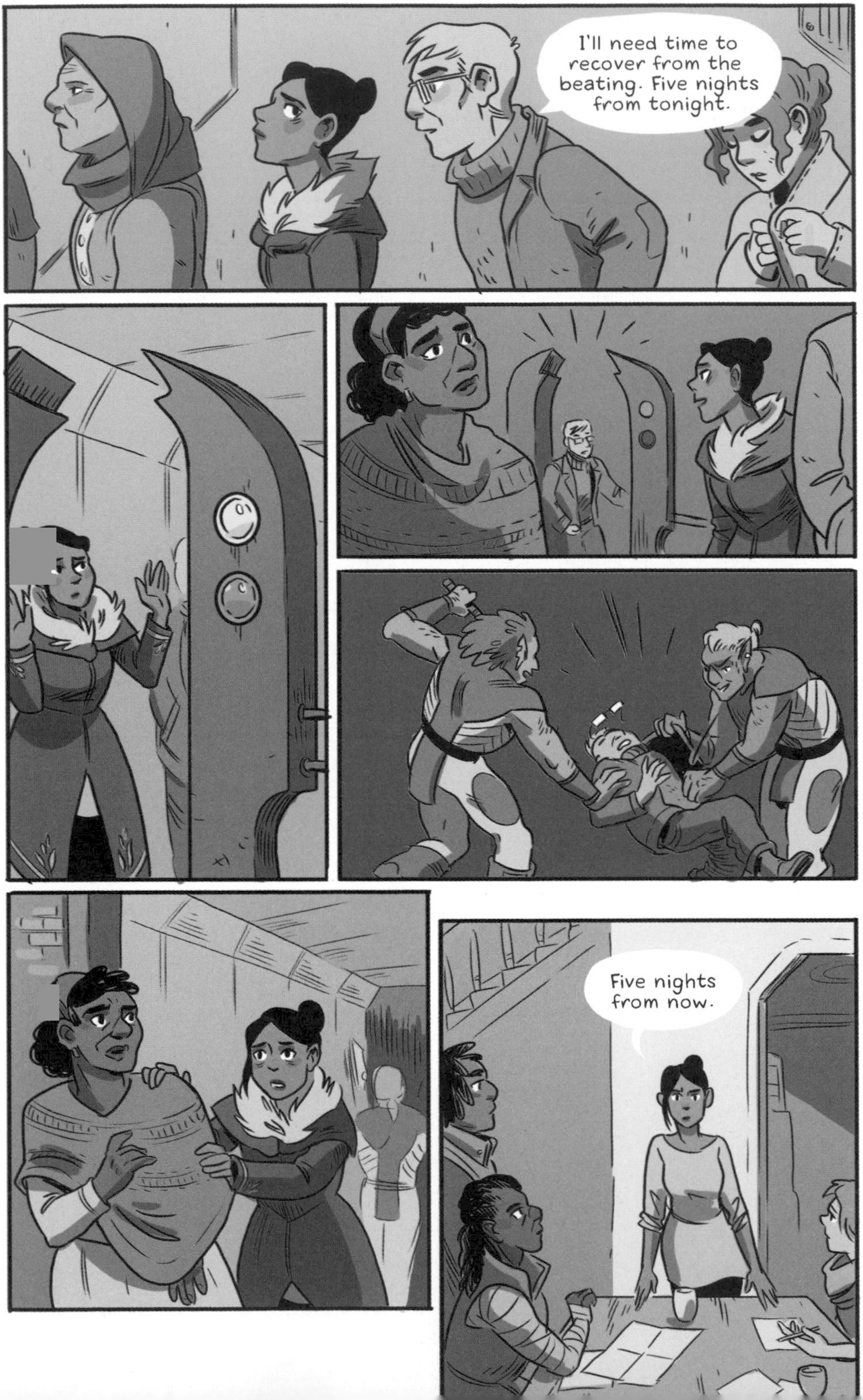
I'll need time to recover from the beating. Five nights from tonight.
Five nights from now.

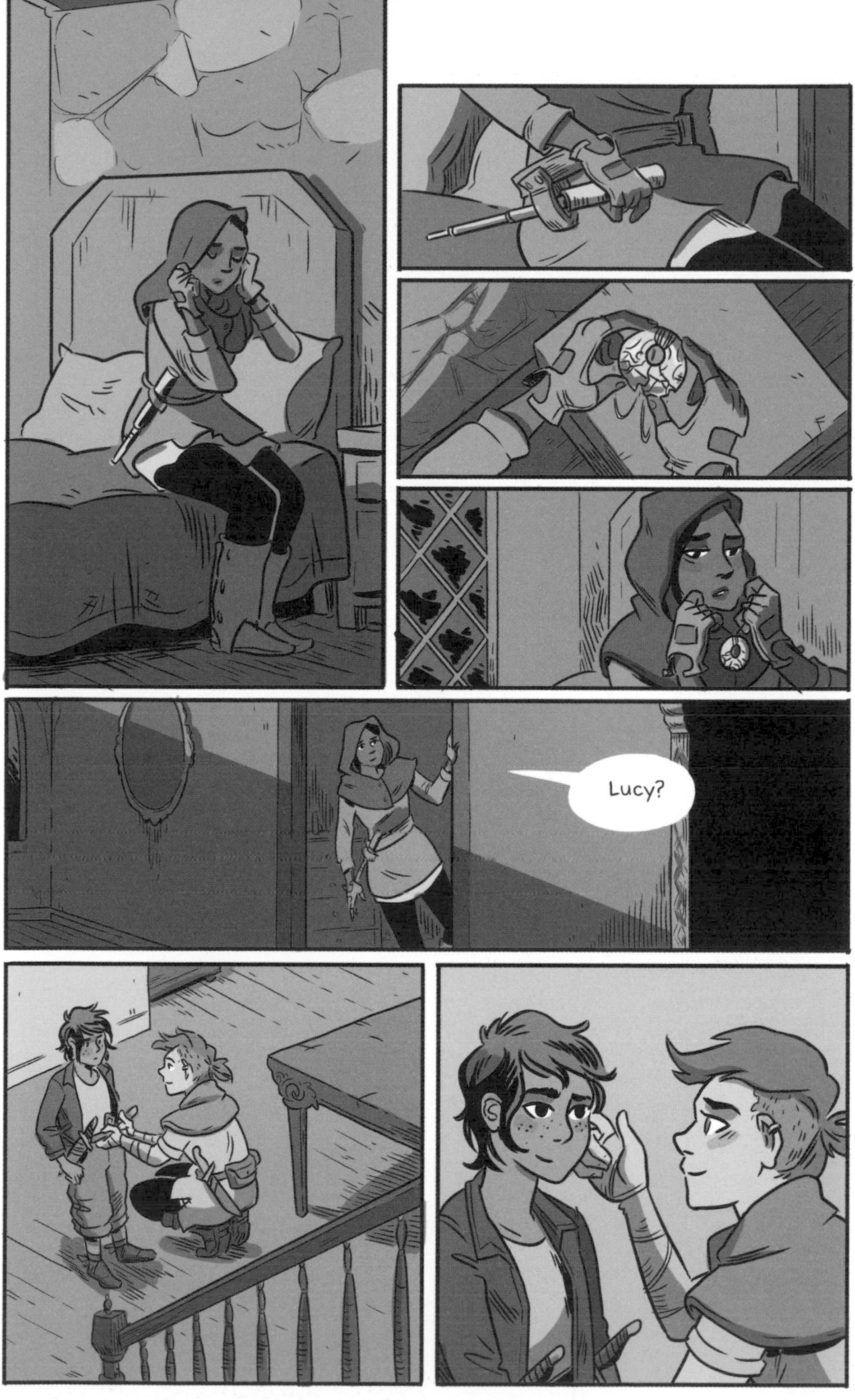
Lucy?

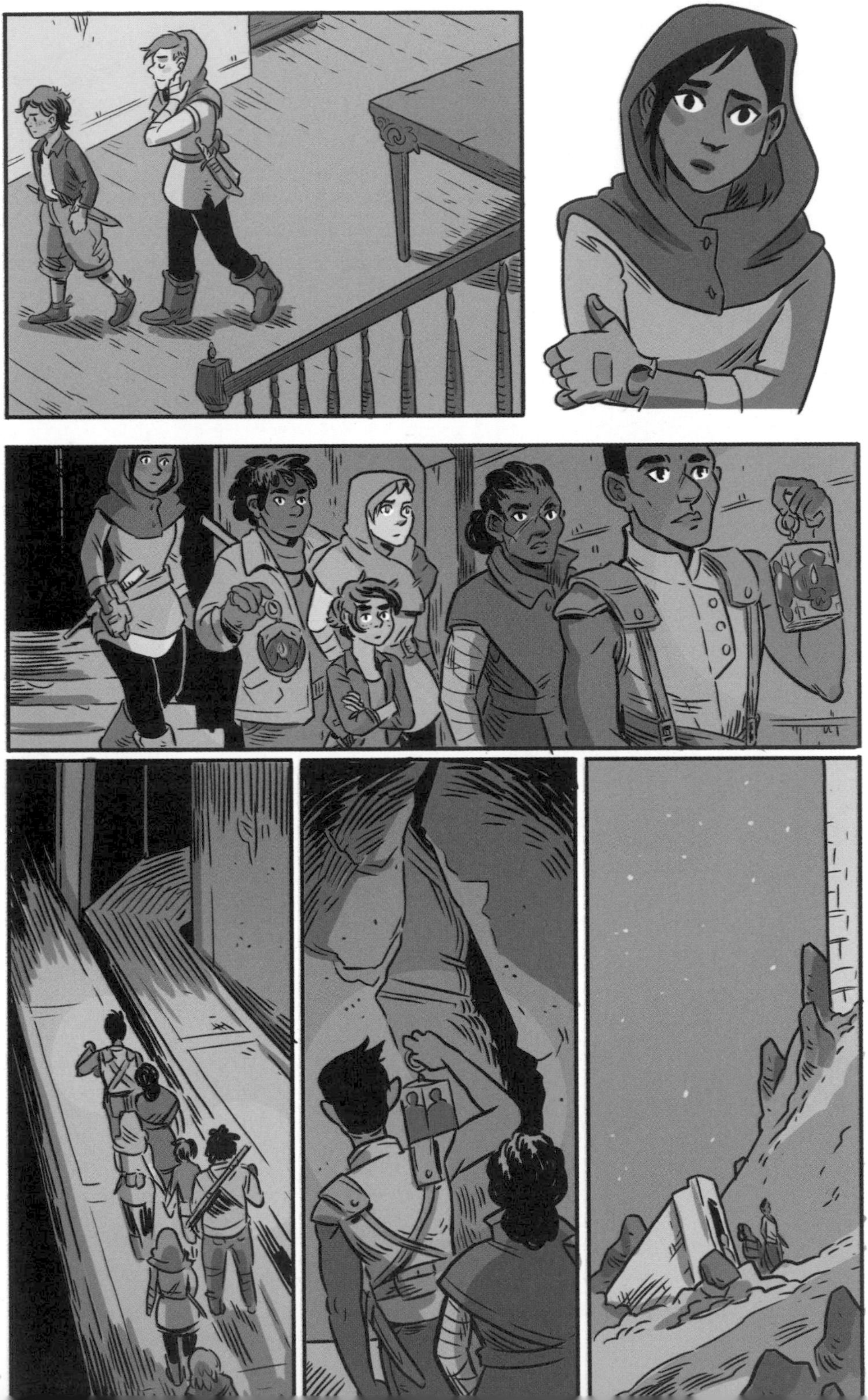

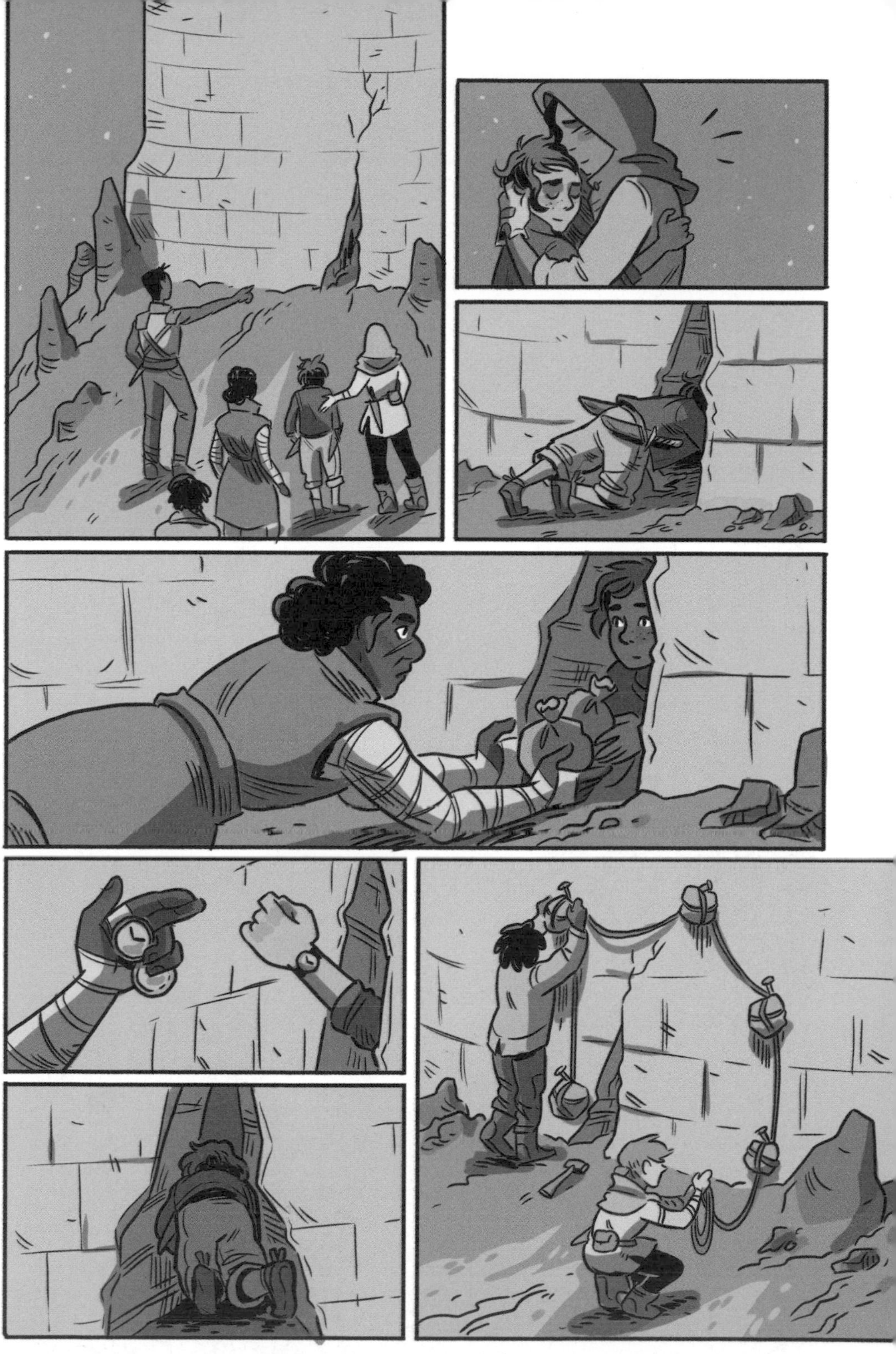

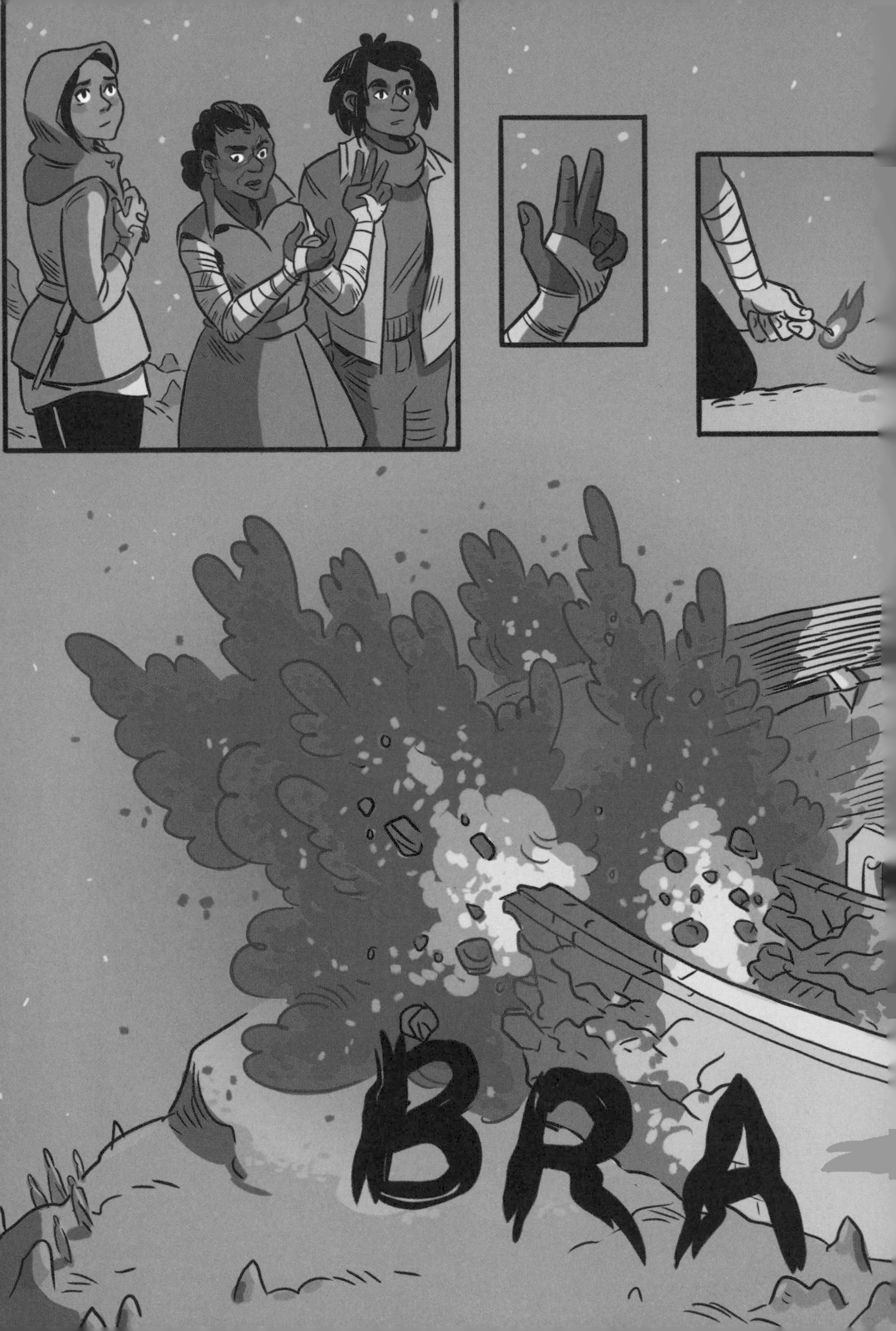
BRA

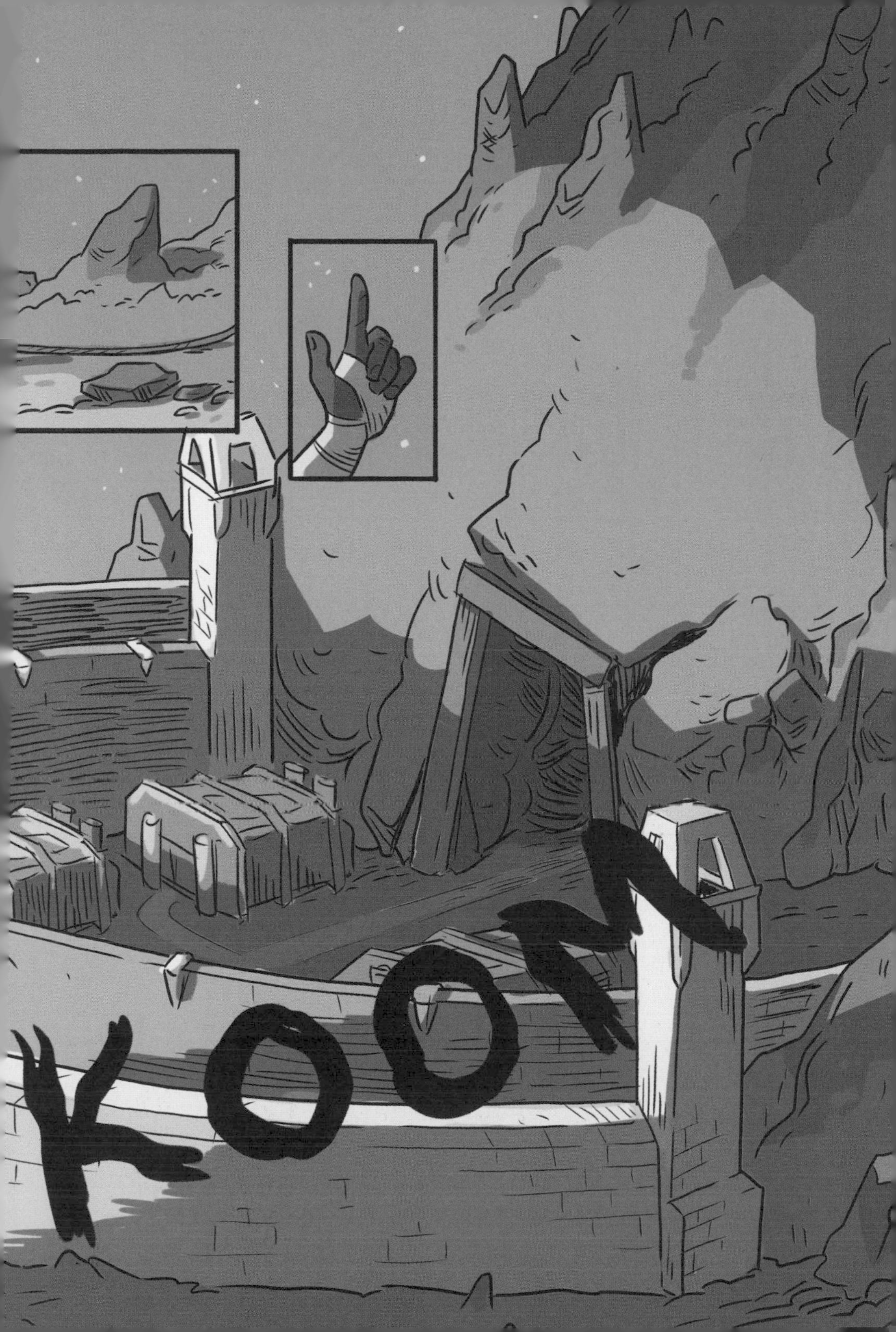
KOOM

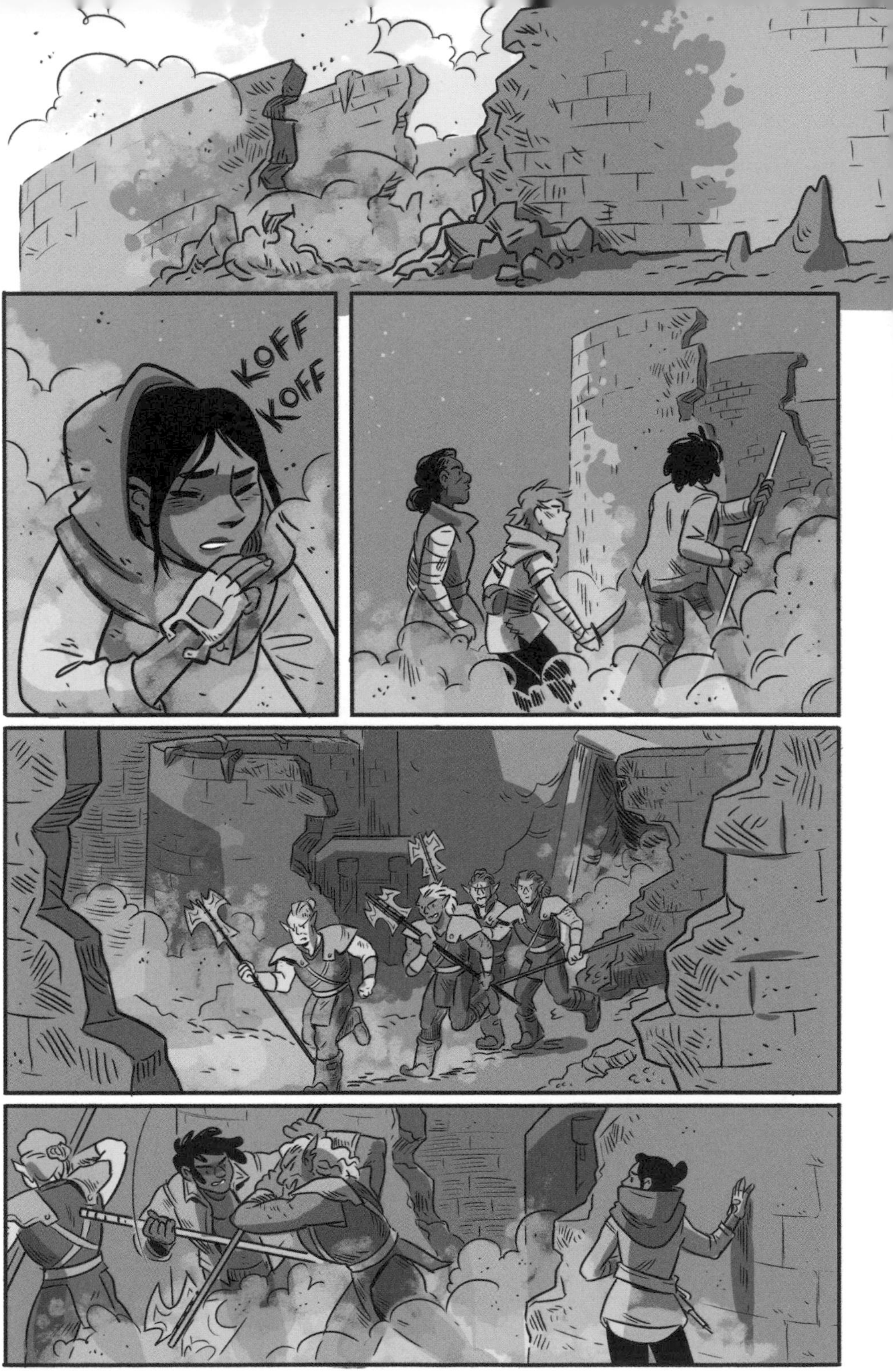
KOFF
KOFF

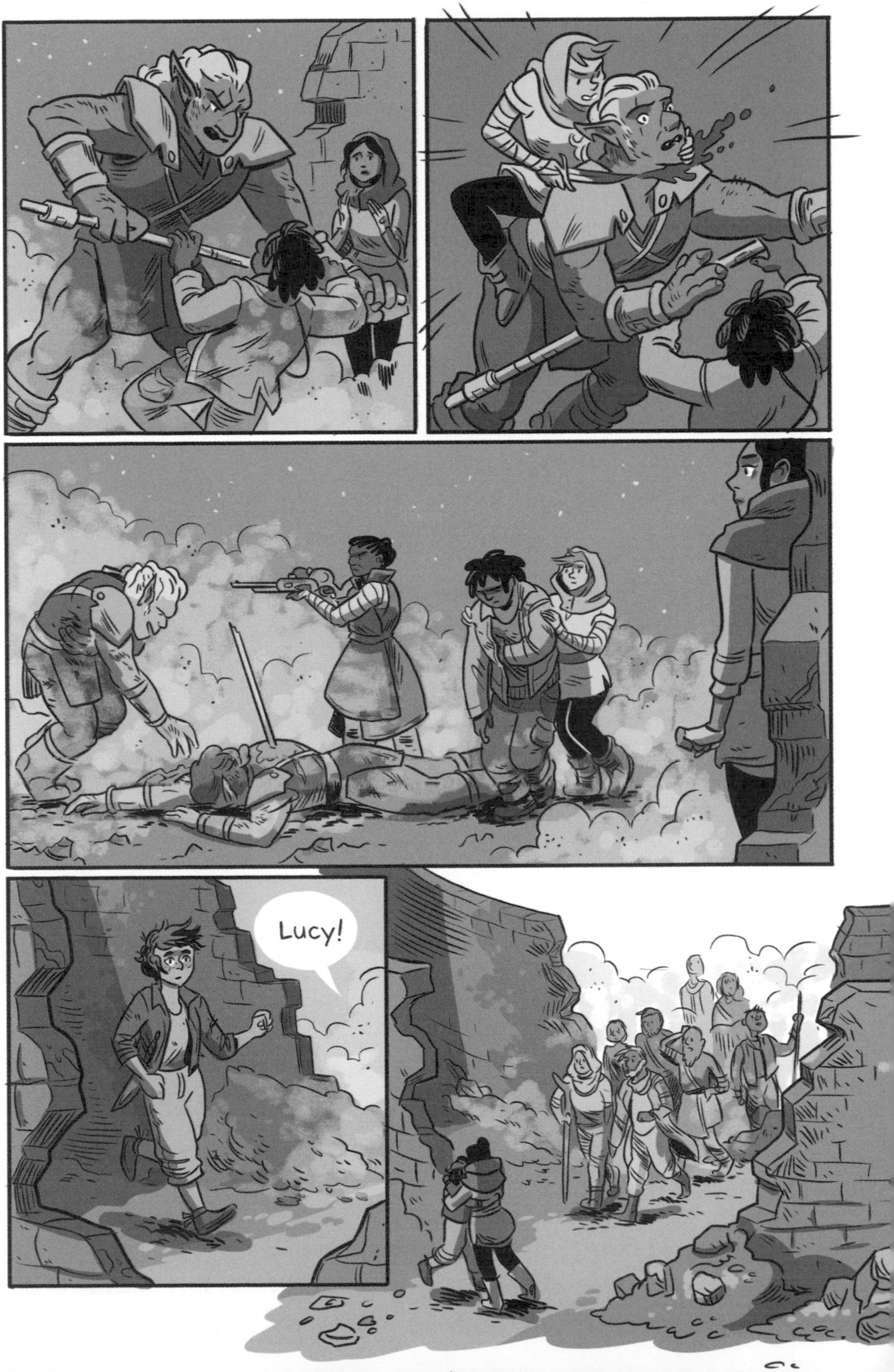
Lucy!

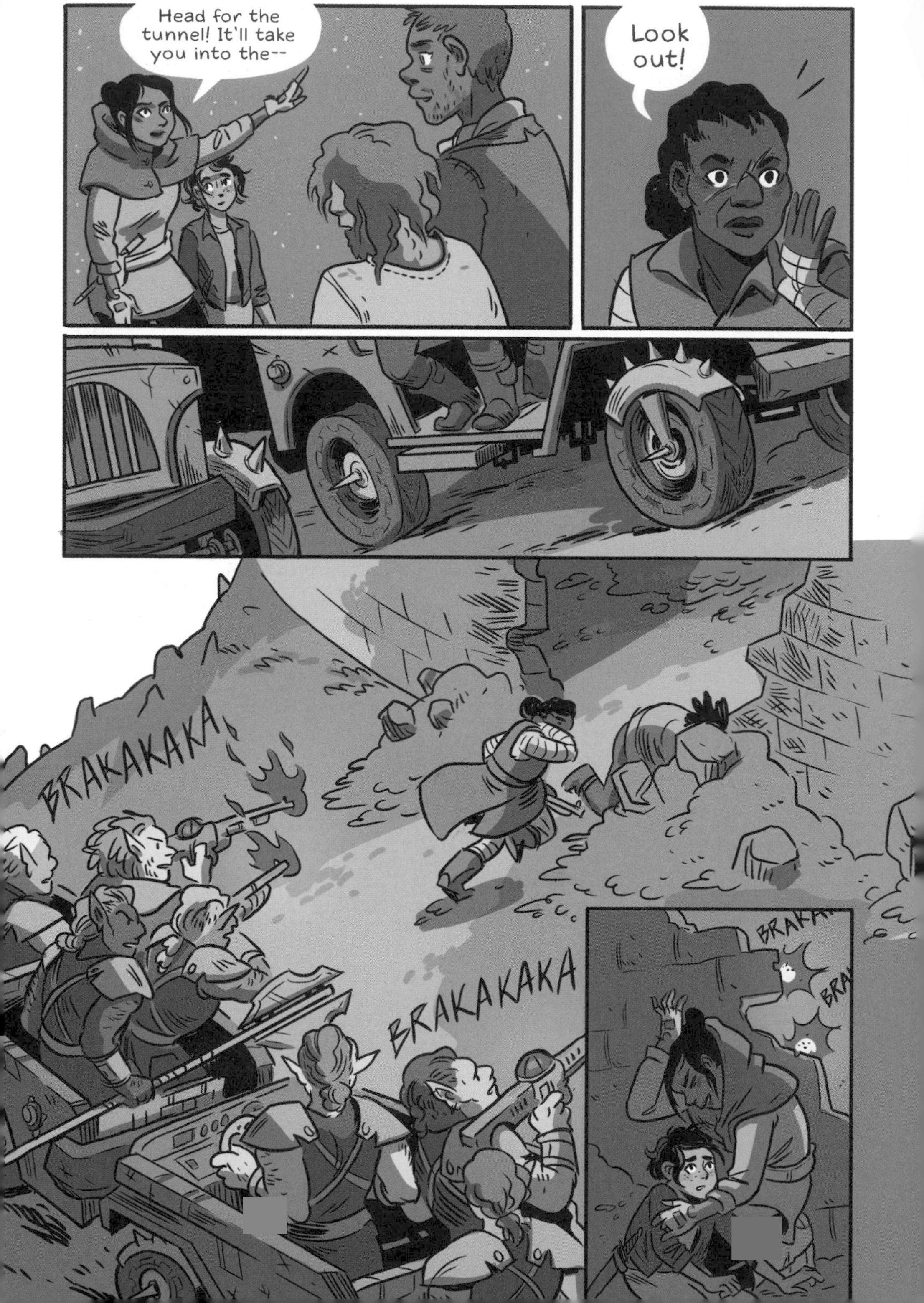
Head for the tunnel! It'll take you into the--
Look out!
BRAKAKAKA
BRAKAKAKA

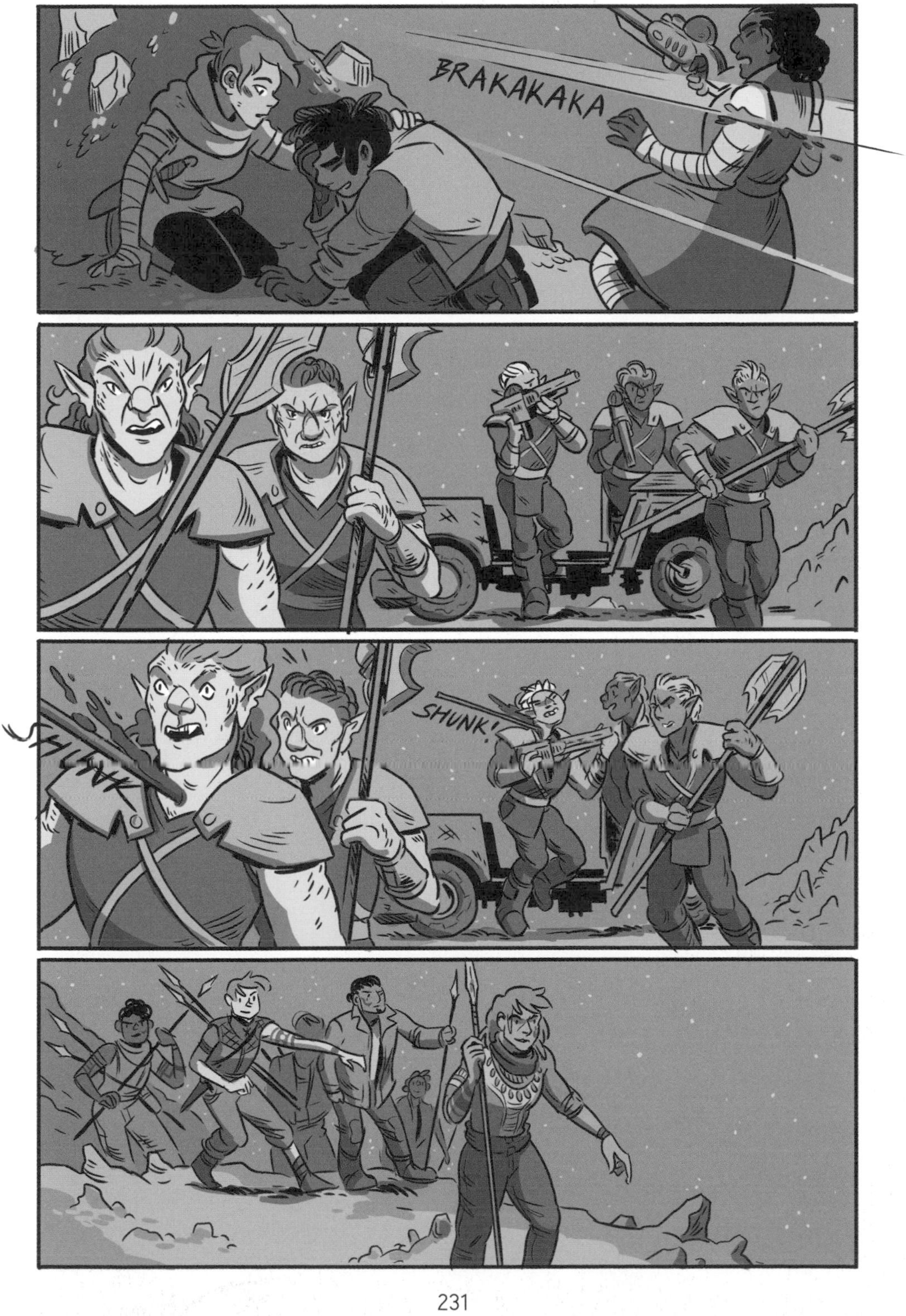
BRAKAKAKA
SHUNK!

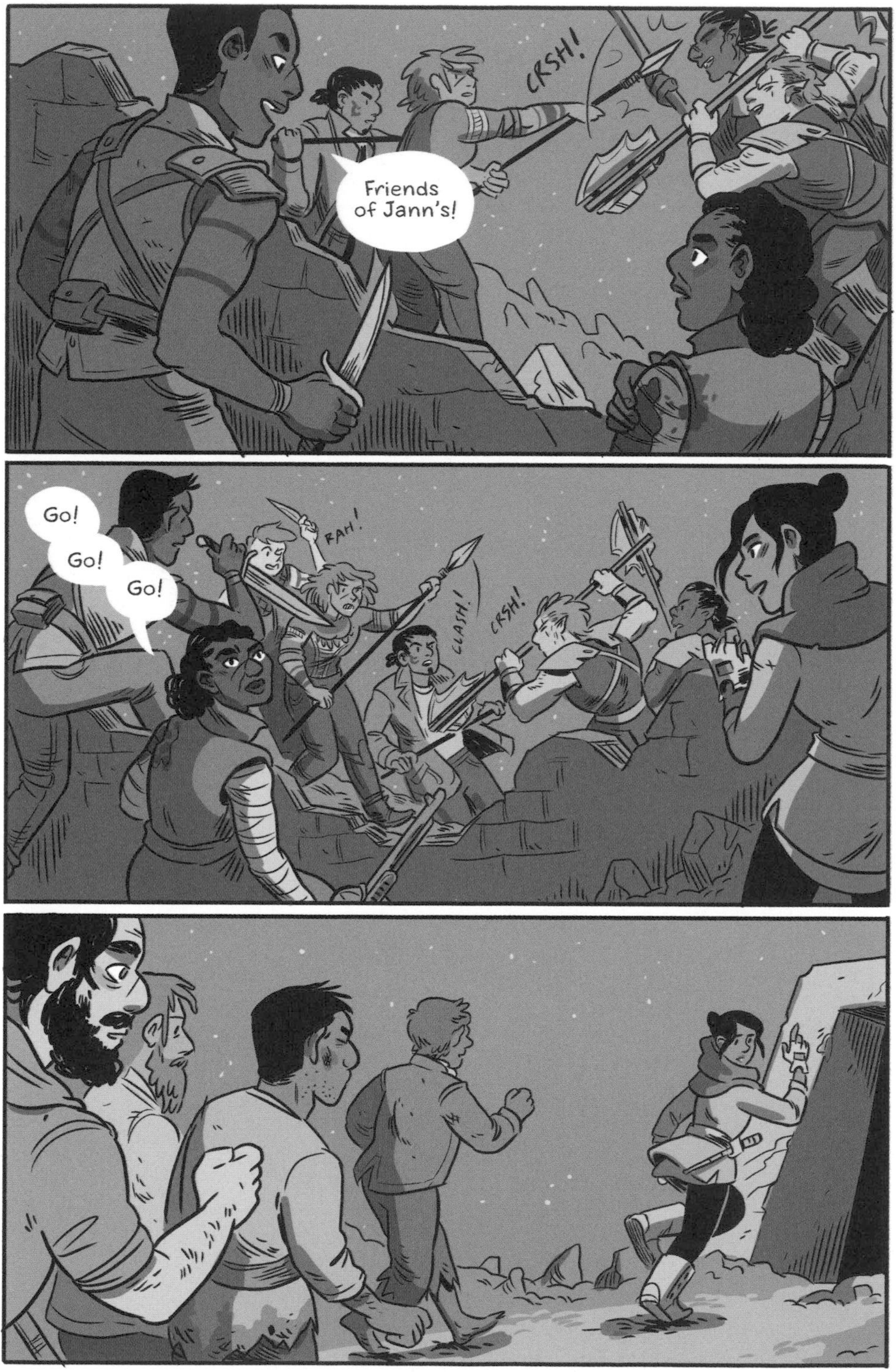
CRSH!
Friends of Jann's!
Go!
Go!
Go!
RAH!
CLASH!
CRSH!

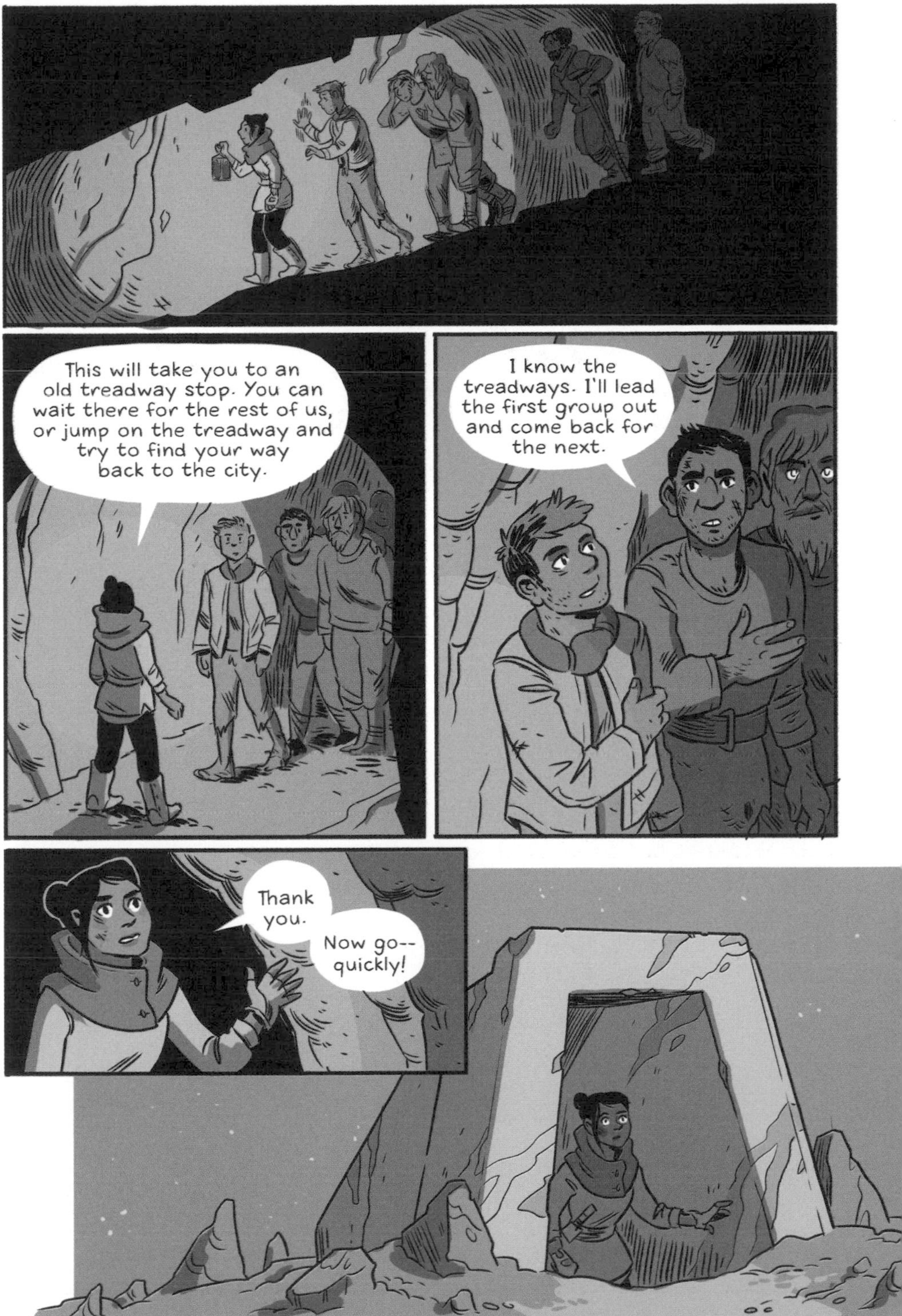
This will take you to an old treadway stop. You can wait there for the rest of us, or jump on the treadway and try to find your way back to the city.
I know the treadways. I'll lead the first group out and come back for the next.
Thank you.
Now go--quickly!

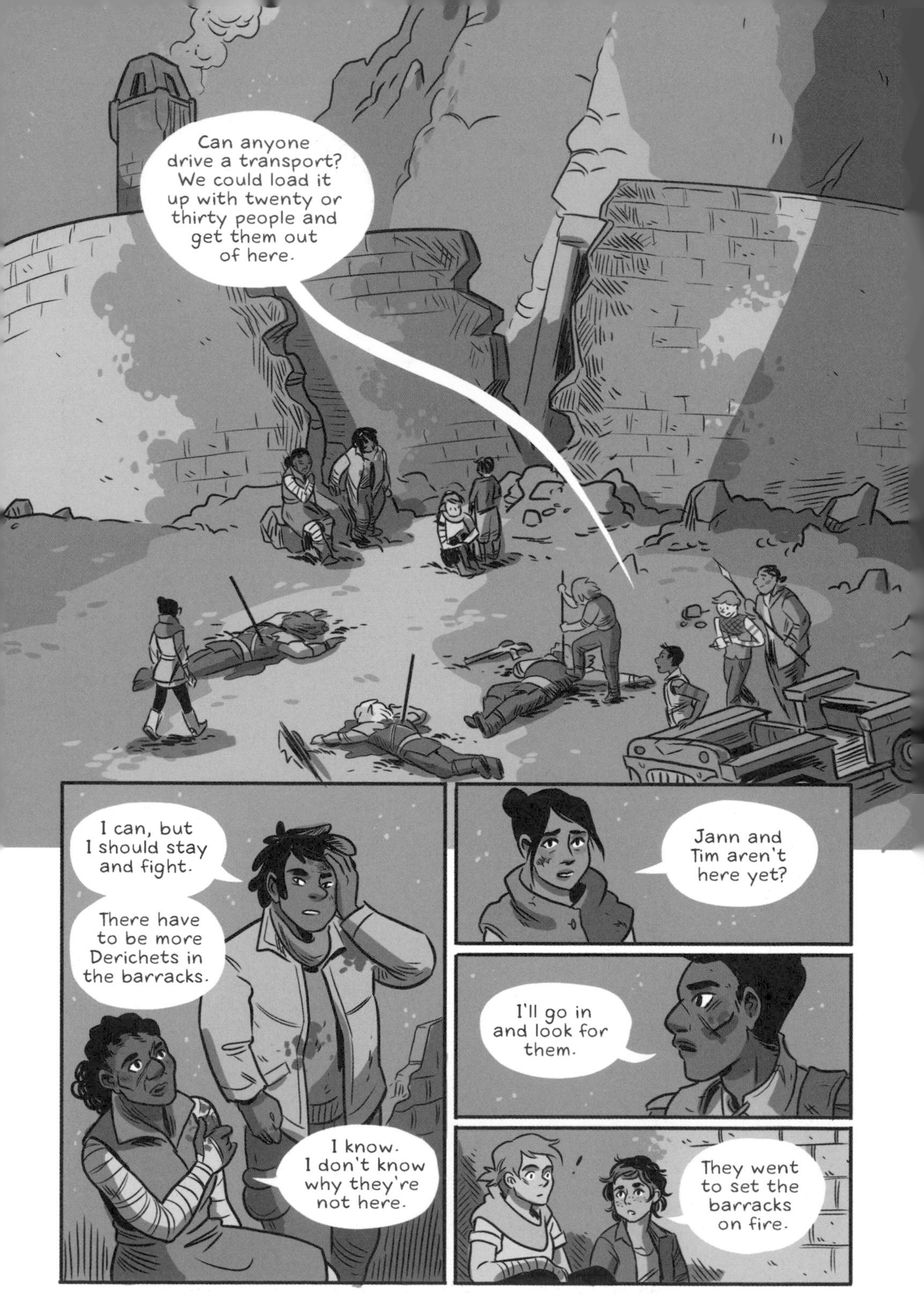
Can anyone drive a transport? We could load it up with twenty or thirty people and get them out of here.
I can, but I should stay and fight.
There have to be more Derichets in the barracks.
I know. I don't know why they're not here.
Jann and Tim aren't here yet?
I'll go in and look for them.
They went to set the barracks on fire.

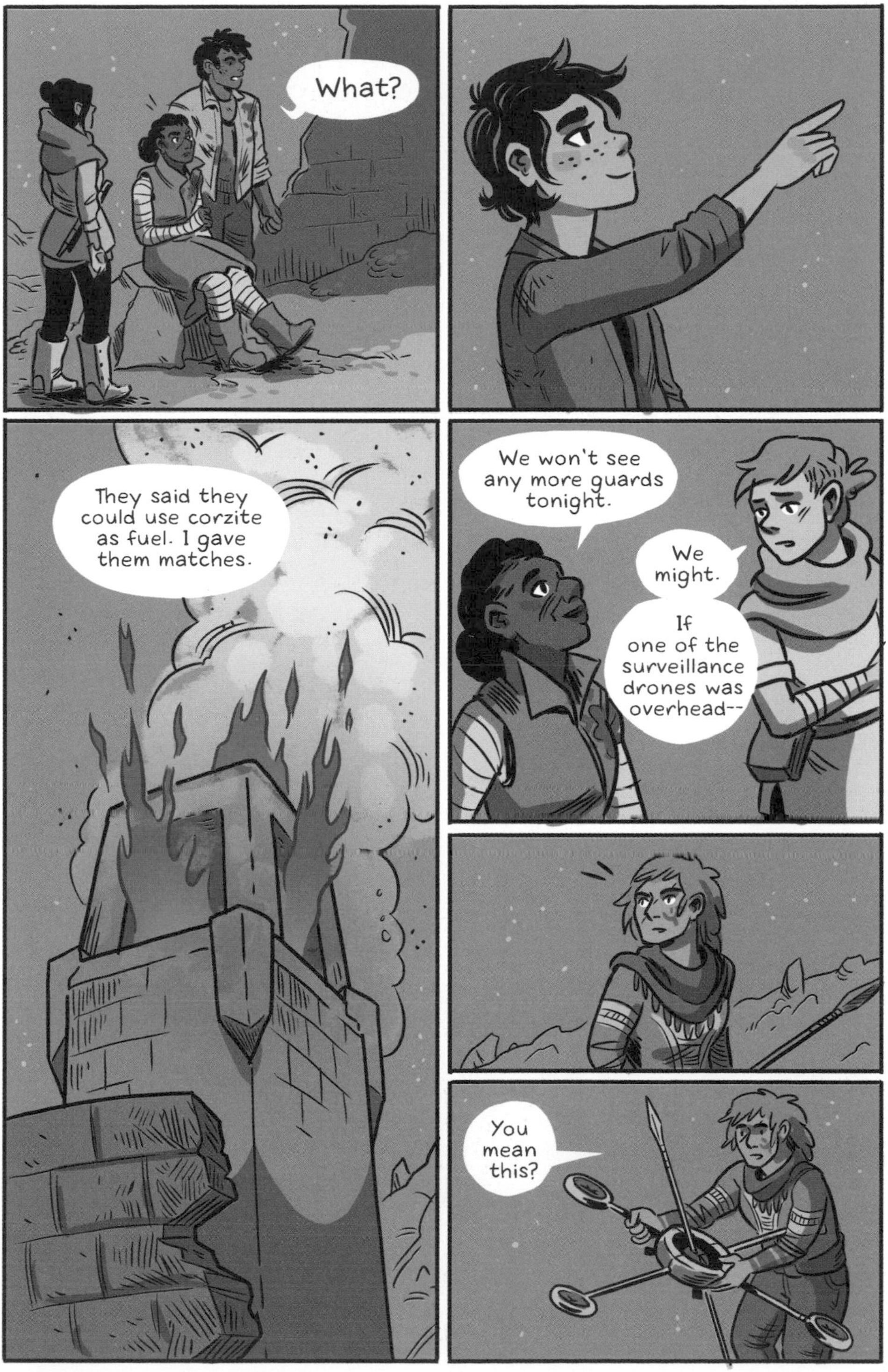
What?
They said they could use corzite as fuel. I gave them matches.
We won't see any more guards tonight.
We might.
If one of the surveillance drones was overhead--
You mean this?

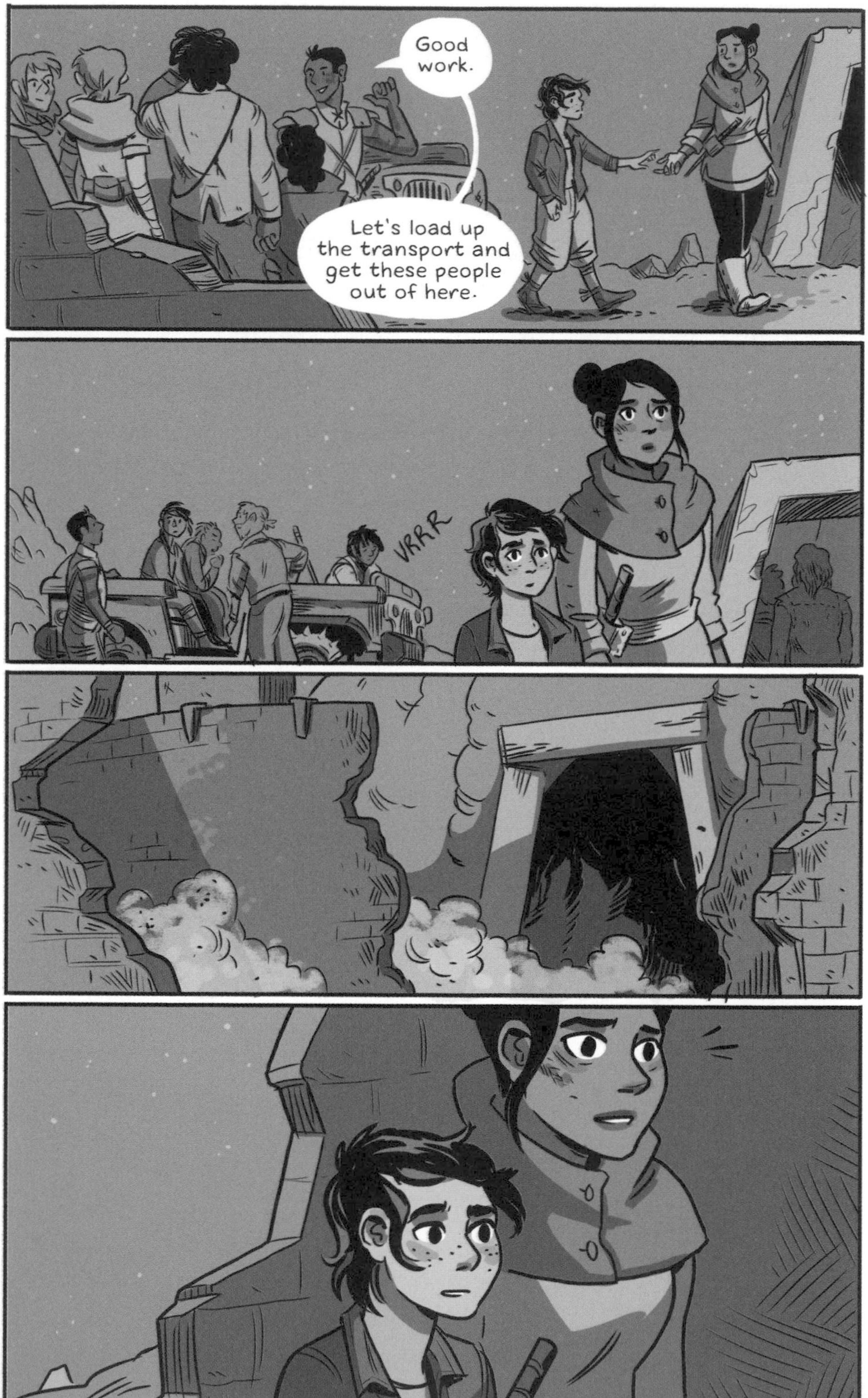
Good work.
Let's load up the transport and get these people out of here.
VRRR

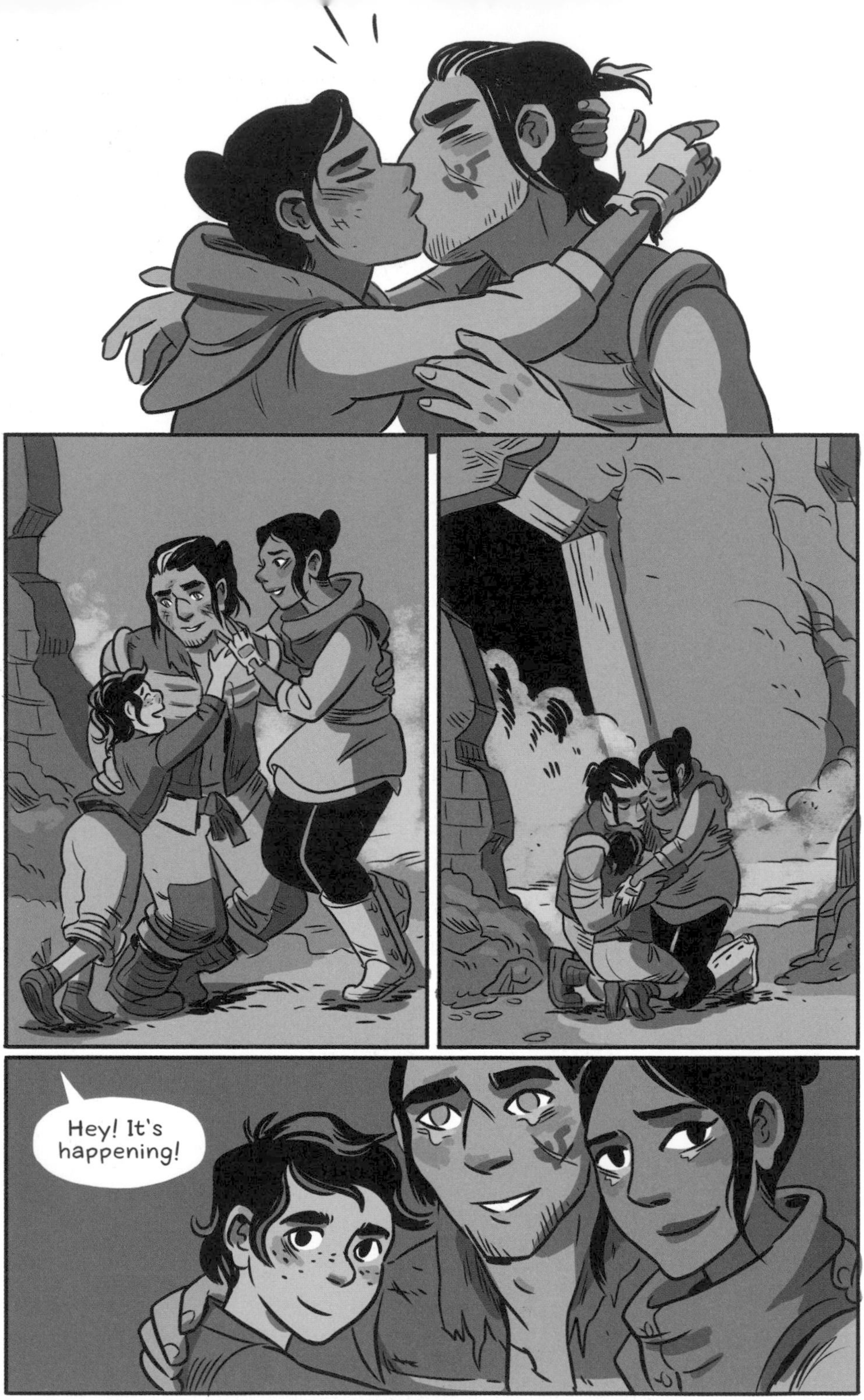
Hey! It's happening!

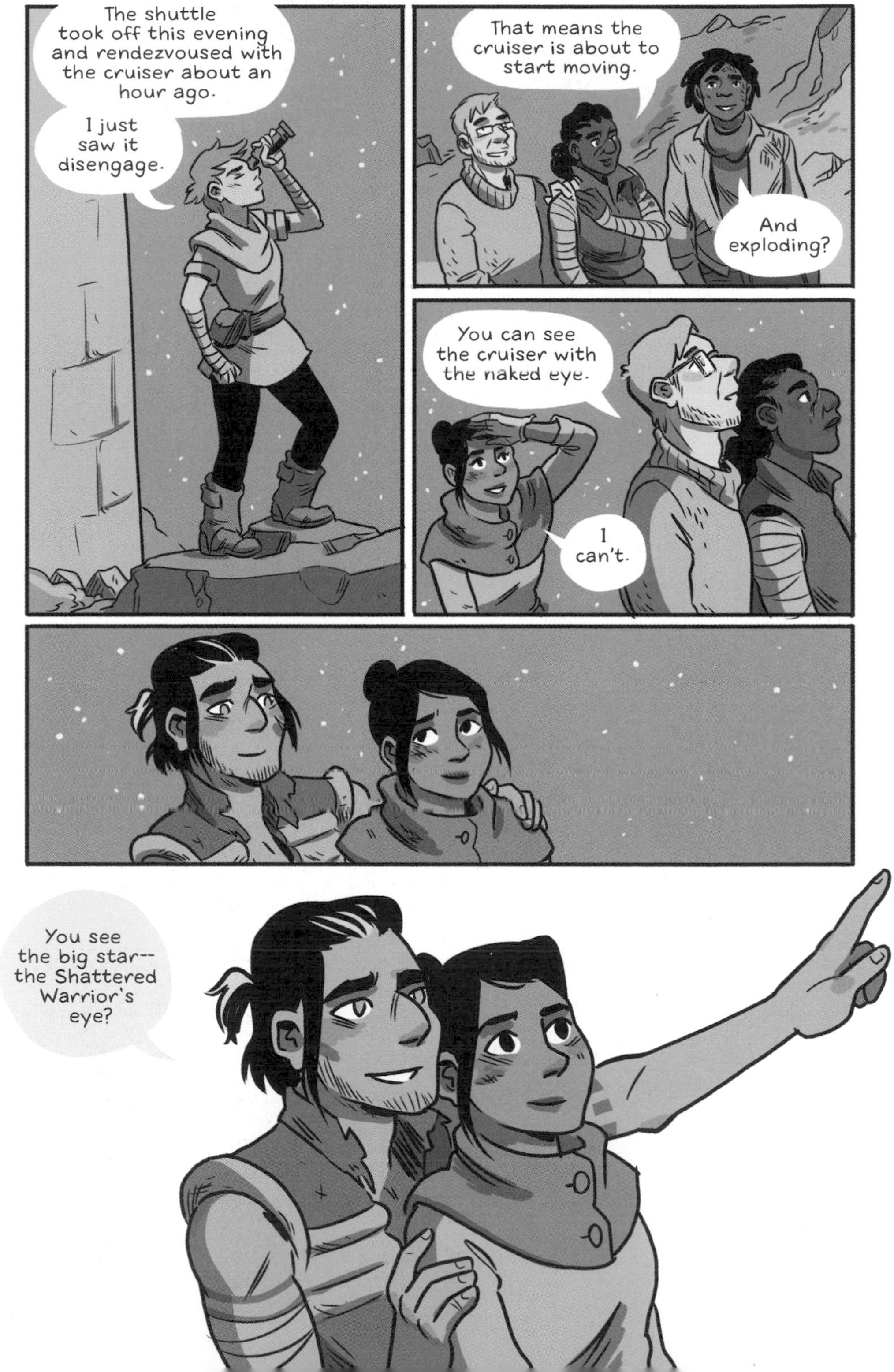

The shuttle took off this evening and rendezvoused with the cruiser about an hour ago.
I just saw it disengage.
That means the cruiser is about to start moving.
And exploding?
You can see the cruiser with the naked eye.
I can't.
You see the big star-- the Shattered Warrior's eye?

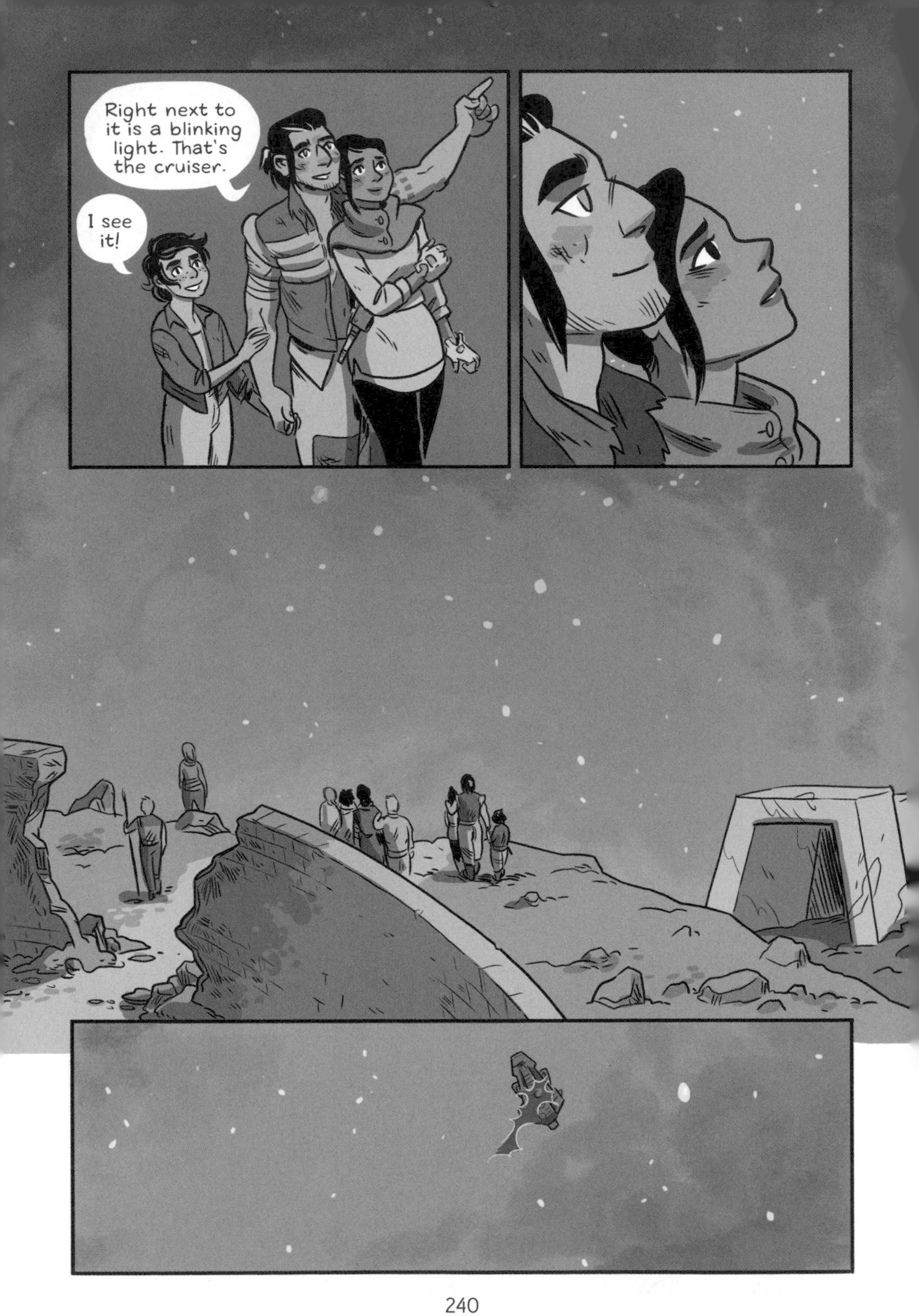
Right next to it is a blinking light. That's the cruiser.
I see it!

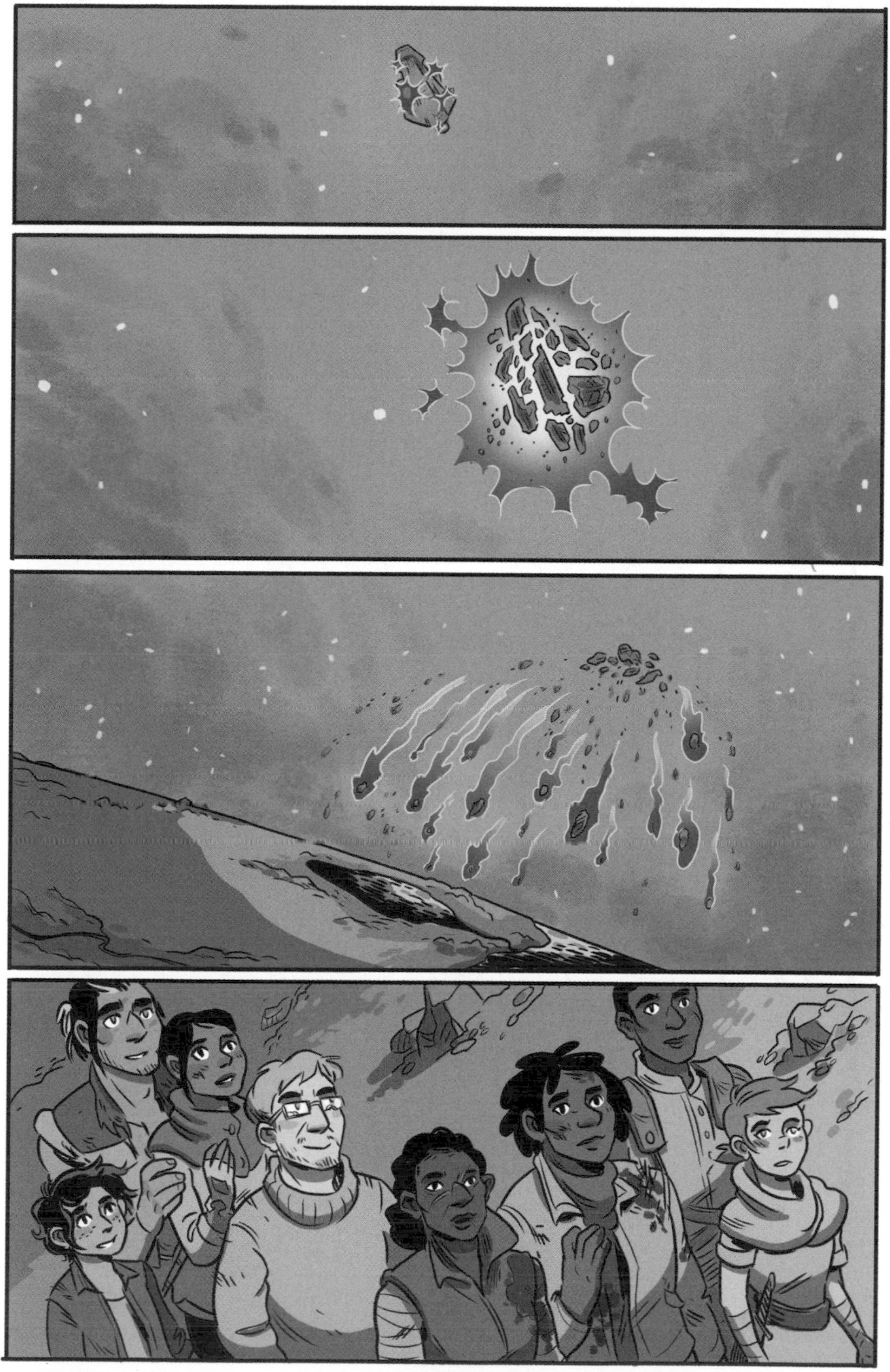

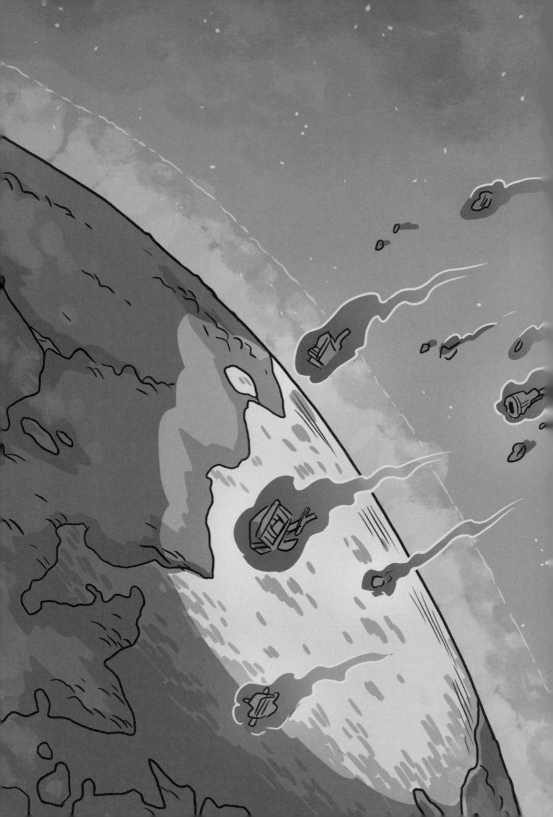

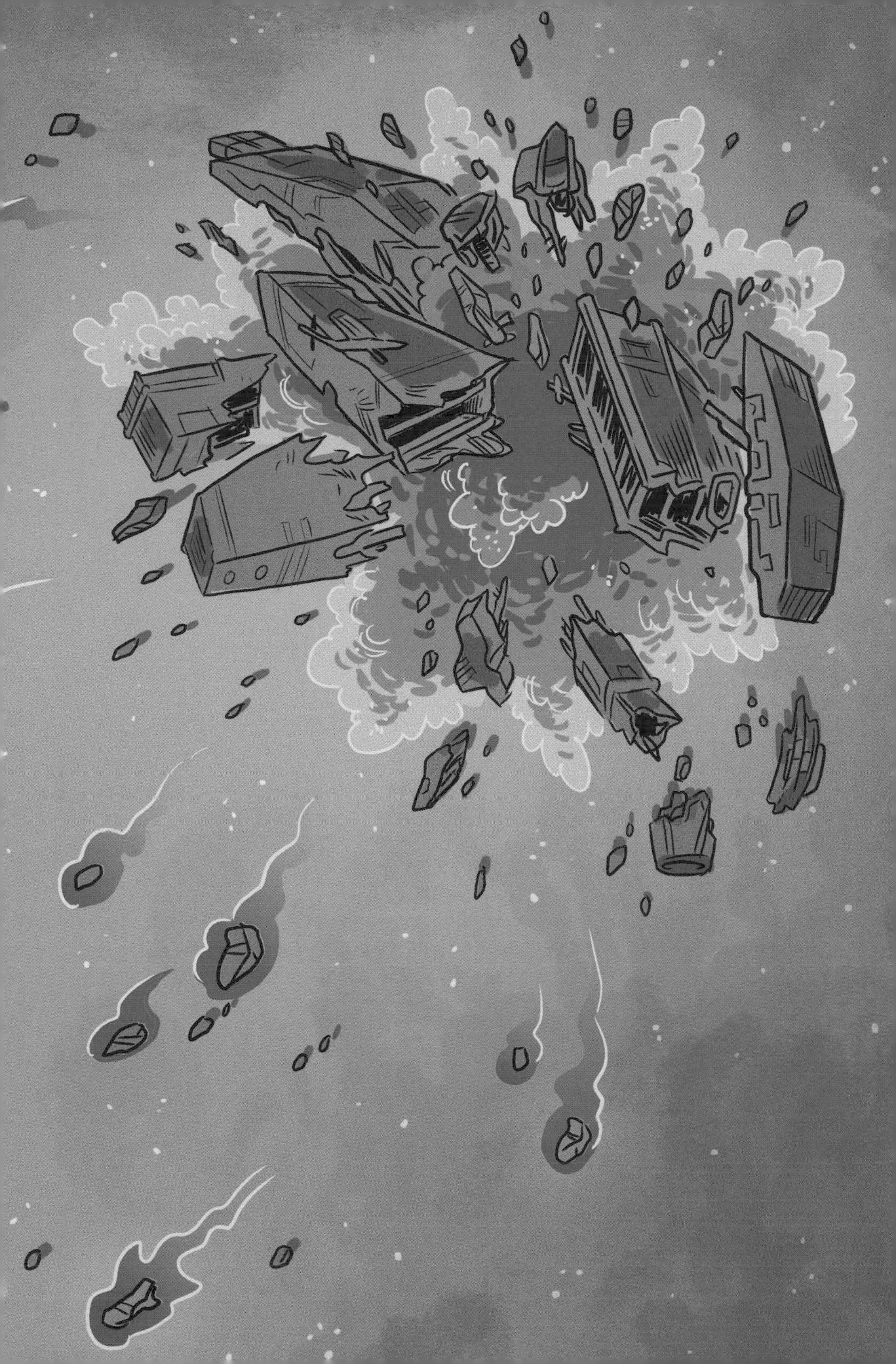

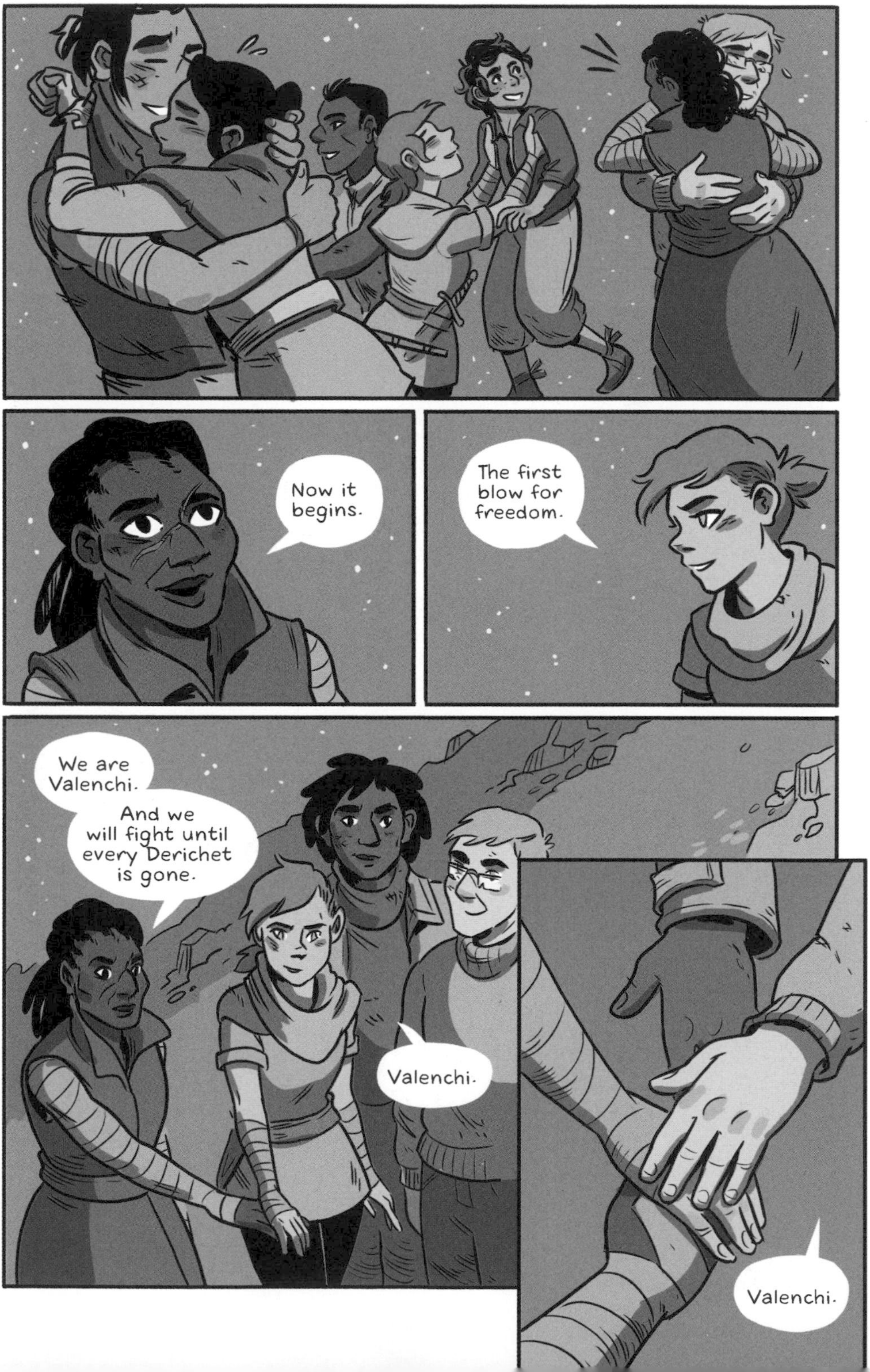
Now it begins.
The first blow for freedom.
We are Valenchi.
And we will fight until every Derichet is gone.
Valenchi.
Valenchi.

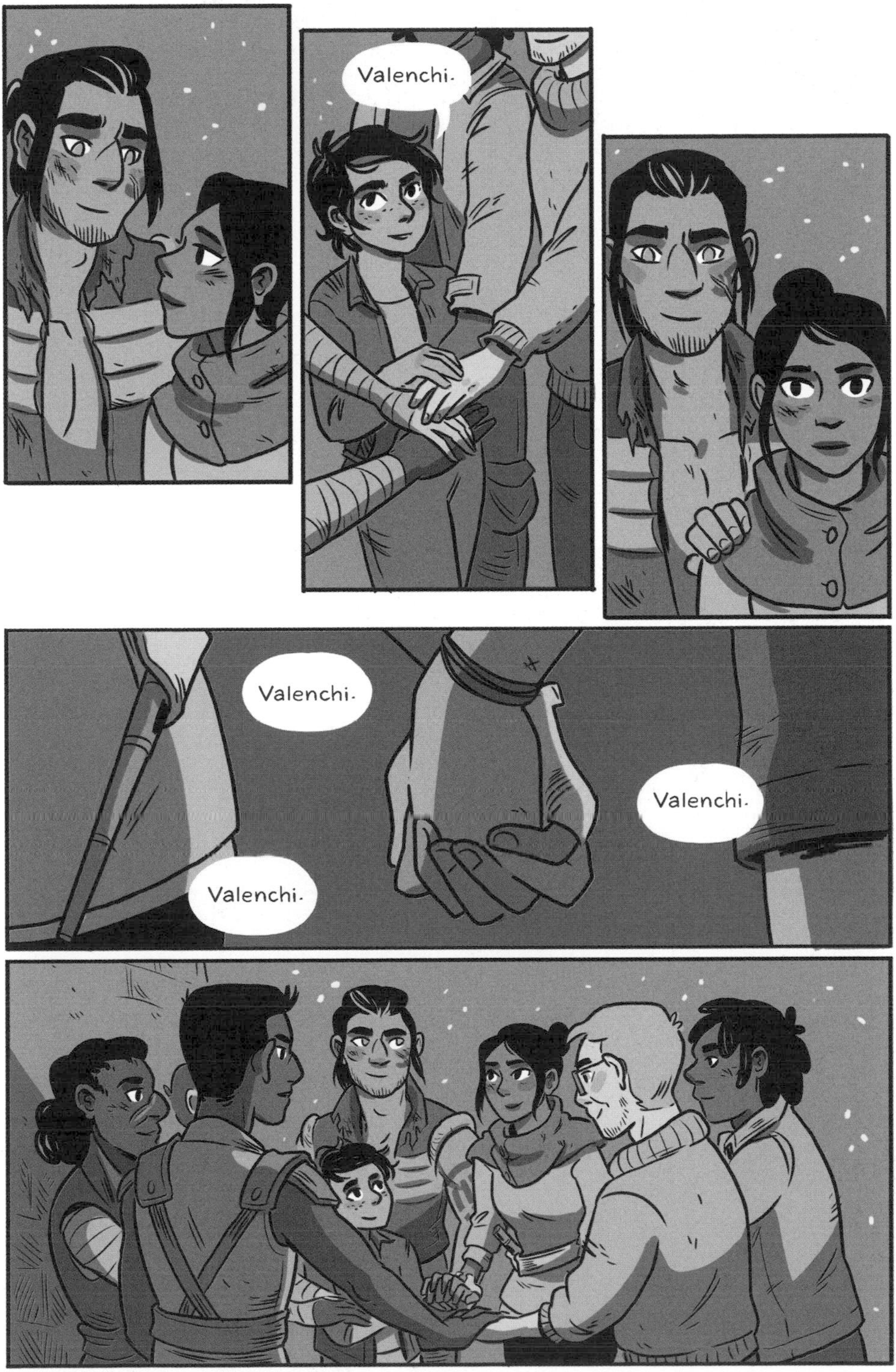
Valenchi.
Valenchi.
Valenchi.
Valenchi.

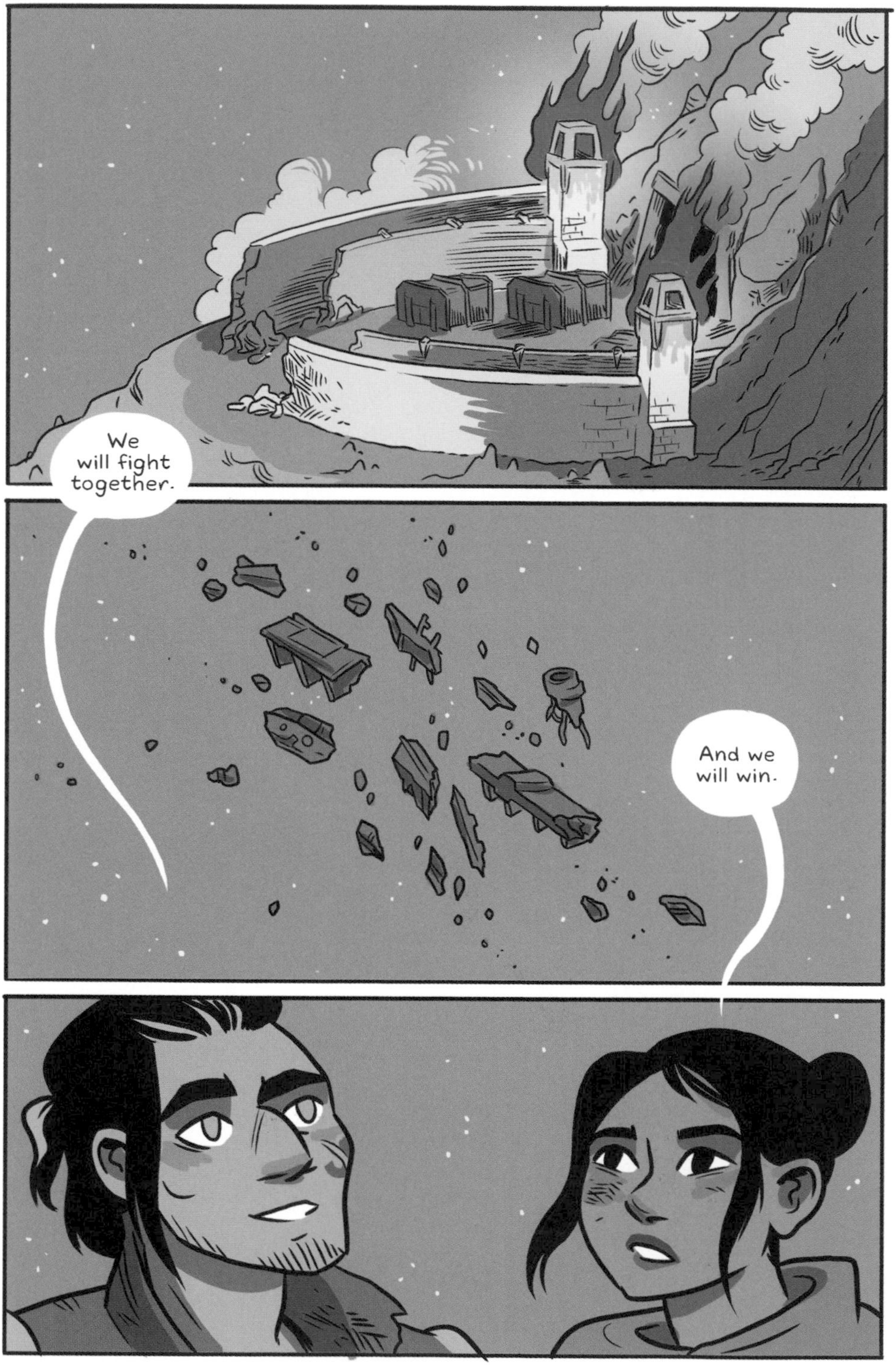
We will fight together.
And we will win.

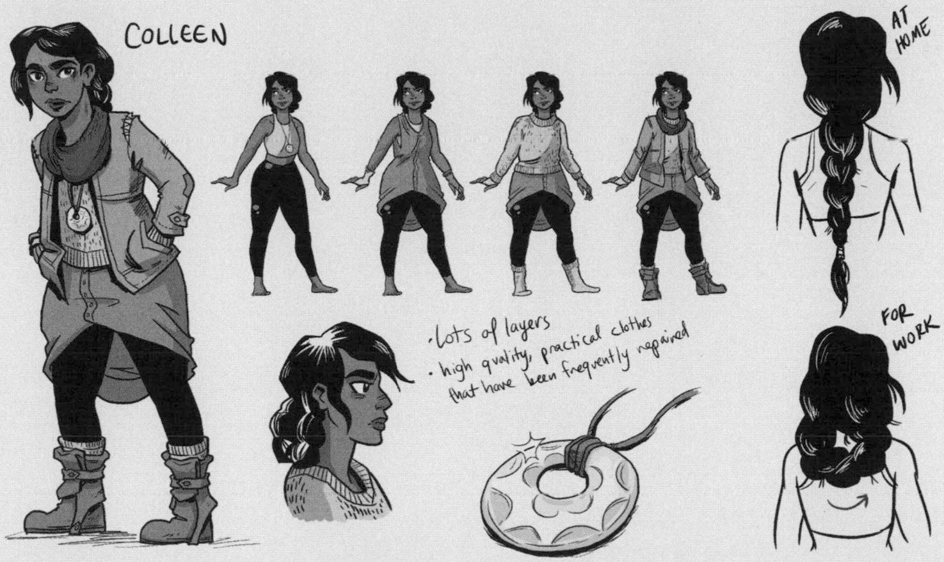
COLLEEN
·Lots of layers
·high quality, practical clothes that have been frequently repaired
AT HOME
FOR WORK

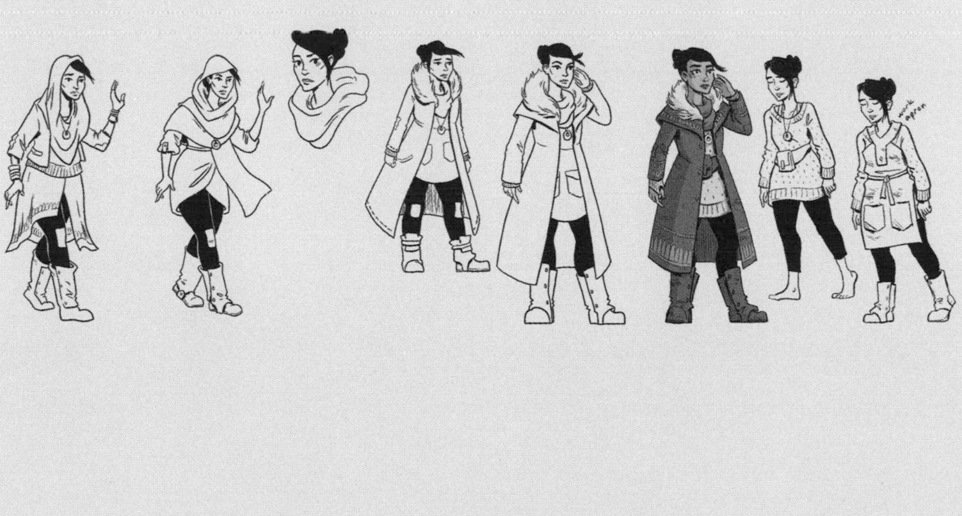
work apron

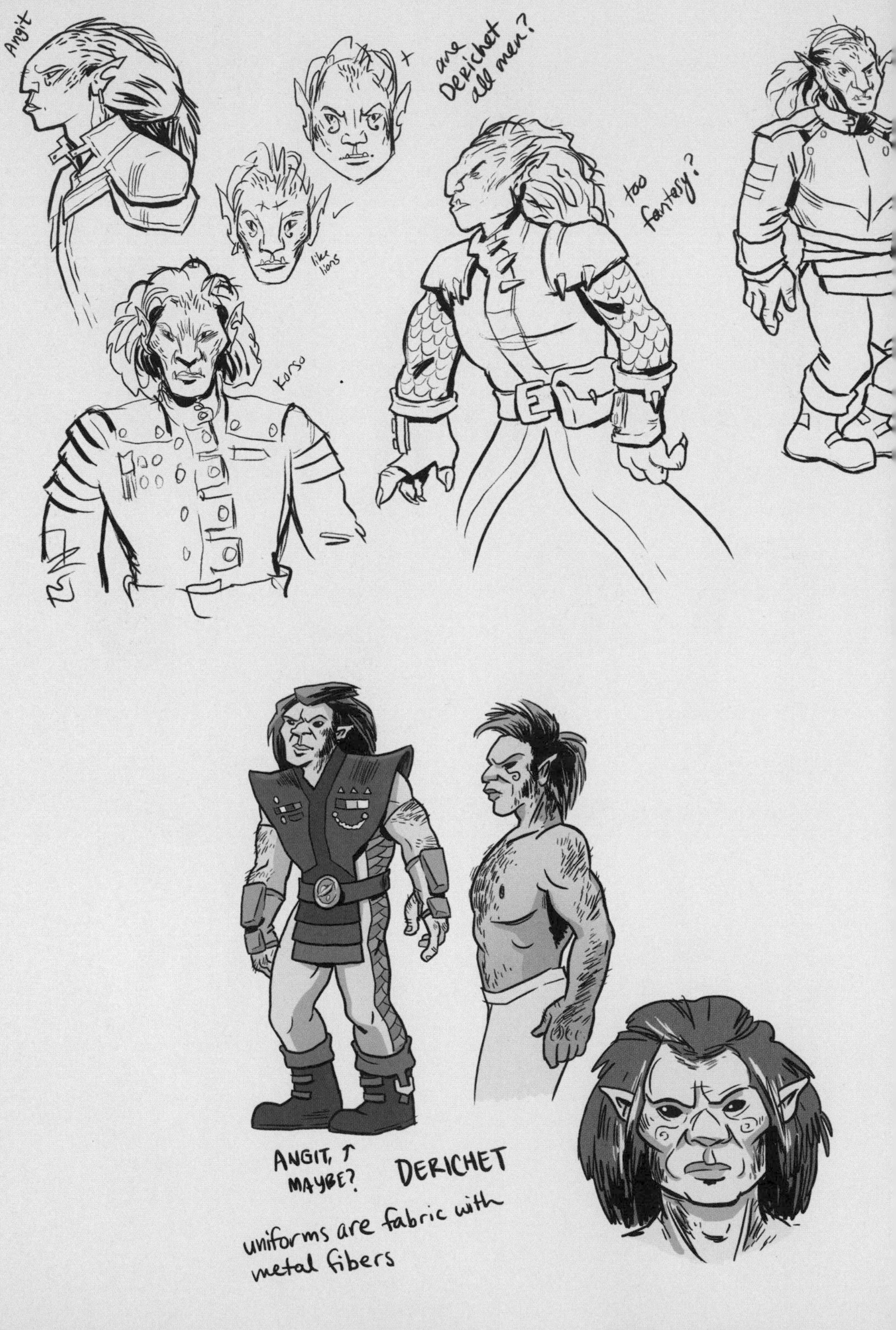
Angit
are Derichet all men?
too fantasy?
like lions
Korso
ANGIT, ↑ MAYBE?
DERICHET
uniforms are fabric with metal fibers

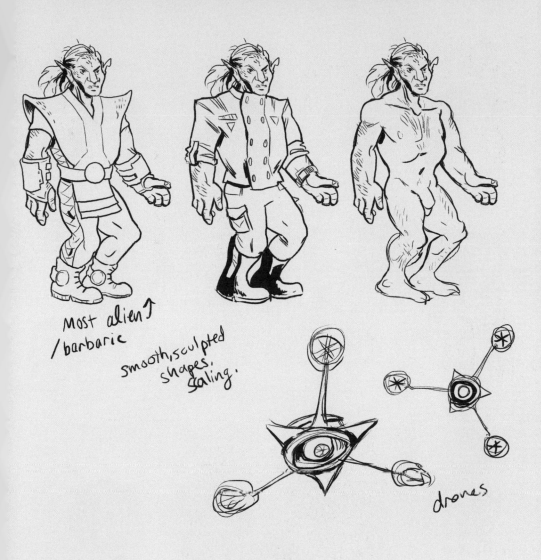

Most alien
/barbaric

smooth, sculpted
shapes,
scaling.

drones

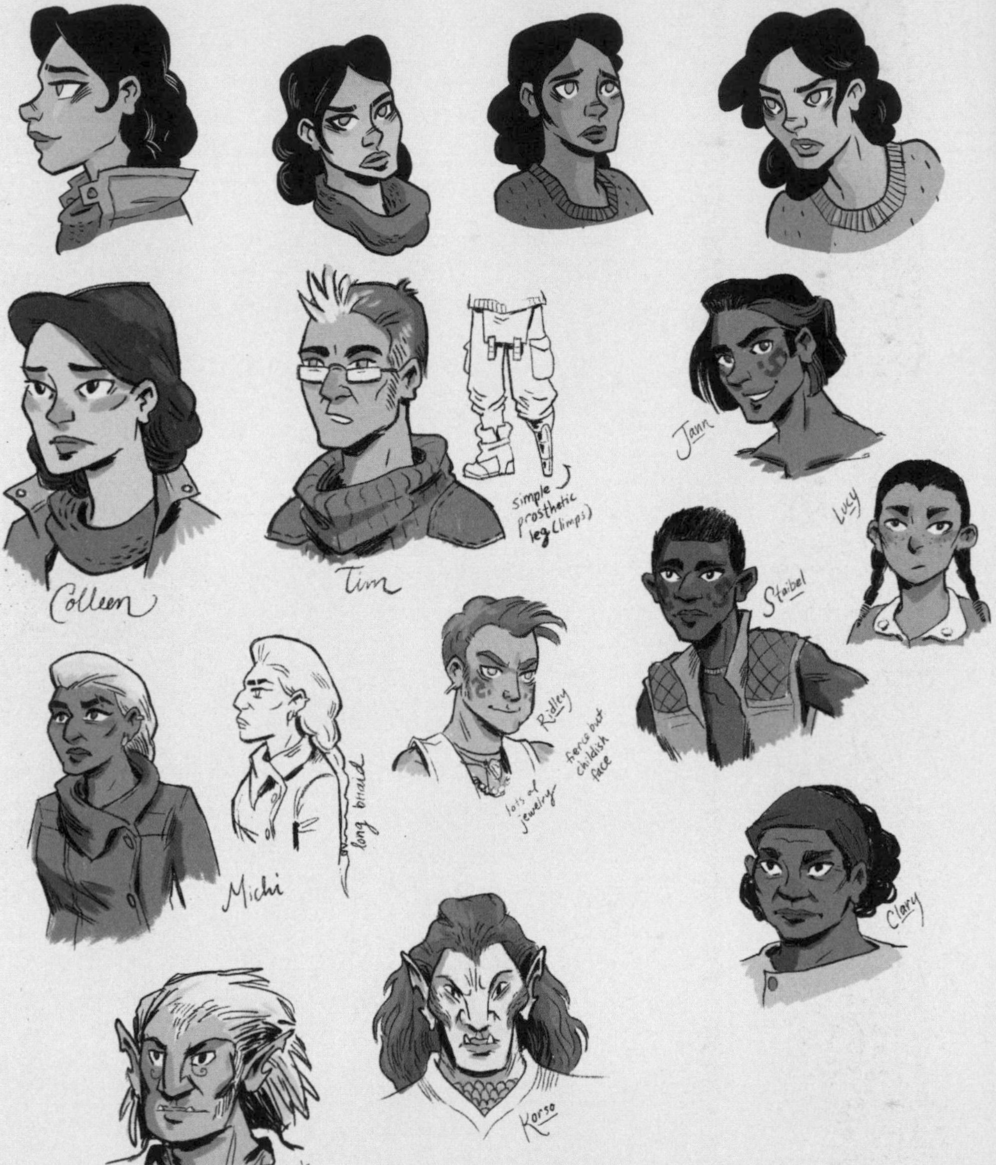
Colleen
Tim
simple prosthetic leg (limps)
Jann
Lucy
Staibel
Ridley
fierce but childish face
lots of jewelry
long braid
Michi
Clary
Korso
Angit

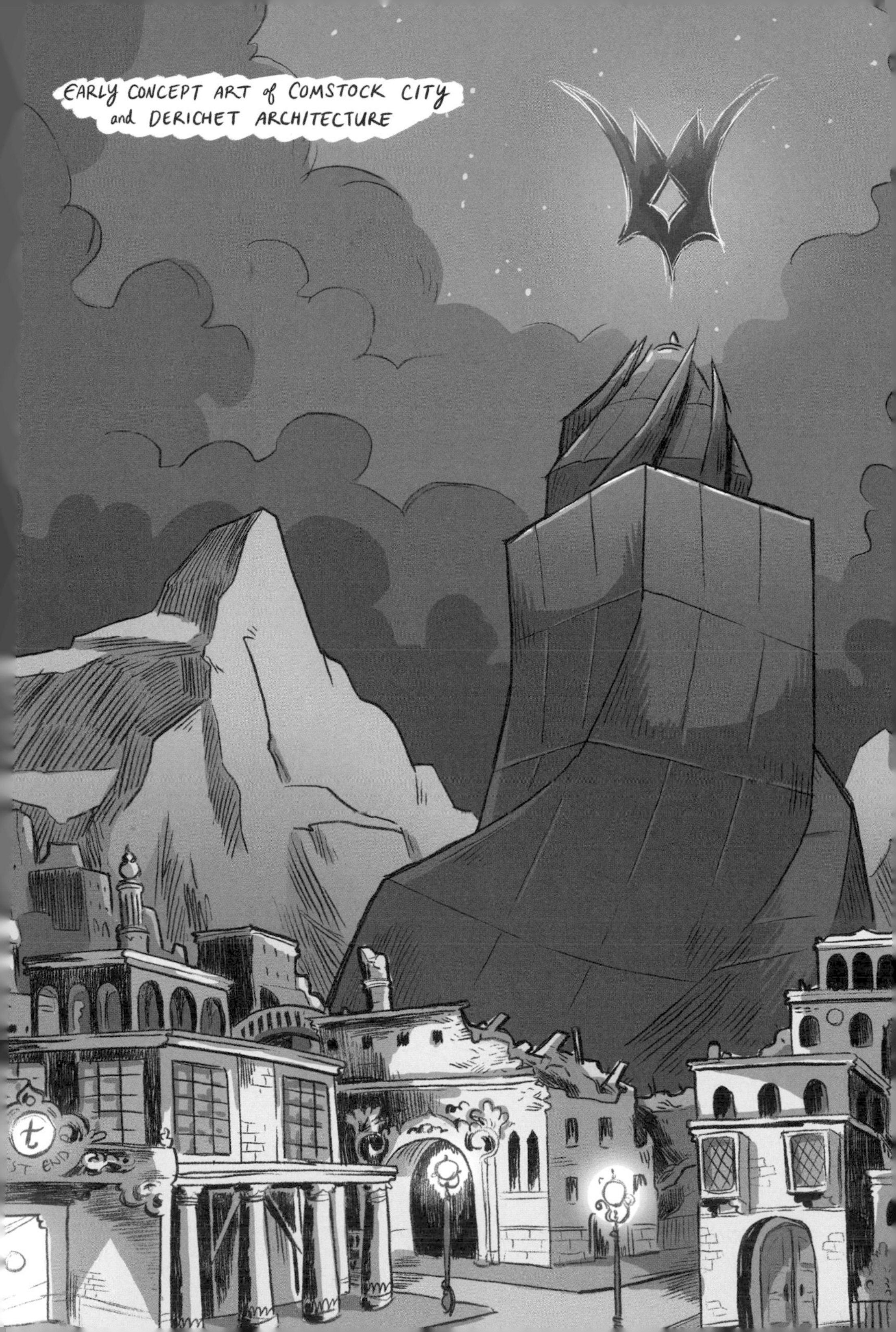

EARLY CONCEPT ART of COMSTOCK CITY and DERICHET ARCHITECTURE

First Second

New York

Text copyright © 2017 Sharon Shinn
Art copyright © 2017 Molly Knox Ostertag
Published by First Second
First Second is an imprint of Roaring Brook Press,
a division of Holtzbrinck Publishing Holdings Limited Partnership
175 Fifth Avenue, New York, New York 10010

Library of Congress Control Number: 2016945554

ISBN: 978-1-62672-089-3

Our books may be purchased in bulk for promotional, educational,
or business use. Please contact your local bookseller or the Macmillan
Corporate and Premium Sales Department at (800) 221-7945 ext. 5442
or by email at MacmillanSpecialMarkets@macmillan.com.

FIRST

EDITION

First edition 2017

Book design by Danielle Ceccolini

Printed in China by Toppan Leefung Printing Ltd., Dongguan City, Guangdong Province

10 9 8 7 6 5 4 3 2 1